Sixty Years of Jump Racing

From Arkle to McCoy

Robin Oakley

with Edward Gillespie

BLOOMSBURY

LONDON · OXFORD · NEW YORK · NEW DELHI · SYDNEY

Bloomsbury Sport
An imprint of Bloomsbury Publishing Plc

50 Bedford Square   1385 Broadway
London   New York
WC1B 3DP   NY 10018
UK   USA

www.bloomsbury.com

First published 2017
© Robin Oakley and Edward Gillespie, 2017

Robin Oakley and Edward Gillespie have asserted their right under the Copyright, Designs and
Patents Act, 1988, to be identified as the Authors of this work.

British Library Cataloguing-in-Publication Data
A catalogue record for this book is available from the British Library.

Library of Congress Cataloguing-in-Publication data has been applied for.

ISBN: Print: 978-1-4729-3509-0
ePDF: 978-1-4729-3511-3
ePub: 978-1-4729-3512-0

2 4 6 8 10 9 7 5 3 1

Designed by CE Marketing
Printed and bound in China by C&C Offset Printing Co

To find out more about our authors and books visit www.bloomsbury.com.
Here you will find extracts, author interviews, details of forthcoming events and the option to sign
up for our newsletters.

Contents

Acknowledgements

One of us is a racecourse impresario with 32 years' experience of running Cheltenham, the other a lifetime racegoer seeking a refuge from politics as *The Spectator*'s turf columnist – we were united in our eagerness to produce this book by a shared passion. For us both there is nothing to rival the wonderful world of jump racing: the colour, the energy, the heartaches, the characters, the courage of horse and rider striving together to prove themselves the best and, above all, the camaraderie of a sporting world like no other, united in its recognition of the risks shared by all.

Our starting point is 1960 because the 60s produced in Arkle the finest jumper ever seen. That decade also saw the introduction of legislation on betting and on financing racing, which has shaped its development since. This is not a comprehensive history of sixty years' racing – it would require something like a volume of the Encyclopedia Britannica to provide that – but a celebration of the wonderful horses, canny trainers and talented jockeys who have given the jump-racing public such joy throughout the period. We have concentrated on British jump racing rather than the worldwide scene; however, since Irish owners, trainers, jockeys and stable staff are such massive contributors, they quite rightly take up a significant proportion of these pages too.

What follows is based not just on the many interviews conducted specifically for this book, but also on experiences and conversations shared over many years in grandstands and winner's enclosures, on the gallops and over trainers' breakfast tables, on weighing-room steps and in racecourse bars. We are, though, especially grateful to many busy people who have found time in their hectic schedules to give generously of their time in aiding our researches. They include Anthony Bromley, Michael Dickinson, Francois Doumen, Peter Easterby, David Elsworth, John Ferguson, Mick Fitzgerald, Andrew Franklin, Nicky Henderson, Henrietta Knight, Richard Linley, David Minton, Paul Nicholls, Dinah Nicholson, Martin Pipe, Jenny Pitman, Richard Pitman, Peter Scudamore, Graham Thorner and Mike Vince. At the British Horseracing Authority, Robin Mounsey, Will Lambe and Paul Johnson were very patient with a range of enquiries, as were Paul Struthers, the chief executive of the Professional Jockeys Association, Nick Craven of Weatherby's and Nigel Payne of the Horserace Sponsors Association.

Of course, none of those above are responsible for any errors or mistakes that may have crept in. Those are down to us.

As ever, special thanks are due to our wives, Carolyn Oakley and Alyson Gillespie, for their forbearance over frequent racing absences, abandoned coffees and late arrivals for meals. We are deeply grateful too to Charlotte Croft, Sarah Skipper, Calvin Evans and Les Glazier at Bloomsbury for their professionalism and wise guidance.

Racing's acronyms and abbreviations

ARC	Arena Racing Company
BHA	The British Horseracing Authority
BHB	The British Horseracing Board, its predecessor
DCMS	Department of Culture Media and Sport
GBR	Great British Racing, racing's chief marketing and promotional group
HRA	The Horseracing Authority, responsible for regulation 2006/07
JCR	Jockey Club Racecourses
NASS	National Association of Stable Staff
NTF	National Trainers Federation
OFT	The Office of Fair Trading
PJA	Professional Jockeys Association
RCA	The Racecourse Association
REL	Racing Enterprises Limited, racing's commercial arm
RHT	Racecourse Holdings Trust, a Jockey Club subsidiary
RMG	Racecourse Media Group, managing the media rights of 34 racecourses including those run by the Jockey Club
ROA	Racehorse Owners Association
TBA	The Thoroughbred Breeders Association

Foreword

by Edward Gillespie

Horseracing is built solidly upon the human condition of differences of opinion. However far back in various cultures the sport can be traced, the principle proves to be timeless.

Two or more people have different opinions about which is the fastest horse over a defined distance and in certain conditions. Money is exchanged on the result of the outcome. Consensus is soon established about which is the fastest and, in order to keep the betting interesting, the fastest horse is slowed down by the allocation of more weight to carry. The handicapper is allowed to hold sway on the balance of differing opinions. A series of separate differences of opinion define the sport of jump racing, how it should be administered, how it should be financed, whether Government has any role to play, how power should be balanced between various professional bodies and amateur associations, even what the sport is called.

AP McCoy celebrates with JP McManus after winning the Ryanair Chase at the 2015 Cheltenham Festival on Uxizandre.

The various names – steeplechasing, National Hunt and jump racing – define various interest groups. Very occasionally and rather disarmingly, regardless of his or her perspective or financial interest, everyone in the sport reaches unconditional agreement. Such a moment occurred soon after 4.30 p.m. on Saturday 25 April 2015 when AP McCoy dismounted from a horse called Box Office at Sandown Park. That moment defined the end of an era. There were still differences of opinion about his number of rides and winners and about which were his best but the sport, let's call it jump racing, agreed that, after winning 20 consecutive British jump jockey titles, the era of AP was over. As Americans add for extra emphasis, period.

In these pages, one of the challenges is to identify the far more complex and mysterious aspect about an era, to define not when it ended but when it began, and how the horses, people and political forces led, directly and indirectly, to that scene in April 2015. The hypothesis that will be tested is that the era began more than five decades earlier, in the very early 1960s.

The Betting and Gaming Act 1960 legalised gambling in the United Kingdom. From May 1961, betting shops laid the foundations for the Betting Levy Act 1961, which established the funding mechanism for racing. Hold that picture of Sandown in your mind and consider how many clues can be investigated. The jockey was a 40-year-old Irishman who had won the 2012 BBC Sports Personality of the Year; the horse was bred in France by an Irish stallion; the trainer, Jonjo O'Neill, is an Irishman based in the Cotswolds; the owner, JP McManus, another Irishman and the owner of the most horses in the sport; the race, The bet365 Handicap Hurdle, was sponsored by one of the world's leading online gambling companies; the racecourse, Sandown Park, is owned by The Jockey Club, for centuries the sport's ruling authority but now primarily a racecourse owner; the broadcaster was Channel 4; the satellite channels, Racing UK and Turf TV, are owned by 34 racecourses. A wider scan will reveal the informal dress of that record crowd, the racecourse equipped with

big screen to enhance the customer experience, and the abundant plastic rails to minimise the risk of injury for horses and jockeys. A year later, that same unsaddling enclosure witnessed the jubilation for Paul Nicholls and 'Team Ditcheat' as they celebrated a remarkable defence of the Trainers' Championship against

Clearing the final fence at Ascot where jump racing was introduced in 1965.

Irishman Willie Mullins. Twenty winners in the season's last fortnight had wrested the title back to Somerset for the tenth time. Many of those winners had been achieved with French imports, notably the Coral Scottish Grand National with Vicente. On the final day at Sandown, two Irish-bred horses, Just A Par and Southfield Theatre, finished in the prize money for the bet365 Gold Cup, crucially swinging the balance of the Championship Paul Nicholls' way.

Irish investment in British jump racing has proved fundamental. The hallmark of the sport is that it is played out on a British stage with many of the leading players being Irish, both equine and human. They set the tone for big occasions, along with spectators who spend the rest of their lives in the likes of London's leafy commuter belt, travelling a hundred miles west to Cheltenham and behaving with the exuberance of Irish aficionadoes. Extending that theatrical metaphor, a glance through the programme will help identify the 'dramatis personae', the characters in jump racing's dramatic work.

The Arkle era

Top billing must go to the thousands of horses that give so selflessly for the pleasure that spectators and punters take from the sport. Right at the beginning of our era, just when, backstage, the structure for a new era had been put in place by racing's civil service, a single horse stepped onto that stage – an Irish horse onto the British stage, a horse destined to remain in the spotlight for many decades. Arkle was a freak, that phenomenon every sport craves, an athlete that can perform at a far higher level than that of his rivals.

Freaks are best recognised by those who watch the sport day-in, day-out. Spectators become accustomed to knowing where and when a winner accelerates and what happens next. Then, quite suddenly, something totally unexpected occurs: that Shane Warne delivery

Anne, Duchess of Westminster, visits Arkle at Kempton Park as he recovers from the bone fracture in his foot.

to Mike Gatting; Jonah Lomu crashing through tackles; Bob Beamon flying out of the long jump pit in the 1968 Olympics. Flat racing had such a moment when Frankel shot into a clear lead in the 2000 Guineas and stayed there. That was

the impact Arkle made in the 1964 Cheltenham Gold Cup. Just when spectators rubbed their hands and nudged their neighbours that the head-to-head battle with the champion Mill House they had come to witness was about to happen, Arkle simply sprinted away and redefined greatness.

British racing went Arkle-crazy. He became the first superstar since Golden Miller, an Irish icon in an era ripe for promoting stardom. His team of jockey Pat Taaffe and trainer Tom Dreaper was topped off brilliantly by the baritone tones of Anne, Duchess of Westminster, from Eaton Hall in Cheshire, who had named the 1,150-guineas purchase after a mountain near her Scottish estate. These were the heady days of 1960s pop music and sport culture. In a *TV Times* magazine poll for the most popular personality of 1966, the Beatles came third, World Cup-winning England captain Bobby Moore was runner-up, and Arkle was voted the winner.

That year's King George VI steeplechase should have been the midpoint of a career that would close with a fanfare three years later when Arkle had gloriously landed a sixth Gold Cup. Still a nine-year-old, he had already won 27 of his 35 races, wrenched the crown that had so long awaited Golden Miller's successor from the head of Mill House – and become virtually unbeatable. In just four seasons since emerging at the 1963 National Hunt meeting, he had taken the sport from the conversation of a sporting fraternity to the forefront of British consciousness.

On Boxing Day 1966, fans had already endured two disappointments. Mill House had suffered a muscle injury while preparing on Christmas Day and would not be running in the 'King George'. Worse still, we awoke that morning to hear that frost had claimed the Kempton Park meeting. How we were to wish the same fate had befallen the racing at Kempton the following day. Only those who travelled to Kempton were to witness the untimely end to Arkle's meteoric era. An early experiment in pay-per-view television prevented the nation from sharing the sight of 'Himself' (as

Arkle was affectionately dubbed by the Irish) dominating his rivals, elation then turning to dismay as his stride shortened after jumping the final fence and he was passed by Dormant. Then there was the mad dash to the unsaddling enclosure to get some idea as to what had befallen our hero, and the long wait until the evening news to learn that he had fractured a pedal bone in a hind foot. Folklore of deliveries of get-well cards and cases of Guinness to his box as he recovered has fogged the memory of quite how close Tom Dreaper got to returning Arkle to the resumption of his racing career, just as, 20 years later, very few recall Dawn Run's final run before her fateful trip to Paris, when she and Jonjo O'Neill parted company at the first fence at Aintree.

The Arkle era effectively closed at Kempton Park. The long vigil had begun for jump racing to bring forth another chaser who could be spoken of in the same hushed tones, a vigil with many false dawns as fans peered eagerly towards the horizon for 'the next Arkle'. Arkle was one side of a virtual triangle, along with extensive television coverage and commercial sponsorship, that projected jump racing into the homes and hearts of the British public in the mid-1960s. In 1957, the inaugural Whitbread Gold Cup at Sandown, later to become the bet365 Gold Cup, and the Hennessy Gold Cup at Cheltenham – which transferred to Newbury in 1960 – heralded a new era for commercial sponsorship. The BBC embraced the sport, whose flat and jump racing fitted brilliantly into the magazine formula of Saturday afternoon's *Grandstand*.

Such was the interest in the possibility of Mill House, jump racing's biggest star since Golden Miller, being challenged by the all-conquering Arkle in the 1964 Gold Cup that the BBC persuaded the Jockey Club, then the Racing Authority and controller of fixtures, to move the race from the traditional Thursday to be included in *Grandstand* on Saturday. Four years later, ITV launched their racing programme, *They're Off*, which was soon retitled *The ITV Seven*; bookmakers responded with a bet of the same name, easily understood and

highly visible. Offered an alternative to the constraints of the format of TV commercials, sponsorship from the widest possible sectors of commerce flowed into the sport. The foundations were laid for jump racing to thrive.

Broadcasters

While the wait for the next Arkle kept fans enthralled, on-screen talent added a dimension that transcended the sport and turned it into entertainment. Presenter John Rickman raised his trilby and greeted us with a civil 'good afternoon'; John Lawrence, the future Lord Oaksey, brought us aristocratic breeding, fine prose and the experience of a champion amateur jockey describing first-hand exactly how it felt to sit astride a tiring front-runner as the favourite bore down on him at the final fence. Often wearing his colours under his tweed jacket, he brought the sport, horse, mud and the occasional near expletive into our sitting rooms. Lord Oaksey continued as a presenter long after race-riding retirement, and only John Francome, of many ex-weighing room colleagues, approached John Oaksey's natural skill for communicating the sport's raw passion, thrill and despair.

Over on the BBC, race-commentator Peter O'Sullevan could take the first mile to run gently through most of the field, perfectly

Peter O'Sullevan, the voice of racing.

complementing the rhythm of a steeplechase, before winding up the pace, subtly mentioning the favourite moving into contention, and riding his trademark commentary finish before pulling up with full details of the placed horses and their owners, trainers and jockeys. As an owner of mixed fortune himself, he never lost sight of who ultimately funds the entertainment. BBC Radio was equally on-message with Peter Bromley ever present, capturing the excitement and sharing his audience's admiration for the extraordinary courage of horse and rider.

Buoyed by enormous Grandstand audiences, frequently over 3 million being attracted to the rugby international coming up after the racing, jump racing's cast became household names. The Grand National, given build-up and coverage from every possible viewpoint, garnered four or five times as many. When Foinavon survived the havoc of 1967, it was no surprise to see his rider, Johnny Buckingham, appear on stage the following evening in ITV's *Sunday Night At The London Palladium*.

It was to be Aintree that forged the next superstar – a horse bred to be a miler and a dead-heat winner over five furlongs, first time out at the same course. He got his head in front in the shadow of the same winning post six years later when running down Crisp and landing the 'National' for the first of three victories. Red Rum had timed his entrance to perfection. Not only did Red Rum win three Grand Nationals and finish runner-up in the intervening years, he also introduced Ginger McCain and his Southport beach to racing's cast of characters and eye-catching locations. To a very great extent, he helped save the National itself.

The tapes go up for the start of the Grand National.

The Grand National

The Topham family had owned Aintree since 1949 and former Gaiety Girl Mirabel Topham, managed the course to great effect, jealously protecting the unique challenge of the world's most famous race. She even gave the commentary herself one year.

The year 1965 brought the first so-called 'last Grand National' after plans were announced to sell the course for development. A commentary was noticeably missing for those of us crammed into the cheap enclosure for the reward of a distant view of American raider Jay Trump denying Scottish-trained Freddie a first win for his country. It took until 1973 for a buyer to be secured in the form of local property developer, Bill Davies. Mirabel Topham shrewdly retained ownership of a car park behind the stands, not to mention a key to the weighing room. Assisting the manager in 1975, I was delegated the formidable task of 'borrowing back' from her the tumble dryer for the valets that had mysteriously vanished the day before racing.

Red Rum kept the flame alive with the help of trainer Ginger McCain, jockey Brian Fletcher, and two gallant defeats – the first by Gold Cup-winner, L'Escargot, and the second by hairdresser Mr 'Teasy-Weasy' Raymond's Rag Trade – before completing a third emotional win under jockey Tommy Stack. David Coleman, BBC's most high-profile presenter of the day, took his annual outing to Liverpool to coordinate the coverage and, gradually, new life was breathed back into the great race. What 'Rummy' had achieved from his stables behind the garage in Southport was now matched by the business acumen of Ladbrokes' boss Cyril Stein.

Fronted by charismatic Clerk of the Course John Hughes and their own publicity chief, Mike Dillon, Ladbrokes managed and sponsored the National until public subscription allowed the steady hand of The Jockey Club to buy the course in 1983. Then followed three decades of investment that has secured and promoted the race and Aintree's three-day fixture way beyond their former glory.

Champion steeplechasers

With calm returned to Merseyside following Aintree's resurgence, the vigil for the next Arkle quietly continued. Two weeks after Scotland had finally won their first National with Rubstic in 1979, a race marred by the death of Gold Cup-winner Alverton at Becher's Brook, a mare called Flower Girl, owned by Jimmy Burridge in Leicestershire, gave birth to Desert Orchid, a grey foal that was to take jump racing to a whole new level. A very decent hurdler, good enough to compete alongside Dawn Run in the 1984 Champion Hurdle, Desert Orchid's conversion from hurdles to fences launched a career that captured the imagination of a public far beyond regular fans. 'Dessie' ran with his heart on his beautiful grey sleeve. In a racing world dominated by more anonymous dark bay horses, there was no mistaking Desert Orchid and where he would be racing – with boundless energy up front.

Thanks to the training skills of David Elsworth, the riding tactics of Colin Brown and others, and to the sporting attitude of his family owners headed by film scriptwriter Richard Burridge, Dessie made regular appearances on Saturdays around London's right-handed park courses: Ascot, Kempton and Sandown. At those tracks he was the winner of the Victor Chandler Chase (when it was a tough handicap), three Gainsborough Chases, a Tingle Creek and a Whitbread, a Racing Post Chase and four King George VI Chases.

Every March, Dessie travelled to Cheltenham, more in hope than expectation, adding thousands to the gate, but ultimately tasting defeat, finding one or two other horses better suited to the Cotswold undulations. Then, in 1989, in conditions that would have caused racing to be abandoned on any other occasion, he fought off a challenge from Yahoo and landed the Gold Cup. Such days make the wait worthwhile. When Her Majesty The Queen returned to the Cheltenham Festival in 2003 after a gap of over 50 years, the line-up of those who had made the Festival such a success in the intervening years included Mill House's rider, Willie Robinson, Fred Winter, Michael Dickinson – and Desert Orchid. For 15 years, Dessie led the parade before both the King George and the Gold Cup. When he passed away in 2006, media coverage reminded those who had been lucky enough to witness his brilliance what a force of nature and game-changer he had been.

However, Desert Orchid was still not Arkle. 1966, the year of Arkle's third Gold Cup and England's World Cup heroics, was beginning to place a heavy burden of expectation on the shoulders of would-be successors. Arkle's Timeform rating of 212 and the 210 allotted to his stable companion, Flyingbolt, were being looked upon as suspiciously inflated. Desert Orchid peaked at a worthy rating of 187, which would have just got him into a 'virtual' handicap on 10 st 3 lb with Arkle carrying 12 stone.

Desert Orchid, ridden by Richard Dunwoody.

A whole new generation had been attracted to the sport and they had to wait only a decade or so for another really good one to arrive. Once again, the darkest hours heralded a new dawn. Less than three weeks before the scheduled start of the 2001 Festival, those dreaded words 'foot-and-mouth disease' were back in common parlance. Everyone who had been around at the time of the previous outbreak in 1967 could recall that racing had been curtailed due to health fears of moving stock. Whether or not such a policy had made any difference was irrelevant; action needed to be taken. Once the Irish and French had announced that they would not be coming to Cheltenham, it came as a blessed relief to discover that sheep had been

Best Mate with Jim Culloty up, jumping at Ascot.

legitimately grazing the infield within a period now thought unsafe by the Ministry. When the racecourse came within an exclusion zone, plans to reschedule the Festival in April were abandoned. Gloucestershire Tourism calculated

a loss of £44 million to the local economy and racing mourned a massive loss from there being no prize-money distribution and betting activity.

Aintree, however, where there were far fewer sheep, continued as part of a carefully orchestrated fixture programme that kept the sport tentatively on the move. Positive by-products from that year's Festival loss included the introduction of the two-mile Celebration Chase on the final day of the season at Sandown, the inaugural running being won by Edredon Bleu for the Best Mate connections, and the elevation of The Open meeting at Cheltenham. For many, the three days of The Open meeting in November 2001 gave them a lower-cost compensation visit to the Cotswolds that soon became a habit.

Just as Golden Miller had been denied his opportunity to run at Cheltenham in his novice-chase season, in his case by frost, Best Mate, hailed by many as potentially the next Arkle, was denied his run, a historic coincidence that quickened the pulse. The team around Best Mate were as much part of his story as the horse himself, being owned by Brummie businessman Jim Lewis, with his passion for Aston Villa and penchant for breaking into song at trophy presentations; trained by former schoolteacher Henrietta Knight; and ridden by Irishman Jim Culloty. Jim Lewis's wife, Valerie, was kept strong through cancer treatment by the Best Mate odyssey. 'Hen' and her partner, Terry Biddlecombe, an unlikely match of personalities, Biddlecombe being a one-time pin-up jump jockey, added a love-story narrative seldom so publicly witnessed in sport.

Best Mate may have sounded British through and through but no, he represented the coming of a new age: horses bred in France. Even though Best Mate's sire, Un Desperado, was by Irish-bred Top Ville, out of a British-bred mare, Katday, the fact that Best Mate had been bred in France meant that the French breeding fraternity were 'all over' the Best Mate story. At last, we hailed a champion who equalled Arkle's three Gold Cups, never looked like falling, and either won or finished second in all 21 starts. Despite all Hen's careful planning, which characterised his immaculate career, on 1 November 2005, in his seasonal debut at Exeter, he lost his action, jockey Paul Carberry dismounted, Best Mate stumbled, fell to his knees and died at his trainer's feet. Jump racing was thrown into a state of shock. We had been denied not just another season or two of the highest-achieving chaser since Arkle but all those glorious, heart-warming years of retirement when Best Mate should have continued his victory parade. Best Mate's career earnings totalled a new record of just over £1 million but the cost of his early death was so much greater.

As we focused on the dreadful end of Best Mate's too-brief life, a horse named Kauto Star galloped past unnoticed to finish second to Monkerhostin in that fateful Haldon Gold Cup. Another French-bred horse, by Grand Prix de Saint-Cloud winner Village Star, Kauto Star was bought by Clive Smith for 400,000 euros on the recommendation of bloodstock agent Anthony Bromley, to be trained by Paul Nicholls. He next appeared on the big stage of Sandown's Tingle Creek Chase, confirming the high expectations of his connections.

Tom Dreaper had skilfully managed the campaigns of the contemporary champions Arkle and Flyingbolt; David Elsworth had been equally clever to get the best from the two champions Desert Orchid and Barnbrook Again. Paul Nicholls was now faced with the enviable challenge of managing the campaigns of two fabulously exciting prospects, Kauto Star and Denman, neighbours at his Ditcheat stables, where Clive Smith also owned Master Minded. In 2008, Nicholls came closer than anyone had to Michael Dickinson's 1983 'Famous Five', when Denman, Kauto Star and Neptune Collonges filled the first three places in the Cheltenham Gold Cup. This was indeed a golden age for steeplechasing. When he retired, Denman's career earnings exceeded Best Mate's by £119,000. Kauto Star, the only horse to have regained the Gold Cup title, and winner of four Betfair Chases and five King George Chases, had earned £3.7 million, which included a couple of valuable bonuses. Kauto Star's Timeform rating of 191 put him level with Mill House and

was the best since that of Arkle. By virtue of the range of his wins from two miles at Sandown to three-and-a-quarter miles round Cheltenham, and his sheer consistency at Grade One level, he was without doubt the best since Arkle and, on his day, would have proved more than a handful for 'Himself'. Frankel was given the courtesy of being promoted above Sea Bird's 1962 best-ever rating on the flat. Sufficient film of Arkle and Flyingbolt exists for forensic research by handicapping experts to reassess whether they were really so much better than any jumper we have seen since. Yet, Kauto Star no longer rubs shoulders with Flyingbolt and Mill House on the all-time ratings. He has been rudely demoted to fourth place by a two-mile specialist, Sprinter Sacre – the French keep coming.

Two-mile chasers

However prodigious their talent, two-mile chasers very seldom catch the attention beyond that of the racegoers who regularly watch the sport. A notable exception was Flyingbolt, who in 1966 very nearly completed an unlikely double of Champion Chase and Champion Hurdle before winning the Irish Grand National. Moscow Flyer, Azertyuiop and Well Chief never resonated with the wider public in the same way as the top staying chasers. Owing to the smaller

Mouse Morris and Skymas, winners of the 1976 and 1977 National Hunt Two-Mile Champion Chase.

number of horses running at this distance, when a single mistake can ruin a winning chance, horses that excel frequently remain at the top for several seasons, giving jump fans a thrilling 'under-card' from December through to April.

Skymas, trained in Ireland by Mouse Morris, was one such champion, winning in 1976 and 1977, and few would swap the experience of watching the likes of Badsworth Boy, Pearlyman or Barnbook Again jumping 12 fences at speed for the ebbs and flows of a race over three miles or more. Trainer David Nicholson specialised in this division with Waterloo Boy, Very Promising and Viking Flagship; Paul Nicholls with Call Equiname, Azertyuiop, Master Minded and Dodging Bullets; and Nicky Henderson with Remittance Man, Finian's Rainbow and Sprinter Sacre.

Sprinter Sacre took his trainer and supporters on a most remarkable journey. At the 2016 Festival cheers greeting his 'Queen Mother' victory raised the roof from the new grandstand. He regained the title after three years that included a diagnosis with a rare heart condition resulting in his only four defeats in 18 appearances over fences. That day at Cheltenham he set a standard for two-mile chaser popularity unlikely to be matched for many years. 'Sprinter' followed that up with an exhilarating Grade One performance at Sandown, a race that was to prove to be his last. The patience and expertise of Nicky Henderson and his team had given us a rare glimpse of equine perfection.

Hurdlers

It is a quirk of jump racing that, for chasers, the stayers' division (for horses requiring a longer distance) is held in far higher esteem and public acclaim than their two-mile equivalent, whereas for hurdlers, the exact opposite holds true. Hurdlers in the stayers' division, covering greater distance and jumping more flights, are considered to be of less merit than those competing over the minimum distance. Those tasked with generating wider media interest in the Festival, away from the Gold Cup, who stray into extolling the virtues of an upcoming clash between Baracouda and Iris's Gift in the long-distance World Hurdle, are likely to be met with the same blank looks as a 'track and field' promoter who suggests that the Olympic pole vault has just as much to offer as the 100 metres. It may be true among the cognoscenti – but not to a wider audience.

Big Buck's very nearly put an end to that perceived order of merit when he went about extending a winning sequence at Grade One level in Newbury's Long Distance Hurdle, at Cheltenham, and at Aintree to four consecutive years, in three of which he also landed Ascot's Long Walk Hurdle. Inglis Drever proved equally dominant over long distances and, passing rivals in a swoop towards the end of each race, brought a special excitement for favourite backers. The connections of another top-class stayer, Baracouda, were frustrated by the cancellation of the 2001 Festival when the horse was primed for the World Hurdle, subsequently lifting the title with style in the following two years. He had proved masterful at Ascot and narrowly prevailed at Windsor in the year when the Long Walk was relocated from Ascot. The 2015/16 'champion' at Newbury, Ascot, Cheltenham and Aintree, Thistlecrack is likely to be returning to those courses over fences as Colin Tizzard turns his attentions to a campaign at the highest level.

Sequences are just as frequently achieved in the Champion Hurdle. Persian War set the trend in the hands of hurdling-specialist jockey Jimmy Uttley and, after Fred Winter had dominated with Bula and Lanzarote (before they went chasing), and Fred Rimell with Comedy Of Errors, there was a group at the top, including Night Nurse, Monksfield, Sea Pigeon and Birds Nest, that delivered a series of the most thrilling contests. 'Peter' Easterby is rueful that his own stable's Little Owl prevented Night Nurse from becoming the first horse to win both Champion Hurdle and Gold Cup, leaving that honour to Dawn Run. Sheikh Mohammed has not yet been sighted at Cheltenham but his Kribensis completed the treble of Fighting Fifth Hurdle, Christmas Hurdle, and Champion Hurdle for trainer Sir Michael Stoute before embarking on a long career as the trainer's hack. Royal Gait, for trainer James Fanshawe, proved that eight flights of hurdles need pose no barrier to converting flat-racing form at the highest level. Winner of the Prix du Cadran and Prix Royal Oak in France, Royal Gait had been disqualified after winning the Ascot Gold Cup for causing the fall of the pacemaker. Following nearly three-and-half years off the track, he took to hurdling, becoming the first novice to win the Champion since Doorknocker in 1959.

An Irish 2,000 Guineas winner for Sheikh Hamdan bin Rashid Al Maktoum was to prove a similar point with no fewer than 23 Grade One hurdle wins. Carrying memories of young trainer John Durkan, who had died of leukaemia, Istabraq was transferred to the stables of Aidan O'Brien by owner JP McManus. Istabraq's reputation preceded him to Cheltenham where he won the 1997 Royal & Sun Alliance Hurdle by nine lengths, the only challenge on the day coming from the racecourse manager mistaking the green-suited trainer for a winner's-enclosure invader and attempting a feeble tackle that, quite rightly, raised the hackles of supporters. Istabraq's connections were back in the winner's enclosure following the next three Champion Hurdles – and may well have matched the four Irish Champion Hurdle wins had not foot-and-mouth disease intervened. Try as they

might, connections were thwarted in their urging to get the race rescheduled.

Istabraq returned in 2002 and was pulled up in front of the stands, to be retired in a race that James Fanshawe won with Hors La Loi III. The crowd's reaction to the favourite dropping out of the race with a circuit to go was spontaneous applause, which had barely faded away when second-favourite Valiramix was fatally injured. Amid all the emotion, winning owner Paul Green felt that appropriate attention had not been given to the presentation – and we did that all over again in the autumn. Istabraq has every reason to be remembered as a Champion Hurdler to sit alongside the very best in the sport. Timeform rated him 180, level with Monksfield, and just below Night Nurse. In Istabraq's case, however, it was not just the races he won but also the support he generated that made him so special.

Willie Mullins has turned up the heat on the opposition in recent years, with Hurricane Fly carrying all before him with 22 Grade One wins, then Faugheen and the remarkable mare Annie Power, prompting thought that she might complete 'a Dawn Run'. That option was never offered to Quevega at Cheltenham, where she completed six wins in the recently introduced OLBG David Nicholson Mares Hurdle, Willie Mullins also training the winner of the following two renewals of the race with Glens Melody and Vroum Vroum Mag. Back home in Ireland, Quevega has landed four World Series Hurdles at the Punchestown Festival.

Owner JP McManus, jockey Charlie Swan, Irish singer-comedian, Brendan Grace and trainer Aidan O'Brien celebrate after Istabraq's victory in the Champion Hurdle in 2000.

Losers

Gallant and serial losers have a particular place in the psyche of jump-race fans. They watched, spellbound, as Richard Pitman drove Crisp over the final fence and towards the elbow at Aintree. With a hundred yards to go, he looked certain to win the 1973 Grand National and then Red Rum snatched glory away from him. Few recall that Crisp was a champion two-mile chaser in his native Australia, where he was dubbed 'the black kangaroo', won the 1971 Champion Chase at Cheltenham and, in 1974, won a specially arranged match race at Doncaster against Red Rum at level weights, a 23-lb turnaround from Aintree. Crisp beat his old foe by eight lengths but honours were hardly even.

Devon Loch remains the unluckiest loser in jump-racing history. His dramatic collapse in the 1956 Grand National won the hearts of the nation.

Wynburgh still holds the record of finishing second in the National on the most occasions, completing the course five times from six attempts, three times being the runner-up. The Jonjo O'Neill-trained Get Me Out Of Here finished second four times at the Cheltenham Festival, beaten twice by a short head, once by a head. His rider on all four occasions was none other than 20-times champion jockey, AP McCoy. Imagine what that did to the atmosphere in the McCoy household. The same stable has the honour of being beaten by the narrowest margin in the Grand National, when Sunnyhillboy went

down by a nose in 2012 to Neptune Collonges. Those narrow losers all won plenty of races and can be remembered as much for the good times.

As a serial loser, Quixall Crossett came from an entirely different parish, retiring at the age of 17 in 2002 after a career of 103 consecutive defeats. Dubbed 'The Sultan of Slow' when he eased past flat-racing legend Amrullah's losing-streak record of 74 in 1998, he never failed to put in his best effort, finishing second twice and amassing career earnings of £8,502. During one particular ten-month period, he ran 31 times. He returned to the track after a 15-month lay-off at the age of 15, to complete his 'ton', amid growing welfare concern from the authorities but to adulation from his army of supporters, particularly in Scotland, where he was trained by Ted Caine.

Harchibald could well have joined the pantheon of great hurdlers if only he had been able to get the job done when perfectly poised to do so. Winner of both the 2004 Fighting Fifth and Christmas Hurdle, he was still on the bridle after the last under Paul Carberry in the Champion Hurdle, looking certain to complete Kribensis' 'triple crown'. The jockey knew he had to leave his challenge until the last 50 yards; otherwise, Harchibald would stop in front. As it turned out, they got no closer than a neck to Hardy Eustace, causing Carberry to be greeted by a rare outbreak of booing. That defeat proved to be not just a one-off when 'enigmatic' became the best way to describe Noel Meade's charge, as Harchibald subsequently went down to Brave Inca at Punchestown and to Straw Bear in the 2007 Christmas Hurdle. The trainer defended Harchibald's attitude by citing a wind problem the horse had suffered all his life, which forced his head to go up in the air when he was sucking for breath.

Most frustrating for connections and intriguing for observers are talented horses that simply refuse to start. Trained by Josh Gifford, Vodkatini got off the mark over fences in December 1985 despite whipping round at the start at Huntingdon and losing many lengths. Two years later, he did exactly the same at

Kempton. Backers were now conscious that the start of a race had become more of a risk than the finish. That proved to be the case in the 1988 Tingle Creek at Sandown, when Vodkatini 'planted' himself at the start, refusing to race and thus allowing Desert Orchid a bloodless victory. The other Vodkatini showed up at Kempton for the King George, getting away without a problem and finishing a good third behind Cavvies Clown and Charter Party. Three months later, at Aintree, the tapes went up and Vodkatini stayed put. He never won another race after running at Kempton, despite 17 attempts.

If there was ever a horse–trainer combination to challenge each other's character, it was that of Mad Moose and Nigel Twiston-Davies. Capable of finishing runner-up to Sprinter Sacre at Grade One level at Cheltenham in January 2013, Mad Moose refused to start on four occasions, including at both the Cheltenham Festival and at Aintree. When he did it again in the Tingle Creek at Sandown, the BHA took a dim view, banning the horse from running. 'The matter was referred to the Authority by the Sandown stewards', read the statement, 'because the gelding had been reluctant to race or tailed itself off, in both flat and jump races, on six further occasions in the previous 14 months. Having considered the evidence, including that from Twiston-Davies, the panel declare that with immediate effect no further entries would be accepted for Mad Moose.' That evidence included the episode of the trainer waving a belt as he chased after Mad Moose at Cheltenham, earning him a £140 fine. There was an outcry among the racing fraternity. 'Enigmatic' and 'quirky' do not deserve a ban, which was duly lifted the following autumn; with much anticipation, Mad Moose subsequently lined up in the International Hurdle at Cheltenham in December. No belt-chasing this time, just despair as Mad Moose refused to start and his stable companion, The New One, won the race. The trainer acted immediately, announcing, 'He's being retired anyway, so it's fine'.

Jockeys

Colonel Bill Whitbread, founder of the 'Whitbread', a major race in the racing calendar, is credited with the saying, 'There are fools, damn fools, and those who remount in a steeplechase'. Remounting is now banned but the denial of the possibility of defeat until the race is over pervades the ethics of the jockeys' changing room. Conditional jockeys, professional jockeys and amateur jockeys share a passion for success in jump racing. They do their job from the same changing room, and alongside each other in races over a range of distances, from two miles to over four miles, often in dire weather, prompting admiration from those who follow the sport, whether it be every day of the year or just one day a year. In no other sporting sphere would you expect to see the winner of the top event turning out the following day to compete at the lowest level.

From Stan Mellor, who topped the table with 68 winners in 1960, to Richard Johnson, who won the title (after 16 runner-up spots) with 235 winners in 2016, there have been 14 champion

Nigel Twiston-Davies, trainer of two Grand National winners, a Gold Cup winner and Mad Moose.

jockeys, who represent a range of riding styles and differing relationships with trainers but all of which have a similar take on courage, dedication, guile, flair, obsession and downright greed. Moments such as when Stan Mellor became the first jockey to ride 1,000 winners; when Jonjo O'Neill reached a total of 149 for a season, which many good judges thought would never be beaten; and when AP McCoy rode his 4,000th winner on Mountain Tunes at Towcester – such moments set the benchmarks that define the development of the sport.

Behind those figures are men who succeed and also men who narrowly fail to reach a level of sustained excellence that might prevail against the best efforts of their colleagues and whatever fate throws at them. Frequently, they operate with visceral energy, striving to convince themselves and others that they are fit to continue, determined to put themselves back at risk in a field of two dozen flailing limbs. Listening to the jockeys' descriptions of, for example, how they outwitted Arkle, how they overcame prejudice and bullying, and how they continued to maintain self-belief when others began to have their doubts takes you right into the mindset of individuals for whom second best is simply not an option.

Time and again, over the decades, those charged with promoting jump racing to a wider audience looked to the leading riders of the day, key rivalries and the jockeys' championship. The 1994 duel between defending champion Richard Dunwoody and 22-year-old former champion conditional jockey Adrian Maguire extended over two months. With the two jockeys never more than a few winners apart in the table, Dunwoody got himself suspended for the Festival when he was found guilty by the Nottingham stewards on 1 March of deliberately obstructing a horse ridden by his rival, causing Maguire to crash through the wings of the second-last hurdle. After falling 40 winners behind Maguire at the beginning of the year, the lead had been cut down to four. The young pretender had been quoted as 1-3 favourite for the title. At last, there was proper enmity in the weighing room. This was national-TV news material and Maguire gained high-profile ground with wins on Viking Flagship and Mysilv at Cheltenham.

On his return from the ban, Dunwoody had the resources of trainer Martin Pipe at his disposal, his battle with Maguire being just the sort of challenge he relished. Maguire relied heavily on Dunwoody's ex-boss, David Nicholson. Chasing each other around the country, not sharing a car, which would have been the case in another era, the physically stronger and more experienced Dunwoody ground down Maguire to gain a winning margin of three.

As the title of his autobiography, *Obsessed,* suggests, this was a champion not given to sharing the spoils. At the time, it was generally thought the inevitability of Adrian Maguire becoming a serial champion had merely been put on hold. As history proved, that was the closest he ever got, with 194 becoming far and away his highest total. With Maguire missing Festivals due to injuries and for personal reasons, it was not Maguire but McCoy who was to wrest the title back from the Brits.

All too often, it is news of the wrong kind that takes jump racing to the back, front and other pages. Jonjo O'Neill and AP McCoy both attracted the attention of the media to their riding style and use of the whip: O'Neill because his style was far more assertive than that of his British contemporaries; McCoy because the authorities called for corrective action. Adrian Maguire had been flown in for his very first ride in Britain when he piloted Omerta to land the Fulke Walwyn Kim Muir Chase as an amateur. His early career was nurtured by Toby Balding and it was the same trainer who mentored AP, the champion conditional jockey in 1995. As one title followed another for AP, and with Richard Johnson soon latching on as the perennial bridesmaid, we appeared to have a promotional dream ticket.

However, with rare exceptions, the public warm far more to a flawed genius – snooker's Alex Higgins and Ronnie O'Sullivan, rather than Steve Davis, being a fair comparison. AP has no flaws. Sure, he rode more losers than anyone else while he was riding more winners, but winning became so relentless and inevitable that media interest focused on how many he would win by, and whether he would beat his own targets, notably the 300 winners in a season, rather than whether he would win the title. Outside of racing, that's really not very interesting. Come 2010 and AP's unrequited passion for the Grand National changed all that. When he and Don't Push It crossed the line at Aintree, everything changed. In a moment, AP, who had so often turned his back on his adoring fans out of frustration and disappointment, allowed them to share his unbridled joy.

The campaign for his elevation to be voted BBC Sports Personality of the Year became over-institutionalised and all a bit embarrassing. Typical of racing, when given a chance to sing the praises of a hero, they do it on an operatic scale. For the next few years, jump racing had a twenty-first-century champion, who engaged brilliantly with his sport and the wider public; this engagement increased dramatically from the moment AP announced his intention to retire at the end of the 2015 season. In the two months leading up to the Sandown finale, AP toured the country fulfilling every engagement, hurting inside but with a smile and a wave, far removed from the moody ghost with hollow cheeks that haunted the ambition of would-be champions for two immense decades.

Opposite: Addington Boy, ridden by Adrian Maguire.

International competition

Jump jockeys are denied the ultimate honour of representing their country, something many of them envy other athletes of equal or lesser talent. That has not always been the case – if one is prepared to stretch the definition of representing one's country to agreeing to ride for Great Britain against a team of jockeys from other parts of the world, even if that invitation comes via a phone call from the manager at Cheltenham. When jockeys enjoyed two months' break in the summer, that representation included away 'Internationals' in the USA and New Zealand, as well as in France and Belgium, organised with Alan Lee, later to become cricket correspondent, then racing correspondent, of *The Times*. Home and away matches against jockeys from Russia brought a visiting jockey in front of the British stewards for riding with his whip between his teeth, the jockey explaining that he needed both hands on the reins, and the morbid sight of a compatriot making deft use of his whip in an attempt to bring back to life his mount, which had collapsed with a heart attack.

British and Irish jockeys of the vintage of Peter Scudamore, who rode extensively in Norway, John Francome, Jonjo O'Neill, Hywel

Davies and Steve Smith-Eccles honed their craft by riding alongside international riders of equal prowess in their own countries. In Britain, overseas jockeys often outrode their hosts, having far greater experience on horses of the low quality offered up by owners and trainers for a ballot that we needed to conduct in private to ensure that British jockeys were allocated horses they were prepared to ride. Most memorably, Japanese champion jockey Shinobu Hoshino travelled to Cheltenham for the modestly titled Rail Freight Jump Jockeys World Championship in April 1984. In a 12-jockey BBC-televised contest over four races, the very public draw for the first race put John Francome on his very own trainer Fred Winter's Don Giovanni. The Japanese jockey was drawn to ride Desert Hero for Winter's friend 'over the wall' in Lambourn, Fulke Walwyn. The 8-stone Hoshino carried 3 stone in lead; the only instruction Walwyn could give that his jockey could understand was that he should finish 'number one'. Hoshino got a real tune out of Desert Hero but Francome tracked him, cat-like, into the straight, ready to pounce. Hoshino then let out a little rein and pulled clear to land a sweet victory. Francome tells of a punter, who had 'lumped on' Fred Winter's 'good

Runners and riders negotiating the Taxis fence during the 117th Velka Pardubicka Steeplechase, Czech Republic, in 2007.

thing', accompanying the winner all the way back to the unsaddling enclosure, hurling every possible abuse at Hoshino, including references to his parenthood and Pearl Harbour, only to be greeted with a grateful 'thank you, thank you'.

The lack of an international dimension to jump racing is a frustration that is likely to continue, despite the best efforts of individuals. The Mullins family have been the most adventurous, achieving the only British or Irish win in the £850,000 Nakayama Grand Jump in Japan, which is run over two-and-three-quarter miles of twists, turns and undulations; Rich Ricci's Blackstairmountain gave Ruby Walsh the winning ride for Willie Mullins in 2013. The race had been opened up to overseas entries in 1999, subject to invitation, and Venetia Williams came close when The Outback Way finished third the following year. Martin Pipe and Paul Nicholls then took up the challenge, taking Exit Swinger and Cenkos out there in 2002, before they returned with Tiutchev and Armaturk the following year, all horses finishing down the field. Australian trainer Eric Musgrave soon had the race in his sights and his three successive wins with Karasi raised the stakes for British raiders. Willie Mullins' post-race quote in 2013 gives an

insight into his typical long-term planning for such a venture: 'I had the Nakayama Grand Jump in consideration back around ten years ago. I had two good jumpers, Florida Pearl and Alexander Banquet – big winners back home – that were invited. But when I came out to check on the conditions here, I decided it wouldn't suit both horses and withdrew the entry. I thought it would suit what we call a "summer horse" and it took me a few years to find a horse good enough.'

It was not the first time a Mullins-trained horse had 'won big' on another continent. In April 1990, the mare Grabel was among a stellar line-up for the inaugural $750,000 Duelling Grounds International, run at the USA course later to be renamed Kentucky Downs. Martin Pipe entered Regal Ambition, and Barry Hills was represented by the super-tough Nomadic Way, winner of the 1988 Cesarewitch and 1990 Irish Champion Hurdle. Having spent more time in quarantine than scheduled, Grabel breezed into the racecourse stables 24 hours before the race and, in the race itself, never looked like getting beaten. Paddy and Maureen Mullins and their rider son, Tony, led the family celebrations in some style.

That same year and in 1991, Toby Balding crossed the Atlantic with Morley Street, landing the Breeders Cup Chase in the hands of Jimmy Frost. Promoted by former amateur jockey George Sloan in the USA, the ambitious Sport of Kings Challenge then strove to establish a credible series between races in America, Britain and Ireland, and it is encouraging that the Brown Advisory Iroquois Cheltenham Challenge tempted Willie Mullins to compete in Nashville, Tennessee, in 2016 with two runners, narrowly being run into second and third. He will be back.

International odysseys have become more the preserve of Irish than British trainers, such forays needing the right horse, trainer, owner and jockey. Ironically, Charlie Mann has landed the only success for either nation in the Czech Republic's Velka Pardubicka, as trainer/rider of It's A Snip in 1995, since that of Chris Collins on Stephen's Society in 1973. Having stood beside Mann at Pardubice on several occasions

since his win, I can testify that his relief, each time another British or Irish attempt comes unstuck, is palpable. It is inconceivable that Cross Country Chase-expert Enda Bolger will not prevail one day. The 'Pardubicka', such a great race, became very much the property of local hero Josef Vana, winning eight times as a jockey and nine times as a trainer, often both at the same time. Such competition prompted the design of Cheltenham's Cross Country Chase course, which has been rewarded with many runners from the Czech Republic. This looked certain to be won by Velka Pardubicka winner, Registana in 2004, only for rider Peter Gehm to take the wrong course two fences from home after doing all the hard work.

Nearer to home, Willie Mullins regularly takes horses to Auteuil in Paris; he has won their Champion Hurdle, the Grande Course de Haies d'Auteuil, four times, following in his father's footsteps, Dawn Run having won in 1984 before she was tragically killed two years later. David Pipe became the first British trainer to win the race with Un Temps Pour Tout in 2015, a feat Paul Nicholls followed up with P'tit Zig in 2016.

Denied the opportunity of officially representing their countries, many jockeys have an ambition to win on foreign soil; this is also the case with trainers such as Martin and David Pipe, Paul Nicholls and, most notably, Willie Mullins, who regard the ultimate test as being global, rather than domestic, competition.

Amateur riders

Very few other major sports continue to embrace the participation of part-time, enthusiastic amateurs all the way to the most high-profile events as jump racing does. All sports grew up in the age of the amateur; one by one, they became professional and, while many continue to encourage amateur participation, there is a cut-off point beyond which amateurs are most unlikely to pass. Golf is a global exception with, very occasionally, the leaderboard in the Majors being headed by one of those who are playing for fun.

In jump racing, Sam Waley-Cohen has proved it is possible not only to compete alongside top professionals but also to beat them. In 2011, he rode his father's Long Run to win the Cheltenham Gold Cup, becoming the first amateur to do so since Jim Wilson on Little Owl 30 years earlier. The previous year, Waley-Cohen and Long Run had beaten Kauto Star in the King George VI Chase. Aboard Oscar Time in the 2011 Grand National, Sam finished second, a rare defeat over the course that has brought him six wins and the best record of any rider in modern times. That same year, he was nominated as Spears Young Entrepreneur of the Year for the development of his Portman Healthcare chain of dental practices. When Sam gets on his phone at the races, he will likely be sealing a deal, not picking up a spare ride. He was back on a winner at the highest level in the 2016 bet365 Gold Cup partnering The Young Master.

The gradation of rider qualification devised by the authorities is a tribute to the Amateur Jockeys Association of Great Britain, one of the most powerful organisations in the complex structure of the sport. That the Cheltenham Festival boasts three amateur-rider races is

The Prince of Wales was 'unseated' by Good Prospect in the 1981 Grand Military Gold Cup at Sandown. They were reunited and returned safely to unsaddle.

wholly down to the defence of this 'right' by a succession of expert lobbyists that included John Lawrence, General 'Monkey' Blacker and Gay Kindersley. What they had when the sport began to modernise, they held, despite a prolonged and ultimately foiled attempt by the Cheltenham Executive to allow conditional jockeys to ride alongside amateurs in one of the three Festival races. Eventually, conditionals – jockeys who have not won more than 75 races – were afforded their own race, named in honour of Martin Pipe.

To measure how far the sport has travelled over six decades and yet remains in a similar place, one need simply look at two remarkable amateur riders: the Duke of Albuquerque and Victoria Pendleton. Beltrán Alfonso Osorio y Díez de Rivera, 18th Duke of Albuquerque, thankfully known more simply as the 'Iron Duke', who became obsessed with the Grand National when watching a film of the race on his eighth birthday, could not be prevented by The Jockey Club from competing at Aintree between 1952 and 1976. A frequent faller with a catalogue of fractures to ribs, wrist, thigh and leg, he rode with a plastered collarbone in 1974, barging into champion jockey Ron Barry at the Canal Turn on the second circuit. In response to Ron Barry's desperate call of 'What the fuck are you doing?', the Iron Duke replied, 'My dear chap, I haven't a clue. I've never got this far before.'

Only a few years later, the heir to the throne, HRH The Prince of Wales, an accomplished horseman, embarked on a race-riding career. Making his debut at Plumpton in 1980 in a charity race won by BBC radio commentator Derek Thompson, His Royal Highness then rode in his first steeplechase at Sandown at the Grand Military Meeting. A year later and still without a win, Prince Charles rode Good Prospect, trained by Nick Gaselee, in the Kim Muir Memorial Challenge Cup Chase at the Cheltenham Festival. The crowd, nation and Commonwealth held its breath as the pair parted company on the second circuit. Hastened to the Ambulance Room, the Prince emerged, unscathed, to a media scrum, and became the only rider ever to remark to the racecourse manager 'how well the jumps are painted on the landing side'.

The sport's open-door policy attracted City-boy Brod Munro-Wilson, 54-year-old John Thorne finishing second to Bob Champion on Aldaniti, and top businesswoman Dido Harding. They competed alongside vastly experienced amateurs Marcus and Gee Armytage, Gee being persuaded to turn professional on account of her level of success. The likes of Ted Walsh, Adrian Maguire, Nina Carberry and Jamie Codd, now four-time winner of the 'Kim Muir' at the Festival, give a flavour of how 'professional' amateurs have come to dominate that division.

Amateur riders visit the sport from all possible directions, some just for a ride or two from their natural habitat of point-to-point, others who ride out at professional yards, some on their journey to becoming professionals, turning fun into finance. Regulations for riding at Aintree, even in the Fox Hunters' Chase, were tightened up as part of the initiatives to reduce risk – but not so for the Cheltenham Foxhunter Chase. An opportunity spotted in 2016 by Betfair to promote Olympian cyclist Victoria Pendleton by persuading her to 'switch saddles', for an incentive reported to be £200,000, captivated the widest audience for the sport since the days of Desert Orchid. With the backing of the most professional team, her fifth place on Pacha Du Polder in the Cheltenham Foxhunter Chase should prove an inspiration.

Trainers

Training yards come in all shapes and sizes. In parallel with other aspects of businesses in the rural economy, the trend over six decades has been towards larger yards dominating the market. Smaller enterprises need to feel 'boutique' to enjoy financial stability. Gradually, there has also been a gravitational pull towards the M4–M5 corridor for much of the activity of jump racing, raising concern for the health of the sport in the north.

Setting up as a professional trainer and pitting oneself against those already established requires substantial investment and determination but, unlike other sports, there is no hierarchy of leagues to prevent self-starters from giving it a go. Every so often, a minnow emerges from the ocean. As the horses returned to unsaddle after the 1990 Gold Cup, a glance at my racecard confirmed the fear that I had absolutely no idea what the winning trainer looked like. Sirrell Griffiths had milked his dairy herd before driving the lorry to the races with Norton's Coin aboard. Sporting miracles at 100-1 do happen but, as their odds suggest, not very often.

The race programme enables a loyal following for trainers who compete at any level. A good example would be that of Henry Daly who, from his Shropshire base, inherited the 'fan base' – not a phrase either might recognise – from his mentor Captain Tim Forster. Over a 36-year career, 'the Captain' sent out 1,346 winners, including three Grand Nationals. Master and pupil built their success on support from owners and supporters who relish their distinctive style and traditional values. On a scale that has 'traditional' trainers at one end and 'game-changers' at the other, Messrs Forster and Daly would hold up the former, along with Fulke Walwyn, Fred and Mercy Rimell, Fred Winter, Josh Gifford, David Nicholson, Henrietta Knight and Nicky Henderson. The game-changers' end would be occupied by Captain Ryan Price, MH (Peter) Easterby, Derek Kent, Michael Dickinson, Jenny Pitman, David Elsworth and Martin Pipe. The most impressive and successful trainers manage to shift along that

Victoria Pendleton switches saddles from cycling to steeplechasing.

*Willie Mullins –
a British trainers
championship on his
mind.*

scale as circumstances demand. That has proved the case with Paul Nicholls and, in Ireland, with Willie Mullins.

Those categories of traditionalists and game-changers can largely be extended to definitions of those who emerge from within the jump racing 'establishment' and those who arrive from outside that establishment. For much of the twentieth century, the establishment included those with military service – Jockey Club Officials and trainers recognising subtle signals of the fraternity, intuitively looking after their own. Since 1964, Cheltenham and the Festival have always been part of the Jockey Club establishment, a citadel that those from outside the establishment plot to storm. Aintree and the Grand National are the reverse, place and race belonging to the people. Since these have become part of the Jockey Club estate, their character has changed. Handicaps – races in which weight is added based on past performance – are a metaphor for socialism, everyone being given an equal chance, compared with championship races, where breeding, upbringing and performance earn advantage.

The popularising of the Festival coincided with handicaps being elevated in prize money and status, affording them more than a supporting role to the gold-standard, level-weight championship races. Jump racing has thrived over six decades through the wide appeal of finding a winner in valuable handicaps all the way up to the pinnacle of the Grand National. Excelling in those handicaps defines the expertise of many trainers from outside the establishment, Ginger McCain and Jonjo O'Neill being prime examples. As the Festival has grown in mass appeal through enhancing the role of handicaps, the Grand National meeting has travelled in the opposite direction, developing a programme of championship races that appeal to the establishment.

Through his prolific achievement in the Grand National with three-time winner Red Rum, McCain established himself as the most recognised jumps trainer in Britain, the first 'personality' trainer, being courted for TV appearances as the 'face of the National'. In the two decades between Red Rum's era and McCain's 2004 win with Amberleigh House, Jenny Pitman inherited that mantle. Twice a winner, with Corbiere and Royal Athlete, Jenny's annual BBC *Grandstand* love-in with Des Lynam became as much part of the race as Becher's Brook.

Jenny Pitman outshone Ginger McCain in two notable areas. First, her fame was not confined to Aintree, having trained two Gold Cup winners in Burrough Hill Lad and Garrison Savannah;

second, she was the first woman to succeed at the very top level in a world dominated by men. Ginger remained comfortable in his skin, encouraged by the media to express his views and not be taken too seriously. Jenny Pitman set her sights much higher; she became a role model for female achievement, comfortable in the company of the Queen Mother but never, quite, acknowledged by the racing establishment. A decade later, Henrietta Knight, a female trainer of more privileged background, rekindled the wider female interest in the Festival, with the same emphasis as that of Jenny Pitman, namely, her care and welfare of the horses, something that male trainers find more difficult to communicate naturally.

Winning the Grand National is as vital a line in the CV for most trainers as it is essential for jockeys. For a trainer, it is as much about status and going down in history as being associated with 'the people's race' as it is about the money. Witness that air-punch by Paul Nicholls, conjoined with pipping Nicky Henderson to the trainers' championship; the glow around Nigel Twiston-Davies; and the unbridled joy of Venetia Williams, Jonjo O'Neill and Mouse Morris. As the years tick by, Nicky Henderson, now elder statesman of the racing establishment, would like a Grand National if it came along but loses less sleep over that gap in his CV than his desire to win another Champion Hurdle.

In stature, voice, geographic context and sphere of influence, it is hard to imagine two men more contrasting than Ginger McCain and Martin Pipe. For all his record-breaking achievements, when he cheered Richard Dunwoody and Miinnehoma crossing that line in front in the 1994 National, Martin Pipe knew he would be remembered for more than mere statistics. Numbers are important for trainers; they drive the business day-to-day. Training 243 winners in a season, as Pipe did in 1999/2000, is a record likely never to be seriously threatened. Much of what Martin Pipe introduced at his stables at Pond House had been done before – but never with such intensity. Michael Dickinson and his parents, Tony and Monica, had the same surgical eye for detail, craving knowledge about each horse's physique and mental ability.

Their level of operation was way ahead of their contemporaries, applying training techniques from a totally different catalogue.

Michael Dickinson trained the first five in the 1983 Gold Cup during his glittering career. He never won the Grand National. The Dickinsons were very much part of the Yorkshire racing establishment, defining their dynasty by winning establishment races – hundreds of them. A Grand National would have been a welcome addition and another pot to polish.

Ever since 1968, almost six decades, when Fred Rimell first won the trainers' championship, only eight others have held that title, all being men. With the exception of David Elsworth in 1987/88, each managed at least two titles, several in substantial sequences. The title is by no means everything but it shows consistency in both quality and quantity. For some, their ambition is focused on establishment, that is, championship races; for others, the people's race, the Grand National, never loses its allure.

Owners

Jump racing is all about partnerships. Establishing a successful partnership between horse and rider is fundamental. The quirky nature of the thoroughbred is such that, for no apparent reason, it may thrive for one rider

Owner Clive Smith celebrates King George success with Kauto Star, Ruby Walsh and Paul Nicholls.

and consistently underperform for another, regardless of the rider's past experience and position in racing's pecking order. Equally, the partnership between trainer and jockey makes all the difference in transferring the proven ability shown on the gallops to a winning performance on the racecourse. Such relationships come in many different guises: from close friendships and family bonds to echoes of 'master–servant' autocracy.

Sheikh Ali Abu Khamsin, owner of Half Free, receives the Mackeson Gold Cup.

The partnership that can give most entertainment to others and is conducted in the public domain of the paddock and unsaddling enclosure is the one between trainer and owner. On one hand, there was the obvious meeting of minds between Martin Pipe and David Johnson; on the other hand, there were the very public differences of opinion between Paul Nicholls and Clive Smith, owner of Kauto Star. Ultimately, it is the owner who pays the bills; very few trainers have the financial security to break that partnership.

The racecourse paddock fulfils the dual purpose of allowing spectators to assess the fitness of the horses and bringing together the 'connections' of owner, trainer and jockey. The fourth party to that brief conversation is the stable lad or girl, the person who spends more time than any of the others with the horse and invests the most anxiety that the horse will come home safely; anything better than that is a bonus.

There is an even wider scale of owners than of trainers, ranging from royalty and multi-millionaires with several hundred horses to members of syndicates with a single share, representing literally a few hairs in the horse's tail. That owner–trainer partnership is often an obvious fit, with Nicky Henderson attracting fellow Old Etonians and bankers, Jonjo O'Neill with a high proportion of Irish owners, and Colin Tizzard appealing to the West-Country farming community. When that match is less obvious, the fun begins for paddock watchers.

Seldom does the entertainment come together so well as proved to be the case when Denman started to build his career. This was a rare case of there being joint owners from entirely different worlds, dairy farmer Paul Barber having sold a half-share to professional gambler Harry Findlay. There was never any doubt as to which partner would become spokesman for the horse, Barber quietly blending into the background beside Paul Nicholls as Findlay held court in the winner's circle.

Very occasionally, an owner's behaviour brings them into direct conflict with the authorities. Such was the case when Anthony Knott, a more colourful dairy farmer than Paul Barber, greeted Hunt Ball after winning at Wincanton in January 2012, leaping up behind jockey Nick Scholfield on the horse's back on his way to unsaddle. That earned him a £100 fine from the local stewards. Two years later, Knott was 'warned off' for three years for supplying inside information, later rescinded.

Fulke Walwyn managed the extreme gambling challenges thrown at him by Dorothy Paget; Fred Winter converted the unusual interest of a Saudi businessman into three seasons as leading owner. In a world where outsiders frequently bid to gain a foothold alongside members of the establishment, Sheikh Ali Abu Khamsin proved more than a curiosity. Winter got to know his motives and objectives very clearly, campaigning his horses where and when the owner could watch them, mainly in the south-west. Exeter, Sheikh Ali's local course, kindly refurbished a private box to his specifications, and protracted discussions to that end were carried out with the management at Cheltenham. Receiving a message from the trainer to take the negotiations slowly, I made regular visits for afternoon tea to the very functional Tattersalls Grandstand box, which we rented to Sheikh Ali on a daily basis. Winter thought this was ideal and guided me carefully to tell his owner quite how long the waiting list was for the 'old' boxes that abutted the Royal Box where Sheikh Ali wished to spend his visits among racing's establishment. Meanwhile, Fifty Dollars More won the Mackeson twice, Half Free won the same race and also the Cathcart twice, and Gaye Brief, trained by Mercy Rimell, won the 1973 Champion Hurdle.

Ownership frequently leads to sponsorship, with investment being embedded in several aspects of the sport. Jump racing provided a means to get close to the establishment for George Ward, boss of Grunwick Film Processing Laboratories in north London. He had taken on the unions in a strike lasting two years between 1976 and 1978, which saw 550 arrests. Jump racing gave Ward an affordable opportunity to be embraced by the establishment through extensive racehorse ownership and by sponsoring the early Bumper series, bringing him into contact with senior members of the Jockey Club and the Royal Family. Over a period of 22 years, Ward invested £25 million into race sponsorship, including the King George, Stayers Hurdle and Tripleprint Gold Cup. Together with Bernard Gover, he took over and relaunched the Horserace Sponsorship Association. Sponsorship for both codes of racing now exceeds £30 million; almost half of all sponsored races promote the betting industry. In addition, sponsorship of trainers' yards allows owners to reclaim VAT, while sponsorship of the jockeys' championship and of individual jockeys spreads investment right across the sport.

As Newbury's Hennessy Gold Cup approaches its 50th anniversary, sponsorship, ranging from local firms to multi nationals, brings far more than the valuable cash investment. Association with sponsors' names promotes the sport to a wide audience and many first-time racegoers who attend as a guest of a sponsor become regular visitors, sharing that experience with their friends and family.

The unexpected

Part of the appeal of sponsoring a horse race is that there is just a chance that something totally unpredictable may happen and what was intended to be seen by a few thousand will 'go global'. There are so many moving parts in a race over steeplechase fences that the likelihood of such moments occurring are far greater than in, say, tennis. As the 'master of the unpredictable', the Grand National rules supreme. Despite all the safety measures, properly introduced over the years, audiences tune in as they do for the start of a Formula One race – just in case there is mayhem. That remains part of the appeal of jump racing.

The 1967 Grand National set the standard. Named, like Arkle, after a magnificent mountain in Sutherland, Foinavon was ridden into the pantheon of unlikely sporting heroes by Johnny Buckingham after Popham Down, running loose since the first fence, veered across the leaders at the 23rd fence. The melee involved 17 horses and riders, one of whom managed to be reunited with the wrong horse in pursuit of the 100-1 shot. Though regarded as a worthy outsider, Foinavon had been good enough to finish fourth in the King George VI Chase and had run in the Cheltenham Gold Cup three weeks earlier, so, once clear of the field, it was not surprising that he held on to win in some style. Key to the worldwide audience that the incident attracted was the good fortune that commentary for that section of the course rested in the hands of Irishman Michael O'Hehir, who described 'a right pile-up'.

An extraordinary moment of a different sort occurred in 1981 when Bob Champion recovered from cancer achieved the most emotional win aboard Aldaniti, himself recovered from a career-threatening injury. Once again, the Grand National hit the headlines for all the right reasons and that particular story became a cinema success.

On two occasions in the 1990s, the non-running of the race brought immense global interest. In 1993, faulty starting equipment caused the race 'won' by Esha Ness to be declared void, and four years later a bomb scare prompted total evacuation, the race being rescheduled to the following Monday, when vast crowds moved heaven and earth to witness Lord Gyllene's victory.

The Cheltenham Gold Cup borrowed from Aintree's stock of fairytales during the 1980s with a sequence comprising Michael Dickinson's 'famous five' in 1983; Dawn Run's double of Champion Hurdle and Gold Cup in 1984 and 1986; The Thinker winning after the race was delayed due to snow in 1987; Desert Orchid in 1989; and Norton's Coin at 100-1 in 1990. Attendances and media interest virtually doubled in that decade.

Not to be outdone by the Grand National, not running the races has proved a winning formula for promoting interest at Cheltenham. The 2001 Festival became a high-profile casualty of the foot-and-mouth outbreak, and high winds caused the Wednesday of the 2007 Festival to be rescheduled to form two elongated days with 19 races between them.

That chance of it all going wrong but nobody getting hurt is part and parcel of staging an outdoor equestrian sport in winter, with risks that will remain so long as there are large numbers of horses and riders, all in their proper zones but, potentially, getting in each other's way.

Aldaniti, ridden by Bob Champion, races to victory after clearing the last fence in 1981.

Racecourses

Racegoers are no different from other sports fans. It is easy to underestimate how passionate and committed they feel about their local 'home' course, just as football, rugby and cricket supporters are about their team and ground. The moment the fixture list comes out, these are the first dates to go into the diary; less important events, such as family weddings, must work around them. Home fixtures are immersed in ritual. For annual members, the car-park label is glued to the windscreen the moment it arrives; the badge is safely secured around the gearstick; and, on race day, that twenty-first-century smartcard is shifted nervously from glove compartment to wallet to trouser pocket. For others, tickets have been bought online and pinned onto the kitchen noticeboard. For major fixtures, texts are exchanged between friends about how many 'sleeps' there are until the big day. Cheltenham fans have greeted me in town from mid-September with the best news possible: that the next Festival was now closer than the previous one! Finally, the moment comes to put on the lucky socks, left foot first, ever since that rank outsider obliged. Racegoers' clothes have changed in parallel with the general trend towards informality. Men tend to dress smartly for the occasion with styled denim and country jacket. Ladies tend to don designer checked coats. The drive, train journey, bus ride or walk to the course is punctuated with unnecessary visits to faded pubs and dodgy coffee shops where father and grandfather always used to pay a visit. Short cuts through farmyards and housing estates throw the satnav into apoplexy and result in the last mile being endured behind the horsebox overtaken on the motorway half an hour back. Once at the course, the rituals really kick in: lucky turnstile, coffee from this stall, first bet with that bookmaker – and so the day continues.

Away fixtures are a totally different proposition. Racecourses are most completely relished when an hour or two is afforded to set them in their context. By the time one arrives at Ludlow or Cartmel, the bucolic countryside has eased tension from your shoulders and

allowing oneself an extra hour to stroll around the village, or visit the castle, will make even greater sense of why the racecourse is there and what it means to its people.

Certain courses, for example Plumpton (but, sadly, no longer Folkestone), have to be approached by train, ideally on a Monday. That is how it has always been and, in Plumpton's case, should remain. The train journey from London is as much part of the day as the racing itself. Overseas, Auteuil needs to be glimpsed through sunlit branches on a stroll through the Bois de Boulogne – not from the window of a cab on the Peripherique; Pardubice in the Czech Republic needs to appear, abruptly, at the end of a walk from the town through thick forests, the intrepid racegoer randomly crossing railway lines, side-stepping express trains.

Urban jump courses have a very important role to play in the heritage and culture of the sport. They defy the origins of the sport, 'steeplechasing', which involved racing across open country from one village to the next using the church steeple as the target. A pause to inspect a nineteenth-century print is likely to be a reminder that Aintree, for example, was once very much part of the countryside and has since been swallowed up by urban sprawl. To fully understand the Grand National meeting, at least one night, prior to the meeting, needs to be enjoyed in the city, with the subsequent journey to the course to be taken by train from Liverpool Central.

City courses have come under pressure from the foibles of racecourse funding. Nottingham and Wolverhampton have both lost their jump racing to allow management to focus on the more profitable flat racing; Newcastle has introduced all-weather flat racing, which some fear may compromise the course's interest in the jump programme.

Several courses are located on the edge of market towns or deep in the countryside – proper places for an outing. Windsor's loss of jumping has deprived the Home Counties of a country track. Ascot introduced jump racing in 1965 and continues to develop its very

considerable impact with top-quality sport. Ffos Las has been a surprising addition, a tribute to civil engineering, the vision of owner Dai Walters and to the popularity of jump racing in South Wales.

The Horserace Betting Levy has been the mechanism through which so many courses have survived and prospered against the odds of free-market economics. Since its introduction in 1961, individual racecourse managements and, from the formation of Racecourse Holdings Trust in 1964, ownership groups have developed their businesses around their relationship with the Levy. Major courses with large capacities and tiny courses with negligible overheads could both argue that they would have survived without the Levy, particularly without the competition of rivals buoyed up by the Levy. However, all courses acknowledge that, by working together, they have a racing product to sell to the betting market and, more recently, to media companies.

With Hereford restored to the fold, 41 courses currently host jump racing in Britain. Since the expansion of summer jumping, this has become a year-round sport with a strong geographic spread. There is, truly, somewhere for everyone. Interest-free loans from the Levy Board encouraged courses to improve facilities for customers and for the 'horsemen' in non-revenue

Ludlow Racecourse, typical of the country setting at the heart of the sport.

earning projects such as stables and weighing rooms. Creature comforts have kept pace with competing leisure venues and the expectations of customers. Revenues from the demand of high-spend individuals and corporates for boxes and luxurious restaurants have been harvested for the less affluent fans.

In the early 1960s, staying at home and watching the racing on television became a popular alternative. Fifty years later, those who have travelled to distant racecourses, paying for admission at great expense, have a clear view of the racing yet sometimes choose to watch it on television screens. Emphasis for those promoting racecourse attendance is now on the experience, the feeling of being at the event itself, enjoying the ambience and atmosphere. There is no value advantage for high-stake gamblers since deductions from off-course betting were abolished and, for many occasional visitors, this is the only time they will bet on horseracing. For a few hours, they share the age-old experience of having a flutter.

Conditions on the course and over the jumps have continued to improve for the horses and riders. Sadly, some injuries suffered by horses, as in every other equine sport, will prove to be career-threatening or even fatal. The statistical risk of a fatality is now well below half of one per cent and, through the efforts of all parties, being reduced all the time. Veterinary expertise now allows more horses to survive, return to active sport and to racing. Plastic rails and fence wings,

irrigation equipment that prevents fast ground, enhancements to turf management and in fence and hurdle design all contribute to reducing risk while retaining the spectacle of the sport.

It is a curiosity of the sport that the winning times of races have not come down despite the advances in training. Much of this is due to courses being watered more efficiently and turf being improved. However, horses are fitter and jockeys 'go for home' much earlier in a race than previous generations will have done. Data from the number and type of falls has prompted the relocation of high-risk fences and hurdles. This was the case arising from the analysis of the second-last fence on Cheltenham's Old Course. The increasing number of falls and injuries, mostly for horses improving their position in the race, had forced reconsideration of that 'signature' fence. Since its move from before the final bend to after the final bend, the improved data makes encouraging reading. Trainers, jockeys, vets, officials and racecourses work together to identify manageable risk and buy into solutions.

Water jumps have been phased out by many courses except, in the main, where they are sited in front of the grandstands. Fewer falls occur at water jumps than at plain fences. However, the fence following a water jump is statistically one where falls are most likely to occur. By removing the water jump, there is no longer that increased risk.

The issue of reduced visibility from low sun

impacting on horses and jockeys is relatively recent. This has proved difficult to manage where the horses run towards the late-afternoon sun, down the back straight or up the finishing straight. Removing an entire stretch of hurdles does the sport no favours. Jockey safety is a priority that has been properly taken on board; the extension of their careers pays tribute to the progress that has been made from working closely, through their appointed representatives, with racecourses and their officials. Risk and injury will never be totally removed. For spectators, witnessing a sport where jockeys accept that pact with fate every time they leave the comfort of the weighing room and are followed around by an ambulance adds to the breadth of the emotional experience. Having a bad day as a punter can quickly and sadly be put into perspective.

Villains

The Rules of Racing and the firm, but fair, British Horseracing Authority deliver a sport of high integrity that has absolute credibility for investors, whether they be owners, sponsors or punters. Those who commit their lives as professionals or amateurs to training and riding horses do so in the full and certain knowledge that the sport will weather an occasional storm and see them through to a day when they can reflect on what they have achieved. They also know that stepping out of line with the rules will result in penalties ranging from a few days' suspension to being 'warned off' for years or even for life. Time and again, those who transgress are reminded that the sport is far bigger than any one individual.

Against that background, the best-known jump jockey, worldwide, is Sid Halley, whose name does not appear in the record books but in the fiction of Dick Francis. Hero of *Odds Against*, published in 1965, British Champion Jump Jockey and private detective Sid Halley returned 30 years later in *Come to Grief*. Since Dick Francis died in 2010, his son Felix has picked up the pen. Translated into more than 30 languages,

this publishing phenomenon has taken the sport to countries with no other contact with the sport. I once saw a Dick Francis paperback in a bookshop in Zimbabwe. His following proves the enormous appetite for reading about skulduggery when it comes to the murky world of jump racing. In 1974, *Dead Cert*, Dick Francis' very first book, was released as a film starring Judi Dench and Michael Williams. That same year, on August Bank Holiday, a real-life drama took place at Cartmel that also became a TV film, with Pierce Brosnan and Niall Toibin in the lead roles. The film was called *Murphy's Stroke,* about a horse called Gay Future.

Low-profile trainer Tony Collins had not sent out a winner for over a year when Gay Future was entered to run at Cartmel to be ridden by a little-known amateur rider. The architect of the coup was Irish millionaire Tony Murphy, who enlisted trainers Edward O'Grady in Ireland and Tony Collins. O'Grady trained the real Gay Future while Collins trained Gay Future's lookalike, a horse of little ability. The horses were switched in a lay-by close to the racecourse. Collins entered two other horses in races elsewhere on the busy Bank Holiday, the races set to start, respectively, five minutes before and ten minutes after Gay Future's race. Murphy and his syndicate flew over to London and laid a vast quantity of multiple bets on all three horses in betting shops across

Jockeys battling each other in a scene from the film Dead Cert, *1973.*

the capital. The two other runners were then withdrawn and soapflakes were rubbed into Gay Future's coat to make out he was 'sweating up', thus appearing unlikely to run well. When bookmakers became aware they were about to be hit, they strove to reduce the starting price of Gay Future. However, in those far-off times, Cartmel had only one public telephone and this was kept engaged by a caller from the syndicate. Ladbrokes sent cash with a motorbike-rider from Manchester to the course in a desperate attempt to lower the odds, but the motorbike got held up in the Bank Holiday traffic – and the horse romped home by 15 lengths at 10-1. The bookmakers cried 'foul' and just one mistake, a stable worker letting slip to a reporter that the other two horses had never left the yard, led the case to Preston Crown Court. Both Collins and Murphy were found guilty of conspiracy to defraud bookmakers and later banned from racing for ten years.

For every 'Gay Future'-style coup that succeeds, several fail, but it remains a key component of the culture of jump racing in Britain and Ireland that a margin for skulduggery continues to exist. In the years I managed Cheltenham, we responded to threats that a Gold Cup favourite would be shot by protecting the horse on his entire route from the stables through the paddock to the start, positioning the huntsmen who lead the parade either side of him. He did not win the race. The weekend prior to another Festival, we discovered that the security cameras in the stables had been tampered with. The camera covering one corner, always occupied by horses from a certain yard, showed clear pictures on the bank of screens but not the pictures of what was actually happening. For example, when a colleague actually opened a box door, the pictures were showing that it remained closed. Someone was up to no good.

Every pound spent on protecting the security and integrity of the sport is well invested but there will always be forces out there bidding to outmanoeuvre the authorities and make a financial 'killing'.

Storytellers

Jump racing has benefited enormously from having media platforms upon which to build heroes and broadcast 'good news' stories. That period of the mid-1980s when there was such a rich seam of activity on the track coincided with ITV bosses calling time on *World Of Sport* and Channel 4 negotiating a deal that started with selected fixtures at Sandown and Kempton in 1986. *The Morning Line* was launched in the autumn of 1989, the title being suggested by commentator Graham Goode from the US term for early odds. The team assembled by producer Andrew Franklin for racing's first magazine show included John McCririck, John Francome and Lesley Graham.

Getting Cheltenham into the Channel 4 stable was identified as a major target in which Chief Executive Michael Grade took personal interest, spearheading the presentation to win the contract in 1995. Andrew Franklin recalls that if that bid had failed, Channel 4 would have walked away from racing. With Cheltenham secured, the executive team at the channel, who had little interest in racing themselves, were kept onside until financial pressures brought the marginal profits of such an extensive outside broadcast under scrutiny. By a stroke of good fortune, that moment coincided with government rules relaxing the prohibition of bookmakers' programme sponsorship – and the Tote's Chairman Peter Jones stepped in to protect their Scoop 6, the popular six-horse accumulator bet.

From the outset, the relationship between Channel 4 and the racecourses was dynamic. That was very much part of the attraction. Far from simply showing up with cameras and crew, which had largely been the style of the BBC's engagement, Channel 4's Head of Sport expected to be involved with everything: from the narrative of the sport, giving viewers a better understanding of how each race relates to the end-of-season highlights, to experimenting with technology such as wire-cams and jockey-cams.

The process of selecting the new races for the Festival when it was decided to expand from three days to four days took Clerk of the Course Simon Claisse and me to many lively discussions with interested parties. The most memorable was to a dinner with the entire Channel 4 team in a smart Newmarket hotel, where the heated debate led to faux fisticuffs between arch-advocate for expansion, John McCririck, and self-proclaimed defender of the status quo, Alastair Down. These are people who were determined to do all they could to protect, challenge and celebrate the occasion they love with a fierce passion.

The arrival of Sky and the revolution for subscribers to access the sport of their choice led to the demise of BBC's *Grandstand*, which had provided a window on racing since 1958. Gradually, the BBC lost interest in covering the sport and 2012 saw their last year at Aintree. From January 2017, ITV will be back as the racing's broadcaster with a four-year contract after a 31-year absence, closing an era through which Channel 4 has championed the excitement, intrigue and issues with a delicate balance between gravitas and good humour. BBC continues to enjoy a large audience through its long-standing radio contract. The combination of national coverage on Radio 5 Live, under the leadership of Cornelius Lysaght, and regional interest in fixtures, trainers and jockeys on BBC Local Radio keeps the sport

familiar to a wide audience. On marquee occasions, such as the Cheltenham Festival and Grand National meeting, programming over several hours takes the flavour of the day and the exploits of key characters into the homes, offices and cars of the nation.

John McCririck, the most recognisable face in racing.

The written media has changed out of all recognition with 24-hour online information supporting and, in some cases, threatening the diet of racing pages in all national newspapers. Local coverage in regions where the sport is strong delivers a constant reminder of who to follow when the local fixture comes along. With no racing within Greater London, the greatest contrast over five decades is in the amount of racing content in the *London Evening Standard*, which once had its own special edition and for years carried all the results as they unfolded during the day. Now there is no racing news in the paper except on very few special occasions.

John Francome, natural talent.

The satellite channels, Racing UK and Attheraces, deliver the most comprehensive coverage of every jump race in Britain and Ireland. Make no mistake; commercial advertising for betting organisations funds the television coverage of the sport. If that were to be threatened, something that remains on certain political agendas, racing would find itself in a precarious situation.

The stable staff

Farrier Ben Parker checks all is well as Trickaway trots up at Philip Hobbs' Sandhill Racing Stables.

Jump racing boasts substantial economic benefit to the rural economy. As farming in Britain becomes an ever more marginal sector, the contribution of training stables has grown in importance, both for the valuable supply chain and as a substantial source of employment.

There is no better barometer of the progress of jump racing over six decades than the development of working conditions and career prospects for the more than two thousand people who choose to work in jump-racing stables. Owners pay the training bills and receive the acclaim but those working with the horses make the greatest emotional investment. Each lad or girl will often look after two or three horses. They get to know the horses' moods and foibles, sharing good times and bad, nursing them back from injury and picking up the pieces when an outing to the races goes dreadfully wrong.

In the twenty-first century, there is a proper structure for building a career for stable staff. They do not need to have any experience of working with horses, as attending the course at The British Racing School will equip them with the skills they need. The Northern Racing School, near Doncaster, provides a foundation

Philip Hobbs' string prepares to move out to the gallops.

course that leads to work experience that will secure an apprenticeship placement in a racing stable. The National Association of Stable Staff negotiates terms for salaries and distribution of pool money from prize money; it also provides guidance on matters such as contracts and maternity rights. Work is hard, hours are long and often unsociable, but conditions are appropriate for a sport that attracts investment from multi-millionaires, that rewards top trainers and riders with decent prize money and enjoys valuable media coverage.

Witness the elation on the faces of stable staff as they rush to greet winners or their anxiety as they run down the course to attend to their stricken charges. Sample the quiet at the stables the morning after a box has returned empty and you will understand what it means to be a proud member of this fraternity.

Especially for those who follow the sport for only a few hours each March or April, the extent of the work that goes on behind the scenes to produce those 500 competitors at the Festival and the 40 runners in the Grand National would appear quite bewildering. For every champion to be produced, several hundred horses need to be bred, 'broken', trained, maintained and found a happy retirement. It takes several years to build that dream and only a few seconds for it to be destroyed. That is the way of this sport.

The future

Jump racing remains very much a sport for participants and fans while generating revenues and delivering an economy that justifies its description as an industry. Unlike flat racing, where the stud fees are the ultimate dividend for investors, over the jumps what you see is what you get. Horses that have won at the highest level might have less pecuniary value after that big win, as the chances of their doing it again are very slim.

Welfare of horses and jockeys is of absolute importance. The BHA works closely with all parties to continually find solutions in order to reduce manageable risk. Newcomers to ownership or those training for a career as stable staff will be encouraged to find out what happens to horses after their racing careers, how retraining racehorses feeds into other leisure activities.

The essence of British jump racing is a sport administered in a highly professional manner for participants seeking credibility, fun and some financial reward. The 2015 BHA Review of Jump Racing set the agenda for the next five years, recommending improvements for the finances, for the supply of horses into the sport, improving opportunities for horses and participants, and how best to promote and be positive about the sport. Delivery of the agenda is the joint responsibility of the BHA, the Horsemen's Group representing the common interests of owners, trainers, jockeys, stable staff and breeders, and the Racecourse Group.

Since the economic downturn in 2008, many of the metrics have moved in the wrong direction. Most crucially, by 2014, the average number of jump horses in training had declined by 850 (14.5 per cent) to below 5,000, while the number of races increased by 7 per cent, leading to smaller field sizes. Trainers may welcome fewer opponents but the betting market demands at least eight runners in each race – and the betting market drives the industry.

With all-weather racing becoming more socially acceptable and offering good prize money, combined with the increased flat-racing activities in the Emirates, the number of horses coming to jumping from a career on the flat almost halved from just under 2,000 in 2009 to just over 1,000 in 2014. At the same time, the number coming from Irish point-to-points rose from 925 to 1,415. Their vendors and sales agents are pleased about that. Despite economic trends, average prize money for jump races dropped only from £11,075 in 2008 to £10,700 in 2014.

Particular attention is being given to how jump racing in the north can be revitalised at a time when flat racing is delivering a quicker return on investment. The quality of horses trained in the north has declined with only 43 of the 495 trained in that region (8.7 per cent) rated 140 or more in 2014, compared with 11.8 per cent in the year 2000, a far cry from the heady days of Peter Easterby and the Dickinsons. With appropriate investment, those days can soon return.

With the long career for high-profile horses and plenty of ultra-competitive handicaps, jump racing remains dominant among the betting public. Jump racing accounts for 19 of the top 25 races by betting volumes. That soon levels out, but still includes 53 of the top 100 races. The challenge remains as to how to convert popularity into long-term economic stability and growth. The sport remains intrinsically linked to the nation's economy, to the Irish economy, and to the relative prosperity of flat racing.

From a strong economic base, equine and human heroes will continue to emerge to capture the imagination of racing fans. Proactive communication will bring these stars to the attention of a wider audience and capitalise on that opportunity. The next era of economic growth, promised by the replacement of the Levy and new broadcasting contract, ensures that the ground has been prepared for the next Arkle, Desert Orchid or Kauto Star to come along soon. The next AP McCoy will explode onto the scene when least expected.

1

The Cheltenham Gold Cup
– Jump racing's holy grail

'He was a bit like I am as a human being. He probably wasn't the greatest horse I'd ridden but he had the greatest will to win.'

Champion jockey AP McCoy on Gold Cup winner Synchronised

Synchronised (white cap) and AP McCoy come to challenge The Giant Bolster and Long Run at the last, en route to winning the 2012 Cheltenham Gold Cup.

Racing is the simplest of sports. To thrill to its colourful spectacle you don't have to understand the intricacies of offside rules, scrum penalties or powerplays: it is about man and beast in unison striving to be first past the post. When they are doing it over obstacles, an extra degree of courage, stamina and technique is required. That is why no sporting event compares with the four-day Cheltenham Festival. Taut-faced jockeys emerge from the weighing room like fighter pilots on a mission. They send their charges hurtling down from the top of the hill, gaining maximum momentum at the last obstacle before their mounts eyeball each other up a final stamina-draining rise to the winning post, enveloped in a wall of sound as the celebrating crowds cheer on their fancies, often with a sharp twist of Anglo–Irish rivalry adding spice to the contest.

Some thrill most to the two-mile 'speed chasers' contesting the Queen Mother Champion Chase, others to the slick techniques and fast finishes of the Champion Hurdle, but it is the three miles two furlongs of the Cheltenham Gold Cup that represents the holy grail of jump racing. Aintree's Grand National invariably provides an enthralling spectacle and has a special place in racing history, but the National is a handicap with horses carrying different weights. There are other key contests for the true staying chasers throughout the season: the Hennessy Gold Cup at Newbury in November, the King George VI Chase at Kempton on Boxing Day, the bet365 Chase at Sandown in the last week of the season, not to mention races like Chepstow's Welsh National or the Scottish National at Ayr. But the Cheltenham Gold Cup, run with all contestants carrying the same weight, is acknowledged as the true championship, the ultimate test of excellence that settles all arguments about who is the best.

As with the Grand National, the Gold Cup creates its own legends. When Welsh farmer-trainer Sirrell Griffiths won the Gold Cup with the 100-1 shot Norton's Coin in 1990, he had milked a herd of cows before setting off for the course. The great steeplechaser Golden Miller was owned by the eccentric Dorothy Paget, who slept by day and lived by night and was allowed by bookmakers to bet on races after they had been run. Golden Miller won five Gold Cups in a row and was second in the following year. In 1983 Michael Dickinson performed the extraordinary feat of training the first five home in the Gold Cup and in 2008 Paul Nicholls was responsible for the first three home. A reformed alcoholic rescued from the gutter rode Captain Christy, the winner in 1974, and Francois Doumen's The Fellow gave France its only victory in the race in 1994 after twice losing out in photo finishes in the previous years. Many great names of the sport made or enhanced their reputations in the Gold Cup.

Some Gold Cup victories in this book are discussed in greater detail amid the profiles of their riders or trainers. Gold Cup winners such as Mandarin, Arkle, Dawn Run, Desert Orchid

and Best Mate merit their own portraits. But as with the Grand National, almost every running of the Gold Cup supplies a story or provides a reminder of a great name of the turf.

If we take 1960 as a starting point, as this book does throughout, then we begin with a thriller. Three horses came to the last fence with a chance but Kerstin, the 1958 winner, fell. Lochroe was best away from the fence up the finishing hill but, 50 yards out, he was caught by Pas Seul, ridden by Bill Rees, who went on to win. Pas Seul was trained by Bob Turnell, who also won two Hennessy Gold Cups and two Whitbread Gold Cups. Turnell was also renowned as a mentor of jockeys, fostering the careers not only of his son Andy but of the likes of Johnny Haine – the ultimate stylist; Jeff King – the iron man feared by all others in a finish; and the popular amateur John Oaksey.

In 1961 the flat-race training centre of Epsom scored a rare success in the Gold Cup when Don Butchers sent out Saffron Tartan to win. His success was notable as the first in the race for champion jockey Fred Winter at the age of 34; Winter scored again the following year riding the brave Mandarin (see page 40.) for Fulke Walwyn, beating the prolific Irish winner Fortria. The French-bred Mandarin had a pedigree more appropriate to a Derby winner and a delighted Madame Peggy Hennessy, Mandarin's owner, declared, 'This is the greatest day of my life. I have kept horses in training over here with only one object to win the Gold Cup.' For Fulke Walwyn it was a brilliant Festival: he achieved the classic double, also winning the Champion Hurdle with Anzio.

Saffron Tartan, with Fred Winter up, clearing the last fence before winning the King George VI Chase at Kempton Park.

Profile: **Mandarin**

*'The comradeship of
dangers shared can
in some sports at least
count for more than
international rivalry.'*

John Oaksey on Mandarin's Grand Prix de Paris

*Mandarin and Willie Robinson take the last before winning the
Hennessy Gold Cup in 1961.*

*Mandarin only just creeps into our
time period but it is impossible to deny
significant space to one of the bravest,
most tenacious horses ever to grace the
British – and French – turf. In 1957, as a
six-year-old, Mandarin, owned by Madame
Peggy Hennessy of the sponsoring family and trained
by Fulke Walwyn, won the inaugural running of the
Hennessy Gold Cup, then run at Cheltenham. Overtaken
by Linwell at the last fence, Mandarin fought back up
the Cheltenham hill, regained the lead and won by three
lengths.*

*That year, and again in 1959, Mandarin won the King
George VI Chase over the sharper, flatter three miles of
Kempton, and in 1961, having three times been runner-up
over the testing three miles five furlongs of the Whitbread
Gold Cup at Sandown, he was in the Hennessy field once
again, up against the rising second-season chasers who
tend to excel in this particular race.*

*The much patched-up Mandarin, who had had his
tendons fired after breaking down, and who had broken
a bone in his stifle when finishing third in another
King George, fenced faster and more slickly than Grand
National winner Nicolaus Silver and the younger
pretenders, eventually pulling away after the last to win
under top weight. He came out once more as an 11-year-
old veteran at Cheltenham in the Gold Cup of 1962,
partnered by Fred Winter. Again, under the greatest
jockey of his time, Mandarin demonstrated his battling
qualities. As with Linwell in the Hennessy, Mandarin
was led over the last by Ireland's hope, Fortria, but once
again he put his head down and battled past the talented
Irish contender up the hill.*

*For Mandarin and for Winter there was to be one more
even greater triumph, a triumph that in John Oaksey's*

*account at the time produced one of the finest pieces
of sporting journalism ever, as Winter and Mandarin
tackled for a second time the fearsome four-mile figure of
eight that constitutes the Grand Steeplechase de Paris at
Auteuil. The 30 fences were not like English park courses:
they included the 9-foot-high hedge of the Bullfinch, and
La Rivière, a massive water jump. Winter was weakened
by ferocious fasting and a stomach bug; the champagne
he drank on the flight over proved no help.*

*In the race, Mandarin, reported Oaksey, was soon in
front, pulling like a train, but then as they tackled the
fourth obstacle the rubber-covered bit broke in half in
Mandarin's mouth. Winter was left without any contact
with the horse's head, his only handhold the reins still
held by the martingale around Mandarin's neck and
the neck strap of the breast-girth. With no means of
steering except that of his weight, Fred Winter had to
rely entirely on grip and balance. Mandarin, with few of
the usual signals coming from his rider, had to rely on
his instinct.*

*Winter did what he could to match the horse's natural
rhythm and the French jockeys sportingly helped to keep
him in on the 180-degree turns, 'Proving gloriously',
in Oaksey's words, 'that the comradeship of dangers
shared can in some sports at least count for more than
international rivalry.' At the fourth fence from home,
Mandarin was heading for the wrong side of a marker*

and Winter had to swing his whole weight to one side like that of a motorcyclist. It was probably at that point that Mandarin's ever-suspect tendon gave way. His action faltered and four lengths were lost. With two obstacles to go they had seven lengths to make up on the leaders but Mandarin, who had, according to Oaksey, gone for the Bullfinch 'like a tank facing tissue paper', passed three horses as if they were walking and landed first over the last fence. Both horse and rider must have been in pain and incurring one of the most fearsome oxygen debts in sporting history as the French challenger Lumino tackled them throughout the last hundred metres, but they held on to win in a photo finish. As Mandarin hobbled to the winner's enclosure, Winter had to be helped from the saddle suffering from stomach cramps. Fellow jockey Stan Mellor had to help him get dressed for the final race, yet 40 minutes later he won that too, on Beaver II.

Mandarin had a long and happy retirement, not with the occasional nip of Hennessy but with Whitbread supplying to the end the beer that he enjoyed mixed into his feed.

The 1963 contest saw Fulke Walwyn succeed again with a horse that he expected to win a series of top prizes. Mill House, who was only a six year old, powered up the hill 12 lengths clear of Fortria. The big chaser, perfectly proportioned and well-muscled, although he was nearly 17 hands, would have dominated the chasing scene in most decades but was unlucky enough to be racing at the same time as the legendary Arkle. Mill House did manage to beat this Irish rival once in a Hennessy but after losing to Arkle (see page 42) in the 1964 Gold Cup he never beat him again. In 1965 Arkle demolished his challenge at Cheltenham and Mill House fell in the Gold Cup he contested after injury forced Arkle's retirement. Mill House did, though, have the consolation of winning the Whitbread Gold Cup at Sandown in 1967 and although he suffered from back problems he won 16 of his 34 races.

Arkle's victories of 1964, 1965 and 1966 are covered in his own profile but it should not be forgotten that Tom Dreaper had in his stable alongside Arkle another horse that might have been a supreme champion. At the 1966 Festival Flyingbolt did not contest the Gold Cup against his stable companion but won the two-mile Champion Chase by an astonishing 15 lengths. The following day Dreaper ran Flyingbolt in the Champion Hurdle, in which he led into the final hurdle but could only manage third place behind Salmon Spray after having uprooted the fourth-last obstacle. A month later Flyingbolt won the Irish Grand National carrying 12 st 7 lb, giving at least 40 lb to all the other runners. Sadly he contracted brucellosis later that year and was never the same horse again.

In 1967 Terry Biddlecombe (see page 211) scored his only Gold Cup success on Woodland Venture, beating Stalbridge Colonist ridden by Stan Mellor by three-quarters of a length in a driving finish. Foinavon, later to be a lucky Grand National winner, finished seventh of the eight runners. Although trainer Fred Rimell sent out 27 Festival winners in all, that was his only Gold Cup success.

The cancellation of racing for six weeks due to a foot-and-mouth epidemic that winter had wrecked preparations for many trainers; only five horses, including the now 11-year-old Mill House, contested the 1968 Gold Cup. Again, Mill House fell when going easily, leaving the Tom Dreaper–Pat Taaffe combination to score again with Fort Leney, for whom rain had softened the ground just in time.

Best Mate jumps the last with Jim Culloty up on their way to win the Cheltenham Gold Cup, 2002.

Profile: **Arkle**

'I couldn't think he would fall. He is as clever as any hunter and would always find a fifth or even a sixth leg.'

Trainer Tom Dreaper on Arkle

Arkle, ridden by Pat Taaffe, in action during the King George VI Chase at Kempton Park, 1965.

Even people who have never watched a horse race have heard of Arkle. In his heyday, Irish graffiti artists daubed 'Arkle for President' on walls. Letters from all over the world addressed simply to 'Arkle, Ireland' used to reach trainer Tom Dreaper's stable and in the season of 1965/6 the horse known to his nation simply as 'Himself' put together a series of steeplechase victories that is unlikely ever to be equalled. The other top steeplechasers of the time must have grown tired of the sight of his elegant backside.

First time out at Sandown in November that season, Arkle won the Gallaher Gold Cup by 20 lengths, despite giving 26 lb to the useful Rondetto and 16 lb to his long-time rival and Gold Cup winner Mill House, who was third.

It was a measure of the extraordinary popularity of both Arkle and Mill House that the two horses were applauded as they left the parade ring, on towards the track down the famous Rhododendron Walk, and again as they cantered past the stands. During the race Mill House was superb, flicking over along the railway fences, and his fans began to hope however, when they turned into the final stretch Arkle strode by the leader as if he were not there. All it took was a shake of the reins at the last fence and he sprinted away up the hill for a devastating win, which broke Mill House's course record by an extraordinary 17 seconds. Rondetto took second and Mill House third; all three were applauded back for their heroic efforts.

Just three weeks later, at Newbury, Arkle won the Hennessy Gold Cup by 15 lengths, carrying 2 stone more than any of his rivals. On Boxing Day at Kempton he won the King George VI Chase by a distance from Dormant. Arkle next raced in Ireland, giving 3 stone to Height O' Fashion and winning the Leopardstown Chase. That was his final warm-up for that year's Cheltenham Gold Cup, due to be run on St Patrick's Day.

In the big race in 1966 the Irish supporters in the crowd, inspired by 1,000 sprigs of shamrock flown over by Dublin's Lord Mayor, got the shock of their lives. With Mill House sidelined by injury, Arkle, who never fell in his career, was going well when he began looking at the huge crowd and thumped into the 11th fence. It was the sort of collision that would have brought down most chasers. The crowd gasped but Pat Taaffe sat still and Arkle didn't stop. His exercise canter continued and he won on a tight rein from Dormant by 30 lengths. Tom Dreaper explained afterwards that the horse was 'a bit of a swank' who had been playing to the crowd. – 'But I couldn't think he would fall. He is as clever as any hunter and would always find a fifth or even a sixth leg.'

That third consecutive Gold Cup was the highlight not just of an incredible year but also of an extraordinary career, which had first caught the public's imagination at Cheltenham in 1963. That year the Gold Cup had been won by Mill House, trained by Fulke Walwyn. 'The big horse', as Walwyn liked to refer to him, jumped like a buck. When he strode imperiously up the hill twelve lengths clear of Ireland's Fortria, he looked like a horse who might emulate Golden Miller with a string of Gold Cup victories. However, on the first day of that year's Festival, form students had already noted how in the Broadway Chase, a traditional Gold Cup stepping stone, an intelligent-looking, athletic six-year-old bay, sporting the colours of Anne, Duchess of Westminster, had won, scarcely taking a breath. That horse was called Arkle.

At the following year's Festival in 1964, amid a brief snow flurry, the racing public had eyes only for two horses. Mill House was the 8-13 favourite. You could get 7-4 against his leaner Irish rival – the one with the inquisitive head – and 20-1 bar the two principals. It was effectively a match of the kind that the Cheltenham crowd likes best: a match between England and Ireland.

Ireland beats England: Arkle leads Mill House at Cheltenham in 1965.

Mill House had given Arkle 5 lb and beaten him by eight lengths in the Hennessy Gold Cup in November, albeit in that race Arkle had slipped badly after one fence. Now Willie Robinson, full of confidence on board Mill House, took him straight into the lead, powering over his fences, ready to test Ireland's hope all the way. Arkle too settled into a rhythm, fencing economically. Mill House had set a good gallop, but as they went out on the second circuit, English binoculars were lowered for nervous enquiries of their neighbour as to why their fellow hadn't shaken him off yet.

Mill House once again jumped well at the ditch on the hill but Arkle was going ominously well, tucked in behind him. Down the hill they came. As they jumped the second-last fence and rounded the bend into the straight, the Irishman moved upsides to challenge Mill House. The pressure was on and Mill House had no extra to offer. Willie Robinson went for his whip and dropped it, but it wouldn't have made any difference if he'd wielded a Star Wars 'lightsabre'. To ecstatic Irish cheers, Arkle and his jockey, Pat Taaffe, were off and away, up to the finishing line five lengths clear. He had not just beaten Mill House, he had crushed him. A shaken Fulke Walwyn declared: 'I can still hardly believe that any horse living could have done what Arkle did to Mill House.'

Walwyn brought Mill House back to take on Arkle once again in 1965, one of only three horses whose trainers were prepared to oppose him. This time it was Arkle who was the 30-100 odds-on favourite and he almost toyed with his rival. From the top of the hill, Arkle began to move away and as he jumped the second-last well clear, Pat Taaffe let him go. Arkle accelerated still further away, cleared the last with feet to spare in an exuberant leap and was 20 lengths ahead of Mill House at the finish. Pat Taaffe declared that Arkle was the best horse he had ever ridden. Arkle finished that season by also winning the Irish National, giving 30 lb to the horse finishing second.

The last time the racing public saw Arkle was in the King George VI Chase at Kempton in December 1966. Arkle jumped the last well clear from Dormant but slowed almost to a walk on the run-in, was caught close to the post and beaten by a length. He was clearly a stricken horse; Pat Taaffe had felt for most of the race there was something amiss. It turned out that Arkle had broken the pedal bone in his off-fore leg, which meant that he

had shown as much courage in finishing second in that race as he had shown class in the rest of his career. After suffering increasingly painful leg problems, Arkle was finally put down in May 1970.

Named after a small Scottish mountain overlooking part of the Westminster estates, Arkle was trained at

Greenogue by the 'quiet man' Tom Dreaper and ridden in every one of his steeplechases by Pat Taaffe. Arkle retired with a record of 27 victories from 35 starts, including 22 of the 26 steeplechases in which he ran. Results alone, however, cannot make a horse as popular as Arkle became. He was in the fullest sense of the word a character. Part of his appeal was the sense of majesty about his parade ring presence, his way of staring intently around the crowd with his ears pricked. Then there was the surge of power he could produce within a race, the sheer exhilaration of his jumping. At home he was a good soldier: while his talented stable companion Flyingbolt would kick and bite as soon as look at you, small children could be sat safely on Arkle's back. Arkle won admiration too for his gutsy competitiveness. He was not kept in cotton wool for championship races like some famous successors but also subjected to weight-carrying tests in big handicaps. Along with his three Cheltenham Gold Cups, Arkle won the Hennessy Gold Cup twice, the Whitbread Gold Cup and the Irish Grand National. He never lined up, though, for the Aintree Grand National: his owner, Anne, Duchess of Westminster, a countrywoman who truly loved her horses, always feared the risk of injury.

The ground had not been considered soft enough for What A Myth in 1968 and, despite his third place the previous year, he was taken out of the race. In 1969, however, the heavy ground was just what suited Ryan Price's twelve-year-old, who, after running unsuccessfully in three Grand Nationals, had been freshened up with a spell of hunter-chasing. The former Whitbread winner was the oldest Gold Cup winner for 18 years.

It was the ambition of American businessman and polo player Raymond Guest, at one time his country's Ambassador to Ireland, to own the winner of three prestigious races: the Derby, the Grand National and the Cheltenham Gold Cup. The inappropriately named L'Escargot (French for snail) helped him realise two of those ambitions, while he won the Derby with both Larkspur and Sir Ivor.

Trained by Dan Moore (Guest's European flat-racing horses were trained by Vincent O'Brien) and ridden by Tommy Carberry, L'Escargot had been voted American steeplechaser of the year before coming to Europe. Moore wanted to run him in the two-mile Champion Chase in 1970 but Guest insisted on his taking his chance in the much longer Gold Cup, which he won by one-and-a-half lengths from French Tan after the hot favourite Kinloch Brae had fallen at the downhill third-last fence. At 33-1, L'Escargot was the joint longest-priced winner ever. (Gay Donald in 1955 was the other.)

Up until 1971, only Easter Hero, Golden Miller, Cottage Rake and Arkle had won more than one Gold Cup. L'Escargot, who had not won a race previously that season, joined the illustrious band in 1971 on ground that had been softened by 15 hours of rain. No horse wins two Gold Cups without having some real quality and the fences always have to be jumped; however, many argued that Raymond Guest was a lucky owner because once again the third-last fence had found out a likely challenger. On this

Halfway in the Gold Cup 1974. Game Spirit (Terry Biddlecombe) in the Queen Mother's blue and buff colours leads Pendil and The Dikler. Captain Christy, in fourth, went on to win in the hands of Bobby Beasley.

occasion it was Glencaraig Lady, who toppled over when going smoothly at that particular obstacle. Those who thought she would have won felt vindicated to say, 'I told you so' in 1972, when Glencaraig Lady, trained by Francis Flood and ridden by Frank Berry, became the first mare to win since Kerstin in 1958. The 1972 field included the bold Australian chaser Crisp, Grand National winner Gay Trip, and The Dikler, winner of the King George VI Chase in the previous December. In one of the most thrilling finishes ever witnessed, Glencaraig Lady won by three-quarters of a length from the outsider Royal Toss, with The Dikler just a head behind in third place. Sadly, Glencaraig Lady, who had struggled with injuries, had broken down again and the new champion was promptly retired.

The following year, 1973, saw The Dikler's famous victory over Fred Winter's highly talented Pendil; Charlie Potheen came third, with L'Escargot fourth once more, as he had been in 1972. Dan Moore had told L'Escargot's owner that the horse should win the Grand National in 1972. He was right about the result but wrong about the year: L'Escargot was third, second

and then first in the Grand Nationals of 1973, 1974 and 1975, thus becoming the only horse, along with Golden Miller, to have achieved the Gold Cup/Grand National double.

The dramatic 1973 contest between Pendil and The Dikler, ridden respectively by Richard Pitman and Ron Barry (see Fred Winter and Ron Barry profiles pages 133 and 218), saw the winner beat Fort Leney's record time by more than 12 seconds. Pendil, a hot favourite, had demolished the Arkle Chase field the previous year and had won all his 11 chases, including the King George VI. Pendil had appeared to be cruising home but there was a twist in the tale: Barry conjured a great leap from The Dikler at the last, and Pendil started to look about him amid the wall of noise as they came up the hill; Pendil was overtaken too late for Pitman's urgings to get him back up again in time and The Dikler was the winner. Grandstand critics blamed Pitman for hitting the front too soon but he had been under orders from his trainer to take the lead when he did – there were no recriminations from Winter. With Crisp and Bula also failing, it was a Festival of ill fortune for the Lambourn maestro.

The year of 1974, however, produced a sensation of a different kind: a heart-warming story of redemption in what even the normally

Al Ferof and Ruby Walsh take a fence during the Arkle Challenge Trophy Steeple Chase.

restrained *The Times* greeted as, 'the greatest comeback since Lazarus.' Pat Taaffe by now was training and in his yard was a talented but impetuous young jumper called Captain Christy. Mutual friends suggested that the man who Taaffe should try in the saddle in order to settle this tearaway was the experienced pilot Bobby Beasley.

Some years back, that might have seemed like sense. Beasley, from one of Ireland's great racing families, was then the glittering meteor of race-riding. In 1959 he had won the Gold Cup on Roddy Owen; in 1960 he had won the Champion Hurdle on Another Flash; and in 1961 he had won the Grand National on Nicolaus Silver. However, the intervening years had not been kind to him. Bad falls, alcoholism and weight problems forced him to quit the saddle. He wasn't just 'yesterday's man' – he was the 'nowhere kid.' Beasley hit rock bottom on the streets and his weight ballooned to over 15 stone. Yet with the aid of friends and Alcoholics Anonymous, he began pulling it together and was back scratching for a few rides. Pat Taaffe gave him a chance. As it turned out, Beasley and Captain Christy hit it off, swiftly winning four races together. They managed only third place in the 1973 Champion Hurdle after Captain Christy had fretted on the journey to England. They went on to win the Scottish equivalent, even though the horse demolished most of the obstacles on the way round. Nevertheless, owner Pat Samuel decided to aim high: the novice, with a record of two spectacular wins in novice chases and a couple of spectacular falls, was sent to take on The Dikler

and Pendil in the Gold Cup.

Coming down the final hill, his race-riding instinct had Beasley pull out from behind High Ken, who cartwheeled and brought down Pendil. Only one serious rival was left but when Beasley asked for a big jump at the final fence, Captain Christy didn't come up for him, buffeting the obstacle with his chest. Somehow, the horse found a leg and his rider regained his balance. With a true horseman's instinct, Beasley allowed his mount a few strides to collect himself before setting out after The Dikler, a strong and consistent horse who always found something on the final hill but now an 11-year-old. Captain Christy passed him as if he were wading through molasses and went away to win by five lengths. The visitors sang, 'When Irish Eyes are Smiling' and the English crowd, who had mostly punted away their money on Pendil and The Dikler, cheered in the near 40-year-old rider with the sportsmanship that is the hallmark of Festival racing. Beasley, visibly touched, noted afterwards: 'As the crowd gave me three cheers, I was thinking less of the actual victory than of my gratitude to Alcoholics Anonymous and the others who had helped me to knock the booze and to use racing as a means of rehabilitation.' Later, he trained a few horses and ran a pub. Pendil, possibly the best horse never to win a Gold Cup, never ran in it again. Pendil was again beaten by Captain Christy in the subsequent King George VI Chase at Kempton, with both horses staying on their feet.

In 1975 the Arkle colours of Anne, Duchess of Westminster, triumphed again as Jim Dreaper

Runners approach the second fence during the Irish Independent Arkle Challenge Trophy in 2004.

followed father Tom's example by training Ten Up to win, with Tommy Carberry on board. Captain Christy and The Dikler, now a 12-year-old, were both pulled up on the heavy ground, which had seen one day of the Festival lost to the weather. Ten Up did not, however, defend his crown in 1976 as the Cheltenham stewards warned Jim Dreaper that the injections he had been giving his horse in Ireland (to prevent his tendency to break blood vessels) could bring about disqualification if used at the Festival. As a result, Dreaper withdrew his horse – and was fined £125 for taking him out so late!

Alverton, trained by Peter Easterby and ridden by Jonjo O'Neill, comes to pass Tied Cottage (who fell) before winning the 1979 Gold Cup in a snowstorm.

Victory went to Royal Frolic, ridden by John Burke and trained by Fred Rimell. The sometimes brusque Rimell could be a diplomat when the occasion required: Royal Frolic's owner, the ailing 86-year-old Sir Edward Hanmer, had been reluctant to run the seven-year-old, maintaining that the horse was too young. Rimell urged him to do so, declaring, 'None of us is getting any younger, Sir, and I think he should take his chance.' Shortly after Royal Frolic's five-length victory, Sir Edward died.

Rimell's success was also welcomed by the more patriotic English punters, who had seen Irish horses win nine of the previous 13 Gold Cups amid a series of reverses for talented horses from Fred Winter's yard. But 'Team Ireland' was back on the winner's rostrum in 1977 when the winner was Davy Lad, ridden by Dessie Hughes and trained by Mick O'Toole, with Tied Cottage, also from Ireland, the runner-up. Winter's misfortunes continued: Lanzarote, his champion hurdler who had been second favourite for the Gold Cup, slipped up and broke a leg. Three weeks later his other champion, Bula, also had to be put down after failing to recover from a Festival injury.

The Fred Winter Gold Cup hoodoo was finally broken in 1978 even if the full Festival audience was not there to see it. Snow on the original Gold Cup day saw the scheduled programme postponed to 12 April, when Midnight Court, ridden by John Francome, at last gave Winter's supporters something to cheer about. The winner of all of his six previous chases, Midnight Court always looked comfortable and when Royal Frolic fell at the last, he went away up the hill to win by seven lengths.

English trainers began to reassert against the Irish invaders with Yorkshire-based Peter Easterby's classy Alverton an easy winner by 25 lengths in 1979. He had already caught the runaway Tied Cottage, who then fell at the last. The following year the highly talented Silver Buck, trained in Yorkshire by Tony and Monica Dickinson, was unbeaten in seven races, including the King George VI Chase. He looked a likely Gold Cup winner but after continuous rain turned the conditions against him he was pulled out. Once again the front-running Tied Cottage set out to run the legs off the rest of the field and this time he succeeded. Five pulled up, two fell and only Master Smudge got within eight lengths of him at the end. Sadly, though, for trainer Dan Moore and jockey Tommy Carberry, post-race testing revealed traces of theobromine in Tied Cottage's urine and he was disqualified, as was Mick O'Toole's Chinrullah, running in the Gold Cup after winning the Queen Mother Champion Chase. No blame attached to the two trainers: the cause was contaminated feed supplies, but it meant that the prize went to Master Smudge, bought by trainer Arthur Barrow from a pig-farmer after seeing him running in a field.

In 1981 a 15-strong field included Tied

Cottage, now a 13-year-old, but he fell at the sixth. Silver Buck was this time allowed to take his chance despite the heavy ground, as decided by former jockey Michael Dickinson, who had taken over from father Tony. Joint second favourites were two horses trained by Peter Easterby, who had already won the Arkle with Clayside and the Champion Hurdle with Sea Pigeon. One was the former Champion Hurdle winner Night Nurse, the other Little Owl, who was ridden by the amateur Jim Wilson after the horse had been left to him and his brother Robin by an aunt.

Night Nurse took over the lead at the tenth and Silver Buck travelled well – but to no avail. From the second-last fence, Little Owl injected more pace and Silver Buck was anchored by the heavy ground. This left only Night Nurse to give Little Owl any kind of competition up the hill. Had the finishing order been reversed, Night Nurse would have become the first horse to win both the Champion Hurdle and the Gold Cup, but Easterby did become the first to train the first two home in a Gold Cup.

That did not stay as an exclusive achievement for long. In 1982 Silver Buck, now a ten-year-old and ridden by Robert Earnshaw, confirmed his class and consistency by beating a big field of 23. The horse who followed him home was Bregawn, also

trained by Michael Dickinson in his second season and ridden by Graham Bradley. The field was towed along for much of the way by Tied Cottage, still in the lead until the third-last fence, despite now being a 14-year-old.

Michael Dickinson's extraordinary feat of training the first five home in the next Gold Cup, the 1983 contest, is described in his profile among the champion trainers. Ever the perfectionist, he still chides himself for not having been able to bring Silver Buck to Cheltenham that year in better shape to defend his crown. By the time the next Festival took place, Michael had been lured away from jump racing by Robert Sangster to become a flat-racing trainer.

That took nothing away from the 1984 Gold Cup in which the feisty Jenny Pitman (see page 184), already the first woman to train a Grand National winner, became also the first woman responsible for a Gold Cup winner. She won the trophy with an outstanding horse. Burrough Hill Lad, already an impressive winner of the Welsh National and the Gainsborough Chase, won his Gold Cup by three lengths in the hands of Phil Tuck, the replacement chosen when his normal partner, John Francome, had to ride Brown Chamberlin for the Fred Winter stable who retained him. The imposing Burrough Hill Lad twice had to be withdrawn

The Queen Mother Champion Chase in 1993: the supreme stylist Richard Dunwoody on Waterloo Boy.

from subsequent Gold Cups because of leg injuries; nevertheless, he still won 21 of his 42 races, including a Hennessy Gold Cup and a King George VI Chase.

In the 1980s, northern trainers were strongly represented at most Festivals and the Gold Cup went to Yorkshire once again in 1985 when Forgive 'N Forget, trained at Malton by Jimmy Fitzgerald and ridden by Mark Dwyer, held off Righthand Man, who was trained by Michael Dickinson's mother, Monica, and ridden by Graham Bradley. Forgive 'N Forget ran in four successive Gold Cups, finishing third the following year and then sadly breaking a leg in the 1988 contest. His ashes were buried near the Royal Box at Cheltenham. Trainer Fitzgerald was famed for his ability to 'lay out' a horse for a big gamble and Forgive 'N Forget achieved a significant coup in the Coral Golden Hurdle final (nowadays the Pertemps Final) at the 1983 Festival – as did Fitzgerald's Trainglot in the 1990 Cesarewitch. Fitzgerald was a good friend of commentator Sir Peter O'Sullevan and he saddled the appropriately named Sounds Fyne in

O'Sullevan's colours to win at Newbury on Peter's last day as a commentator. We can be certain that neither of them let the horse go unbacked.

In 1986 the Gold Cup focus was very much back on Ireland as the big mare, Dawn Run, followed up her Champion Hurdle success of two years earlier by becoming the first horse to couple that with success in the Gold Cup.

On a day when weather conditions were the biggest talking point, the Gold Cup went back to the north of England in 1987 when WA Stephenson succeeded with The Thinker, ridden by Ridley Lamb. A snowstorm, which had started during the previous race, quickly covered the course, which meant that the Gold Cup runners were sent back to their boxes for an 80-minute wait before the ground was considered raceable. Forgive 'N Forget was a hot favourite to regain his crown and northern horses (used to the colder weather) seemed to handle the conditions best with Peter Easterby's Cybrandian, Forgive 'N Forget, Monica Dickinson's veteran, Wayward Lad, and The Thinker prominent, along with

Profile: **Dawn Run**

'Once you had her up and running she'd go through fire – no problem.'

Jockey Jonjo O'Neill on Dawn Run's Gold Cup

They say that elephants never forget. It is also amazing, given how swiftly things happen in the saddle, how much jockeys remember of the races in which they have ridden. Considering that it produced one of the most famous race finishes of all time, it is probably less of a surprise that Jonjo O'Neill should remember in minute detail the running of the 1986 Gold Cup won by the mare Dawn Run, making her the first and only horse to have won both the Champion Hurdle and the Gold Cup. What is truly impressive, though, when Jonjo talks you through that epic race, is not just the detail but the passion with which it still comes across.

Jonjo O'Neill on Dawn Run, winners of the Gold Cup, Cheltenham 1986.

'At the end of that Gold Cup, I thought coming down the hill we were after going a right gallop. I missed the water jump and that kind of messed us up a little bit. There were three or four front-runners. There was Cybrandian, herself [Dawn Run], Run and Skip, and Forgive 'N Forget, all going for the lead, all good horses. We were going so fast, I missed the water and I couldn't give her a breather when I wanted to. Then she got headed. She didn't like being headed and I had to motivate her out of it, motivate her from every angle.

'We were going some lick. She missed the fence after the ditch going up the hill – she walked through that one – and then I was in trouble trying to get her back as the race was really on at that stage. I was lucky enough that Run and Skip missed the one at the top of the hill and so I got upsides – we were back on top again.

'We were flying down the hill and I could hear them coming behind us. I thought we'd gone a right gallop and couldn't believe they were so close to us. We jumped the third-last and they were jumping up my backside, and I thought, "Jesus, if we don't ping the second-last, we're going to get beat." She did ping the second-last but they passed me as if I was stopped. I couldn't believe it. I thought, "Oh, we're beaten," so I left her alone for a few strides. Then, just between the second-last and the last, I could feel her filling up and I thought, "We ain't done yet."

'We rallied to the last and we were flying and she picked up; she picked up outside the wings herself in fairness to her. Wayward Lad was in front of me and he hung in across. I thought, "He won't get home," because I'd ridden him the year before and Forgive 'N Forget had had enough of it at that stage. I just kept going across the track on her now, and the more on her own she

was, the better she was. She came up the hill like a tyrant. The funny thing was that halfway going down to the last I knew I was going to win. I just knew she'd keep going once I'd got her motivated. I know it didn't look that way but I knew she'd get up the hill.'

Passed by two horses going to the last fence, Dawn Run, with all of Ireland cheering for her, got up to Wayward Lad, ridden by Graham Bradley, some 40 yards from the line and went on to win by a length. No horse has ever looked so beaten in a big race and yet summoned up the reserves to get back up and win. Even 'Brad' on Wayward Lad, three times a winner of the King George VI Chase, called it one of the greatest races he has even ridden in.

In personality terms, Dawn Run, a moody mare built on masculine lines, was not the most attractive. It took two men even to get a blanket on her and, just like her owner, Charmian Hill, who won a bumper on the mare and continued to race-ride until the Irish Turf Club refused her a licence at 62, she had her own way of doing things. As Jonjo puts it, 'If you hit her before she was ready to be hit, she'd pull up and she'd let you know. But if you got her motivated, then once you had her up and running, she'd go through fire – no problem.'

Dawn Run had already joined a select group by winning the Champion Hurdle in 1984. The last mare before her to perform that feat was African Sister, ridden by Keith Piggott, in 1939. Prior to that success, Dawn Run had won a number of races with the trainer's son Tony aboard, but Mrs Hill more than once insisted on his being 'jocked off' for big races in favour of a more experienced rider. Thus it was Jonjo who was in the saddle when she beat Champion Hurdler Gaye Brief in the Christmas Hurdle at Kempton. When Gaye Brief was pulled out of the Champion Hurdle, the mare started as the odds-on favourite at Cheltenham and, having beaten off Buck House, she resisted a challenge from the 66-1 outsider Cima to win by three-quarters of a length, despite having hit the last and landed flat-footed. She had already won the Irish Champion Hurdle and went on to Auteuil to collect the French

version too, the Grande Course de Haies d'Auteuil. Trainer Paddy Mullins noted: 'She has that will to win. When a horse goes past her, she fights back and simply won't give in. That's the one thing that makes her stand out.' In combination with Jonjo's racing style, it made them into a formidable combination.

Dawn Run won a chase in the autumn of 1984 but then injured a leg and had to have a year off. When she returned in December 1985, she won chases at Punchestown and Leopardstown. Things didn't go so smoothly in her Cheltenham trial race in January 1986 when she walloped the last open ditch and gave jockey Tony Mullins no chance of staying in the saddle.

Once again, Mrs Hill insisted that Paddy Mullins had to 'jock off' his son and, as a result, Jonjo, who had never ridden her in a chase before, was booked for Cheltenham. When he trialled her, he didn't even think she should be entered in the race. As he says now: 'She was desperate. God, she was "novicey" and she was such a moody old devil, a moody old thing to get her going.' It was therefore a less than harmonious camp that brought the mare to the Festival. She was having only her fifth race over fences; she was running over a distance she had never tackled before; and she was facing opponents of the calibre of Wayward Lad, the previous year's winner, Forgive 'N Forget, and the Welsh National winner, Run And Skip. Yet she was also a national heroine and Irish money had made her the favourite, adding to the pressures on all connected with her.

Wayward Lad was a classier chaser. He had ground to suit and a Gold Cup-winning jockey. But he was by then reaching the veteran stage. Dawn Run fortunately didn't read and she still had one thing going for her – that precious will to win, in what became as much a test of character as of racing ability. And now we all know the story.

To this day, Festival regulars have never heard a noisier reception for a winner and no clips of any Cheltenham Festival finish have ever had so many replays. Peter O'Sullevan's vivid commentary that day captured every nuance of the occasion and at the moment when he declared, 'The mare's beginning to get up,' a whole small nation rose to its feet.

Jonjo O'Neill is mobbed by the crowd after riding Dawn Run to victory in the Cheltenham Gold Cup.

As Jonjo puts it, 'It was a magical day. It was fantastic. The whole of Ireland wanted her to win and knew she could win. It was great that she did it and it was great how she did it. I've met a lot of people since who've told me what inspiration it gave them at times when they were down in their lives. She gave a lot of people inspiration.'

Sadly, Dawn Run did not get the chance to nurture foals with her fighting qualities. After winning at Cheltenham, she next ran at Aintree where she and Jonjo parted company at the first fence. She then won a specially arranged match against Buck House at the Punchestown Festival. Later, against Paddy Mullins' wishes, Mrs Hill insisted that the mare should be sent back to Auteuil once more to win another French Champion Hurdle. Tragically, during the race at Auteuil she fell and was killed. Dawn Run will, of course, never be forgotten, being one of only a few horses to have their own statue at Cheltenham. She was perhaps a little lucky to win her Champion Hurdle: it was the first year in which mares were given a 5 lb allowance. Yet there is no doubting the quality of her Gold Cup performance: former champion jockey Peter Scudamore, for one, calls it 'the greatest performance I have seen in a steeplechase.'

the southerner Josh Gifford's Door Latch. Twelve-year-old Wayward Lad led them over the last but faded as The Thinker, Cybrandian and Door Latch came home 1-2-3. The Thinker's trainer, Arthur Stephenson, had chosen to go to Hexham instead that day, so a nephew picked up the prize. The trainer also owed a debt to his travelling head lad who had thoughtfully sought out a pat of butter from the catering stores and rubbed it into The Thinker's feet to help him manage the snowy conditions. As for the favourite, Forgive 'N Forget, who finished seventh, trainer Fitzgerald quipped that he'd had him trained to the minute and the 80-minute wait for the race had seen him go over the top!

The favourite in 1988 was Playschool, one of a batch of horses imported from New Zealand by West Country trainer David Barons and ridden by the future champion trainer Paul Nicholls, who had partnered him to victory in the Hennessy and the Welsh National. Playschool ran unaccountably badly and his trainer believed he had been 'got at' by dopers, although Nicholls does not share that view.

The race went instead to Charter Party, a faller in the previous year's event, who was ridden by Richard Dunwoody for the familiar racecourse figure of trainer David 'the Duke' Nicholson (see page 166). Cavvies Clown had cut out the pace but when he made a mistake at the second-last, Charter Party strode away up the hill to win by six lengths. A blood disorder and jumping errors had hampered Charter Party's career after a Festival win two years previously but Nicholson had him at his best on the day that mattered.

The following year's Gold Cup, won by Desert Orchid, was one of those 'were you there when...?' occasions, which has been talked about by racing folk ever since. The David Elsworth-trained chaser was one of the three or four most popular jumpers ever; the fact that he was an almost-white grey drew attention to his spectacular, zestful jumping. But 'Dessie', as his stable knew him, never liked left-handed tracks (he had only ever won going left-handed on one occasion and had run five times at

Cheltenham in various races without ever winning). When snow and rain that morning turned the ground heavy, which was not reckoned to suit him, many wondered if Desert Orchid would be pulled out of the race. Trainer David Elsworth, though, has never lacked courage in campaigning his horses. Despite owner Richard Burridge's qualms, Elsworth

increased his bet and sent Dessie out to run in a field that included previous winners The Thinker and Charter Party.

The 1990 Gold Cup contest produced an almost equally heart-warming story in a very different way. In flat racing, if you want to win the bigger prizes, you generally have to spend big money on your ammunition. One of the joys of jump racing, although perhaps it is now happening less often, is that big prizes are still won some of the time by relatively cheap horses, little stables or unfashionable jockeys.

As the field of 12 lined up, with Desert Orchid the odds-on favourite to defend his crown on much better ground than in the previous year, Yahoo was back to challenge again. Up against them were Martin Pipe's Bonanza Boy, twice a winner of the Welsh National, and Jenny Pitman's progressive fencer, Toby Tobias. Also in the field was the 100-1 shot Norton's Coin, who was only running in the Gold Cup because

Looks Like Trouble, winner of the Cheltenham Gold Cup in the year 2000, jumping ahead of Ireland's hope Florida Pearl.

Profile: **Desert Orchid**

'With Dessie pulling against you you could only harness his power. Controlling it wasn't an option.'

Jockey Richard Dunwoody

When readers of the Racing Post *and a panel of experts were asked a few years ago to vote on the Hundred Greatest Races, the Gold Cup of 1989 came out on top, not just because 'Dessie' was such a popular horse but also because it was an utterly absorbing contest.*

It came as something of a surprise that 16 March 1989 was a day of heavy rain, sleet and snow. Only after a midday inspection was the ground ruled fit to race. Many racegoers feared that Desert Orchid would be pulled out and, with conditions against him, the grey drifted out in the betting. Trainer David Elsworth responded like the American general who was urged to retreat in the face of overwhelming odds and who declared, 'Retreat? Retreat? Hell, we only just got here.' Elsworth declared Dessie to run, saying, 'The ground is horrible and conditions are all against him, but he is the best horse.'

In the race Dessie was up against two previous winners in Charter Party and The Thinker, as well as Ireland's top novice Carvill's Hill, and Ten Plus, winner of four races that season and rated highly enough by Fulke Walwyn to be occupying the box previously tenanted by both Mill House and The Dikler. Rider Simon Sherwood was bold too. Instead of nursing Desert Orchid at the back of the field, he took him out in the lead, his fluent jumping helping to conserve his energy. On the second circuit, he was joined by Elsworth's other runner, Cavvies Clown, second the previous year, and by Ten Plus,who passed Desert Orchid at the 14th of the 22 obstacles. Tragically, three fences out, Ten Plus fell, fatally injured.

Approaching the second-last, the mud-loving scrapper, Yahoo, came through on the inside to take the lead. But Desert Orchid was ready for a fight and set out to tackle him. Reaching the last fence, they were almost level. Somehow, Desert Orchid and his equally exhausted jockey summoned up what was, in those dire conditions, the equivalent of a burst. Simon Sherwood, who lost only

Richard Dunwoody on Desert Orchid.

one of the ten races he rode on Desert Orchid and entitled his autobiography, Nine Out Of Ten, *said afterwards, 'I have never sat on a horse that showed such courage. By hook or by crook he was going to win.' Desert Orchid drifted left to eyeball Yahoo as the mud-spattered pair's surge took the two horses eight lengths clear of Charter Party in third; inch by inch, Dessie and Simon Sherwood clawed their way past Tom Morgan's equally willing mount to win in the end by a length and a half. Horse and jockey were applauded every step of the way to the winner's enclosure.*

Desert Orchid had many other notches on his gun barrel besides his Cheltenham victory. One of the other major tests of a top chaser's ability is the King George VI Chase over the flatter, right-handed three miles at Kempton on Boxing Day, which Desert Orchid won four times. Richard Dunwoody, who inherited the ride on him when Simon Sherwood retired, said, 'He seemed to know the course so well at Kempton. You would encourage him to take a breather down the back straight but he was already doing so, and as you turned for home he would move up a gear.'

The sturdily built Desert Orchid, who remained remarkably injury-free through a packed racing schedule, had a bigger, harder neck than most horses, which gave his riders a sense of enormous strength. Said Dunwoody: 'With the reins in your hands and Dessie pulling against you, you could only harness his power. Controlling it

wasn't an option.' In all, Desert Orchid won 27 of the 50 races in which he participated, including a Whitbread Gold Cup. His bold jumping and heart-on-the-sleeve, front-running style gave him equine charisma, and although he retired in 1992 his subsequent racecourse-parade reappearances were enthusiastically applauded. On such occasions the veteran often seemed to want to stay on for the actual race as well.

Simon Sherwood, who rode Desert Orchid to victory nine times in ten races.

his trainer Sirrell Griffiths hadn't realised he was ineligible for the Cathcart Chase in which he had been runner-up the year before. It had already been a long day for Griffiths: before driving the cattle truck to Cheltenham from his three-horse permit-holder's yard at Nantgaredig near Carmarthen (he didn't own a horsebox), he had milked 70 cows at 4.00 a.m.

Norton's Coin was well bred and had won four races to the value of £23,000. He had run respectably at Cheltenham in January to finish second over two-and-a-half miles and he had an effective pilot in the shape of Graham McCourt, but he was at an extravagant price because the betting public were besotted with Dessie and few had ever heard of Sirrell Griffiths. In the race, Kevin Mooney was on Fulke Walwyn's Ten of Spades and Richard Dunwoody on Desert Orchid, as the bookies, who stood to lose £2 million if Desert Orchid won, gnawed their satchel straps with anxiety. Down the hill, as they approached the second-last, Toby

Tobias, ridden by Jenny Pitman's son Mark, and Desert Orchid took charge, but just coming into the action behind them was Norton's Coin. Suddenly there were sharp intakes of breath in the huge crowd as Desert Orchid visibly ran out of steam. Toby Tobias led over the last two fences but suddenly there was Graham McCourt challenging on the 100-1 shot just 50 yards from the post. As Norton's Coin swept past Toby Tobias to win by three-quarters of a length, the packed stands were almost silent with shock. Perhaps the kick that Toby Tobias had given him before the start had added to Norton's Coin's determination to prove a point, but this was no fluke: on good-to-firm going he had broken Dawn Run's course record time by four seconds. Their betting tickets shredded, the crowds then applauded Norton's Coin and his trainer and jockey into the winner's enclosure, recognising the romance of the achievement by a permit-holder with just two other horses.

Sirrell Griffiths revealed in the aftermath,

The 100-1 shot. Norton's Coin, trained by Sirrell Griffiths and ridden by Graham McCourt captures the 1990 Gold Cup from Toby Tobias in the last fifty yards.

'A local bookie knocked on my door last night and asked if I wanted to have a bet of £25,000 to £200 each way, but I refused.' When the trainer and his wife drove home from Cheltenham, the local pub, The Railway, had a welcome banner out: the minibus of regulars had returned from Cheltenham with winnings of £17,000 between them. Griffiths had to send out for ten bottles of whisky to lubricate the celebrations.

Jenny Pitman's record as a trainer of staying chasers is discussed elsewhere but it was further underlined by the 1991 Gold Cup, which she won with Garrison Savannah, ridden by her son Mark. That was despite the fact that three of her horses, namely Royal Athlete, Toby Tobias and Golden Freeze, were all denied a chance to run through injury. In the formidable field of 12 who did run that year were the previous winners Norton's Coin and Desert Orchid, along with Yahoo, who had run Dessie so close in 1989. Not only did Garrison Savannah beat them, with Desert Orchid once again occupying third place, he also defeated a future Grand National winner in Party Politics and two future Gold Cup winners in The Fellow, who finished second, and Cool Ground. It was one of the closest finishes ever with Mark Pitman, later to follow his mother into the training ranks, securing consolation for Toby Tobias's narrow defeat the previous year by beating The Fellow by a short head.

Famous for spotting and developing the talents of young jockeys, including Richard Linley, Bob Champion and a certain AP McCoy, Toby Balding was also one of the few trainers to achieve the Holy Trinity of jump racing, sending out winners of the Grand National (Highland Wedding and Little Polveir), the Champion Hurdle (Beech Road and Morley Street) and the Gold Cup, which he won in 1992 with Cool Ground. Cool Ground was ridden by another of his finds, Adrian Maguire, whom everybody expected to win a champion jockey title but who never quite managed it in a distinguished career cut short by injury. After jumping the last only in third place, he conjured a storming run from Cool Ground to get up and beat the unfortunate Frenchman, The Fellow, by a short head.

The Gold Cup that year was overshadowed by a controversy about race tactics involving Jenny Pitman's Golden Freeze and Carvill's Hill, the even-money favourite trained by Martin Pipe and ridden by Peter Scudamore. An official inquiry cleared Mrs Pitman and Golden Freeze's jockey Michael Bowlby of all allegations but Carvill's Hill never ran again after injuries incurred in the race. The inquiry was into whether Golden Freeze, ridden by Michael Bowlby, had run on his merits or as a 'spoiler' to hinder the chances of Carvill's Hill. It was found that no breach of rules had taken place and trainer Martin Pipe and jockey Michael Scudamore accepted that pulled muscles in his chest and a tendon injury were responsible for Carvill's Hill's below par performance.

On much firmer going, Cool Ground was back to defend his Gold Cup title in 1993. This time the favourite was Francois Doumen's The Fellow, who had had the worst of photo finishes in the two previous years, and who faced two Jenny Pitman contenders in the shape of Garrison Savannah and Royal Athlete. The Fellow had won a second King George VI Chase in that season after only just failing to give 2 stone to Sibton Abbey and Jodami in the Hennessy at Newbury. Jodami was a strong, old-fashioned chaser with a big stride, who had won the Irish Hennessy for Yorkshire trainer Peter Beaumont, who operated from Foulrice Farm near Brandsby. Uncharacteristic jumping errors this time proved The Fellow's undoing and the race developed into a duel between Rushing Wild, ridden by Richard Dunwoody, and Mark Dwyer on Jodami, who could be read as the winner from two fences out, and who prevailed by a comfortable two lengths, with the 66-1 Royal Athlete taking third place. No northern-trained chaser has, to date, won a Gold Cup since that time.

In 1994 The Fellow finally came good at Cheltenham for the popular French trainer Francois Doumen. Only The Dikler had managed to win a Cheltenham Gold Cup at his fourth attempt and The Fellow had finished only third in the latest King George VI and in the Racing Post Chase. As a result, Doumen, criticised for continuing to use the Polish-born Adam Kondrat rather than an experienced Cheltenham jockey, fitted the horse with blinkers. By the second-last, the serious contenders had been reduced to four: Young Hustler, Bradbury Star, Jodami and The Fellow. Bradbury Star cracked first and Young Hustler was soon only hanging on. Jodami was less than perfect jumping the last, and The Fellow was first away up the hill, maintaining his advantage to the line to win at last by a length-and-a-half.

Not since 1950 had any trainer secured victory in the Champion Hurdle and the Gold Cup in the same year – but that was the achievement in 1995 of Kim Bailey. His ex-flat racer, Alderbrook, in just his third race over obstacles, showed a sharp turn of foot to win the Champion Hurdle and Kim Bailey advanced

on the Gold Cup with Master Oats, ridden by Norman Williamson, the clear favourite in a mixed-bag field of 15. Opponents included Young Hustler, Jodami (who had won his third Irish Hennessy), the previous King George VI Chase winner Barton Bank, former Champion Hurdler Beech Road, and Grand National winner, Miinnehoma. Master Oats's rider truly earned his fee because after several small jumping mistakes and a bad error at the 11th fence, Norman Williamson switched his mount to the outside. Seeing his fences better, Master Oats jumped well after that, moving into the lead two fences out and coming away to finish 15 lengths clear of Dubacilla.

Ireland had been without a winner of the Gold Cup for nearly ten years, having failed to score since Dawn Run's victory in 1986. The

Cleeve Hill forms a spectacular background to racing at Cheltenham.

Profile: **Francois Doumen**

'In France they bet numbers. People here know what they are talking about.'

Francois Doumen on the Cheltenham crowd

At the Cheltenham Festival of 2016, a distinguished spectator parked his car to head for the admission gate. Two or three racegoers spotted him and within a minute a group of 20 had clustered round to break into a spontaneous rendition of the Marseillaise, a gesture that brought tears to the celebrity's eyes. The focus of the group's attention was Francois Doumen, British jump racing's favourite Frenchman.

His regular raids on Britain's top jumping prizes began with Nupsala in 1986 and the man to blame for all the prize money that Francois Doumen took back across La Manche with him over the years was his friend Oliver Sherwood. The Lambourn trainer had travelled to France in 1986 to try to buy Nupsala, a horse that had run second in the French Gold Cup. Francois Doumen couldn't be persuaded to sell but complained to Oliver that in France there was nothing he could do with Nupsala, who hated soft going, since from November onwards, Auteuil became a bog. Oliver said, 'There is a racetrack in Britain which if it goes three days without rain becomes good ground and that is Kempton Park.' Doumen later confirmed, 'I was lucky. I tried that and it worked. That's it.'

Francois Doumen smiles as he recalls Nupsala's achievement as the first French-trained winner of the King George VI Chase that year: 'It was my first race and his first race [in Britain]. If it hadn't worked, I might not have come back at all with other horses except that I always liked to run my horses abroad. I backed Nupsala at 50-1. They didn't give 50-1 against me after that!'

Five years later, Kempton's Thameside track raised the French flag when The Fellow, a winner of the Grand Steeplechase de Paris at home, became Doumen's second winner of the King George, and they had to do it again when he repeated the feat the following year. Two more years for Tricoleur-wavers were provided by Algan in 1994 and First Gold in 2000. However, at Cheltenham, Francois Doumen and his Polish jockey Adam Kondrat

had to live with both agony and ecstasy over the years.

In 1991 The Fellow, a 28-1 shot, was the youngest horse in the race at only six years old. Coming to the last, Mark Pitman conjured a huge leap from Garrison Savannah, trained by his mother, Jenny, meaning that The Fellow landed four lengths behind. Coming up the final hill, Garrison Savannah, whose preparation had been hindered by a shoulder injury, began to tire and, with Kondrat urging on his mount for all he was worth, the two horses flashed past the post together, neither jockey knowing which had won. The photo gave it to Garrison Savannah by a short head.

The following year, The Fellow, now 7-2 second favourite, was narrowly in the lead at the last, pressed by Docklands Express and Cool Ground. Docklands Express went into the lead then wandered across the course. The Fellow took over but then faced a challenge from Adrian Maguire on Cool Ground. With Adam Kondrat's response limited by the fact that The Fellow's owner, the Marquesa de Moratalla, did not like jockeys to use the whip on her horses, The Fellow once again went down by a short head in a photo finish.

In 1993 The Fellow, with Kondrat once more aboard, was installed as the 5-4 favourite in a big field of 16. On this occasion, however, after a couple of jumping errors, he seemed to be caught out when the leaders accelerated down the hill. He could manage only fourth as Jodami beat Rushing Wild by two lengths.

Jodami was favourite to repeat his victory in 1994 as The Fellow sought to win the Gold Cup on his fourth appearance in it, a feat only ever achieved previously by The Dikler. Equipped with blinkers after finishing only third in the King George and in the Racing Post Chase, The Fellow was among a dozen horses still left with a chance four fences out. Come the last, it was three in a line again, as Jodami, Young Hustler and The Fellow rose at the fence together. The Young Hustler had shot his bolt and The Fellow was quickest away. He forged on up the hill to hold off Jodami and this time no camera was needed: he scored a much-deserved victory by a length and a half.

Francois Doumen, always loyal to his jockey when Kondrat had faced criticism over his tactics from the English press, was able to heap praise on him that year. Now, he reflects that it did make it harder for his horse

Francois Doumen leads in Snowdrop after winning the 2000 Triumph Hurdle at Cheltenham.

that his jockey's Cheltenham experience was limited: 'If you have a jockey like Micky Fitz [Fitzgerald] or AP McCoy or Ruby Walsh, it is worth lengths, so when you get beaten two inches, a nose twice, the horse really deserves enormous respect. Four years later he had learned a lot about the track. It was just bad luck the first two.'

There is, he says, a big contrast between race-riding in France and in Britain: 'Especially with hurdle races there is a huge difference. Your hurdles are ridden like tierce races on the flat in France. When Thierry [his jockey, then trainer, son] came here and rode in the Triumph Hurdle, he said, "I only saw the last two hurdles. Everybody packs together as if they were in a flat race." It is ridden as a flat race. In France there is always room. The hurdles are probably more severe and they probably need more of a good view so it is probably less hectic than it is here. The fences are more severe here and the undulations and the hills are very hard for the horses so jockeys have got to be more efficient riders all the way, not only strong at the finish. The only tracks in France where the fences are equally severe are at Craon and Auteuil.

'There are fewer jumping meetings in France so French jump jockeys ride less often than in Britain and are not so fit. Here the guys are so fit because they ride so many times a week. Our jockeys are not as experienced as your jockeys.'

If M Doumen remains a truly popular figure at Cheltenham, the feeling is mutual: 'There is no other place like it in the world. It is amazing, the quality of the public. People here know what they are talking about. In France they bet numbers. "Who is going to win? Oh, Number One." It is a different mentality altogether.' But it was not only at Cheltenham where he won respect. He recalls, 'In the Grand National, The Fellow was brought down at the Canal Turn. Kondrat jumped on him again immediately after the race – he didn't want to walk back – and he cantered back in front of the stands. Some chaps recognised him – he had won the Gold Cup just a month before – and the crowd began to call, "The Fellow, The Fellow." It was the last time Sir Peter O'Sullevan called the Grand National and he had a tape done of it and gave it to me, saying, "I am sure you will love this."'

Another Doumen veteran who became popular with the British racing public was the staying hurdler, Baracouda. 'He had a ridiculous head and his hips

2000: Trainer Francois Doumen with jockey Thierry Doumen after First Gold landed The King George VI steeplechase.

stuck out but he was a good horse. All he needed was to have a clever jockey to put him at the back and to relax him, otherwise he was too keen and would not finish the same way.' Baracouda was still a novice when he won the first of his four Long Walk Hurdles: 'I wasn't sure what was a novice, so I thought, "Well, that's a nice race." I didn't think, "With a novice, should I go against the old boys?" I had no complex at all.' Baracouda may not have been beautiful but he was good for the Doumen bank balance – he won two Stayers Hurdles (now the World Hurdle) at Cheltenham.

At the urging of his elegant South-African born wife, Elizabeth, Francois Doumen gave up training jumpers on reaching the age of 70 in 2010. He has had considerable success on the flat too but there is one question to which he does not really have an answer. Given the vogue for French-bred horses in Britain and given his success in big races here, why has there not been a flood of French trainers following him to contest the big jumping prizes?

'Everybody asks me that and I cannot answer it. It takes a lot of organisation to do a winter season in

England, moving your horses back and forth all the time because you are not allowed to leave them here for more than a month. The Jockey Club said, "We will give you a licence any time but you will have to hand in your French licence." You can't have a licence in both countries at the same time.

'All the moving backwards and forwards is difficult. At the end, we had the Tunnel. But when The Fellow won the King George, we were still waiting for the ferry and the ferry boat was cancelled and cancelled and cancelled because of bad weather. We had to take him back to Le Bourget and fly over. It was never easy.'

British champion-trainer, Paul Nicholls, has an explanation too: 'It's mostly because they sell them. It's a business. It depends what you want to do and what your owners want to do. Prize money for their top horses is phenomenal. The timing of their calendar doesn't fit in with Cheltenham and the prize money is terrific for their top horses, they're better staying over there.'

man who got them back on the score sheet was Fergie Sutherland, an Eton-educated Scotsman born in England and domiciled in Ireland after an earlier training career in Newmarket. A former soldier who had lost a leg in Korea when a soldier tripped a landmine, he never let it impede him, keeping separate artificial limbs for riding, fishing and dancing.

The Irish knew they had a good one when Sutherland's Imperial Call beat Master Oats comprehensively in the Irish Hennessy. In the Gold Cup, Gordon Richards's grey, One Man, and Imperial Call came to the second-last together but suddenly One Man's tank emptied, as it also would the following year. As it turned out, the one to chase Imperial Call home was Rough Quest, who went on to win the Grand National a few weeks later. Surprisingly, Imperial Call was Sutherland's first-ever runner at the Festival. Ireland greeted a new hero but within a few years Sutherland had wound down his operation to concentrate on country pursuits.

The following year it was a different kind of Irish talent that emerged in the Gold Cup as AP McCoy rode the winner of both the Gold Cup and the Champion Hurdle. His long-time employer, Martin Pipe, sent out Make A Stand to win the Champion Hurdle, while Noel Chance in Lambourn was responsible for Mr Mulligan, a powerful chestnut whose relentless galloping style had his rivals in trouble on the second circuit. Once again, One Man, impressive all the way to the second-last, ran out of fuel in the closing stages. A year later, Gordon Richards decided to enter One Man in the two-mile Champion Chase instead – and at last he gained the Cheltenham victory he deserved.

In 1998 the Gold Cup went to Cool Dawn, a former hunter chaser on whom Andrew Thornton had taken over in the saddle from his diminutive owner, Dido Harding. The pair stayed on more strongly up the hill to hold off Norman Williamson and Strong Promise. Reports of the race, though, were dominated by an incident when Cyborgo, trained by Martin

Pipe, sustained an injury. In the process of pulling him up, AP McCoy carried out the outsider, Indian Tracker, and the strongly fancied See More Business. Although bridges have been largely repaired since then, See More Business's trainer Paul Nicholls, yet to train a Festival winner at the time, was furious over what he perceived as Pipe's attitude to the affair. Fortunately, Cyborgo did race again; for See More Business, there was to be another day.

Much of the focus in the 1999 Gold Cup was on Teeton Mill, another popular grey, who had emerged from the hunter-chasing ranks to be the best horse trained by Venetia Williams. After beating a strong field in the Hennessy and easily winning the King George, Teeton Mill was made second favourite to Ireland's star, Florida

Bobs Worth and trainer Nicky Henderson celebrate winning the Gold Cup, 2013.

Opposite: Newmill and AJ McNamara in the lead over the water: Queen Mother Champion Chase 2007.

Profile: **One Man**

'Twice I have said to myself, "Yes, Gordon, you've got a Gold Cup" but from the second-last, it was sad to see him.'

Trainer Gordon Richards on One Man

There are champions: horses whom we will always admire, whom we thrill to see in action and whom we will remember when they are gone. But there are some 'personality' horses who pass beyond that: horses whose victories and setbacks tug at the heartstrings, horses who are adopted by the race-going public and willed home in their races by those who have never had a penny on them, horses whose passing leaves a void that can never quite be filled by the next chasing star.

One Man, a brilliant, athletic grey in the mould of Desert Orchid who was trained by Gordon W Richards, seized the public imagination early in his career. Before the great WA Stephenson died One Man had been in his charge, winning three times over hurdles. Stephenson knew he had something special and had told Richards, his friend as well as his rival, that once the muscular, bounding grey started jumping fences, the world would recognise that.

At the dispersal sale in 1993 following Arthur Stephenson's death, Richards, determined to get One Man, took along toy manufacturer John Hales as his potential owner. They had hoped to acquire him for between 20,000 and 40,000 guineas but Hales stuck with the trainer's judgement as the bidding soared and eventually signed a cheque for £68,000. It proved a brilliant purchase: the best grey since Desert Orchid became the King of northern steeplechasing. Not only did he win 20 of his 35 races, amassing £456,649 in prize money, but he won the hearts of racegoers. It was not just his sheer class that did it. One Man was brilliant, but he was not invincible: part of his appeal was his fallibility and the way he bounced back after setbacks. On the roller coaster ride, his fans had to take the dips as well as the mountains climbed.

With Gordon Richards he won five novice chases in a row, already displaying the high cruising speed, the exuberant jumping and the speed away from his fences

that were his trademarks. Then he went to Cheltenham as favourite for the Sun Alliance Chase at the Festival, where to the dismay of connections and his growing fan club he was well beaten.

The next season, back at his best, he beat off 15 others to win the Hennessy Gold Cup at Newbury, a chase that often falls to second season chasers likely to figure in future Gold Cups. But then in the Racing Post Chase he took a crashing fall that had John Hales fearing he had lost his pride and joy.

After that it was on to the 1995 King George VI Chase at Kempton Park, the traditional Boxing Day highlight and the second most important race in the calendar for a champion chaser. It was the race that Desert Orchid had made his own, winning it four times, and Gordon Richards, who used to ride One Man himself at exercise, had no doubt his bonny grey was worthy of comparison with the old stager who was to parade before the Kempton showpiece. In fact, snow and frost cancelled the holiday event, which was then run at Sandown Park in January 1996, thus making One Man the answer to a typical pub quiz question: which horse won the King George TWICE in 1996?

One Man not only won the first of those two races but, ridden by Richard Dunwoody, he simply blew away a high class field with his speed and spectacular fencing, coming home 14 lengths clear of his field. The pair were then back on Boxing Day the same year to produce another record-breaking effort and dominate the King George field once again.

But Desert Orchid had also won a Gold Cup and Gordon Richards wanted his 'bouncing rubber ball' to demonstrate he was the best by winning that too. He sent him back to Cheltenham for the 1996 Gold Cup. Running down from the top of the hill, with the crowds starting to cheer for their hero, One Man was going as well as any and appeared to have every chance. At the third last, Richard Dunwoody shouted across to Conor O'Dwyer on Imperial Call that they had the race between them. But suddenly, as push came to shove, it was as if a switch had been flicked: the lights went out, the tank emptied. One Man had nothing left for the final drive up the finishing slope and limped home in sixth place, 30 lengths behind the winner.

Gordon Richards and John Hales gave it one more go, only to see precisely the same thing happen in the

One Man and jockey Brian Harding, winners of the 1998 Queen Mother Champion Chase with owner John Hales (left).

1997 Gold Cup. Once again One Man emptied out at the crucial point. Richards acknowledged: 'I have seen One Man come down the hill in the last two Gold Cups and I have said to myself, "Yes, Gordon, you've got a Gold Cup" but from the second-last it was just sad to see him.'

One Man, who had been winning races elsewhere in his usual exuberant style, seemed to be the victim of a Cheltenham hoodoo: it appeared he just could not do it in the Cotswolds, certainly over the Gold Cup distance. The Gold Cup, over Cheltenham's undulations, is measured at three miles two and a half furlongs, whereas the King George at Kempton is just three miles on a flat track.

In 1998, however, Gordon Richards, by then a very sick man, played a masterstroke. Always convinced of his horse's quality and determined to defy the critics who had doubted One Man's courage, he entered One Man not for the Gold Cup but for the Queen Mother Champion Chase, the championship for speed chasers over just two miles, a far shorter distance than he was accustomed to running.

One Man had a new jockey, too. Richard Dunwoody had ridden One Man to many of his successes but was unavailable so the ride was handed to stable jockey Tony Dobbin, only for him to fracture his thumb on the first day of the meeting. So the stable number two, Brian Harding, was given his chance of the spotlight and he did not waste his opportunity.

The decision to drop One Man back in distance proved to be a brilliant one. He was able to go with the pace and test the others with his jumping skills with no fears about lasting the trip. Coming round the final bend, Brian Harding was able to put daylight between One Man and his pursuers and this time the grey did not run out of gas on the hill, winning comfortably from Or Royal and Lord Dorcet. The Cheltenham stands erupted: he was a Cheltenham winner at last in a championship race and the emotional owner, John Hales, was not the only one to shed tears of joy.

Tragically, that Cheltenham triumph was One Man's last success. At Cheltenham he had been saddled by Nicky Richards, the trainer's son. Sixteen days later he went to run at Aintree and Gordon Richards came too, the desperately ill trainer being applauded by racegoers lining the paddock rail.

Brian Harding rode again, but this time there was no triumph. After fencing impeccably to that point, when coming up to the ninth fence in the Melling Chase One Man veered right, failed to achieve any height and crashed into the obstacle, breaking a hind leg in a way that left the vet with no option but to put him down. The tears of joy that John Hales had wept at Cheltenham became tears of anguish at Aintree. Richards, One Man's greatest fan of all, died that September.

War of Attrition trained by Mouse Morris and ridden by Conor O'Dwyer wins the Totesport Cheltenham Gold Cup in 2006.

Pearl. Sadly, in that year's Gold Cup, Teeton Mill injured a tendon so badly that he was never to race again. See More Business had run disappointingly earlier in that season and was less fancied than his stable companion, Double Thriller, but the fitting of first-time blinkers did the trick. As the leaders headed for the last two fences, Florida Pearl could not stay with the outsider, Go Ballistic, and See More Business who, partnered by Mick Fitzgerald, showed greater staying power up the run-in to win by a length, thus topping off a breakthrough Festival for Nicholls, who had also won the Queen Mother Champion Chase with Call Equiname, and the Arkle Chase with Flagship Uberalles.

The year 2000 was to provide another triumph-and-tragedy scenario. Florida Pearl was back for Ireland, along with Dorans Pride and Rince Ri; Strong Promise and Go Ballistic were contesting again, and See More Business was the 9-4 favourite. The most intriguing participant, though, was the front-running Gloria Victis, who had shattered a high-class field in the Racing Post Chase at Kempton with rapid-fire, athletic jumping. After much debate and amid much unsolicited advice from the media, Martin Pipe and owner Terry Neill had decided on the bold strategy of sending the brilliant novice to play against the big boys in the Gold Cup, rather than keeping him in the novice version.

Gloria Victis, seemingly unabashed by the company he was keeping, led them through the first circuit. At the third-last, See More Business began to drop away from the leaders; Rince Ri unseated Ruby Walsh as both Looks Like Trouble and Florida Pearl began to make progress. Then came the hideous blow. Jumping the second-last, Gloria Victis crumpled on landing. Initially, he got to his feet but after he was taken away in a horse ambulance, it transpired that he had broken a canon bone and he had to be put down. Pipe and rider AP McCoy were both in tears. Back in the race, meanwhile, with the Irish roaring on Florida Pearl, it was Looks Like Trouble, who had been pulled up in the King George with a suspected injury, who

stormed up the hill to clinch a second Gold Cup in a short period of time for Noel Chance, later to become the jockey's father-in-law when Richard Johnson married his daughter Fiona.

There was no Gold Cup in 2001 due to a foot-and-mouth epidemic, but 2002 saw the rise to fame of another of those horses who have captured the hearts of racegoers and left an indelible, hoof-shaped impression – the handsome Best Mate.

Following Best Mate's three consecutive victories, it was Ireland's turn again in 2005 with Kicking King, an exciting young chaser

trained by Tom Taaffe, son of Arkle's rider, Pat, and ridden by Barry Geraghty. Kicking King had been second at successive Festivals in the Supreme Novices Hurdle and in the Arkle Chase but he signalled his arrival at the top level by winning the King George VI Chase at Kempton as a mere six-year-old in 2004. A couple of weeks before the race, his stable had confirmed him as an unlikely runner after a bad 'scope' (the mucus from a horse's lungs examined with a probe) and briefly he could be backed at 999-1 on the betting exchanges. However, he not only recovered well enough to take his place in the race but was exuberantly full of running at the top turn under Barry Geraghty, before pulling clear to win by five lengths and eight lengths respectively from Take A Stand and Sir Rembrandt, who had made it such a test for Best Mate the previous year. Kicking King won the King George again at the end of that year but, in narrowly seeing off Monkerhostin he suffered a tendon injury that kept him off the track until January 2008 – and he was never the same force again.

Irish connections were back in the winner's enclosure again in 2006. Beef Or Salmon,

Profile: **Best Mate**

'Terry and I always liked to have a horse with a nice head because you are going to see it a lot sticking over the stable door.'

Henrietta Knight

Henrietta Knight is a renowned judge of a horse, but it isn't all science. What she looked for in an animal when she and her husband, Terry Biddlecombe were buying horses to train was, 'the way they moved. Athleticism is incredibly important, watching them jump – and sound legs. Terry and I always liked too to have a horse with a nice head because you are going to see it a lot looking over the stable door and if you don't like it you are going to get fed up by the end of the winter!' All those qualities were obvious in the best horse they ever trained, Best Mate, who emulated Arkle by winning three consecutive Cheltenham Gold Cups from 2002 to 2004.

Best Mate may have worn the colours of Aston Villa fanatic Jim Lewis through his racing career but as with Desert Orchid or Arkle he became public property in the minds of many racing folk. He was a national emblem, the People's Horse. He not only helped to fill racegoers' wallets but flicking silkily over his fences he engaged their emotions too.

Hen and Terry, affectionately dubbed 'the Odd Couple' because she was an ex-debutante, ex-schoolmistress from the top drawer and he was a battered, earthy, ex-champion jockey who had lost a few rounds with the bottle until the pair rescued each other's lives, were true horse people who typified the quirky mix of graft, skill and romance that unites what we used to call National Hunt racing. Hen's superstitious reluctance to watch her horses run concealed a deep attention to detail and a well-honed instinct for timing a horse's preparation for the big day. Terry, who had ridden even better than he

Jim Culloty holding three fingers in the air after riding Best Mate to a third successive Cheltenham Gold Cup victory.

roistered in his cavalier phase, could read a race better than anybody and his instructions to their jockeys were a model of tactical nous.

Says Henrietta, 'Terry did all the schooling with Fred Rimell but he always said a lot of jockeys were better not riding out the horses at home because it gave them preconceived ideas when it came to the racecourse. The way we school horses, if it makes a mistake you can correct it. If you put a pro jockey on it schooling then when they go to the races the jockey will think, "That horse made a howler at home" and may be wary. If you go to the racecourse and tell them, "This horse is a good jumper" they will believe it.'

Hen and Terry found Best Mate, like many of their horses, at an Irish point-to-point and persuaded Jim Lewis to strike a deal with horse-dealer Tom Costello. Following an early hurdling career, the son of Un Desperado and Katday would have been fancied to win the Arkle Chase at Cheltenham in 2001 but the meeting was cancelled after a foot-and-mouth disease outbreak. In the 2002 Gold Cup the seven-year-old Best Mate was the baby of an unusually large field of 18, and having been beaten by Florida Pearl in that year's King George, with AP McCoy substituting for suspended stable jockey Jim Culloty, he started only as the 7-1 third favourite. The previous year's winner, Looks Like Trouble, was at 9-2 and Nicky Henderson's Bacchanal was at 6-1 but it was Ted Walsh's Irish outsider Commanche Court, ridden by his son Ruby, who first came to dispute the lead with former winner See More Business. Best Mate quickened impressively under Jim Culloty on the inside rail and drew away from Commanche Court up the run-in to win by one-and-three-quarter lengths. Culloty went on to complete a rare double, winning that year's Grand National on Bindaree.

At the end of 2002 Best Mate did win a King George, under AP McCoy. Terry Biddlecombe's instructions to the great rider were bold and simple, 'For God's sake don't fuck it up again today.' Henrietta Knight is a great admirer of AP but says he wasn't necessarily the best jockey for Best Mate, who liked to make his own decisions. 'AP was brilliant because he always wanted to win but he wanted to win at any cost and he would put the gun to the horse's head. A horse like Best Mate, although he was always first or second, was a bit of a thinker as well. He was very sensitive. If you put the gun to his head he didn't particularly like it.'

In 2003 it was a stronger Best Mate who came to Cheltenham. His biggest threat this time seemed to be Beef Or Salmon, trained in Ireland by Michael Hourigan, but he fell at only the third fence. This time, at the top of the hill Valley Henry set the pace along with Best Mate's stable companion, Chives. But Best Mate and Culloty had simply been playing with them, jumping flawlessly and economically. At the second-last his jockey pressed the go button and up the hill he surged clear of Truckers Tavern to win by ten lengths. It was the first time since L'Escargot in 1971 that a champion had successfully defended his crown and the biggest winning margin since Arkle.

But if Best Mate's first two Gold Cups had demonstrated his high cruising speed and sheer class, his third and final victory was the one in which he proved himself a scrapper too. Technique is vital but the best jump racing demands bravery, too, from both horse and rider.

The course having suffered a late soaking, Terry Biddlecombe and Jim Culloty had agreed that the best ground was down the inside. But if you stick to the inside you risk being denied a clear run. Culloty

had Best Mate in a good rhythm, taking the fences in his usual neat way. But others were determined not to yield him any advantage. At the last ditch Best Mate was pocketed by Sir Rembrandt, ridden by Andrew Thornton, on his outside with Paul Carberrry on Harbour Pilot deliberately hemming him in at the front.

Culloty admitted they were legitimate race-riding tactics. With roles reversed he would have done the same: 'You wouldn't get many rides in this game if you were a perfect, "after you, Sir" gentleman.' It was a test of resolve for the jockey and his horse. But whatever Best Mate thought of it he never became flustered and they forced their way out of the scrimmage. Best Mate jumped the second-last with élan. But then at the final fence, with his jockey making safety the priority, they were a little slow, a touch flat-footed. Best Mate's usual fluency was not there and on ground that he loved Sir Rembrandt was battling.

It was no time for gentleness and driving up the finishing slope Jim Culloty was as hard on his partner as he had ever been. Best Mate, though, had the courage to respond up the demanding finish slope and in the

end they prevailed, though only by half a length. An emotionally drained Henrietta Knight greeted the result by saying, 'Everyone wanted him to win. He has been taken over by the country and I just couldn't bear the thought of letting anybody down.' Said Jim Culloty, 'We knew he had the class and the ability. Now we know he's got the bottle too.'

Sadly, there were to be no more Gold Cups. Best Mate missed the 2005 Gold Cup, having suffered a burst blood vessel shortly before the race. Making his seasonal comeback that autumn in the Haldon Gold Cup at Exeter, partnered by Paul Carberry because Jim Culloty had retired, Best Mate was clearly not himself and his rider pulled him up. As they started trotting back, he collapsed and died of a heart attack. Best Mate's career lasted 22 races. He won 14 of them and finished second in 7. That last race at Exeter was the only time he did not finish in the first two.

From 'Best Mate' by The Racing Poet, Henry Birtles.

A death that robbed a nation,
but upon it we won't dwell
Let's celebrate the life of one
who served his sport so well
Best Mate, you never let us down,
you lived up to your name
You ran your rivals ragged,
showed 'em how to play this game

He won with ease and nonchalance;
he won with craft and style
He won the hearts of England
and the mighty Emerald Isle
He gave us what we'd waited for,
a Gold Cup crown retained
An undisputed Champion,
a King who proudly reigned

Don't judge him upsides Arkle,
if you don't judge man by God
But see him as a Winter King,
who never spared the rod
Who poured it on at Prestbury Park,
with smiling Jim aboard
And left this world with three Gold Cups,
Best Mate by all adored

the winner of eight Grade One races, was the Irish-trained favourite but, for the fourth time, he flopped at the Festival. It was instead War of Attrition, owned by the Ryanair magnate Michael O'Leary and his Gigginstown House Stud, trained by Mouse Morris and ridden by Conor O'Dwyer, who on St Patrick's Day led home the first-ever Irish 1-2-3 with Hedgehunter, subsequently a Grand National winner, and Forget the Past occupying the places. Ireland had to wait until 2014 for a further success because for the next five years much of the Festival focus was on Paul Nicholls' two great chasers, Kauto Star and Denman, as they battled with each other, and with the young pretenders who followed them, for Gold Cup supremacy.

After Kauto Star had won back his title in 2009 racegoers had looked forward to 2010 as the ultimate showdown, hopefully with Kauto Star and Denman both fully fit. But warning signals flashed in the 2009 Betfair Chase when Kauto Star only just beat Imperial Commander

and it was the younger Imperial Commander, trained locally by the popular Nigel Twiston-Davies and ridden by Paddy Brennan, who took the 2010 honours, running away up the hill to win by seven lengths. Twiston-Davies, who had been somewhat irritated before the race by the scarf-waving mania surrounding Kauto Star and Denman, despite what Imperial Commander had shown in the Betfair Chase, was proved absolutely right in his claim that his champion had been undervalued.

In that 2010 race Kauto Star took a horrible fall, the kind that can often lead to maiming or death. Thankfully, he survived, which meant that in the 2011 Gold Cup the two stablemates were back again. This time, with Imperial Commander absent through injury, it was Robert Waley-Cohen's Long Run, trained by Nicky Henderson and ridden by Waley-Cohen's son Sam as an amateur jockey, who represented the up-and-coming generation's threat. Had any screenwriter supplied it as a script, such a scenario would have been

Jockey Ruby Walsh and trainer Paul Nicholls enjoy Master Minded's victory in the Queen Mother Champion Chase in 2008.

Profile: **Kauto Star**

'Whatever beats Kauto Star will have to be a superstar.'

Trainer Paul Nicholls

No horse can ever do more than beat his contemporaries and comparisons between racing eras are always a little unreal, but if ever there was a horse to rival Arkle's reputation in his overall performance it was Kauto Star, who won his first Gold Cup in 2007. Arkle won a higher proportion of the races he contested and was a more dependable jumper but his career was shortened by injury. Kauto Star won back his Cheltenham title after losing it. He was fast enough to win two Tingle Creek chases over two miles as well as durable enough to drive up the Cheltenham hill at the end of three miles plus. He won no fewer than 16 Grade One races and he was still winning top class chases at the age of 11, eight years on from his debut in a modest hurdle in France. In racing the best things come in fives, like Golden Miller's Gold Cups, and when on 26 December 2011 Kauto Star won the King George VI Chase at Kempton Park for the fifth time, he joined the racing immortals. Even Desert Orchid had only managed four of those.

Kauto first won the three-mile Kempton classic, despite a last fence blunder, in 2006, just three weeks after winning the Tingle Creek, a specialist event for speed chasers over two miles at Sandown. In 2007 Kauto Star won the King George in a stroll and he was eight lengths clear of Alberta's Run in 2008 despite once more tangling with the last fence. In 2009 he won with almost unbelievable majesty, 36 lengths clear of Hennessy winner Madison du Berlais. In 2010, after a troubled year, he was only third but amazingly came back at the age of 11 to win the King George again in 2011.

Paul Nicholls probably knew he had the 2007 Gold Cup in his grasp when he watched a grinning Ruby Walsh enter the winner's enclosure at Haydock Park on 18 November, 2006. That was Kauto Star's first Grade One run over three miles and he had defeated by 17 lengths a cluster of top horses lured to Lancashire by the exciting £1 million bonus Betfair were offering

to any horse that won their race plus either the King George or the Lexus Chase in Ireland and the Gold Cup. The race is now a regular target for potential stars.

Kauto Star looked the perfect horse, bar one worry. He seemed to have a habit of making jumping errors, in particular seeming to panic at the last obstacle and dive through it. The media fastened on to this tendency and the public had what they liked best – a spectacular hero with just a hint of soap opera fallibility about him, likely to turn every race he ran into a drama, although in practice the jumping errors became fewer and farther between.

Kauto Star not only won two Gold Cups and five King Georges but he also won the Betfair Chase on four occasions and twice triumphed in the two-mile Tingle Creek Chase. In all, for 23 victories in 41 races he won £3.7 million in prize money. Timeform, who in the past allotted a rating of 212 to Arkle and 210 to his stable companion, Flyingbolt, put Kauto Star on 191, equal to Mill House and the highest since then.

In the 2007 Gold Cup itself, Kauto Star did not disappoint either his fans or the worriers. Accelerating round the final bend he went clear of his pursuers, but then he lost concentration, got too close and launched himself at rather than over the final fence. Somehow he got through it and somehow Ruby sat tight. They were pursued up the hill by McCoy on Exotic Dancer but once Kauto Star had found his feet the result was clear. He duly collected the £1 million bonus to add to the £242,335 first prize.

As Kauto Star and his stablemate, Denman, prepared to meet in the 2008 Gold Cup, they took different routes to Cheltenham. Kauto Star returned to action in the Old Roan Chase at Aintree in October but suffered a shock defeat, going down to the smart grey, Monet's Garden.

Ruby Walsh and Kauto Star winning at Kempton.

With Ruby Walsh injured and Sam Thomas in the saddle, Kauto Star then ran more like his old self when again winning the Betfair Chase. Meanwhile, under top weight, Denman had slaughtered a field of top-class handicappers, winning the Hennessy by eleven lengths.

Kauto Star reaffirmed his credentials with a King George victory; Denman further burnished his by flying to Ireland to win the Lexus Chase. Denman powered his way to victory at Newbury again in the Aon Chase; Kauto Star put in a flawless performance winning the Commercial First Ascot Chase. It was 'game on' for the Festival and the 2008 Gold Cup with Paul Nicholls predicting 'Whatever beats Kauto Star will have to be a superstar.' Back at his Ditcheat yard, as it turned out, he had that superstar in the adjacent box. In the Gold Cup a dominant Denman turned the screw on the whole field. Taking over a circuit from home and steaming on like a rail express under Sam Thomas, Denman forced Kauto Star into jumping errors as he drove on to an emphatic victory.

rejected as being too obvious, but racegoers saw the three best-known chasers in the country, Kauto Star, Denman and Long Run, rise as one at the second-last fence. Long Run then forged ahead at the last before steaming on up the hill ahead of Denman, who finished second for a third successive year, with Kauto Star in third. Surprisingly, given that Nicky Henderson is the most successful trainer of all time at the Festival, this was his first Gold Cup winner and, in an ever more specialised and professional age, Long Run's convincing victory was a remarkable achievement for an amateur rider.

After the 2011 contest the two Nicholls stars remained in training with contrasting fortunes:

while Denman sadly suffered the tendon injury that led to his retirement, Kauto Star became the comeback king with stunning victories over Long Run in the Betfair and in the King George that winter. But time was catching up with him too and, in the 2012 Gold Cup, Kauto Star was pulled up after Ruby Walsh felt that something was amiss.

That 2012 Gold Cup may have seemed an ordinary race after the glamour of the preceding few years – but it was not: it was a race in which Synchronised, a relatively small horse, bred more for the Derby than for the Gold Cup, won the supreme championship thanks to his own courage and thanks to a memorable ride from AP McCoy. His Gold Cup victory was applauded

Profile: **Denman**

'We'll have him in the rematch.'

Kauto Star's owner Clive Smith,
after Denman beat him in the Gold Cup

Denman and the horse who lived in the adjacent box to him in Paul Nicholls' Ditcheat yard always encouraged sportswriters' comparisons. If Kauto Star was a Mod, then Denman was a Rocker. If Kauto Star was the Cassius Clay of the racetracks, then Denman was the Sonny Liston. If Kauto Star was an athlete, then Denman was a powerhouse. The pair even epitomised the constant debate in breeding circles as to whether traditional Irish-bred horses or the more rapidly advanced French chasers were the best investment for the British chasing scene. (Kauto Star, purchased from France for 400,000 euros by owner Clive Smith, had run in ten races before Denman had even been broken in. Denman had yet to jump a fence when Kauto Star was beginning his third season.) All that was really proved was that Paul Nicholls was equally happy handling either type.

As for Denman's breeding, he was by Presenting out of a mare called Polly Puttens. Denman, a liver chestnut, was a massive foal and a big yearling, who was purchased by Nicholls' patron Paul Barber after a point-to-point victory in County Cork for former top-jockey-turned-trainer Adrian Maguire. Both Henrietta Knight, who had acquired Best Mate in the same way, and Willie Mullins had previously had the chance to

buy him but decided against, probably because Denman had undergone a hobday operation to improve his wind. Barber sold a half-share to professional gambler Harry Findlay, once affectionately described by Nicholls as 'a mouth in search of a microphone.' After a couple of novice hurdle wins and victory in the Challow Hurdle, Denman went to his first Cheltenham Festival in 2006 but he and Ruby Walsh lost to Nicanor and Paul Carberry in the RSA Novices Hurdle.

In the 2006/7 season, he won his first four novice chases by a total just short of 60 lengths and, as a Festival favourite once again, this time he won the RSA Novice Chase by ten lengths. The exuberant Harry Findlay, who had been backing his horse for months from 10-1 down to 6-5 , won almost £1 million. What all the world realised from Denman's performance, up with the leaders all the way until he took over, was that he was capable of sustaining his relentless ground-devouring gallop until he burned off all opposition. What Paul Nicholls had come to realise was that the hefty Denman was so stuffy that it took an enormous amount of preparation to get him race-fit.

Weather conditions having prevented a 'prep' run, Denman's first engagement the following season was in the Hennessy Gold Cup at Newbury, where he sent his reputation soaring skywards. Under top weight of 11 st 12 lb, he demolished a classy field, earning from Harry Findlay the soubriquet of 'The Tank'. He went to

Cheltenham unbeaten over fences, having won 13 of his first 14 races.

In his first Gold Cup, Denman was always travelling well. On the second circuit, he took over and ground out a pace that kept the others constantly on the stretch. Four fences out, Denman and Sam Thomas stepped it up again and went ten lengths clear. From that moment he never looked in any danger; although Kauto Star eventually closed the gap to a more respectable seven lengths, it was Denman's day. After that 2008 Gold Cup, some pundits argued that Denman would always beat Kauto Star at Cheltenham, but that Kauto would always be superior in the King George at Kempton. However, Paul Nicholls warned people not to write off Kauto Star, while his owner, Clive Smith declared, 'We'll have him in the rematch.'

They were prophetic words because it transpired that Denman's overpowering 2008 effort might have left its mark. Denman missed much of the next season when an irregular heartbeat was discovered and had to be treated. Only at the last minute did his trainer decide to let him run in the 2009 Gold Cup, in which he ran a less spectacular but respectable second to Kauto Star.

Kauto Star (white blaze) and Denman together on Paul Nicholls's Ditcheat gallops.

Preparing for the 2010 Gold Cup, Denman went back to Newbury for another Hennessy. Given top weight again, although he had not won since his Gold Cup, he once more pounded his rivals into the ground. Next stop was Cheltenham, where he took over the lead at halfway after Kauto Star had crashed out early. Could Denman too win back the Gold Cup crown? For a moment it looked likely as he wound up the pace. Yet Denman had no answer when the younger Imperial Commander sailed past, so he had to be content with another second place.

It was another younger-generation story in 2011. Denman and Kauto Star were now both aged 11 and no horse older than ten had won since 1969. As Kauto Star led from halfway before Denman took over three fences out, the crowd cheered what they were beginning to imagine as the final battle for the crown between the two veterans. Denman got the better of Kauto Star, but then at the second-last fence, Long Run appeared and ran on up the hill to beat the old guard. Second once more, Denman at least had the satisfaction of being seven lengths clear of his old rival.

He was retired later that year after injuring a tendon, the winner of 14 of his 24 races and of more than £1.1 million in prize money. Denman ran eight times at Cheltenham, four times in the Gold Cup, and was never out of the first two.

because his owner, JP McManus, is hugely appreciated by the jump-racing community, not just for the money he puts into the sport spread across many, many training yards, but also for his sportsmanship and for the way he ensures that his horses have a happy retirement. Says Nicky Henderson: 'He's passionate about his horses. If you go to Martinstown (McManus's Irish estate), there are fields and fields of retired horses. He goes out there with his carrots and his dogs, just to see his old friends. He hardly ever sells a horse.' McManus has, of course, also been famous for some significant gambles, albeit rather less detail is available about those.

The irony was that JP McManus had spent a fortune over the years trying to buy Gold Cup winners and Synchronised was bred at home by his wife, Noreen; Synchronised was by Sadler's Wells out of a mare, Mayasta, who was AP McCoy's first winner for JP. His victory made Sadler's Wells the first sire to have bred both a Derby winner and a Gold Cup winner and it also took Jonjo O'Neill into the exclusive club of those who have both ridden and trained a Gold Cup winner.

After the race, McCoy explained that Synchronised simply didn't have the physique to travel comfortably at Gold Cup pace. 'It was just about tagging on to the back of them for as long as I could … I just wanted not to ask him too many big questions as far as jumping was concerned. I was niggling, slapping and cajoling him all the way round.'

Sadly, there was no happy ending for Synchronised, who went on to run in that year's Grand National, ridden by McCoy. They fell but although Synchronised was unharmed by that tumble, he then broke a leg when galloping loose and had to be put down. McCoy admits that he cried for days and when he was asked on his retirement to list his ten favourite horses, he put Synchronised, on whom he had won a Lexus Chase and a Welsh National as well as the Gold Cup, at the top of the list, saying, 'He was a bit like I am as a human being. He probably wasn't the greatest horse I'd ridden but he had the greatest will to win.'

The 2013 Gold Cup also went to a popular horse, who epitomised the honesty of the true staying chaser. Owned by the Not Afraid Partnership, headed by Malcolm Kimmins, and trained (like

Amateur rider Sam Waley-Cohen celebrates winning the Cheltenham Gold Cup of 2011 on Long Run.

Profile: **Amateurs and Sam Waley-Cohen**

'Once you've been legged-up, it doesn't matter who gave you a helping hand.'

Rider Sam Waley-Cohen

Champions who began as amateurs include Terry Biddlecombe, seen here (above) on the Queen Mother's Game Spirit, and the 2015–16 champion jockey Richard Johnson (above right)

Amateur jockeys do not ride against professionals in flat racing but they are allowed to over the jumps. Professional jump jockeys who gained their early experience as amateurs, often starting in the point-to-point field, have included the likes of Dick Francis, Tim Brookshaw, Michael Scudamore, Stan Mellor, Terry Biddlecombe, Bob Davies and, more recently, Peter Scudamore and Richard Johnson. Adrian Maguire's first ride in England was as Mr A Maguire (signifying his amateur status), partnering Omerta to win the Kim Muir amateur riders' chase at Cheltenham for Martin Pipe. And on the day when trainer Nigel Twiston-Davies won the Gold Cup with Imperial Commander, he looked even more thrilled by the victory of his then amateur-jockey son Sam, now number-one jockey to Paul

Nicholls, in the Festival Foxhunter Chase on Baby Run.

The authorities have long sought to strike a balance, encouraging rider development, while trying to ensure that those dependent on riding fees for their living are not harmed by exploitation of the system. One well-known 'olden days' amateur, when asked by owners what he would like for a 'present', would mention a gold cigarette case in the window of a famous London jeweller. He already had one, so the jeweller would credit the sum to his account. Another was asked by the stewards to show his bank passbook. Since the latest entry in it was a cheque for £100 from a gossip-column celebrity owner, he

Left: *Stan Mellor.* Right: *Dick Francis*

announced instead, 'It's been a hard decision, gentlemen, but I have finally decided today to turn professional.'

Since 1961, amateur riders have been required to have permits, and rules now stipulate that after an amateur has had 75 rides in races against professionals, owners have to pay the same fee for their services as they would for a professional.

Top-class amateurs not seeking a professional career in the saddle have scored some famous successes. Jim Wilson's Gold Cup victory on Little Owl was not his only Festival success that year: he was the only amateur ever to have been the Festival's leading rider. Alan Lillingston won the Champion Hurdle of 1963 on Winning Fair, and trainer's son Marcus Armytage, nowadays a leading racing journalist, won the Grand National in record time on Mr Frisk in 1990.

In recent years, Sam Waley-Cohen, son of Cheltenham Racecourse Chairman Robert Waley-Cohen, and himself a millionaire entrepreneur with a string of dental clinics, has had a remarkable record. He has scored six victories over the Grand National fences, more than any professional. He has scored three times in the Fox Hunters' Chase, restricted to amateurs, on Katarino in 2005 and 2006, and on Warne in 2014. He won the Topham Chase in 2006 on Libertine, and on Rajdhani Express in 2015. His best performance so far in the Grand National itself was second place on Oscar Time.

Sam Waley-Cohen riding Rajdhani Express.

A picture of determination: Terry Biddlecombe on Parkland at Stratford in 1963.

To top that, he has made his father's chocolate-and-orange colours familiar, winning two King George VI Chases on Long Run, and in 2011, on the same horse, he secured a famous Gold Cup victory over Denman and Kauto Star. You could say that he is fortunate in having

Little Owl ridden by his owner Jim Wilson.

a father wealthy enough to buy him good horses to ride, but it is still a remarkable achievement that, despite his limited number of rides, he has secured at least one Graded race victory every year. As he puts it, 'Once you are legged-up onto the horse, it doesn't matter what helping hand you've been given.' If there were weighing-room resentment, we would soon hear of it – and we don't.

An inveterate thrill-seeker who pilots his own helicopter and goes mountaineering, white-water rafting, and road cycling in Tour de France conditions, Sam Waley-Cohen fell at the first fence on *The Young Master* in the 2016 Grand National. He then made amends by winning the bet365 Gold Cup on the same horse at Sandown in a pulsating photo finish against *Just A Par*, the previous year's winner, ridden by Nick Scholfield.

Modestly, Sam declared: 'I have to be on the right horse, have plenty of luck and just put your head down and go for it. It's a privilege to be with these great jockeys and I'm lucky to have some nice rides.' His proud father, noting, 'He's quite good value for a claiming amateur,' added accurately, 'It's an unbelievable performance. To take on the most capable people in their profession takes a lot of dedication and a lot of practice and hard work.'

Sam Waley-Cohen and proud father, Robert Waley-Cohen after Long Run's success in the 2012 King George VI Chase at Kempton.

Long Run) by Nicky Henderson, Bobs Worth was the first horse since Flyingbolt to win three different races at the Cheltenham Festival: he won the Albert Bartlett Hurdle at the Festival in 2011, the RSA Chase in 2012, and then the Gold Cup in 2013. It was a real battle to the line on rain-softened ground with Bobs Worth's determination, under a drive from Barry Geraghty, getting him there ahead of Sir Des Champs and Long Run. Geraghty and his brother had actually bred Bobs Worth and when they sent him to the sales, Nicky Henderson bought Bobs Worth on spec. 'We buy 20–30 three-year-olds in the summer (it used to be four-year-olds) and most of them will be on spec – though not the expensive ones. Then, hopefully, somebody will want a horse. Kimbo [Malcolm Kimmins] came along and needed a horse. It was the last horse standing, the one everyone else had discarded, and that was Bobs Worth. As long as that happens once, you're fine. When somebody else comes along and there's only one left, you can say, 'Don't worry, look what happened the last time!'

Bobs Worth, who provided Henderson with his 50th Festival victory, also scored brave successes in the 2012 Hennessy Gold Cup and in the 2013 Lexus Chase. He was famed for his refusal ever to give up; when he retired, his trainer explained, 'He wasn't a horse who took too much racing because he put so much into it.

Whatever he lacked in natural class, if you like, he was the greatest workman.'

Ten years on from Best Mate's third victory in the Gold Cup, his jockey Jim Culloty was back on the winner's rostrum after an equally thrilling contest: this time as trainer of Lord Windermere, after a scrambling finish that had the stewards deliberating for 15 minutes before confirming the 2014 result. Bobs Worth and Silviniaco Conti had both veered off a straight line coming up the hill to the post, while David Casey on On His Own and Tom Scudamore on The Giant Bolster, the eventual second and third, were trying desperately to get to the winner. Lord Windermere had stayed on after being no better than eighth around the final bend and trailing the field on the first circuit. It was a sweet moment for winning jockey Davy Russell, who had been taken for a cup of tea by owner Michael O'Leary at Punchestown ten weeks earlier and sacked as Gigginstown House Stud's retained rider in favour of 21-year-old Bryan Cooper. Asked soon afterwards for his advice to young jockeys, Russell replied, 'Never go for a cup of tea!' Davy Russell rode two other winners on Gold Cup day, one of them for O'Leary.

By contrast, the result of the 2015 race looked assured a long way out, as the long-striding Coneygree, trained at the small

Barnbrook Again (black and gold colours) ridden by Hywel Davies and Waterloo Boy, ridden by Richard Dunwoody, fight out a typically pulsating finish in the Queen Mother Champion Chase of 1990.

The setting sun lights the steam rising from the runners as they return after finishing at Cheltenham.

Letcombe Bassett yard by Mark and Sara Bradstock, and bred by Sara's father, the revered Lord Oaksey, had dominated his field Denman-style in the hands of Nico de Boinville. Having led from the start and been foot-perfect in only his fourth race over fences, the exciting Coneygree won comfortably from Djakadam and Road to Riches. He was the first novice to win a Gold Cup since Captain Christy in 1974. Lord Windermere, Bobs Worth and The Giant Bolster were all pulled up, while the subsequent Grand National winner, Many Clouds, and Silviniaco Conti trailed in to occupy sixth and seventh place respectively.

Coneygree was denied the chance to defend his title after suffering a hock injury and Djakadam once again found one to beat him in 2016. This time it was Don Cossack, trained in Ireland by Gordon Elliott and ridden by Bryan Cooper. It gave Michael O'Leary and his Gigginstown House Stud their second Gold Cup, and the same colours were on the third, Don Poli, Cooper having made the right choice in opting to partner Don Cossack. Racegoers will long debate, though, whether the popular Cue Card would have won if he had not fallen at the third-last when being brought through to challenge by jockey Paddy Brennan. He had won the King George VI Chase in which Don Cossack fell in the previous December.

The Gold Cup may be the biggest draw but part of the delight of the Cheltenham Festival is its sheer range. It isn't always the blue-riband race that provides the biggest thrill; other times, it might be the three-mile World Hurdle for staying hurdlers, or the two-mile Queen Mother Champion Chase that provides the most nail-biting finish or the most intriguing duel between several fancied combatants. There are, it is true, a few owners and trainers who consider hurdle racing no more than a briefly beguiling appetiser; nevertheless, it has often been the Champion Hurdle, a feature of the Festival card since 1927, that has underlined one of the biggest joys of jump racing: familiar characters, each with their own band of loyal followers, returning year after year to renew battle.

Profile: **The Queen Mother Champion Chase**
The race AP McCoy used to call 'the professionals' race'

'This horse knows what he is, he knows what it is all about and he wants to do it – so you have to let him. We owe it to the crowd.'

Trainer Nicky Henderson on superstar Sprinter Sacre

The Cheltenham Festival prize that AP McCoy sought above all the others was success in the Queen Mother Champion Chase, a contest run usually at breakneck pace over the minimum distance of two miles and which he used to call 'the professionals' race'.

Few races for the two-mile crown, renamed in 1980 to mark the Queen Mother's 80th birthday, fail to excite. Although fields are often quite small, the speed at which the downhill fences are negotiated is terrifying, magnifying the results of any errors. Over the longer distance of the Gold Cup, a horse can be given a breather, allowed time to recover from a mistake. In the Queen Mother Champion Chase, it is pell-mell all the way and, more often than not, the finish is fought out between well-established stars who have previously clashed, with little quarter given or received, in races like the Tingle Creek Chase at Sandown.

As well as One Man's famous victory (see page 64), horses of the quality of Dunkirk, Flyingbolt, Crisp, Badsworth Boy, Pearlyman, Barnbrook Again, Viking Flagship and Moscow Flyer have earned their place in racing history or burnished their considerable reputations in the race that has become known in short as 'the Queen Mother.' Special qualities of verve and courage are required. A dozen horses have won it twice since 1960, while the electric Badsworth Boy won three Queen Mothers in a row for Michael, and then Monica, Dickinson from 1983 to 1985. Irish trainer Tom Dreaper sent ten horses to contest the race through the 1960s and won it no less than six times.

Regular racegoers rated the contest in 2000 between Edredon Bleu, in the Aston Villa stripes of Jim Lewis and

In a driving finish, the eventual winner Klairon Davis (Francis Woods) leads Viking Flagship after the last in the 1996 Queen Mother Champion Chase.

made famous by Best Mate, and Direct Route as one of the best races ever seen at Cheltenham. McCoy was riding 'Edredon,' who had run second the previous year, while Norman Williamson was on Direct Route, trained in the north by Howard Johnson. Edredon's electric jumping put pressure on Direct Route early on but as the pair shook off the previous year's winner, Flagship Uberalles, at the last of the eight fences, the northern-trained horse came level. As McCoy said: 'I didn't worry coming down the hill at Cheltenham flat out at 38 miles an hour – it never occurred to me that this fellow might not take off.' Both horses jumped the last fence well and 50 yards later Direct Route was a head in front. Both riders and horses really went for it, heads down, locked together up the hill in the ultimate nostril-to-nostril duel, neither giving an inch. Neither horse ever changed its stride pattern and, at the finishing line, McCoy and Edredon Bleu had it by a short head. Yet another classic running of the Queen

Mother was the battle between Barnbrook Again and Waterloo Boy in 1990, as was Pearlyman's victory over Very Promising in 1987.

Very Promising, ridden by Richard Dunwoody, led Pearlyman over the second-last but Pearlyman was gaining ground; coming to the last, Peter Scudamore drove him between Desert Orchid and Very Promising. Dunwoody, however, conjured a leap at the last from Very Promising that put him back in the lead. Very Promising was a neck up and had the greater momentum but as Scudamore drove his mount, Pearlyman began creeping ever closer. There was uproar from the stands and white knuckles clenched on binoculars as Very Promising's half- length leading margin became a neck, then a head. Finally, in the shadow of the winning post, Pearlyman's nose inched ahead; at the post, he was half a length up on the brave Very Promising, with Desert Orchid three lengths back.

The race was won in 1962 by Piperton, a horse that had been so lame that a previous owner had been planning to shoot him! The winner in 1971 was Crisp, the giant 'black kangaroo' from Australia, who had scarcely had time to get used to the British weather before scoring by 25 lengths on tacky ground. In 1992 Nicky Henderson won the Queen Mother for the first time with Remittance Man, a truly spectacular jumper, who provided one of five riding successes at that Festival for the stylish jockey Jamie Osborne.

In 2006 one of the contestants was the French mare Kario de Sormain. When it was suggested to her trainer, Jean Paul Gallorini, that it was a 'tough ask' bringing her to Cheltenham for her first race in England, he replied romantically, 'She will take to the English fences like a young girl discovering love.' Sadly, she fell at the first fence.

A horse that was pretty well unbeatable in his prime over the two miles – provided that he didn't fall – was Moscow Flyer, trained by Jessica Harrington and ridden by Barry Geraghty. He jumped perfectly and coasted home in 2003 and 2005.

In recent years, amid all the quality of the two-mile-chase winners, two horses have stood out as being in a class apart – Master Minded and Sprinter Sacre. Neither of them had to make their mark as battlers in a tight finish; they did it with such awesome demonstrations of

Barry Geraghty and Moscow Flyer.

cruising speed and spring-heeled jumping through a race that they totally dominated the opposition. Both horses won the race twice, albeit in rather different circumstances.

Master Minded, trained by Paul Nicholls and ridden by Ruby Walsh, was a mere five-year-old when he won the race in 2008, the first of his age group to do so. He did not merely win; his breathtaking exhibition round destroyed a high-class opposition including the previous year's winner, Voy Por Ustedes. Master Minded simply coasted to victory and Ruby Walsh could have extended his winning margin of 19 lengths if he had wanted to. Former champion jockey John Francome called the performance 'scary', suggesting that Master Minded on that form could have won any race at the Festival. He became the highest-rated chaser in the world; in the aftermath of a 16-length victory in the Victor Chandler Chase at Ascot the following January, Paul Nicholls, with

Kauto Star and Denman also in his yard at the time, called Master Minded the best horse he had ever trained.

In the 2006 running of the Queen Mother Champion Chase, Nicholls reckoned that Master Minded was only 95 per cent fit; it made no difference and it was all over from several fences out. He scored with a winning margin of seven lengths over the veteran Well Chief. From then on, though, the special spark that ignited Master Minded's talent no longer seemed to generate. He finished fourth in 2010 and, at only seven years old, proved to be past his peak. It had certainly been a remarkable peak.

We did not have to wait too long for another sperhero. One of the most handsome horses ever to grace a racecourse with his big, strong neck and bold head, the dark-brown, almost black, Sprinter Sacre appeared to be a force of nature. Trained by Nicky Henderson, he was unbeaten in five chases in 2011/12, including the Arkle Challenge Trophy at Cheltenham. The following season he set himself apart from the other two-mile chasers, winning the Tingle Creek and the Victor Chandler, before becoming the first horse since Istabraq to win at all three Spring Festivals, taking the Queen Mother Champion Chase, the Melling Chase at Aintree, and the Punchestown Champion Chase.

His victory in the 2013 Queen Mother, by 19 lengths over Sizing Europe, meant that in his

first eight races over fences he had beaten his opponents by a total of 114 lengths, earning him the highest Timeform rating since Arkle's day. His proud trainer, as prone to anthrop-omorphism as the rest of us about a true champion, declared: 'He's got that wow factor about him and he knows it. He's got that thing about him that says, "look at me, now watch me."' He added about the big jumper who was so neat on his feet: 'You don't school him because I can't teach him anything. It's just pure natural talent.' Then, alas, came nemesis with knobs on. On his first outing of the following season, Sprinter Sacre was pulled up and found to be

AP McCoy wins on Edredon Bleu.

Sprinter Sacre with Barry Geraghty in full flight.

suffering with heart problems. Back problems followed, which meant that he ran only four times in two seasons, pulling up in the 2015 Queen Mother. Henderson, though, kept the faith. Slowly and quietly he and work rider, Nico de Boinville, worked to bring their champion back and in 2015/16, he did come back. Sprinter Sacre won the Shloer Chase and the Desert Orchid Chase, before coming back to Cheltenham to face the hot favourite from Ireland, Un de Sceaux, in another Queen Mother Champion Chase.

'Sprinter', a 5-1 shot, made swift progress to go clear approaching the second-last and stayed on up the hill to win by three-and-a-half lengths, receiving a rapturous reception from the crowd. His previous Queen Mother victory in 2013 had been greeted respectfully but quietly, partly because few would have backed him at 1-4, the lowest odds at the Festival since Arkle. There is, though, something special about a king regaining his crown, about an ex-invalid returning to top form. The cheering was ecstatic and the emotion flowed.

Master Minded, ridden by Ruby Walsh, comes home clear of his rivals.

Sprinter Sacre's trainer put himself through further stress sending the horse out again soon afterwards to win Sandown's Celebration Chase, after which he revealed both the joy and the scary responsibility of handling a national treasure. 'Why did we have to put ourselves through it again?' he pondered aloud. 'I was looking for every possible excuse not to run him but there weren't any. His work was good, his schooling was good, he looked brilliant ... This horse knows what he is, he knows what it is all about and he wants to do it – so you have to let him. We owe it to the crowd. I'm dying to say, "Stop. Let's go and open more supermarkets and attend open days" – he loves doing that too, but this is what makes National Hunt racing.' In November 2016, however, Sprinter Sacre damaged a leg and this time around Henderson decided on an honourable retirement for the horse who had personified the sport's appeal.

Barnbrook Again with jockey Simon Sherwood.

The Champion Hurdle

– *From the 'pigeon who couldn't swim' to the 'aeroplane who hijacks himself'*

'The horse would have to be dead two days to stop battling and McCoy would carry on riding if he had no arms or legs.'

Trainer/commentator Ted Walsh on McCoy's Champion Hurdle victory aboard Brave Inca

Champion hurdler Night Nurse in action in 1976.

The Champion Hurdle grew in popularity after the Second World War, starting with National Spirit's two successive victories, followed by Vincent O'Brien's trio of victories with Hatton's Grace. Our period begins with Another Flash in the 1960 Champion Hurdle, which first brought jockey Bobby Beasley to the notice of the Cheltenham public when riding for trainer Paddy Sleator. The next year, Ryan Price won with Eborneezer, an entire (ungelded) horse named after a butler and owned by a Dr Burjor Pajgar from Croydon, whose wife had brought Eborneezer up on a diet supplemented with whisky, eggs and milk.

In 1962 Lambourn maestro Fulke Walwyn, a trainer since 1939, finally succeeded in winning a Champion Hurdle with the fast-finishing roan Anzio, ridden by Willie Robinson. Winning Fair, first past the post in 1963, was ridden by the amateur Mr Alan Lillingston and was blind in one eye, having once run into an apple tree. His Irish trainer, George Spencer, who had only three other horses in his yard, enquired with a grin, 'If he had two eyes, wouldn't he be good enough for the Derby?'

Magic Court, trained by Tommy Robson, struck a blow for the north when he won in 1964. Then in 1965, in line with the London-bus principle, Willie Robinson and Fulke Walwyn followed up their 1962 success when they were back on the rostrum with the 50-1 shot Kirriemuir.

In 1966 it was the turn of the consistent Salmon Spray, trained by Bob Turnell and ridden by Johnny Haine, to be Champion Hurdler, with the great Flyingbolt only finishing third, after being asked to run his second race within 48 hours. In 1967 Peter Easterby (see page 137) introduced himself to southern racegoers by sending Saucy Kit down from Yorkshire to become the first of the Great Habton trainer's five Champion Hurdle winners. The next three years, though, were to be dominated by one of Cheltenham's best-loved

characters: Persian War, trained by Colin Davies and ridden each time by Jimmy Uttley, took three championships from 1968 to 1970.

The Cheltenham crowds adored Persian War – not just for his honesty and courage, but also for his ability to come back patched up from one injury after another to deliver his best. He finished third in one race despite biting through his tongue and losing two teeth. Another time, Persian War was given up for dead after knocking himself out when hitting his head on the top bar of a hurdle!

Owned by the opinionated Henry Alper, who changed trainers as often as others changed their shirts, Persian War was faced in his first Champion field by Salmon Spray and Saucy Kit, as well as the favourite, Chorus, who was known to relish the prevailing firm ground. Persian War led down the hill to the second-last, but even though Saucy Kit landed awkwardly at that one, he still won untroubled.

In 1969 Persian War had not enjoyed the ideal preparation. On his seasonal debut he had fallen, fracturing a femur, and was off the course for three months. He had also been beaten in a prep race at Wincanton; it transpired that he had been running a temperature. In the Champion Hurdle itself, Drumikill took up the running three flights out. Rounding the bend for

Bula (left) and Paul Kelleway, who went on to win the Champion Hurdle, at the third obstacle from home in 1971.

home, Persian War was still four lengths behind, already being hard driven, but when Drumikill then sprawled, Persian War had enough left to drive up the hill and win by four lengths.

Coming to the 1970 Festival, 'Persian' had not won a race since the previous Easter. This time, Colin Davies, his fourth handler, had tied down Persian War's tongue to prevent the champion from swallowing it, as he had become prone to do – an affliction that leaves a horse effectively running on an empty tank. The trainer later commented, 'When we put a tongue strap on Persian War, a few people said it was a pity we didn't put it on the owner.'

Jimmy Uttley took his brave companion into the lead at the fifth hurdle – and there they stayed until passing the winning post, resisting the challenge of Josh Gifford on Major Rose.

Two old favourites battle it out in 1979. Monksfield (nearest camera) comes to beat Sea Pigeon and win his second Champion Hurdle. Sea Pigeon took the title in 1980 and 1981.

The patched-up old warrior then had an operation on the 'soft palate' condition that had been inducing his tongue-swallowing and vets discovered that he had a broken wolf tooth, which must have been causing him severe pain. Before he ran again in the 1971 Champion Hurdle, differences between owner and trainer saw him removed from Davies to the Epsom yard of Arthur Pitt. Persian War was to pass

through the hands of two more trainers before he was allowed a deserved retirement.

From his new Epsom base, Persian War won the Irish Sweeps Hurdle at Christmas but a new generation was on the way and he was beaten ten lengths by Bula at Wincanton. At the 1971 Cheltenham Festival, he responded to the crowds once again and managed, once more, to beat his old rival, Major Rose. However, Bula, the new kid on the block, joining the leader at the last hurdle under Paul Kelleway, left Persian War four lengths behind as he stormed up the hill to take the title.

In all, Persian War won 18 of his 51 hurdle races, including a Schweppes Gold Trophy, when he carried the massive burden of 11 st 13 lb, and a Welsh Champion Hurdle. He won at Cheltenham on every kind of ground and was the first hurdler ever to earn the 'Horse of the Year' title. Bula also set up a Cheltenham sequence, winning again for Paul Kelleway and trainer Fred Winter in 1972.

If Persian War was a tank who would have happily carried a gun turret, then Bula was a racing car, one who coasted most of the way and could then accelerate fast enough to settle any race in a matter of a hundred yards. Crowds

thrilled to the sight of the ice-cool Kelleway letting his mount snooze at the back of the pack in top hurdle races, confident that when he activated the booster after the second-last, his mount would power past them. Sometimes, he left it agonisingly late: for example, in the Benson and Hedges Hurdle at Sandown, Bula sprinted past seven horses after the last hurdle to win by two short heads.

The brown horse, whose name was Fijian for 'Hello', won his first 13 hurdle races and 25 in all. When he turned to chasing, he won 13 of his 25 contests over the bigger obstacles. His place in racing history means that he still has a Cheltenham race named after him.

The following three seasons saw a fascinating battle for supremacy between two superbly talented hurdlers: the next Fred Winter machine in the sleek shape of Lanzarote, and the strapping sprinter-sired Comedy Of Errors, trained by Fred Rimell. They clashed eight times and each won on four occasions. It was a civilised competition. When both horses headed to Ireland for the Sweeps Hurdle, the two trainers' families travelled over together and their horses exercised alongside each other at the track on the morning of the race.

In 1973 Comedy Of Errors beat Bula to win his, and his trainer's, first Champion Hurdle, although Rimell had won it previously as a rider. In 1974 Lanzarote beat 'Comedy' but in 1975 Comedy Of Errors became the first horse to regain the top prize after having lost it, with Lanzarote trailing home only seventh in the mud. Only Hurricane Fly has equalled Comedy's feat since. Ironically, neither Lanzarote nor Comedy seemed to like Cheltenham: Lanzarote's Champion Hurdle was his only victory there in four attempts, while he was unbeaten in eight races at Kempton. Comedy Of Errors, who tended to jump to the right, lost half of his ten races at Cheltenham, whereas he won three Fighting Fifth Hurdles at Newcastle. Lanzarote, reckoned by Winter to be the best horse he ever trained, and the winner of 20 of his 33 races, lost his life in the 1977 Gold Cup. Comedy Of Errors, who won 23 of his 48 contests, retired to become Mercy Rimell's hack.

By now, we have arrived at what most aficionados acknowledge as an exquisite, vintage period of the Champion Hurdle. The domination of the training centres of Lambourn and Kinnersley was now over, which left the way open for two champions from the north of England and one from Co. Meath, Ireland, to monopolise the race for the next six years, each of them winning it twice: Night Nurse, Sea Pigeon and Monksfield.

All were Cheltenham favourites but most experts give the ultimate accolade to Night Nurse. Sired by a sprinter and trained, like Sea Pigeon, by Yorkshire's Peter Easterby, he not only went on to be a successful chaser too, but he also won his Cheltenham crowns against both superstars: Monksfield and Sea Pigeon. Against that, it was Monksfield who finally dethroned Night Nurse and then twice held off Sea Pigeon; whereas Sea Pigeon had the sheer class and speed to beat them both – if his jockey got the tactics right…

A bold front-runner, who skimmed his obstacles with precision and nipped away from them swiftly, Night Nurse was ridden for most of his career by Paddy Broderick. In 1975/6 he was unbeaten in eight races, including the English, Irish, Welsh and Scottish Champion Hurdles.

Having led all the way to win the 1976 Champion Hurdle, the next year, on very heavy ground, Night Nurse faced not only his old rival, Bird's Nest, but also Sea Pigeon and Monksfield. Despite the appalling conditions, Ron Barry opted to make the pace as usual on Night Nurse, hoping in that way to find the best ground. At the hurdle at the bottom of the hill, Monksfield hit it hard; Night Nurse jumped cleanly and was off up the rise to the winning post to record an authoritative win by two lengths. Dramatist was third and Sea Pigeon fourth. Monksfield rallied but could not get to the leader.

The tough little 'Monkey' (as Monksfield was affectionately dubbed), trained in Ireland on the Co. Meath border by Des McDonagh, had already performed in 52 races over four years by the time he came to the 1978 Champion Hurdle. That season, Monksfield, who had a taste for Granny Smith apples and kept other stable inmates awake with his snoring, spent two months in the autumn out of action with a leg infection. Maybe the unaccustomed rest did him good.

In the 1978 event, Night Nurse was in trouble, not skating over the hurdles with his usual fluency. Aboard Monksfield, 43-year-old Tommy Kinane, aware of the need to draw the speed from fast finishers like Sea Pigeon, committed for home early. Frank Berry, who was deputising on Sea Pigeon for the injured Jonjo O'Neill, brought his mount up to challenge but it was too soon and Monksfield, who always responded when a rival came alongside, drew away again up the hill to win by two lengths.

In 1979 it was déjà vu all over again, except that Jonjo O'Neill was back on Sea Pigeon, and Dessie Hughes was riding Monksfield. Just as Frank Berry had done in the previous running, Jonjo also got it wrong. He attacked Monksfield on the final bend and jumped the last in the lead. Both horses took the last obstacle perfectly, but halfway up the run-in, Sea Pigeon began to 'empty' on the sticky going. His stride shortened and, in clinging mud, Monksfield, his head lowered almost to his knees as he clawed his way back, passed him 50 yards out to win by three-quarters of a length. 'It's a pity pigeons can't swim.' observed Easterby.

If racegoers are excited by brave front-runners who set sail for home and defy the others to catch them, they thrill even more to the 'hold-up' horses who swoop like a predator with a well-timed burst of speed at the death; so it was that in 1980 Sea Pigeon, who had once finished seventh in the Derby, produced just that kind of finish.

His work having been held up by an injury, Sea Pigeon was only 90 per cent fit. At the top of the hill he was wheezing, so Jonjo switched him off, gave him time to get his second wind, and this time he jumped the last a length down on Monksfield. They landed level but Sea Pigeon produced such a surge of power that he was clear halfway up the run-in, sooner than his jockey had intended. He went on to win by seven lengths to the roars of an ecstatic crowd.

When Sea Pigeon came to defend his crown in 1981, Jonjo was sidelined with a badly broken leg. This time it was John Francome who provided a silk-smooth ride, delivering Sea Pigeon halfway up the run-in to pip Pollardstown and Daring Run. Francome declared that he had never ridden a jumper with such acceleration.

Sea Pigeon lived on in his Yorkshire retirement to the ripe old age of 30. He and Night Nurse won 70 races between them, Night Nurse once going ten races and 21 months without a defeat.

The year of 1982 may have seen a temporary end to the cluster of multiple winners, but the race didn't lack for drama as For Auction, the subject of an audacious old-fashioned betting coup and ridden by the amateur Colin Magnier, ran out a convincing winner by seven lengths. Irish celebrations continued late into the night.

In 1983 it was the turn of Gaye Brief, making Mercy Rimell, who had taken over the Kinnersley yard on the death of her husband, the first woman to train a Champion Hurdle winner. Gaye Brief was ridden by Richard Linley and owned by Sheikh Ali Abu Khamsin, that year's champion owner. His victory and that of Sheikh Mohammed's Kribensis in 1990, trained by flat-racing supremo Michael Stoute (who was then yet to be knighted), had some National Hunt traditionalists fearing that the jumping world was about to be transformed by Arab-oil money. However, Middle-Eastern owners have shown little interest since in travelling to Britain in the winter months; Sheikh Ali, who was in fact a Saudi, retreated to Riyadh after his business interests were hit by the first Gulf War.

Dawn Run's 4-5 victory in the 1984 race was predictable after the withdrawal of Gaye Brief. She had already beaten Mercy Rimell's hurdler at Kempton earlier in the season. Dawn Run vied for the early lead with Buck House (later to become a Champion Chase winner), and with Desert Orchid (later, like Dawn Run, to become a Gold Cup winner), and despite making a bad mistake at the last when she was distracted by the tumult of the excited crowd, she ran a copy-book race to win by three-quarters of a length. That year the tough mare won eight of her nine starts. In her career, Dawn Run collected the English, Irish and French Champion Hurdles.

Perhaps the finest training feat among the series of multiple Champion Hurdle winners was that of Nicky Henderson in preparing See You Then to win three times from 1988 to 1990. Apart from being a brute in his box who would take chunks out of lad, trainer or vet, given the slightest opportunity, See You Then had legs like china and could be raced only at rare intervals. He was in consequence less a public icon than a mystery horse. A son of the Derby winner Royal Palace, See You Then had plenty of quality – he won ten of his 15 races over hurdles – but the problem was keeping him sound. After he won his first title in 1988, See You Then ran only six more races but they included two more Champion Hurdle victories.

In the 1985 Champion Hurdle (the year the favourite, Browne's Gazette, whipped round at the start under jockey Dermot Browne, who was later to earn notoriety in racing circles and be 'warned off' after being named in a doping scandal as 'The Needle Man'), See You Then was a 16-1 shot but he stormed home seven lengths clear under Steve Smith-Eccles. The jockey had acquired the ride on See You Then for his first Champion Hurdle at a mere ten minutes' notice: John Francome had originally been booked to ride but was now unavailable, having suffered a scary fall in the previous race, which had left him hanging upside down from a twisted iron.

See You Then won by the same distance (seven lengths) in 1986 from former champion Gaye Brief, after the two had jumped the last hurdle together. In 1987 See You Then was barely fit – trainer and jockey acknowledge that he 'blew up' as expected on the run-in – but he was simply in a different class to the other runners. He won by one-and-a-half lengths after America's champion jump jockey, Jerry Fishback, misjudged the last obstacle on Flatterer.

Celtic Shot was the champion hurdler in 1988, providing Peter Scudamore with his first victory in the race. Although Celtic Shot ran in Fred Winter's name, the great trainer had by then suffered a stroke and fractured skull in a fall down stairs; his assistant Charlie Brooks and head lad Brian Delaney were largely responsible for Celtic Shot's preparation.

The grey Kribensis beats Nomadic Way in record time in the 1991 Champion Hurdle.

Conor O'Dwyer and Hardy Eustace (right) having cleared the last flight in company with Paul Carberry riding Harchibald and Brave Inca (left) ridden by Barry Cash.

The next three years were to see two Champion Hurdle victories for one of the most popular trainers in the sport, the gregarious Toby Balding. Beech Road, the 1989 victor in the hands of Richard Guest, was a 50-1 surprise, although not to his trainer. The media labelled him 'the winner back from the dead' because, two months previously, the green screens had been erected around Beech Road's seemingly inert body after a fall in a novice chase. Come the Champion Hurdle, he had recovered well enough to beat a field including Celtic Shot, Celtic Chief and flat-racing trainer Michael

Stoute's previously unbeaten grey, Kribensis. Balding was to win again in 1991, this time with a 4-1 favourite in the handsome, athletic shape of Morley Street, ridden by Jimmy Frost.

The Champion Hurdle prize was by now worth £50,000 to the winner. That not only tempted a return by Kribensis in 1991, but also a comparatively rare foray into jump racing by Barry Hills, with the Cesarewitch winner, Nomadic Way, owned by Robert Sangster. The flat-racing pair of horses jumped the last together in company with Beech Road and Past Glories; however, on that year's better ground,

Kribensis found his speed and the resolution he had appeared to lack the previous year – and Richard Dunwoody drove him past Nomadic Way to victory in a new record time.

The training centre of Newmarket was to the fore again in 1992 as Stoute's lanky former assistant, James Fanshawe, ran Royal Gait, formerly an accomplished stayer on the flat. The nine-year-old, owned by Sheikh Mohammed, had once been controversially disqualified after winning the Ascot Gold Cup. When he bumped a contestant in the Champion Hurdle after six tired horses had jumped the last hurdle virtually together, the stewards had to huddle together to see whether the result should stand: this time, Royal Gait and jockey Graham McCourt kept the prize they had won.

The 1993 contest saw the first Champion Hurdle victory for Martin Pipe (see page 158) with Granville Again, ridden by Peter Scudamore; Pipe did it again with Make A Stand in 1997, the man in the saddle by then being AP McCoy. In 1994 the race was won by the mare Flakey Dove for Leominster trainer Richard Price, the Mark Dwyer-ridden winner providing welcome evidence that the small battalions could still fight their way into the Cheltenham Hall of Fame. At 6.15 that morning, Richard Price had been lambing ewes. His Oh So Risky having finished second once again, trainer David Elsworth sportingly observed, 'Flakey Dove is a much more romantic tale than old Elzee making a few quid.'

In 1995 trainer Kim Bailey's Alderbrook gave the race a touch of class. An entire horse by the great stayer Ardross, he had won Group 2 and Group 3 races on the flat; now at Cheltenham over the jumps, he accelerated smoothly under Norman Williamson after the last and simply cruised clear of Large Action. He was an odds-on favourite to repeat his victory the following year and, with regular pilot Williamson injured, Kim Bailey booked the talented but wayward Graham Bradley. Bailey then sacked him after he failed to turn up on time for a training gallop. Bradley, after a party the night before, had overslept when a power cut was said to have disabled his alarm call – the unimpressed trainer handed the

plum ride to Richard Dunwoody instead.

Bradley was then booked by Jim Old for Collier Bay. The pair took control of the 1996 race rounding the home turn and went on to win by two-and-a-half lengths from Alderbrook, whose trainer and owner felt he had been left with too much ground to make up. Richard Dunwoody disagreed. Graham Bradley, ever the humorist, pointed at a non-existent watch on his wrist as he rode triumphantly back into the winner's enclosure.

The horse who ran second to Make A Stand in 1997 was the 33-1 outsider, Theatreworld. He occupied the same position for the next two years. In retrospect, he had no serious chance of improving on that position because, from 1998 onwards, he was competing against the phenomenon known as Istabraq, who raced in the green-and-gold hoops of JP McManus.

With Istabraq out before much of the 2002 race had been run, Hors La Loi III, ridden by Dean Gallagher, provided a second Champion Hurdle victory for trainer James Fanshawe, who could clearly have prospered as a jumps trainer had he chosen that route.

The winner of the Champion Hurdle in 2003 had spent most of his racing life not in prestige events, but humping big weights in handicaps. Rooster Booster, trained by Philip Hobbs, had won the County Hurdle in 2002 for owner Terry Warner, who has a penchant for greys. In 2003 he came to the Festival with four wins from four races and, with Hors La Loi III refusing to start, 'Rooster' led much of the way and scorched up the hill to crown his career with the big prize he merited, winning by 11 lengths.

Fanshawe and Hobbs, the only two English trainers to get on the Champion Hurdle scoresheet in a period of nine years, provided a brief interlude between Istabraq's domination of the event and a series of wins by some intriguing Irish contenders. At that time it seemed that England simply could not produce a horse to rival those of the Irish over the smaller obstacles. In one particular year the first nine in the ante-post betting were all trained in Ireland and in 2005 there was only

Profile: **Istabraq**

'Only if he kicks him at the start.'

Jockey Chris Maude, asked by an owner if his horse had a chance of beating Istabraq

Istabraq won 18 of his first 20 contests over hurdles, including the 1997 Royal & Sun Alliance Novices Hurdle. Even so, before the first of Istabraq's champion hurdles in 1998, jockey Charlie Swan was startled to hear the horse's trainer, the normally shy, soft-spoken Aidan O'Brien, declare: 'Istabraq will destroy them.'

Swan reckoned that Istabraq, having won over two-and-a-half miles, might lack a true Champion Hurdler's speed. He resolved to ride him for stamina, forcing the pace. But he need not have worried. By the time they got to the top of the hill, Istabraq's high cruising speed had demolished his rivals and they came home 12 lengths clear. Jockey Chris Maude, asked by an owner the next year if his horse had a chance of beating Istabraq, replied, 'Only if he kicks him at the start.'

The most respected of all racing assessors, Timeform, gave Night Nurse a rating of 182 in 1976/7. The only other hurdler ever to reach 180 was Istabraq in the 1999/2000 season. Had there been horses to push him, he might have soared higher but with Istabraq we did not enjoy a series of duels with regular rivals; there was simply nobody around capable of duelling with him. His winning margins over his three Champion Hurdle victories amounted to nearly 20 lengths. Istabraq was responsible for introducing British racegoers to the latest Irish genius – Aidan O'Brien. Ireland's champion amateur rider, O'Brien began training as assistant to his wife, Anne Marie Crowley; however, once he took out his own licence, he set a new record for stakes won in his very first year and in 1994/5 sent out an incredible 138 winners.

Similar to his unrelated predecessor, Vincent O'Brien, he has an uncanny ability to divine a horse's potential and devotes massive attention to detail. He discovered that the key to Istabraq, who was highly strung and easily upset, was to keep him happy without letting him get too far above himself, as he was otherwise inclined to do when approaching race-fitness.

Istabraq – the highest rated hurdler since Night Nurse,

Istabraq had scored only two wins from 11 starts on the flat for John Gosden before being sold on by Hamdan al Maktoum. When JP McManus bought him, he sent him to O'Brien, whose reports on the horse soon had JP declaring: 'Whenever he runs, whatever Istabraq is doing, I'm there. I'll never take my holidays to miss anything he is doing.'

The horse could hold his own at home with any of O'Brien's flat-racing stars over a mile-and-a-half and McManus must have laughed when bookmaker Victor Chandler gave him odds of 3-1 against Istabraq for the Champion on a £30,000 investment. Istabraq toyed with his field and the 12-length margin by which he won was the biggest since 1932.

When he came back to the Festival the following year, Istabraq's trainer said that he was heavier, stronger and quicker; he was 4-9 to defend his crown. At the second-last, Charlie Swan sent him on and he strolled to victory three-and-a-half lengths clear of poor old Theatreworld.

In theory, the 2000 contest should have been a lot tougher for Istabraq. Among those lining up against him was Hors La Loi III, who had won the Supreme Novices Hurdle at the previous Festival in a time three seconds faster than Istabraq's in the Champion. There was a scare, too; the day before racing. At the course, Istabraq had bled from one nostril. If it were a sign of an internal haemorrhage, that could be serious, but it could equally be as a result from just a knock on the nose. So close to a race, he could not be sedated and 'scoped' (the mucus from his lungs examined with a probe) and, because it was the Champion Hurdle with a third consecutive title at stake, 'Team O'Brien' chose to run. In the event, there was no problem. Make A Stand, back in action, tried to repeat his all-the-way win from three years previously but faded after the fifth hurdle. Nicky Henderson's runners, Katarino and Blue Royal, then took it up. However, by the turn for the straight, every jockey's whip except Charlie Swan's was in action. On good ground Istabraq won by four lengths from Hors La Loi III in a new record time. Sadly, the foot-and-mouth epidemic wiped out the Festival of 2001, thus depriving Istabraq of the chance that year of becoming a four-time champion.

He was back for the Festival of 2002 but by then it was rumoured that he had problems. It did not stop many hundreds of Irish fans wearing rosettes in McManus's green-and-gold colours, demanding 'Gimme Four' and backing him down to favourite once again. But soon after they set off, Charlie Swan felt something amiss and before the second hurdle he pulled up Istabraq. The extraordinary

thing was that the crowd applauded. It was a tribute to the horse himself and it was further evidence of the sporting crowd that Cheltenham produces. Many of those applauding would have lost their bets yet they did not want anybody to run risks with such a great horse.

Charlie Swan celebrates Champion Hurdle triumph.

Charlie Swan (right) riding Istabraq and Conor O'Dwyer (left) riding Finnegans Hollow at Leopardstown.

one English-trained horse in the first seven home – from the yard of Jonjo O'Neill – hardly a Home Counties man.

The pattern was set in 2004 when the 33-1 shot, Hardy Eustace, trained by Dessie Hughes and ridden by Conor O'Dwyer, scooted away from Rooster Booster to win by five lengths. It was a reminder to many of the perils of the trade: at the previous Festival, Hardy Eustace had won the Royal & Sun Alliance Novices Hurdle, when ridden by young Kieran Kelly, who was killed at Kilbeggan in August that year.

In 2005, travelling ominously well, the talented Irish-trained runner Harchibald simply cruised up to Hardy Eustace after jumping the last hurdle. It seemed only a question of when his rider, Paul Carberry, would press the button to go past Hardy Eustace into the lead. But when he did press it, Harchibald simply ignored the message, leaving Hardy Eustace to battle on to win, with another Irish runner, little Brave Inca, just a neck away in third.

The winner's trainer, Dessie Hughes, admitted, 'I thought we were cooked when Harchibald cruised alongside.' But never was it so obvious that horses are not machines. Both jockey Carberry and trainer Noel Meade insisted that there was no other way to ride Harchibald. His jockey's only regret was that he hadn't made his challenge even later: 'He's a bridle horse. That's the only way you can ride him. If he hits the front, he stops.' Carberry later said of the talented but complicated Harchibald that he was, 'Like an aeroplane. But the trouble with this aeroplane is that he hijacks himself.'

Most of the same cast returned in 2006, except that AP McCoy was now riding Brave Inca. The pair were well suited: as the veteran trainer/commentator Ted Walsh put it, 'The horse would have to be dead two days to stop battling and McCoy would carry on riding if he had no arms or legs.' Brave Inca was not one of those horses to go ten lengths clear in a race. When anything came at him, he responded. Said trainer Colm Murphy: 'He sticks his head out and anything that went by would know he's had a race.' Brave Inca claimed the crown and on this occasion Hardy Eustace was relegated to third,

with Mac's Joy, trained by Jessica Harrington and ridden by Barry Geraghty, in second place.

Come 2007 and it was Ireland again, but with a new name. Few knew much about John Carr's Sublimity, ridden by Philip Carberry in only his sixth hurdle race. Only after he had come home the 16-1 winner from Brave Inca, with Afsoun in third and Hardy Eustace fourth, did racegoers recall that Sublimity had previously shown good form on the flat when trained by Michael Stoute, and that he had been an unlucky fourth at the previous year's Festival in the Supreme Novices Hurdle. Sublimity was going so well that he could be called the winner from half a mile out.

Ireland's Sizing Europe was favourite for the race in 2008 and he and Sublimity were both very much in contention coming down the hill. However, this was to be the year of England's comeback. Katchit, a little horse bought from Mick Channon in a racecourse bar by his trainer, Alan King, and ridden by Robert 'Choc' Thornton, was the winner, beating two more English candidates in Osana and Punjabi. It used to be felt that it was too much to expect five-year-olds to win a Champion Hurdle – they were considered to be too young – but both Katchit and Punjabi were only five. Channon had told his purchaser that the horse might win him 'a couple of little summer jumps races' but Katchit never stopped improving. He won five out of his first six races on the Cheltenham track.

Nicky Henderson has the best Cheltenham record of any trainer still in business; there was a reminder of the glory days of See You Then as Henderson prepared Punjabi to win in 2009. The surprise for the Cheltenham crowd was that Punjabi was something of a long shot at 22-1, whereas the horse he beat into third, Binocular, ridden by AP Mcoy and also trained by Henderson, was the 6-4 favourite. The horse who divided them by a neck and a head was Paul Nicholls' Celestial Halo.

That year, a betting-exchange company offered a £1 million bonus for any horse winning the Champion Hurdle, the Fighting Fifth Hurdle at Newcastle and the Christmas Hurdle at Kempton. Punjabi had won the Newcastle race but had fallen at Kempton when, in the words of his owner, Raymond Tooth, 'he was cantering.' After the Champion Hurdle, Punjabi's trainer ruefully called it, 'probably the most expensive fall in the history of racing.'

Following Punjabi's victory, Nicky Henderson warned: 'Binocular is a year younger and I still think he is a horse with a big future.' They were prophetic words because in 2010 McCoy did score on JP McManus's horse. Binocular had run some poor preparatory races and was nearly scratched at a time when he mysteriously decamped briefly to Ireland, a series of events that explained his generous starting price of 9-1.

In 2011 a new star burst upon the Champion Hurdle scene, a hurdler that trainer Willie Mullins later hailed as 'the horse of a generation,' namely Hurricane Fly (q.v.).

In the Mullins yard at the same time as Hurricane Fly was winning his Champion Hurdles, a remarkable mare also entered the record books. Quevega ran six times in the OLGB Mares race at the Cheltenham Festival over two miles three furlongs and 200 yards – and she won every time, often by wide margins. As the only horse ever to win at six consecutive Festivals, she beat the record held by five-times Gold Cup-winner Golden Miller. Like Hurricane Fly, Quevega demonstrated tenacity as well as talent. In the 2014 mares race, she stumbled at the top of the hill and lost her place but she still came back with a late burst of speed to win from Sirene d'Alnay. Not always easy to prepare for racing, Quevega three times won at the Festival while making her seasonal debut. She was retired in May 2014 after just failing

Make a Stand ridden by AP McCoy comes in first in the Smurfit Champion Hurdle, in 1997.

Profile: **Hurricane Fly**

'Guts, determination, stamina.'

Ruby Walsh, taking just three words to sum up Hurricane Fly's comeback victory in 2013 after the horse had appeared to struggle mid-race

Hurricane Fly, a gelding by the Prix de l'Arc de Triomphe winner Montjeu had won only two of his ten flat-racing starts in France but once transferred to Willie Mullins for a jumping career, he became a phenomenon. Jousting regularly with horses of the quality of Jezki, Solwhit and Rock On Ruby, Hurricane Fly won five consecutive Irish Champion Hurdles and four consecutive Punchestown Champion Hurdles. He was unbeaten in five races in the 2010/11 season, in which he beat Peddler's Cross in the Champion Hurdle.

In 2012 he was not quite the same horse and finished third at Cheltenham behind Rock On Ruby from the Paul Nicholls yard, but in 2013 the nine-year-old Hurricane Fly was back to his best, beating Rock On Ruby and becoming the first horse since Comedy Of Errors to regain the Champion Hurdle crown after losing it. He had appeared to struggle during the race and rider Ruby Walsh summed up his victory in three words: 'Guts, determination, stamina.' Hurricane Fly could also show plenty of aggression, having painfully grabbed his trainer's backside during his preparation.

At the Punchestown Festival that followed, Hurricane Fly equalled Kauto Star's record of 16 Grade Ones; he then became the sole holder of the record when winning the Morgiana Hurdle in Ireland that November. Although Hurricane Fly was only fourth in the 2014 Champion Hurdle, he took his total of Grade One victories to 22 before being retired, boasting victories in 24 of the 32 hurdle races he contested and amassing winnings of £1.8 million.

Hurricane Fly, with Ruby Walsh.

to record a fifth successive victory in the three-mile World Series Hurdle at Punchestown. It was her first defeat since May 2009 but she had run in only ten races – a testimony to her trainer's skill and patience.

In the 2014 Champion Hurdle at Cheltenham, owner JP McManus had the first two home in a thrilling finish as Jezki, trained by Jessica Harrington, beat My Tent Or Yours, trained by her regular Cheltenham house-party host Nicky Henderson. With a choice of JP's horses, champion jockey AP McCoy had picked My Tent or Yours, leaving Barry Geraghty as the beneficiary in Jezki's saddle for Jessica Harrington's first Champion Hurdle winner. The New One, supported by many British punters, lost his chance when hampered by the fatal fall of Our Conor.

Although My Tent Or Yours was absent injured, the next year saw Jezki, The New One and the now 11-year-old Hurricane Fly renewing their rivalry but it was the new kid on the block, Faugheen, who prevailed, sporting the colours of Susannah Ricci; these colours – pink with green spots – were now appearing on the backs of so many quality horses. Faugheen's trainer, Willie Mullins, was responsible for the first three home. Jezki could manage only fourth and The New One fifth, as the impressive Faugheen powered home from Arctic Fire and Hurricane Fly.

Aided by the buying power of American banker Rich Ricci (husband of Susannah), Willie Mullins had now become a dominant figure at the Cheltenham Festival and he trained two of the first three again in 2016. This time it was Faugheen who was absent injured but the mare Annie Power, who had lost the Mares Hurdle in 2015 by tumbling at the last obstacle with the race at her mercy, proved a more than able substitute, winning authoritatively from My Tent Or Yours, running his first race for 703 days, and the Mullins second-string, Nichols Canyon. Annie Power was only the fourth mare ever to win the race.

Cheltenham is the biggest draw and the constant target, of course, for racing's professionals and for regular racegoers.

However, for many people who take only an occasional interest in racing, there is a different focus: the Grand National, run at Aintree, is Britain's nearest equivalent, in terms of nationwide interest, to the Melbourne Cup down under; the Grand National is the race that tempts all but the parsimonious and the disapproving to have a flutter on a 40-horse contest over a marathon course, and which puts racing on the front pages, if not always for the right reasons.

Ruby Walsh celebrates Champion Hurdle victory on the mare Annie Power in 2016.

3 The Grand National
– Racing's magnifying mirror

'If it had been anywhere else in any other sport, there would have been a riot.'

Jenny Pitman on 'The National That Never Was'

The Grand National is both jump racing's crown jewel and its potential poisoned chalice. Watched live by 600 million people across the world and gambled on by hundreds of thousands who never strike another bet in the year, the breathtaking spectacle over nearly four-and-a-half miles is a unique test of horse and rider. It has a rich history of heart-warming stories; every jockey, trainer and owner in jump racing yearns to acquire the prefix of 'Grand National-winning ... X' – not to mention a share of the biggest slice of prize money for jump racing available outside Japan.

The National's ups and downs, its triumphs and tragedies, its successes, its blunders and its controversies sometimes seem to be a magnifying mirror in glorious technicolour, reflecting the fortunes of the whole sport. That is largely because the Grand National is also the supreme focus for those who regard racing as animal cruelty and who see the National as the weapon with which they can persuade legislators to ban the whole sport. It thrills the sporting nation, yet such is its potential for producing the wrong kind of headlines that some senior racing figures watch it in trepidation from behind the sofa and some leading owners are reluctant to let their horses participate.

This history began with Arkle who, unlike

Runners start the race and head towards the first fence.

Golden Miller, one of the few horses with a record to compare with his, was never permitted by his owner, Anne, Duchess of Westminster, to tackle Aintree's then admittedly fearsome obstacles (although she did win the race later with Last Suspect). Since Arkle's days in the 1960s, however, the National has changed: realists would admit that it has been forced to change in response to public and media opinions. Nevertheless, even though the fences, the qualifications for running, and the distance of the race are not exactly what they were, it remains a focus of the nation for ten minutes every April, with the bookmakers enjoying a turnover of around £500 million on the great race alone.

The 1960s were a time of trial and torment for the Grand National. Although it had become a national institution, Mirabel Topham, the owner of the huge course and its then decrepit buildings, could not make it pay, even when she added motor racing to the mix. In 1949 she had bought the course, long run by her family company, from Lord Sefton for £275,000 with a mortgage of £220,000, probably reckoning that as a leaseholder she would have nothing if Aintree went under, whereas if she owned it she would still have an asset to sell.

In 1964, having created Grand National Steeplechase Ltd to retain the rights to the great race, she tried to sell Aintree to developers while hoping to stage the National at another course, her preference apparently being Ascot. Her aims were thwarted by a condition written into the original deed of sale and the refusal of the local authority to grant planning permission. In 1965, and again for the next few years, the media run-up to the great race depicted it as 'the last Grand National'. At one stage, Mirabel Topham tried to persuade the Labour Prime Minister Harold Wilson, a local MP, to create a national lottery linked to the Grand National. Revealingly, her letter contained the admission: 'Like you, I am not a racing fan.'

In 1973 Bill Davies, a millionaire builder, bought Aintree for some £3 million in the hope of turning a profit and using 40 acres for a shopping complex. However, he had taken out so many loans to finance the deal that he too could not afford to improve the course's outdated facilities. He hiked up admission charges and thinned the crowds still further with some clumsily staged

flat racing. He was receiving a poor return on his investment. It was then that the bookmakers Ladbrokes, headed by Cyril Stein, came to the rescue, leasing the course for seven years from 1974 for £1.6 million and bringing in sponsors such as the *Sun* newspaper. The key Ladbrokes figure was the Leeds-born PR Director, Mike Dillon. Stein told him that his northern accent would ensure that he was understood! A crucial part was also played by the astute racing executive John Hughes, whom they installed as the Aintree manager. Others who became involved included the leading amateur rider and businessman Chris Collins, and Peter O'Sullevan. The 'National' had been televised since 1960 but the famous commentator noted that 1976 was the first time that TV coverage of the National was properly marketed worldwide. As a result, the income from sales exceeded the aggregate of TV's previous 15 years at Aintree 'when negotiations were headed by a less than universally admired outfit inappropriately styled BBC Enterprises.'

Thanks particularly to the exploits of Red Rum over the next few years, the National became even more of a nationwide sporting icon but the sky was still cloudy when Ladbrokes' option expired. Finally, the Jockey Club set about securing Aintree's future by buying out Bill Davies and taking control of the National themselves. Davies, however, asked for £7 million, more than the course was worth and more than racing's chief authority could lay its hands on. The Jockey Club negotiated options running to 1983 and paid Davies £250,000 to rent the course and run the Grand National that year,

while launching an appeal to raise the £4 million that he was eventually persuaded to settle for. In order to raise funds, racing personalities ran the London Marathon, Jockey Club stewards competed in a sponsored bike ride in Hyde Park, and Red Rum and Corbiere contributed to the appeal fund with personal appearances. Such efforts raised £2 million; the Betting Levy Board lent the cause another £1 million, repayable over 15 years; and the drinks company Seagram's agreed to put up £400,000 to sponsor the National after the company chairman, Ivan Straker, had read an impassioned plea on the National's behalf by journalist and leading amateur rider, John (Lord) Oaksey. In the end, Bill Davies collected £3.4 million for passing over control of the course and the race to a new subsidiary of Racecourse Holdings Trust.

Fortunately for racing, through the years of uncertainty about the National's continuation we saw some of the most thrilling contests ever in the history of the race, notably the years from 1973 to 1977, during which Red Rum triumphed three times and came second on two other occasions.

The National has never been short of heroes. Year after year, it seems to produce a human story that takes it from the sports pages to the front pages, or a result that adds something new to the record books.

In 1960, the year when the BBC first began televising the race, it was won by Merryman II, the third National winner trained by the Yorkshire-based Captain Neville Crump. Rider Gerry Scott broke his collarbone a week before the race and rode heavily strapped – but that did not stop him winning by 15 lengths. The next year saw the first of a series of modifications over the years to the National fences: the take-off sides of the fences were sloped out to form an apron, making them easier to negotiate. That did not prove enough to help a contingent of three horses from Russia in that same year: they were outclassed and failed to finish.

People used to say there was a hoodoo on greys, no horse of that colour having triumphed in the race since The Lamb won his second National in 1871; however, trainer Fred Rimell (q.v.) proved them wrong in 1961 by winning his second Grand National with Nicolaus Silver. Twelve months later, in 1962, it was the turn of older horses to score: the winner was Kilmore, trained by Ryan Price and ridden by Fred Winter; Wyndburgh, the runner-up in 1957 and 1959, was second yet again and Mr What, the Arthur Freeman-trained victor in 1958, was third. All three of them were 12-year-old veterans.

Despite the fact that the National fences were daunting, there was often an added

incentive for top jockeys to ride in the race – in addition to the normal riding fee. Owners keen to obtain the services of top riders would offer special inducements. Fred Winter told Richard Pitman that he was once given £5,000 for riding a particular horse in the race, with another £5,000 promised if he got round. In those days, that was big money.

In 1963, Lester Piggott's father, Keith, sent out his only National winner, Ayala, who won a particularly thrilling race from Carrickbeg, ridden by the popular amateur jockey John Lawrence, later to become Lord Oaksey. Ayala took the lead only in the last 100 yards to win by three-quarters of a length. The next year, Fulke Walwyn, who had ridden Reynoldstown to victory 28 years previously, won the race with Team Spirit, who was running in the race for the fifth time.

In 1965 a Lambourn yard struck for a third year when Fred Winter, who had ridden Sundew to victory in 1957 and Kilmore in 1962, won the National in his first year as a trainer with Jay Trump, ridden by the American amateur jockey Tommy Smith, a feat Winter repeated with Anglo the next year. Anglo had previously run under the name of Flag Of Convenience.

In 1967 the National was a story of chaos. At the 23rd fence, the blinkered Popham Down, who had himself been brought down at the first fence and was running loose, then brought down much of the field by running at right angles across the fence. Even those horses that did not fall or get knocked over were brought to a standstill; thus it came about that Foinavon, who had been toiling in the rear under John Buckingham, was able to pick his way through the melee to go on and win, at odds of 100-1, before any of the casualties could catch him. After that famous shambles, on the day that a certain Red Rum first ran at Aintree, dead-heating in a five-furlong sprint, the 23rd fence became known as the 'Foinavon Fence'. Foinavon, who had been accompanied to Aintree by his goat companion, Susie, paid a staggering 444-1 on the Tote.

When Brian Fletcher won the 1968 contest on Red Alligator, much of the attention went to 68-year-old American Tim Durant, a former Hollywood actor, who still had the determination, at his age, to remount after a fall at Becher's on the second circuit to come home 15th on his third attempt. He had backed himself to finish the course.

In 1969 former Olympic show-jumper Eddie Harty won on Highland Wedding for trainer Toby Balding. In 1970 Pat Taaffe won his second National on Gay Trip, his final ride in the race, 15 years after winning on Quare Times. Gay Trip marked another training victory for 'Mr Grand National' himself, Fred Rimell.

In 1971 Specify won by just a neck for holiday-camp supremo Fred Pontin, his victory inspiring Trevor Hemmings, who later led a management buyout of the Pontin holiday camps, also to become a proud owner of a National winner. Mr Hemmings didn't just achieve that ambition in 2005 with Hedgehunter, and in 2011 with Ballabriggs, but made it a three-timer with Many Clouds in 2015.

In 1972 trainer Captain Tim Forster won with Well To Do – a wise choice when an owner bequeathed him the pick of her five horses. Ridden by Graham Thorner, the lighter-weighted Well To Do, who had only been declared to run fifteen minutes before the race entry deadline, prevailed in a thrilling duel after the last fence with Gay Trip, ridden by Terry Biddlecombe. Fellow jockeys noted that the superstitious Thorner continued race-riding in the blue underpants sported for Well To Do's National even when they were in holes and had to be held together with a pair of tights. Along with his victory on Well To Do Thorner was famed almost as much for his incredible recovery in 1978 when Tamalin belly-flopped at Becher's the second time around, getting him back up with the leaders won him a prize for the best ride in the race.

The next five years were dominated by Red Rum and L'Escargot before Lucius won for jockey Bob Davies and trainer Gordon W Richards in 1978 – in one of the most exciting finishes ever: a mere two-and-a-half lengths covered the first five horses home. The next year, Rubstic became Scotland's first National winner, leading home just six more finishers; things were even worse

Profile: **Red Rum**

'Respect this place, this hallowed ground, A legend here his rest has found. His feet would fly, our spirits soar. He earned our love for ever more.'

The inscription on Red Rum's grave in the shadow of the Grand National winning post

The legendary Red Rum makes a point back in the yard after another National victory.

Racegoers will never forget Red Rum, owned by octogenarian Noel Le Mare and trained on the nearby Southport sands by Ginger McCain, who was then combining training with taxi-driving. Bred as a flat-race miler, 'Rummy', as he came to be known, ran 100 times and only ever fell once, when another runner collided with him in mid-air. More than a decade after his death at the age of 30, when a national poll asked people which horse's name they could recall, Red Rum still topped the list (ahead of the fictional Black Beauty and the kidnapped Derby-winner Shergar).

The first National that Red Rum won, in 1973, provided one of its greatest contests. The giant, black Crisp, imported from Australia, put in one of the most extraordinary front-running displays ever under Richard

Red Rum exercising on the Southport sands.

Pitman, the top weight at one stage being 40 lengths clear of his field. Red Rum, made joint favourite by Merseysiders' money and ridden by Brian Fletcher, was the only one to hunt Crisp down. At the last fence, Fletcher and Red Rum still had 15 lengths to make up, but through the 465 heartbreaking yards from the last fence to the winning post, past the famous 'elbow' in the track, Crisp was toiling, having given his all. Almost in the shadow of the winning post, Red Rum, carrying 23 lb less than Crisp, finally caught the leader and went on to win by three-quarters of a length. In doing so, he broke the record time for the race, which had been set way back in 1934 by the great Golden Miller.

Those who dismissed Red Rum as a fortunate beneficiary of the handicapping system had to eat their words the next year. Red Rum, having run a close second in that season's Hennessy Gold Cup, was now himself the 12-stone top weight, set to give weight to the two-time Cheltenham Gold Cup winner L'Escargot, who was trained in Ireland by Dan Moore. Red Rum forged into the lead at Becher's the second time around and although he pitched on landing at the fifth fence from home, he was never headed again, coming home by seven lengths from L'Escargot and becoming the first horse to win two consecutive Nationals since 1936. Three weeks later, he won the Scottish Grand National too.

In 1975 'Rummy', who had not been running with the same verve in some of his prep races, was set by the handicapper to give his old rival L'Escargot 11 lb but, once again, he came to lead the race four fences from home with The Dikler and L'Escargot close behind him. At the final fence, to the roars of the crowd, Red Rum and L'Escargot touched down together. L'Escargot, who had earlier nearly come down at the smallest fence on the course, causing jockey Tommy Carberry temporarily to lose his irons, this time proved to have more in the reserve tank, striding on to win by 15 lengths. L'Escargot thus became only the second horse, after Golden Miller (who took both in the same year), to win both the Cheltenham Gold Cup and the National; he was immediately retired by his American owner, Raymond Guest.

Red Rum, however, was back at Aintree in 1976, the year the meeting became an all-jumping card rather than a mixed event with some flat racing. This time 'Rummy' was ridden by champion jockey Tommy Stack after Ginger McCain and Brian Fletcher had fallen out over how much ability Red Rum retained. Among the horses he faced was the Welsh Grand National winner of that year, Rag Trade,

Red Rum catches the top weight Crisp in 1973 after one of the most thrilling Nationals in history.

trained by Fred Rimell, who already had three National victories to his credit. Between the last two fences the race appeared to be a duel between Red Rum and Eyecatcher, ridden by Red Rum's previous partner, Brian Fletcher, but after the last fence, Rag Trade appeared on the stands side, gaining rapidly on the leading pair. Aware of Rag Trade's challenge, Red Rum fought back but went down by two lengths to be second once again.

The year 1977 proved to be Red Rum's final appearance at Aintree (he was prepared for the 1978 race but had to be withdrawn just before it with a foot injury). In the same year that Charlotte Brew became the first woman to ride in the Grand National (her mount, Barony Fort, refused after 26 fences), Red Rum, at the age of 12, had his easiest victory in the race, coming home under Tommy Stack 25 lengths clear of Churchtown Boy, another Aintree regular, followed by Eyecatcher. That meant that in his five runs over the Grand National course, jumping 150 fences, only two horses ever beat him. Many in the Aintree crowds who continue to thrill to this unique race make a point of visiting Red Rum's grave in the shadow of the winning post where the inscription reads: 'Respect this place, this hallowed ground, a legend here his rest has found. His feet would fly, our spirits soar. He earned our love for ever more'.

in 1980 when Captain Forster's Ben Nevis beat only three other finishers in dreadful conditions. That was another success for trainer Tim Forster and another one for American amateurs too: Ben Nevis was ridden by merchant banker Charles Fenwick, who had twice won the Maryland Gold Cup on the horse in his native country.

One of the most popular winners ever was Aldaniti in 1981. Trained by the former champion jockey Josh Gifford, the horse had been a virtual cripple but was nursed to recovery after a series of injuries. His jockey, Bob Champion, having at one stage been told he had only months to live, had fought a long battle against cancer and it was only his huge determination that brought them together on the racecourse. If there were any other horse that the crowds could have cheered home that year with nearly equal enthusiasm, then it would have been Spartan Missile, who was ridden by amateur John Thorne. Thorne had once retired with a broken back to let his son Nigel take over but Nigel was killed in a car crash in 1968 and Thorne, now aged 54, had returned to the saddle. In both 1978 and 1979, he had ridden Spartan Missile to victory in the Aintree Fox Hunters Chase, in the first of those years negotiating the last eight fences without stirrups after a leather had broken. In this 1981 National, they came with a storming run at the end but Bob Champion and Aldaniti still had four lengths to spare at the post. Tragically, there was a sad ending to the story. Champion survived his

cancer and, with Aldaniti's assistance, went on to raise huge sums for charity – but John Thorne lost his life the following year in a point-to-point riding accident.

In another compelling story, an amateur was to triumph once more in the following year's National in 1982. At the age of 48, Dick Saunders, a member of the Jockey Club, which by then owned the course, became the oldest Grand National-winning jockey on the 7-1 favourite Grittar, trained and owned by permit-holder Frank Gilman. Ironically, Saunders had been due to ride Steel Bridge, second in Highland Wedding's Grand National, but was 'jocked off' in favour of the professional jockey Richard Pitman when he could not do the allocated weight. In Grittar's year, ten horses came down at the first fence and Geraldine Rees became the first woman to complete the National.

There was another 'female first' the following year: Jenny Pitman became the first woman to train a Grand National winner when Corbiere, ridden by Ben de Haan, won the 1983 contest, holding on by three-quarters of a length from the fast-finishing Greasepaint after an impressive round of jumping.

The following year saw a victory for the north of England in the shape of the Gordon W Richards-trained Hello Dandy, with a record number of 23 horses completing the course. In 1985, Tim Forster, a famously pessimistic trainer whose alleged instruction to one National contestant's rider was merely 'Keep remounting', won again with Last Suspect, a 50-1 chance. He owed this success, with a horse whose own willingness for the task at hand was often under suspicion, to his loquacious jockey, Hywel Davies. When Hywel heard that Captain Forster and the horse's owner, Anne, Duchess of Westminster, had determined after the horse's latest mulish non-performance to scratch Last Suspect from the race, he tracked down the owner to a ladies' hairdresser and successfully pleaded with her to let him take his chance. Her response was: 'It's your neck, young man, if you want to bloody break it ...' When Hywel went to see Forster, the trainer pushed aside his breakfast kipper, lit a cigarette and said, 'I

The massive Limeking and Pat Buckley amid the chaos of the 1967 Grand National. Limeking eventually walked away intact.

suppose I'll have to start training the bugger.' On the second circuit at Aintree, Last Suspect's tail was going round like a rotor blade and he ploughed through the third-last, but on the run-in he collared Mr Snugfit, on whom Phil Tuck 'felt like a drowning man' as he saw the Duchess's yellow-and-black colours looming.

In 1986, the National victor was West Tip, trained by Michael Oliver and ridden by Richard Dunwoody. He was another who proved that some horses thrive on the challenge of the Aintree fences: although he had fallen at Becher's, second time around, in the previous year, West Tip finished fourth both in 1987 and 1988, and second in 1989. He finished tenth in 1990.

In 1987, the 92-year-old Jim Joel became the oldest winning owner when Maori Venture, trained by Andy Turnell, won the National in the hands of Steve Knight. The owner was on a flight from South Africa at the time of the race but joined the celebrations at the stable the following day as one of the select band who have owned both a National winner and a Derby winner (his Derby success was with Royal Palace in 1967). There and then, he revealed that he was retiring the horse immediately and bequeathing him to his rider.

Twenty-two horses finished in that 1987 race but the next year only seven finished behind Rhyme'N'Reason, ridden by Brendan Powell, who made a remarkable mid-race recovery. David Elsworth had brought back Rhyme'N'Reason from a barren spell to win three chases through the winter but when he had run him in the Cheltenham Gold Cup he had fallen when still in contention four fences from home. The Grand National punters who backed him down to 10-1, despite that fall, must have started tearing up their betting tickets when the horse made a shocking blunder at Becher's. His trainer says, 'It was a blessing in disguise because if you didn't produce him late he was useless. When Little Polveir fell four out, Rhyme'N'Reason and Durham Edition were left clear, but luckily for Brendan Powell, Durham Edition pinged the last fence and took the lead. Brendan Powell was able to come from behind and pass him on the run-in.'

As in 1988, there was a false start again in 1989 before Little Polveir, ridden by Jimmy Frost, became a second National winner for trainer Toby Balding on heavy ground. Two horses died at Becher's that year and the Jockey Club set up an inquiry after a media outcry. The landing side of Becher's was levelled out considerably as a result.

In 1990, the year the course changed its name from Liverpool to Aintree, the National was won once again by an amateur rider, the journalist Marcus Armytage, son of the trainer Roddy Armytage and brother of the leading female rider of the day, Gee Armytage. His mount, Mr Frisk, trained by Kim Bailey, set a new record National-winning time of 8 minutes

Early stages in the 1967 Grand National. The 100-1 winner Foinavon, ridden by John Buckingham, is at the extreme right.

Aldaniti and Bob Champion clear the final fence in 1981.

47.8 seconds. No amateur has won since, despite the outstanding record over the Aintree fences of Sam Waley-Cohen.

Through the years since the 1960s, various companies had been involved with Grand National sponsorship, including bookmakers Ladbrokes, the *News Of the World*, Vaux Breweries and Schweppes, but the longest connection was with Seagram's, who sponsored between 1984 and 1991. In the last year of their sponsorship before Martell Cognac, a Seagram's subsidiary, took over, the race was won coincidentally by a horse called Seagram, trained in Devon by David Barons and ridden by Nigel Hawke. In a painful echo of Crisp's defeat in 1973, when ridden by Richard Pitman, his son, Mark Pitman, was also thwarted in a similar way when riding Garrison Savannah. Mark and Garrison Savannah were seeking a famous double after winning that year's Cheltenham Gold Cup, despite Mark having broken his pelvis on Gold Cup day. Garrison Savannah, whose preparation for the National had been interrupted, led over the last but was caught and passed on the run-in. Ironically, Ivan Straker, the Seagram's chairman, had twice been offered the chance to buy the winning horse but had declined; the owner was Sir Eric Parker.

Coincidence backers did well in 1992, when the race was held just days before a general election: first home at 14-1 was the giant Party Politics, trained in Lambourn by Nick Gaselee and ridden by Carl Llewellyn. Party Politics won the 1992 race without breathing through his mouth or nostrils: he had been fitted with a steel pipe that ran from his windpipe to his neck, a particular wind-operation practice finally banned by the BHA in 2012.

Nothing went right in 1993 as 39 horses lined up to be despatched by starter Keith Brown, officiating at the National for the last time. Initially, there was a delay of eight or nine minutes as animal-rights protesters staged a protest at the first fence and had to be cleared away by police and security men. Then, when Keith Brown did start the race, the antiquated starting tape became caught up around some of the runners. Mr Brown declared a false start and, as the excited horses and their riders galloped towards the first fence, they saw the 'recall man' Ken Evans waving a red flag to stop them. That time the system worked: the riders, some more successfully than others, pulled up their horses, turned and cantered back. With the adrenalin pumping and the normal anxieties before the great race by now well magnified, horses and jockeys were kept milling around for what seemed like an age to trainers, owners and spectators. Eventually, the 'off' was called again, only for the tape once more to become entangled with some runners and for another false start to be called by Mr Brown. But this time, some allege, Mr Brown's flag did not fully unfurl and the 'recall man' did not wave his red flag: while nine horses remained at the start, some of them enmeshed in the tape, the other thirty set off at full pelt. There was pandemonium – with some calling for the race to be physically stopped, others urging that it should continue. The race commentary continued, leading some riders who heard snatches from the loudspeakers to assume that the race really was on. As officials tried to wave the riders down and placed cones across the course, some jockeys pulled up their mounts. Others thought that those gesticulating at them were protesters. In heavy rain, a number of horses continued on the second circuit and, eventually, seven horses, led by the Jenny Pitman-trained Esha Ness, ridden by John White, finished the full course. Esha Ness's time was the second fastest in history. Mrs Pitman, deeply upset by the sight of Esha Ness's ashen-faced owner, as he realised that his dream of owning a National winner had just evaporated in the 'race that never was', had no doubt that the race would be declared void. At first, the starter told jockeys that all except the nine who had stayed at the start would be disqualified and that there could be a rerun for the nine later that day. The stewards soon scotched that idea and, with the race declared void, bookmakers had to start the tortuous process of refunding some £75 million worth of bets. Esha Ness had won no more than a place in a thousand future pub-quiz question sheets. It was the biggest public-relations disaster in Aintree's history, with millions left wondering why, with all the improved technology available, the correct procedure for a steeplechase to be broadcast to 300 million people depended on one man waving a red flag.

An official inquiry was held, chaired by High Court Judge Sir Michael Connell, himself a former amateur rider. It criticised Ken Brown for letting the horses get too close to the tape but attached most blame to 'recall man' Ken Evans. Changes – including a stronger starting tape and a narrower width for the starting line-up – were introduced, following a Jockey Club review led by Andrew Parker Bowles. He concluded: 'You start 7,000 races a year with flagmen and it went wrong just three times last year, but one of them was the Grand National. It won't happen again.'

Party Politics' trainer, Nick Gaselee, was particularly frustrated, having been robbed of the chance of a repeat victory for his horse: he had won the race the previous year after constant problems training the horse. In 1993, he believed, Party Politics was a better horse by 14 lb: 'Nothing went wrong with his preparation even for ten minutes. It will never happen to us with a horse again.' But his Lambourn neighbour, Jenny Pitman, was equally convinced that it was going to be her big year with the Gold Cup winner, Garrison Savannah and she remains angry with the then Aintree authorities over more than that.

'After the second shemozzle, I'm thinking, "This can't be right: they've got to be called back." I ran out of the Owners And Trainers, out to the weighing room and I don't know what was in my mind. The clerk of the scales was behind the scales looking terrified – I don't know if it was the look on my face – and I knocked on the stewards' door although, of course, they were all elsewhere. I was looking at the screen in the jockeys' room. There was the clerk of the scales, Johnny Buckingham [the jockeys' valet, once rider of Foinavon] and somebody else. He went

Cheltenham Gold Cup winner L'Escargot, ridden by Tommy Carberry, completes a rare double by taking the 1975 Grand National – 15 lengths clear of Red Rum.

and found me a chair and I just couldn't believe it. All these years you prepare these horses. I had thought "Gary" [Garrison Savannah] is going to prove his point and you lot are going to beg for mercy – 'Can I photograph you, can I touch you?' Then John White and Esha Ness are going round and he pulls up, peeping through his fingers, and I think, "No. It's not happening."

'My son Paul was at Aintree and he said if it had been anywhere else in any other sport, there would have been a riot. There's this big scaffolding tower the stewards were in and the crowd stood around the bottom of it baying for them. He said it would have taken the smallest thing to have kicked off a riot. My sister came into the weighing room and I said, "I can't go on doing this any longer. I can't put myself through this, I can't do

it." She was saying, "Shush, don't say that."

'What I was gutted about was Patrick [Esha Ness's owner, Patrick Bancroft]. He'd been racing with his Mum and his Dad from when he was a little tiny boy and all he'd ever wanted was to have a runner in the National. It was just such a pathetic mess. On top of that, when I was interviewed by Des Lynam, there was a little boy there, thanks to the Starlight Foundation, who do dreams for terminally ill children, and this little boy's wish was to meet Jenny Pitman, who was his favourite trainer, and Peter Scudamore, who was his favourite jockey. He was such a lovely little boy. I remember he was as cold as a frog and I refused to go on air without him.

'Afterwards, I rang the Starlight Foundation and asked about David. They said he wasn't very

The 1997 bomb scare. The crowds, which would have packed the stands, are cleared – and some try their luck over the fences.

well, and I asked if they'd like to come down. We had the Starlight Foundation down to the yard for the Open Day, the following Friday, Good Friday. I'd asked Aintree if we could have the rug [special rug for National winners] to parade Esha Ness in, because I wanted to give it to him. They said "no" so I went down the saddlers and got one made. Sadly, the poor little boy was dead on the Monday. When you've got kids yourself, it wasn't just about finance and whether Gary had won it or not, it was about a little kid's dream.'

In 1994, the next year, Richard Dunwoody again demonstrated his prowess as a Grand National jockey. He added to his 1986 victory on West Tip by winning on Miinnehoma for Martin Pipe, holding off Just So after being left in the lead at the elbow as Moorcroft Boy faded. Dunwoody, whose career was ended prematurely by a shoulder injury, made the frame in the National on eight occasions.

In 1995, Jenny Pitman made up for Esha Ness's 'victory that wasn't' by winning the big race for a second time with Royal Athlete, who had spent 14 months off after a fall that left the skin of one leg rolled up like a sock. He was nursed back from his injury to win at 40-1 with his jockey, Jason Titley, instructed to ride him, 'as if his reins were threads of cotton.' By contrast, the next year saw Rough Quest become the first winning favourite for 15 years in the hands of jockey Mick Fitzgerald. He famously declared in the excitement of his post-race interview with Des Lynam, 'After that, even sex is an anti-climax.' An informed TV commentator himself since then, Mick had the good humour to give his autobiography the title, *Better Than Sex*.

The 1997 Grand National was the 150th running of the race. Many would have remembered it as the occasion when the revered broadcaster Sir Peter O'Sullevan gave his 50th and final commentary on the race – but there was greater drama than that. The Saturday race-day had to be cancelled: after a coded bomb warning from the IRA less than an hour before the start of the race, police and course officials began a total evacuation of around 60,000 people, including film-star owner

Gregory Peck and Labour frontbenchers Robin Cook and John Prescott. Those parked at the course, including owners, trainers and jockeys, were not allowed to go to their cars or coaches; an estimated 20,000 people, including jockeys in their racing colours, were stranded in and around a city where all the hotels and B&Bs had long been booked up. With Radio Merseyside helping to match the willing and the stranded, Merseysiders responded with a 'blitz' mentality, many of them providing hot meals and taking total strangers into their homes for the night. One stable lad, Phil Sharp, who was at Aintree to look after Charlie Brooks's entrant Suny Bay, insisted on getting back into the stables to water the horses, but nobody else was allowed to penetrate the cordon after the police had blown up two suspect devices (although no explosives were ever found). Eventually, the horses were moved out, many of them being stabled for the night at nearby Haydock Park.

Thanks to huge efforts by the Aintree authorities, the 150th National was finally staged on the following Monday, when a crowd of 20,000, including the Princess Royal and Prime Minister John Major, turned up to see Lord Gyllene triumph in the hands of Tony Dobbin. Merseyside police received another bomb threat on the day of the rerun, again with an authenticated code name, but decided that it was a hoax.

In 1998, the National was won by Earth Summit, ridden to his second victory by Carl Llewellyn and trained by Nigel Twiston-Davies, who had been contemplating giving up his training licence. Fortunately for the sport, he changed his mind after that. A co-owner of Earth Summit was Nigel Payne, who as Aintree's press officer had to cope with many of the National's ups and downs. Earth Summit is one of the few horses to have won the National wearing blinkers; in addition, he was the first Grand National winner to have also won both the Scottish and Welsh Grand Nationals, staged respectively at Ayr and Chepstow.

In 1999, Tommy Carberry, who had ridden the 1975 winner L'Escargot to victory over Red Rum, trained the winner Bobbyjo, who was ridden by his son, Paul. In the millennium year of 2000,

Ireland secured its 20th victory in the race when the Walshes, trainer father Ted and jockey son Ruby, scored with Papillon, a horse backed down from 33-1 to 10-1 on the day of the race.

The Grand National of 2001 provided another controversy when Red Marauder won by 'a distance' (racing parlance for more than 30 lengths) in the hands of Richard Guest, assistant to the owner and permit-trainer Norman Mason. That year's race was run in atrocious conditions, with the result that only four of the runners completed the course – and two of those had been remounted. Mason had backed the horse at 80-1 and 66-1 when Richard Guest told him they would be in the first four as Red Marauder was a terrible jumper but the kind of horse who would scramble round! The contest was notable too for trainer Martin Pipe's contingent: he sent out ten of the 40 runners, out of which Blowing Wind did best by finishing in second place.

The following year, Jim Culloty became only the sixth jockey in the National's long history to have won both the National and the Cheltenham Gold Cup in the same season. Best Mate's partner in his three Cheltenham Gold Cup victories, Culloty was a last-minute choice for Bindaree, trained by Nigel Twiston-Davies, after Jamie Goldstein, Bindaree's planned partner, broke his leg that week in a fall at Ludlow.

In 2003, the media devoted almost as much attention to the bets landed by the Dee Racing Syndicate as they did to the victory by Monty's Pass, trained by Jimmy Mangan in Ireland, and ridden by Barry Geraghty to a comfortable 12-length success. One of the syndicate owners, Mike Futter, put his total winnings at £800,000, and the group, who had backed the horse down from 66-1 to 16-1, won more than £1 million between them.

In the following year, Ginger McCain, Red Rum's trainer, who was now based at Cholmondely in Cheshire, showed that he could achieve success at Aintree without the assistance of 'Rummy', sending out Amberleigh House to win in the colours of the Halewood family (who were later to become sponsors of the Grand National through their Crabbie's Alcoholic Ginger Beer company). The winning jockey on this occasion was Graham Lee. Subsequently, in 2012, he switched with great success to riding full-time on the flat.

Jockeys have different ways of coping with Aintree. Trainer Michael Dickinson recalls that one year, when an old friend was coming to the National with him, he told him, 'I'll get Graham Lee to walk round [the course] with us, he's won a National and got round about six times.' When he approached Lee, the jockey declared, 'Walk round? Walk round? You must be joking. Those fences are bloody unjumpable. I wouldn't go near them on my feet. They look all right from the back of a horse, but on your feet they're entirely different!'

That decade was largely dominated by Ireland. In 2005, the National was won by Hedgehunter, trained by Ireland's long-time champion trainer Willie Mullins and ridden by their champion jockey Ruby Walsh, although the horse was owned by England-based Trevor Hemmings.

In 2006, Irish trainer Martin Brassil notched Ireland's 23rd victory in the big race with Numbersixvalverde, ridden by Niall 'Slippers' Madden. (His jockey father had been known as 'Boots' Madden.) When Gordon Elliott matched that achievement in 2007 with the 33-1 shot Silver Birch, ridden by Robbie Power, it meant that Ireland had won six Nationals in nine years. Gordon Elliott has since become a leading figure in Irish racing but, at that stage, he had not trained a single winner in his homeland.

England struck back in 2008 when David Pipe, Martin Pipe's son, matched his father's 1994 victory with Miinnehoma, when Timmy Murphy rode Comply Or Die to victory. Like those other 'major-player' owners, Trevor Hemmings and JP McManus, multi-horsepower owner David Johnson had long been in quest of a National victory and Comply Or Die duly obliged.

The following year may have delighted more bookmakers than punters when Mon Mome, ridden by Liam Treadwell, won at 100-1, after two false starts to the race; his stylish trainer, Venetia Williams, thereby became only the second woman to train a National winner.

A truly popular victory came in 2010 when Don't Push It scored a trio of firsts. It was the first victory in the race at the fifteenth time of trying for long-time champion jockey AP McCoy, later to become Sir Anthony McCoy. Perhaps more than any other moment in his remarkable career, it was his reception by the adoring Aintree crowd that made AP realise just how much he was loved and treasured by racing's followers. It clearly helped to clinch his election that year as the BBC Sports Personality of the Year, the first time the award had ever gone to someone from horseracing. Not only that, the success for Don't Push It, a quirky character who spent much of his time out in a field alone, was a first victory as a trainer for Jonjo O'Neill, who had never succeeded in riding a National winner during his years in the saddle. Indeed, he never completed the course. Many racing folk were delighted, too, that it was a first National win for the prolific owner JP McManus.

There was another father-and-son achievement in 2011 when Donald McCain, Ginger McCain's son and his successor at the Cheshire yard he had moved to some years earlier, gave Trevor Hemmings another National success as an owner by sending out Ballabriggs to win in the hands of Jason Maguire. Ginger McCain died only a few months later.

A National victory was one thing missing from Paul Nicholls's CV as the champion trainer over the previous seven years, but he finally rectified that by winning with Neptune Collonges in the hands of Daryl Jacob in 2012, again after the race had suffered two false starts. Neptune Collonges, only the third grey ever to win the race, did so by the narrowest margin in its history, scoring by just a nose from Sunnyhill Boy, ridden by Richie McLernon for trainer Jonjo O'Neill and owner JP McManus. Third place went to rider Katie Walsh on Seabass, who thus achieved the highest place yet for a female jockey. Three other milestones were reached in 2012: this was the last Grand National run over a full four-and-a-half miles; the last in which horses younger than seven could run; and the last to be broadcast on BBC television.

In 2013, the first National to be televised by Channel Four, there was another shock for punters when the 11-year-old Aurora's Encore

'Look no horse!' Tom Doyle parts company with Esprit de Cotte.

won at 66-1 for trainer Sue Smith, wife of former show jumping star Harvey Smith. That made her only the third female trainer to succeed in the race and also the first Yorkshire-based trainer to win since 1960. The Smiths' successful young jockey, Ryan Mania, surprisingly retired within 18 months, having been struggling with his weight for some time.

A contrast to Ryan Mania was Leighton Aspell, the winning rider on Pineau de Re in 2014, the first occasion on which Grand National prize money, then sponsored by Crabbie's, rose to £1 million. Aspell had retired from riding in 2007 and become an assistant trainer, only to return to the saddle with his batteries recharged 18 months later. His National victory came at the age of 37 and was remarkably to be repeated the next year aboard Many Clouds, trained in Lambourn by Oliver Sherwood. Pineau de Re was trained by Richard Newland, a qualified GP and businessman, who keeps only a dozen boxes full in his yard. Paul Moloney, stable jockey to the Welsh yard of Evan Williams, also cemented a remarkable record in 2014. He had then been placed for six consecutive years in the National, riding Evan's horses for Angela and William Rucker: State of Play was fourth in 2009, third in 2010 and fourth again in 2011; Cappa Bleu was fourth in 2012 and second in 2013; while Alvorado, trained by Fergal O'Brien in Gloucestershire, was fourth in Pineau de Re's year. Moloney made it seven in a row when Alvorado was fourth again in 2015.

Many Clouds' victory in 2015 followed a hugely popular win in the Hennessy Gold Cup at his local Newbury track for the Oliver-Sherwood-trained horse, yet another National winner owned by Trevor Hemmings. Leighton Aspell, his 38-year-old jockey, equalled the feat of Brian Fletcher (on Red Rum in 1973 and 1974) and of Bryan Marshall (on Early Mist in 1953 and on Royal Tan in 1954) in riding two successive Grand National winners, as he held off the challenge of Saint Are.

If experience was the keynote that year, it was a different story in 2016: in testing conditions, 19-year-old rider Danny Mullins brought home the 33-1 shot Rule The World in first place for trainer Mouse Morris and owner Michael O'Leary. It was a first National ride for Mullins, who had not even jumped a fence 12 months earlier, and Rule The World, although seven times being placed second, had never previously won over fences. Rarely have so many Irishmen been so lost for words as owner, trainer and jockey struggled to come to terms with their success on an emotional occasion, trainer Mouse Morris having lost his 30-year-old son Tiffer in tragic circumstances not long before. Despite the worst conditions in the National since 2001, 16 horses finished and, for the fourth year running, there were no equine fatalities.

There were 17 finishers in 2013 , 18 in 2014, and 19 in 2015 – so the significant changes to the course and race, made in 2013, seem to have been vindicated. No fatalities have occurred in the past three years. In 2013, the start was moved forward 90 yards, closer to the first fence and further away from the noise of spectators, and starting procedures were altered. Crucially, the timber central frames in the fences were replaced with softer plastic or natural birch, and the landing side of Becher's was further levelled.

Animal Welfare organisations, such as Animal Aid and the League Against Cruel Sports, have long sought the scrapping of the Grand National, and the RSPCA has regularly made representations about various aspects of the race, including the number of runners, the length of the course, and the severity of the fences. The traditional Jump Sunday, when many local families used to visit the course the weekend before the big race, was cancelled in the 1960s for fear of sabotage to the course by those with extremist views.

The televising of the National from 1960 onwards seemed to reduce some of the pressure for change as many more people actually witnessed the race. However, with the media highlighting animal-welfare aspects in the last few decades, Aintree and the racing authorities have become much more responsive to such concerns. In the 1960/61 season, bigger, sloping 'aprons' were built out in front of the fences. Becher's was significantly modified several times, especially in 1989 and 2004, with the levelling-off of the landing area. The use of gorse was banned for the fences from 1971 and, in the 2000/01 season, additional padded guard rails and deeper toe boards were provided. In the last few years, a purpose-built cooling-down area for the horses has improved the post-race treatment of exhausted participants, especially in warmer years.

Some old-school riders and trainers say that the changes have gone too far and the race is not what it was. But plenty of veterans approve of what has been done. Says Peter Easterby: 'It's gone far enough but Lord Daresbury and his entourage have made a good job of it with the National. They are still big fences, the best horse still wins, and there aren't as many casualties.'

The BHA says that equine fatalities in jump racing have fallen by a third in recent years; Aintree historian John Pinfold put things into context by noting a 2012 Liverpool University study that found that 62 per cent of traumatic injuries to horses occur when they are turned out in fields, compared to only 13 per cent when being ridden. Between 1997 and 2014, horseracing fatalities fell by a third from 0.32 per cent to 0.22 per cent.

The National will always, though, have the capacity to highlight welfare issues. When Jason Maguire, who rode Ballabriggs to victory in 2011, was penalised for excessive use of the whip on the horse, the case helped to precipitate a BHA inquiry into the wider issues, which resulted in controversial changes to the regulations on the use of the whip (see page 202).

Compromises have been made but the Grand National is still a special challenge for rider and horse. As AP McCoy has pointed out, the additional element of danger or risk is one of the reasons why ten million people in Britain – and 600 million worldwide – tune in to watch it. Comparing the race to people's desire to climb Everest, he noted, 'It is the job of those in charge to strike the balance between ensuring safety for all and maintaining the magic and fascination of the special challenge for horse and rider.'

Runners prepare for the world's greatest steeplechase in front of grandstands that do justice to the occasion.

4 The Champion Trainers

'Courage is like a bank account. If you draw too many cheques, sooner or later one bounces.'

Trainer Fred Winter to amateur jockey Tommy Smith

Trainers, whose careers tend to last longer than those of jockeys, are the backbone and mainstay of horseracing, providing much of the continuity. Some have been traditionalists, others innovators, and a few have been revolutionaries. The period from 1960 to the present has seen some things simplified, such as the composite feeds for horses available to trainers today, with their carefully balanced nutrients, and the arrival of jockeys' agents, who have made it so much easier for the top yards in booking riders. Less welcome to many has been the concentration of power in a handful of big yards, all in the southern half of the country, containing most of the horses of the wealthier owners, able to afford the 'Saturday horses' (competing for bigger prizes). The increase in the number of richly sponsored handicaps has made it easier to become champion trainer without winning a top race such as the Grand National.

Fulke Walwyn won a Grand National as a jockey before becoming a champion trainer. Here, he is led in on Reynoldstown in 1936.

With more and more jumpers undergoing operations to improve their breathing, there are questions to be asked about the robustness of today's performers; the debate continues as to whether the more precocious French-bred horses or the traditional Irish 'store' horses provide the best jumping material. What will become clear, though, from the detailed interviews with top trainers that follow, is that there is no magic formula. Some top trainers constantly test their horses' blood, others swear by weighing them regularly, some do neither …

From the end of the Second World War, for more than 20 years the trainers' championship table, determined by prize money won, was mostly headed by southern handlers such as Fulke Walwyn, Ryan Price, Peter Cazalet and Fred Rimell, albeit the Irish-based Vincent O'Brien was champion in 1952/53 and in 1953/54. Only two northern-based trainers, in this era, topped the table: one was the Middleham-based Captain Neville Crump, who won three Grand Nationals (with Sheila's Cottage, Teal and Merryman II) and who was champion trainer in 1951/52 and in 1956/57; and the other was Denys Smith in 1967/68.

In the 1960s, Fulke Walwyn took the last of his five championships, and the Sussex-based Ryan Price won three titles, while another went to Lambourn's Keith Piggott in the year he

trained Ayala to win the Grand National.

Between 1968 and 1978, the championship became 'the battle of the two Freds' with either Fred Rimell, based in Worcestershire, or Fred Winter, from Lambourn, coming out on top. In the following six years, however, things changed: first, the Yorkshire-based Peter Easterby won the championship for three consecutive years, and then Michael Dickinson repeated the feat. Since then, northern-based trainers have scarcely had a look in, while, conversely, the West Country in particular has prospered.

In 1984/85, Fred Winter won the title back, and then the young Nicky Henderson, who had spent four years as Winter's assistant, wrested it from his mentor in 1985/86 and followed up in 1986/87. David Elsworth, champion in 1987/88, had his year of glory at the height of Desert Orchid's fame.

Starting in 1988/89, Martin Pipe then took the title to Somerset for 15 consecutive years, punctuated only by the two seasons when David 'the Duke' Nicholson, based in Gloucestershire, triumphed in 1993/94 and in 1994/95. Another West Countryman, the ex-jockey Paul Nicholls, won it for the first time in 2005/06 and has won the championship every year since, from his Somerset stables, with the exception of 2012/13, when Nicky Henderson triumphed again after a break of 26 years. It has been a similar story in the saddle. His association with Pipe and with the top owner JP McManus helped the phenomenal AP McCoy, based in Lambourn, to be champion jockey throughout his 20-year career.

For the last 30 years, jump racing has been increasingly dominated by the powerful stables in the south of England and in Ireland. The yards of Martin Pipe (later handed over to his son, David), David Nicholson, Paul Nicholls, Nicky Henderson, Philip Hobbs, Alan King and Jonjo O'Neill, together with the Willie Mullins juggernaut in Ireland, have accumulated a lion's share of the big-spending owners, the expensive horses and the prizes in the top races. There was, though, one decade when trainers in the north of England dominated the record books.

Back in the 1960s and 1970s – and through into the 1980s – northern-based trainers and riders frequently figured among those with championship chances. It was Red Alligator's Grand National victory in 1968 that clinched a title for Denys Smith that season, and the powerful stables of Peter Easterby and Michael Dickinson faced plenty more competition in the north in that era. The canny Arthur Stephenson, with a big string of horses based in Bishop Auckland, Gordon W Richards in Penrith, Jimmy Fitzgerald in Malton and Ken Oliver in Scotland were all trainers who turned out winners aplenty in big races; meanwhile, Ron Barry (1972/73 and 1973/74), Tommy Stack (1974/75 and 1976/77), and Jonjo O'Neill (1977/78 and 1979/80) all won the jockeys' championship while riding for northern yards. In the most exciting period in the history of the Champion Hurdle, it was the northern-trained stars, Night Nurse and Sea Pigeon, who dominated; and, in terms of northern success, no horse has figured more gloriously in Grand National history than Red Rum, trained not far from Aintree by Ginger McCain.

WA 'Arthur' Stephenson. The first jumping trainer to send out more than 100 winners in a season.

Fred Rimell

Champion Trainer 1950/51, 1960/61,
1968/69, 1969/70, 1975/76

A man who helped to set the tone of racing in his time, Fred Rimell was four times champion jump jockey and five times champion trainer, earning himself the title in the media of 'Mr Grand National' by training four winners of the great race.

A Worcestershire boy and the son of trainer Tom Rimell, Fred rode his first winner on the flat at the age of 12 and also 'whipped-in' the Croome foxhounds. Riding at the same time as his later training rival Fulke Walwyn, Fred Rimell was champion National Hunt jockey in 1938/39 and retained his title the next year when racing was significantly cut back. When racing resumed in the 1944/45 season

Trainer Fred Rimell leads in his National winner Gay Trip, Pat Taaffe up.

he shared the title with Frenchie Nicholson, and Rimell won it again, outright, in 1945/46. He took out a training licence in 1945 while still riding, hoping that his popularity as a rider would help him to attract owners. He quit the saddle after breaking his neck for a second time on Coloured Schoolboy in the Cheltenham Gold Cup in 1947, but with

the aid of his wife, Mercy, he soon became a shrewd and successful trainer.

At first, he admitted, no jockey could ride a race to satisfy him. He complained of races cluttered with incompetent riders and reflected on how changing styles in racing required a different kind of horse: 'Before the war you could win over hurdles with a six-furlong horse. Now you have to be up with the leading bunch all the way to keep out of trouble, so you need one that gets a mile and a quarter on the flat.'

He may have looked and acted 'old school' but he was always ready to adapt in the cause of winning races. When he and Mercy visited Australia in 1952, they saw horses being taught to jump unridden in 'loose schools', learning how to correct themselves when tackling obstacles. They were sufficiently impressed to come back and build a loose school at Kinnersley. Perhaps that was one reason why Rimell had particular success at winning 'first time out' with novice chasers. He was fond of quoting former trainer, Atty Persse: 'A jumping trainer means a trainer who teaches his horses to jump. If they fall, you are falling down on the job.'

Rimell won two Champion Hurdles with Comedy Of Errors but some criticised him for persevering too long over timber with hurdlers who might have made good chasers. His top hurdlers included Gaye Brief, Coral Diver and Normandy. Comedy Of Errors was by the sprinter Goldhill.

Fred Rimell certainly proved himself sharper than a number of his contemporaries when his yard was targeted by the infamous doping gang led by Bill Roper in the 1960s. Roper's glamorous scout, Micheline Lugeon, visited Kinnersley in her usual way, posing as a would-be owner and taking the opportunity to make a note of which box Nicolaus Silver (Rimell's star horse) occupied; however, when Rimell saw her at Stratford Races in the company of some unsavoury characters, he notified the authorities and switched Nicolaus Silver to a different box. The dopers did break into the Kinnersley yard and reached their targeted box – but it was another horse who suffered their malign attentions.

Fred Rimell was one of the generation that had to adapt to a fast-changing world and, as 'nods and winks' gave way to a more rigid rule-book officialdom, Rimell was aware that when he first started riding, there had been a kind of rough justice. Officials who lived their lives on the racecourse were inclined to turn a blind eye to possible misdemeanours. For example, regular racegoers knew that the horse that appeared with boots or bandages all round was likely not to be trying to win the race or, in racing parlance, was 'not off.' He once noted, 'Although jockeys even then were forbidden to bet, it was sometimes better to safeguard yourself by letting it be known that one of your close associates had a financial interest in your mount winning.'

Among his many victories, Rimell won the Mackeson Gold Cup four years in a row with Jupiter Boy, Gay Trip (twice) and Chatham. He won a Whitbread Gold Cup with Andy Pandy; Welsh Grand Nationals with Fearless Fred and Rag Trade; and the Scottish Grand National with The Fossa. Yet it is as a trainer of Grand National winners at Aintree that Fred Rimell is most remembered: he took the 1956 race with ESB when Devon Loch collapsed close to home, and the 1961 contest with the grey, Nicolaus Silver. He won it again with Gay Trip in 1970, and, in the 1976 running, it was his Rag Trade who beat the great Red Rum into second place.

Fred Rimell was champion trainer five times (1950/51, 1960/61, 1968/69, 1969/70 and 1975/76). It was in that final year that he became the first jumps trainer to earn his patrons more than £1 million in prize money. After he died in 1981, his widow, Mercy, took over the training licence and sent out Gaye Brief to win another Champion Hurdle for Kinnersley in 1983.

Ryan Price

Champion Trainer 1954/55, 1958/59, 1961/62, 1965/66, 1966/67

If ever a man was defined by the way he wore his hat, it was Ryan Price. The trilby tipped at a rakish angle, combined with his outspoken views, his contempt for authority, and his capacity for vigorous overstatement – together with the clouds of controversy that overhung his Schweppes Hurdle victories – have combined to ensure that he has never been given credit for

Ryan Price with characteristic headgear.

what he was: a truly great trainer, both over the jumps and on the flat, who made his formidable reputation without ever having a great horse.

Born in 1912, the son of a Surrey 'gentleman farmer' whose life centred on rearing and training horses and whose motto for his children was, 'Die rather than cry', the young Price was an outstanding and fearless point-to-point rider and had launched out on a training career before volunteering at the start of the Second World War. Talent-spotted for the early commandos, he led the survivors ashore when half his D-day troop died as their landing craft was blown up on the run to the beach. Often involved in hand-to-hand fighting, the man who was to become universally known to the racing world as 'The Captain' won an MC and, at one stage, became one of General Montgomery's bodyguards. But being a war hero does not pay the bills in civilian life. Returning to training with no money behind him, Price and his wife, Dorothy, began with a caravan and a handful of low-grade horses. It is a measure of the times that as they struggled to survive the vicious winter of 1946/47, the seven races Price won were together worth just £862.

That year, however, Price acquired Gerry Judd and his brother Bill as patrons. They began buying better-class horses in France, and Price, who knew how to condition them, began to win some more valuable races. He was aided in doing so by taking on as his jockey a young man who had come out of the parachute regiment at the end of the war, one Fred Winter, who was to stay with him for 15 years.

The ability had always been there and, given better ammunition, Price had by the 1954/55 season become champion trainer. Early on, however, there was an indication of the kinds of trouble that were to dog his career. In the summer of 1948, one of Price's owners heard of a good chasing prospect, Priorit, in France. Price flew to Chantilly, liked Priorit and bought him for the then considerable sum of £4,000. In March 1949, Priorit landed a successful gamble (in which Price himself was not involved) by winning the Blagrave Memorial Chase at Cheltenham. Officialdom is always suspicious of what are seen to be gambling yards or gambling trainers and, when they are effective self-publicising personalities as Price was, oblivious to convention and happy to feed good lines to the media, such suspicions soon take wings.

In those days there was virtually no sponsorship, prize money was limited, and the only way for an owner to recoup the sort of money paid for a two-mile chaser like Priorit was by gambling. The racing community knew that and, within bounds, it was quietly accepted. The problem at Cheltenham that day was that the indiscreet Gerry Judd had been boasting to the racing press about what a killing he had made.

According to the form book, Priorit had come home ahead of a horse that had beaten him impressively three weeks earlier at Lingfield, thus reversing the form by 20 lb. Priorit's trainer was called in by the stewards and cautioned as to the future running of his horses. In fact, Priorit was entitled to improve. His first race in Britain had been the three-mile King George VI Chase at Kempton in which he had patently failed to stay. He had then run over two miles at Lingfield, ridden by Bryan Marshall, and faded, but next time out at the same course had finished

third. He was acclimatising and improving physically in Price's care. At Lingfield the going had been holding; at Cheltenham it was good. But the stewards, not liking his style, had been watching Price, and they had been given the opportunity to show him who was in charge.

Price and Winter won three Champion Hurdles in seven years, the first of them in 1955 with Gerry Judd's French import Clair Soleil, who also won the longer race, now known as the World Hurdle, in 1959. That year, Fare Time, also owned by Gerry Judd, won the Champion Hurdle, as did Eborneezer in 1961. Based at The Downs in Findon, and with his clientele steadily growing, Ryan Price was the champion National Hunt trainer in five seasons (1954/55, 1958/59, 1961/62, 1965/66 and 1966/67), and it was his hurdlers who provided the bulk of the winnings to gain him those titles. As well as those three Champion Hurdles, Price also won the last two Triumph Hurdles run at Hurst Park before that friendly track became a housing estate.

There were some big chasing successes too. In 1962, he won the Grand National with the 12-year-old Kilmore, owned by a trio including Nat Cohen and Stuart Levy, who were responsible for producing many of the 'Carry On' films. Before the Grand National of 1961, Nat Cohen had asked what Fred Winter was riding in the race and Price told him that he didn't have anything good enough. 'You haven't got a ride for the best jockey in the world in the best race in the world? You must find him one.' 'Can I use your money?' asked Price. 'Yes.' The upshot was that little Kilmore was found in Ireland after a good lunch with fellow trainer Vincent O'Brien, and he then ran promisingly in the National on ground that was too fast for him, coming fifth at 33-1. The next year, Kilmore ran poorly in his prep races and went off as a 50-1 shot for the National, despite having Winter in the saddle. But it rained all night and all morning, and the ground turned soft – just the way he liked it. Come the day of the race, Nat Cohen and his friends were missing, having been struck down with the flu, but the now 12-year-old Kilmore, ridden by Winter, took the lead approaching the last fence and ran on well to beat Wyndburgh.

Price might well have trained another National winner with Honey End, the favourite in the year of the pile-up at the 23rd fence. Honey End was going well in 1967 when he became one of the victims of the melee induced by Popham Down and was remounted to finish a fast-closing second to Foinavon.

Price won a Mackeson Gold Cup with Charlie Worcester (1967), Whitbread Gold Cups with Done Up (1959) and What A Myth (1966), and he took a Welsh Grand National with Bora's Cottage in 1948. But his other really big chase success came in the Cheltenham Gold Cup of 1969 and, as in his Grand National success, that too was won by a 12-year-old veteran.

The mud-loving What A Myth had run in three Grand Nationals and had been third in the 1967 Gold Cup. In 1969, he was given a spell hunter-chasing to prepare him for Cheltenham where The Laird, trained by Bob Turnell, and Domacorn, trained by Fred Rimell, were joint favourites at 7-2 in a larger than usual field of 11. At the eighth fence, The Laird was brought down by the fall of the outsider Dicky May. On the second circuit, the six-year-old King Cutler led from the outsiders Kellsboro Wood and Arab Gold, with What A Myth, Domacorn and the Gordon Richards-trained northern raider, Playlord, tucked in just behind them. Five fences from home, with most of the field clearly tiring in the conditions, jockey Paul Kelleway took the lead on What A Myth, who ran on well up the hill to become the oldest champion for 18 years, after which he was promptly retired.

It was, though, the performance of Price's horses in the Schweppes Gold Trophy (in its modern form: the Betfair Hurdle) that made him either famous or notorious, according to which camp you embrace. The richly endowed handicap carried prize money worth almost as much as the Champion Hurdle, seven times the average handicap-hurdle prize, and Price won the race four times in its first five years, twice in highly controversial circumstances.

In 1963, Price won the Schweppes with Rosyth, ridden by Josh Gifford, who had become his first jockey when Fred Winter retired. Price

then won the race again the next year with the same horse, but this time the stewards held an inquiry into what they called the horse's 'abnormal improvement' on its previous runs. Unconvinced by his explanation, they removed Price's licence to train for the rest of that season and imposed a shorter ban on Gifford. Of the horses that then had to be boxed out to other trainers, some never returned: they included Anglo, winner of the Grand National in 1966, trained by Price's former jockey Fred Winter.

Rosyth, with Josh Gifford in the saddle, at the last flight in the Schweppes Gold Trophy.

Rosyth had been bought after losing his form on the flat while trained by Ryan Jarvis. Price eased his jarred-up shoulders by towing the horse behind a rowing boat and swimming him off Selsey Bill. In his first Schweppes, Rosyth, who had finished fourth in the Imperial Cup only five days earlier, carried only 10 stone. The next year his form was indifferent. Rosyth was a 'bleeder' – a horse who occasionally broke blood vessels – and had to be brought along to fitness carefully. Price was also convinced he was a 'spring' horse, who only showed his best form at that time of year. Rosyth was an

Profile: **The horse who doped himself**

There has never been a racing cause célèbre like the Hill House affair, which took the sport off the back page and into the news pages for almost six months in 1967.

Hill House had been trained on the flat by Bernard van Cutsem, but did not seem to have the temperament to cope with racing. When Ryan Price trained him for Len Coville, taking a half share in the horse, he was nervy and excitable and 'ran up light' (lost weight) after his races. Price noted, 'When he was nine-tenths fit he was brilliant, but ten-tenths fit and he had gone over the hill. He just couldn't take it.' But the quirky Hill House obviously had talent. He won the Cambridgeshire Hurdle at Kempton and was then fourth in the Mackeson Hurdle

at Cheltenham, despite losing many lengths when almost brought down. He then went for a spot of hunting with his owner to freshen him up, but when produced at Kempton for his Schweppes prep race in the Lonsdale Hurdle, for which he was made favourite, Hill House became stirred up and refused to start. They had to have another go at Sandown a week later, when owner Coville, who had previously trained Hill House himself, decided to lead the horse up to the tape. After mistakes at the fourth and fifth hurdles, which had him in last place, Hill House was brought round the outside of the field and stayed on to finish fourth in what was his first proper race in three months. The Sandown stewards were happy,

Hill House spreadeagles his field to win.

seeing nothing untoward in the horse's performance, but when the media asked Price, 'What about the Schweppes?' he replied simply, 'I will win.' There was already much speculation about the always newsworthy Schweppes and the next development was a curious one. Major Derek Wigan was a member of the National Hunt Committee and a loyal owner with Price; his wife had Burlington II, a fancied Schweppes entrant, in Price's yard, and Wigan was overheard by ex-trainer and Daily Mail correspondent Tim Fitzgeorge-Parker, warning Price that if Hill House won the Schweppes, he would be in trouble with the stewards. The Mail ran the story under the headline: 'Trainer warned: your horse must not win' and quoted Price as saying, 'They've told me that if Hill House wins the Schweppes, I'll be warned off for life.' Had it been an official warning or merely the action of a friend, a friend who was also trying to persuade Price to put stable jockey Josh Gifford on Burlington II? Nobody could be sure, especially when Ryan Price then issued a statement contradicting the Mail report and saying there had been no warning.

In the event, at Newbury, Hill House not only won the 1967 Schweppes but did so imperiously, almost ridiculously, jumping the last alone and being driven out by Gifford to win by a dozen lengths. Burlington II was unplaced. With a section of the crowd making obvious their disapproval, there was no great surprise when Price was summoned by the stewards and, with Major-General Sir Randle Feilden the senior steward taking charge, asked to explain the improvement in his horse over just one week. Price told them that the horse had 'blown up' (run out of breath) at Sandown and had improved since, but the case was referred on to the National Hunt Committee. Then, as fellow trainers contacted Price to show their support, a bombshell exploded: the Jockey Club investigation officer telephoned him to say that Hill House's dope test had proved positive for the steroid cortisol: it was now a doping case. A stunned Price, who had this time engaged legal assistance, contacted all those who had agreed to give evidence for him; in those days a positive dope test almost inevitably meant a trainer being 'warned off.' He had given the horse nothing and he trusted his staff. Price had private scientific tests conducted on Hill House, which confirmed cortisol levels in excess of those found on race day.

The trainer's livelihood now depended on complicated scientific analysis and debate; he had expensive legal assistance, but his lawyer would not, he was told, be allowed into the inquiry to present the case, although he would be allowed to sit in a nearby room.

After rounds of discussions with the National Hunt Committee and the scientists on both sides of the argument, Hill House was taken eventually to Newmarket's Equine Research Station for further tests, with the results of these tests being made available to the Jockey Club. One of Price's owners, Lady Weir, as well as helping to meet Price's legal costs, turned up several instances of horses manufacturing cortisol naturally, and scientific evidence on how that was possible. The Newmarket testing finally proved conclusively that the cortisol that the authorities had initially insisted had to have been administered to Hill House was being produced naturally by the horse. Finally, on 10 August, Price was pronounced to be in the clear. There was no remaining suggestion that the horse had not been run on its merits at Sandown or that there had been abnormal improvement in his performance between his race there and in the Schweppes. (None of the horses he had beaten so emphatically that day achieved anything later, and Get Stepping, the only horse with whom Hill House had reversed fortunes between the two races, had to undergo an operation having 'gone in his wind' – i.e. suffered a breathing impairment – in the Schweppes.)

After Price declared, 'It is an ordeal I would not like to have to undergo again,' Lord Willoughby de Broke looked towards his fellow stewards, Lord Leverhulme and Captain Miles Gosling, and assured him, 'I can guarantee that goes for us too.'

The media were appalled at the length of time taken by the inquiries with the threat of racing execution hanging over the trainer, and they demanded improvements. Two of the lasting legacies of the case were an improvement in the sophistication of dope testing, and a recognition that, in future, trainers facing a threat to their livelihood should be entitled to legal representation at the inquiries.

Hill House himself was bought by the flamboyant Scottish bookmaker John Banks. In two appearances for Malton trainer Frank Carr, Hill House whipped around and refused to start. After an unsuccessful attempt at showjumping with Harvey Smith, he was retired back to the Findon Downs to be cared for by Price, the man for whom he had caused such trials and tribulations.

entire, not a gelding, and Price maintained that colts did not start 'to come in their coats' until the breeding season approached. Rosyth had seemed frightened after hitting a hurdle in a Liverpool race, then developed flu, and finished tailed off at Newbury. He showed some improvement to finish third in a Boxing Day race at Kempton and, in his final race before the 15 February Schweppes, had blinkers fitted for a race at Sandown Park, in which he finished behind Salmon Spray. When, at odds of 10-1, Rosyth triumphed again, carrying 10 st 2 lb, in the Schweppes, reversing the form with Salmon Spray by 7 lb, the stewards called in Price over what they again insisted was the horse's 'abnormal improvement' between the two races and they referred the case to the National Hunt Committee. When that committee met, Major-General Sir Randle Feilden, the senior steward at Newbury (the Berkshire course to which the Schweppes had been transferred), made much of the fact that Price, who habitually escorted his horses from the parade ring to the track, had led out Rosyth rather than his other runner, Catapult II, who was the favourite for the race. The National Hunt Committee took away Price's licence to train and made him a 'disqualified person', barred from setting foot on a racecourse. At first, it seemed that the ban was timeless but when the official notice appeared in the racing calendar, a term had been set – to the end of that National Hunt season. Gifford was banned for six weeks.

Price received 2,000 letters of sympathy and there was much press comment to the effect that if improving a horse by 7 lb over a month was illegal, it virtually meant that no horse could ever be allowed to win with a 7 lb penalty. Interestingly, in the following year, Rosyth, now trained at Lewes by Tom Masson, ran once more in the Schweppes after three lacklustre performances in the meantime. Carrying 14 lb more than in 1964, he finished second to Elan; Rosyth was, indeed, a spring horse.

With his licence restored, Price won the Schweppes once again in 1966 with the champion novice Le Vermontois. But when Price did it yet again with Hill House in 1967, the contemptuous ease of his victory in such a competitive field had a section of the crowd booing loudly, even before he had jumped the last hurdle, and again when he reached the winner's enclosure. Almost inevitably, Price was again tapped on the shoulder for a word with the stewards.

In 1970, at the age of 57, Ryan Price called in Josh Gifford and told him that, from then on, he was going to concentrate on the flat. He was already a dual-purpose trainer who had three times won the Cesarewitch, on one occasion with his classiest jumper, Major Rose, who had twice been placed in the Champion Hurdle in the vintage era of Persian War and Bula. Price sold The Downs to Gifford and moved to the appropriately named Soldiers Field next door. He never had expensive horses but was successful enough with his switch to flat racing to be compared to the likes of Vincent O'Brien, André Fabre and Aidan O'Brien. He won two Classics, the Oaks with Ginevra in 1972 and the St Leger with Bruni in 1975, and he also trained the champion sprinter Sandford Lad.

His clashes with officialdom and the Schweppes shenanigans ensured that Price was the ultimate victim of those who insist that there is no smoke without fire. He died in 1986 and would probably have been uncomfortable in the modern racing world: he once ended a threatened 'strike' by stable staff by knocking out the ringleader with a single punch and giving him his cards. What remains certain is that Price was a master of the art of preparing a horse for a race. Sir Peter O'Sullevan said: 'He had a gypsy instinct for producing a horse at its peak on an appointed day. It was a talent that made him vulnerable, not crooked.' Peter would also have approved of another of Price's qualities: he was a genuine animal lover who kept many of his old racing heroes, including Kilmore, Clair Soleil, Le Vermontois, Persian Lancer, Major Rose and Hill House, in a paddock up on the Downs and looked after them as long as they could enjoy their retirement, feeding them oats from August onwards to maintain their body weight. He declared, 'These horses have been my life and the least I can do is to offer them decent retirement.' If only all trainers took such trouble.

Keith Piggott
Champion Trainer 1962/63

Never mind the breeding of horses: the breeding of horsemen too is an intriguing study. Keith and Iris, the parents responsible for the birth of a certain Lester Piggott on Guy Fawkes Day 1935, were always destined for the racing life. Iris was a Rickaby from another great racing family. Her great-grandfather, Fred, trained a Derby winner; her father, Fred, and her brother, also Fred, rode Classic winners; and she herself twice collected the pound of sausages and bottle of champagne presented to the winner of the Newmarket Town Plate, then the only race open to women.

Keith Piggott's father, Ernie, with a Cannon and a Day, two more great racing families, in his maternal pedigree, rode successfully on the flat in France and Belgium, and settled in Britain permanently only after his increasing weight forced him to turn to riding over the jumps. It was a successful switch: he won three Grand Nationals – one on Jerry M in 1912, and two more on Poethlyn in 1918 and 1919. Both Keith and his brother, Victor, rode over fences between the two world wars and Keith's five-hundred-plus winners in the saddle included the Champion

Hurdle of 1939 on African Sister, the first mare to compete in the race. She was trained by his uncle, Charles Piggott, whose yard on Cleeve Hill overlooked the Cheltenham course. Keith Piggott might have ridden, as well as having trained, a Grand National winner: Grakle, who won in 1931 for trainer Tom Coulthwaite, was his intended ride but Keith was laid up at the time of the race with a broken thigh.

A significant success came in the Welsh National of 1925, then run at Cardiff's Ely Racecourse. Riding Vaulx, Keith beat Jack Anthony on Old Tay Bridge. Keith Piggott was one of the key contributors to that delightful chronicle of departed racecourses, *A Long Time Gone*, and he told author Chris Pitt that as they pulled up in that 1925 race, Anthony had asked him where he had finished. 'I won,' said Keith. 'Don't talk nonsense,' said Anthony, the senior rider, 'I did.' They had finished spread across the course, with the two jockeys on either side of the track at the finishing post, and Keith Piggott noted wryly, 'He probably hadn't seen me because he had drunk a ginger-beer bottle full of port before he went out to ride.'

Keith Piggott, who rode a number of horses for John Goldsmith, a wartime secret agent as well as a successful trainer, was clearly not without a touch of style: he drove an open-top Bugatti. It was Keith who, as a trainer in Lambourn (at a yard later purchased by Barry Hills with his legendary Lincoln gamble on Frankincense), put up his 12-year-old son Lester to bring home The Chase at Haydock in August 1948. That was the first winner of Lester's phenomenal career and it was Keith who trained 14 of the 20 winners Lester rode over hurdles before Lester's increasing opportunities on the flat took him away from the jumping game.

Lester rode four winners over hurdles from four rides for the 'Swinging Sixties' hairdresser 'Teasy Weasy' Raymond, who was a friend and patron of the Piggott family; it was Keith Piggott's success in training Raymond's Ayala to win the Grand National that enabled him to head the trainers' championship list in 1963.

Piggott had seen some potential in the chestnut Ayala, who had at one stage been

12-year-old jockey Lester Piggott reads the racing newspaper The Winner *on the balcony of his family's home in Lambourn. Lester's father, Keith Piggott trained the Grand National Winner in 1963.*

sold as a hunter for just £40. His trainer kept a half share in the gelding, which he purchased for 250 guineas. Even Lester was involved: he had schooled Ayala shortly before the race and reckoned he had come to his peak.

Jockey Pat Buckley, who was, unromantically, approached for the ride in the toilets at Newbury, recalls that Keith Piggott came down to the start with him, tapped him on the knee, and said, 'There's £1 million riding on you today.' The connections had backed the horse at 100-1 ante-post, and Buckley recalls that they rewarded him generously after the race.

The 1963 contest was not the only National on which Keith Piggott had an influence: he happened to own a film projector and he had made a collection of recordings of recent Grand Nationals, which he loaned to Tommy Smith as the American amateur prepared to ride Jay Trump at Aintree. The model that Smith took as the way to ride Jay Trump, on trainer Fred Winter's advice, was that of Bobby Beasley winning on Nicolaus Silver in 1961.

Fulke Walwyn

Champion Trainer 1946–49, 1957/58, 1963/64

Two racing greats in the Lambourn of the 1960s shared initials: Fulke Walwyn and Fred Winter. They were racing legends in adjoining stables who helped the 'Valley of the Racehorse', as Lambourn is known, to dominate the jump-racing scene and who nurtured many future racing careers in the process.

Walwyn rode 133 National Hunt winners as an amateur, including his success in the Grand National on Reynoldstown in 1936. He then turned professional while still an officer in the 9th Lancers, but a 1939 fall at Ludlow left him with a fractured skull, a stutter and scarcely the ability to write his own name.

He recovered sufficiently to begin training that year and returned after war service to buy Saxon House Stables in Lambourn in 1944. By the second season after the war, he was champion trainer and, in all, he sent out 2,009 winners over jumps and another 184 on the flat. Joining that rare band who have both ridden and trained a Grand National winner, he won the Aintree classic as a trainer in 1964 with Team Spirit. Perhaps Walwyn's greatest successes, though, were at the Cheltenham Festival. Between 1946 and 1986, he won 40 races at jump racing's Mecca, a record that stood until Nicky Henderson passed that total in 2012.

Fulke Walwyn won four Gold Cups: with Mont Tremblant (1952), Mandarin (1962), Mill House (1963) and The Dikler (1973). He took Champion Hurdles with Anzio (1962) and Kirriemuir (1965). His greatest horse, the giant Mill House, would assuredly have taken Cheltenham's supreme prize on more occasions had he not been a contemporary of the phenomenal Arkle. Walwyn also won the Stayers Hurdle, nowadays also one of the 'Big Four' at the Festival, with Crimson Embers (1982 and 1986) and Rose Ravine (1985).

Walwyn, though, was more than just a Cheltenham specialist. Cheltenham's turns and gradients do not suit all horses; some judges regard the King George VI Chase over the flatter Thameside track of Kempton Park on Boxing Day as a better test of a champion jumper. Walwyn won the King George five times: with Rowland Roy (1947), Mandarin (1957 and 1959), Mill House (1963) and The Dikler (1971). His record was just as good at other top tracks. He took the Hennessy Gold Cup seven times: he won the inaugural Hennessy at Cheltenham with Mandarin in 1957, and he took it again at its settled Newbury venue with Taxidermist (1958), with Mandarin once more in 1961, and with Mill House (1963), Man of The West (1968), Charlie Potheen (1972) and Diamond Edge (1981). Walwyn also won Sandown Park's Whitbread Gold Cup seven times: with Taxidermist (1958), Mill House (1967), Charlie Potheen (1973), The Dikler (1974), Diamond Edge (1979 and 1981), and Special Cargo (1984).

Trainers, however, all have their foibles and favourites. On one occasion, when jockey Barry Brogan broke his leg a week before the Hennessy, Fulke Walwyn put up

Richard Pitman on Charlie Potheen on the recommendation of his next-door neighbour, Fred Winter. The big horse was a headstrong character and Walwyn told the rider: 'You won't be able to stop him. Just humour him.' When they passed the stands, Charlie Potheen tried to 'duck out' so Pitman gave him a slap. Pitman remembers, 'He went mad, like a spoiled child, and ran all over the place, but we still won the race.' Pitman then had eight or nine rides for Walwyn in the next week: most of them won and the trainer then said, 'You'd better come and school some.' Such an invitation usually means you are 'in' with that trainer – with a prospect of further rides.

When the eager Pitman arrived for the schooling session, there alongside the trainer was the travelling head lad holding Rags, the little terrier that Fulke Walwyn adored. 'I want you to school this horse first,' said Walwyn, adding less than encouragingly, 'He's the one that broke Brogan's leg.' Another 'character' to cope with. The Mandown fences included seven rows of three obstacles abreast, and Pitman was told that he should go down the middle row, so that even if the horse tried to 'duck out', he would have to jump something. Pitman recalls, 'We got over one, somehow, then the horse cocked his jaw. Walwyn was standing in the wings of the second row and

the horse was running straight at him. I still remember his horror-stricken face as we loomed up. At the last minute, the horse veered, but unfortunately the lead attached to Walwyn's terrier got wrapped around the horse's leg – and we went over the fence with the dog attached. Walwyn was furious. He pulled me physically off the horse and declared, "You'll never ride for me again – and what's more, you can walk home..."' Walwyn never did give Pitman another ride.

Among Walwyn's patrons was the eccentric Dorothy Paget, who slept by day and studied form at night, and whose nocturnal habits he curbed by refusing to take phone calls after 9.00 p.m. Former champion trainer Martin Pipe has a collection of Paget memorabilia bought at auction, which includes correspondence with Walwyn in which the high-rolling Paget demands a 'banco' to beat the bookmakers. She instructed Walwyn: 'I want a banco. I don't want any mistakes and I don't want anything to go wrong. You won't be able to get me, so if anything goes wrong don't run it.' The strain must have been considerable. Pipe's collection includes one particular Paget betting slip for a wager of £120,000 – a fair sum of money in the 1940s!

Walwyn once sent out five winners in a day for Dorothy Paget at Folkestone but instead of

Ron Barry on The Dikler, trained by Fulke Walwyn on whom he won the Cheltenham Gold Cup in 1973.

praising his achievement, she abused him for not winning the sixth. On one occasion, owner and trainer were not on speaking terms but communicated through a go-between (Dorothy Paget's showjumping protégée, Peggy 'Pug' Whitehead) moving between the two separate rooms in which they sat. Having dictated her final instruction for Pug to relay to her trainer, Dorothy Paget demanded '... and if you've got the guts, kick him in the balls.'

Whatever the opinions of that one unusual owner might have been, Fulke Walwyn was a giant on the jumping scene and a revered figure in Lambourn.

Walwyn was part of a racing family. His twin sister Helen Johnson Houghton also trained, and was one of the first women to be elected as a member of the Jockey Club. His cousin Peter Walwyn, who also trained in Lambourn, won the Derby with Grundy.

Denys Smith, who trained 145 winners at Sedgefield, celebrates his 91st birthday at the course.

Denys Smith
Champion Trainer 1967/68

Not all its leading figures have entered racing by a traditional route. Denys Smith, who was based in Bishop Auckland, was the top dual-purpose trainer of his time and the first to score a half-century in consecutive seasons, with 54 wins over jumps in 1969/70 and 52 wins on the flat in 1970. As well as his jumping successes, he had two Group One successes on the flat,

and he remains one of only three people to have trained winners of both halves of the famous 'spring double' – winning the Lincoln Handicap with Foggy Bell, ridden by Sandy Barclay, in 1969, as well as taking the 1968 National with Red Alligator.

Smith was entirely self-taught. He had been a taxi-driver but when he married his wife, Joan, his father-in-law, Bert Richardson, persuaded him to join him as a cattle dealer and help out with his hobby – trotting horses. Before that time, Denys Smith had never even put a saddle on a horse, but he soon moved on to point-to-pointers. People told him that you could not mix flat racing and jumping, but he was determined to go his own way. He was no respecter of officialdom or reputations. Learning that Lester Piggott had taken an alternative ride for Newmarket trainer Bernard van Cutsem after having agreed to ride Smith's horse, called Baldur, with Piggott claiming that he had a retainer with the Newmarket trainer, Smith accosted the great champion jockey. He told him, 'Everyone knows no one has a retainer for you, Lester, but it doesn't matter, we'll finish in front of you anyway..' Smith then booked Alan Bond to ride – and Baldur beat Piggott's mount by five lengths.

When Red Alligator, with Brian Fletcher in the saddle, won the 1968 Grand National, having been brought down in the famous Foinavon race the year before, yet still finishing third, he earned a civic reception that saw him paraded down Newgate Street to Bishop Auckland Town Hall. His trainer later recalled: 'It took all night to do it because people kept coming out of the pubs with buckets of beer for the horse. I think he enjoyed himself.' Denys Smith, who died in November 2016, was still enjoying a pint, well into his 90s, at the South Church pub near Bishop Auckland, which used to be the Crown and Anchor but which was renamed the Red Alligator in the horse's honour. Smith was able to remind people that no one had a record to match his at Sedgefield, Catterick or Redcar.

Other leading figures from the North

There were other leading figures in the north who figured prominently in the trainers' tables without actually winning a championship. Ken Oliver, based at Hassendean Bank, Hawick, ran the most successful stable in Scotland for 30 years. A larger-than-life character, he was a gregarious, bonhomous man whose motto, according to friends, was 'Win or lose, we'll have the booze.' When he went into hospital for a triple heart bypass, friends joked that it was two tubes for the blood and one for the Tio Pepe.

The energetic Oliver was also a successful farmer and an all-round sportsman who played rugby, tennis, squash and golf to a high standard, alongside his hunting. On top of that, he was a shrewd businessman. With the aid of his friend Willie Stephenson, the Royston-based trainer who bought Sir Ken for £1,000 on a holiday in Paris and won three Champion Hurdles with him. Oliver also played a significant part in the development of the Royal Highland Show.

Although he joked about his first winner, the one-eyed Delman, 'I think we had only one eye open between us, coming to the first two fences. Mine were both tight-shut,' Ken Oliver was a capable rider before he became a trainer. In 1950, he rode his own Sanvina to win the Scottish Grand National. He went on to win the race five times as a trainer. He also trained half a dozen Cheltenham Festival winners, and sent out Fighting Fit to win the Hennessy Gold Cup in 1979. His wife, Rhona, very much part of the team, owned Wyndburgh, who finished second three times in the Grand National (in 1957, 1959 and 1962). Wyndburgh, the winner of 13 races, was also fourth in the 1958 National.

Wyndburgh's unluckiest venture was in 1959 when, as they jumped Becher's for a second time one of Brookshaw's stirrup irons snapped. He slipped the other foot out of the irons and shouted across to Michael Scudamore, who was on the Willie Stephenson-trained Oxo, 'Look, no feet!' With a fine piece of horsemanship,

Brookshaw somehow managed to keep his horse in touch with the leaders, and then drive Wyndburgh after Oxo over the last two fences. Oxo, who had a long lead, hit the last and, with Brookshaw urging on his mount as if pursued by a Mongol horde, they got within a length-and-a-half of Scudamore on the winner. Wyndburgh ran at least five times for eight consecutive seasons – and then lived on for 20 years, ten of them spent hunting.

Oxo was another young prospect who had caught the eye of the shrewd Willie Stephenson. Six years after he won the 1951 Derby with Arctic Prince Stephenson saw Oxo in a point to point and bought him for £3,000. Asked what he planned to do with him his reply was succinct: 'Win the National.'

It seems strange that Willie Stephenson's cousin Arthur, better known by his initials 'W.A.' never won a championship not least because, until Martin Pipe re-wrote the record books, Stephenson figured in them as trainer of more jumping winners than anyone before him. In all, WA Stephenson trained 2,632 winners over 40 years, both over the jumps and on the flat, his jumping stars including such well-known names as Credit Call, Celtic Gold and Durham Edition, the last-named being a major player in several Grand Nationals. Stephenson's most famous victory was with The Thinker, ridden by Ridley Lamb, in the Cheltenham Gold Cup of 1987.

Following victories at Wetherby and Haydock, The Thinker had been backed down from 10-1 to 13-2 second favourite, but the race nearly did not take place. On the day of the race, as the jockeys mounted in the parade ring, it began to snow. By the time the horses reached the start, Cheltenham was in the midst of a full-scale snowstorm – and the snow was settling. The stewards called the runners back, but instead of cancelling the race, they waited, assured by weather experts that the storm would pass through. Their patience was rewarded: the skies cleared and the race, originally scheduled for 3.30, eventually took place 81 minutes later at 4.51. As they jumped the last fence, The Thinker, after a mistake two fences out, was in only third place, but he stayed on strongly up the hill to beat Peter Easterby's Cybrandian by one-and-a-half lengths. Stephenson was not at Cheltenham to witness the victory: he had gone to a humdrum Hexham meeting that day instead.

Stephenson trained plenty of winners on the flat but his first love was jumping. Although he never won a Grand National, he won a Mackeson Gold Cup with Pawnbroker, a Welsh National with Rainbow Battle, and a Scottish National with Kinmont Wullie. He also sent out Stephen's Society to win the testing Velka Pardubicka in the Czech Republic with the

Gordon W Richards with One Man, the horse he called his 'bouncing rubber ball.'

amateur rider Chris Collins on board, making Collins the first Englishman to win the race for 50 years. Collins was also associated with Stephenson's consistent Credit Call, who won 37 chases, including both the Cheltenham and Liverpool versions of the Foxhunter Chase in 1972. Stephenson himself had been a successful amateur rider before he took out his first training licence in 1959, based at Leasingthorne near Bishop Auckland in County Durham.

In 1969/70, Arthur Stephenson became the first jump trainer ever to turn out a century of winners in a season and he went on to repeat the feat many times.

Another leading figure in the north was Gordon W Richards, who acquired his 'W' not from a county registrar, but from a clerk of the scales who wished to differentiate the then apprentice rider from his famous namesake, the flat-racing jockey Sir Gordon Richards (after whom he had been named). Gordon W Richards was riding as an apprentice to Jack Waugh at the time of the added initial; the W was for Waugh. Gordon W Richards lived up to his name, sending out nearly 2,000 winners as a trainer and becoming the second man to train more than 100 winners in a season. He was never champion trainer, a title determined by the total value of stakes won; however, in 1975/76, he did train the winners of more races than anyone else. On one particular day at Carlisle, he had five winners on the same card.

His riding career having been ended by a broken back, Richards began training at Beadnell on the Northumberland coast in 1964 and then moved to Greystoke Castle in the Cumbrian fells near the Lake District. His voice was distinctive: although he characterised all the famed grittiness of the region he made his home he never lost the soft burr of his West Country origins. Tough with his fellow human beings – Richards had been a successful boxer and was famous for his bollockings of jockeys, even in the winner's enclosure – he adored his horses, especially the bounding grey One Man, referred to by Richards as his 'bouncing rubber ball' and who became one of the most popular chasers in history.

Early success for Richards came with Playlord, the horse who enticed him into training, and who won the Great Yorkshire Chase and the Scottish Grand National as well as finishing third in the Cheltenham Gold Cup. Having fallen out with a previous partner, Richards sold a half share in Playlord to millionaire builder Philip Cussins; the canny trainer then persuaded Cussins to pay a record £14,750 to buy Titus Oates from the yard of his friend WA Stephenson. It was money well spent: the handsome chaser went on to win 17 races, including the 1969 Massey Ferguson Gold Cup, in which he beat the subsequent Grand National winner Gay Trip; the King George VI Chase, in which he beat Flyingbolt; and the 1971 Whitbread Gold Cup, in which he held off Young Ash Leaf.

Richards won the Grand National twice: in 1978, ridden by Bob Davies, Lucius scored in a thrilling finish with Sebastian V; six years later, Richards repeated the feat with Hello Dandy, ridden by stable jockey Neale Doughty. Many felt that Richards slightly underachieved at Cheltenham for a man of his ability, but he did have one glorious success at the Festival with One Man, and might have had a couple of Champion Hurdles to add to his tally, had he not fallen out with owner Pat Muldoon. Among the horses Muldoon took away from Richards – after a dispute engendered by Richards' readiness, from time to time, to run two horses in the same race – was the great Sea Pigeon. Richards reasoned that he sometimes needed to 'educate' his horses on the track, not to organise a future betting coup, but to prepare them for the proper job. Owners tend not to like their pride and joy being beaten by another horse from the same stable, especially if they have not been tipped the likely winner.

In his brown trilby and well-polished shoes, Gordon Richards was a dominant figure at northern courses such as Ayr, Hexham and Carlisle. In their early days, running horses on the flat as well for owners like Jimmy McGhie, formerly associated with Tommy Robson, the Greystoke operation had a reputation as something of a gambling yard. All this changed in the 1980s when the stable reverted to being a full-time jumping stable, from which Richards was responsible for launching several riders into the big time. He never made it easy for his jockeys and always put the horses first: after one angry dispute, long-time stable jockey Ron Barry left, albeit, after a break, he came back again.

Jonjo O'Neill, who became champion conditional jockey when based at Greystoke, used to sit in the back of the car listening to Richards' lengthy instructions to 'Big Ron' – and the arguments between the two racing greats as Ron Barry drove them back. In 1972/73, Ron Barry, the stable jockey from 1966 to 1983, apart from that one break, was champion jockey (having won the Gold Cup on The Dikler and the Whitbread on Charlie Potheen for Fulke Walwyn); Jonjo O'Neill was champion conditional jockey; and Nicky Richards, Gordon's son, was champion amateur jockey. Nicky Richards, who has followed his father as a successful trainer at Greystoke, is the only jockey to have won on his first ride on the flat, over hurdles, and over fences, and the travelling head lad in those days was Malcolm Jefferson, who went on to train successfully too.

Richards' longest-serving jockey, after Ron Barry retired, was Neale Doughty, who, despite their mutual respect, spent 14 years happily tussling with the trainer. Doughty put this into perspective, after Richards' death from cancer at the age of only 68, by explaining: 'The boss loved the game and lived it to the full with such intensity that we were bound to fall out at regular intervals.'

Peter Cazalet

Champion Trainer 1949/50, 1959/60, 1964/65

One of racing's biggest debts to Peter Cazalet was the role he and his good friend Anthony, Lord Mildmay, the second Lord Mildmay of Flete, played in introducing Queen Elizabeth The Queen Mother to racing (see section on The royals and racing, page 250).

Cazalet and Mildmay had both spent the Second World War in the Welsh Guards, and they shared the belief that jump racing was very much the poor relation. They were determined to lift the profile of a sport that had been condemned as a pursuit purely for the 'needy and greedy' – and they did just that. Part of the profile-raising was down to their success rates: in 1946/47, for example, Cazalet had 40 winners from around 30 horses, while the talented Mildmay was the leading amateur rider in each of the first five post-war years. Furthermore, they helped to change jump racing's image because they were boosted by royal patronage.

At a dinner during Royal Ascot one year, Mildmay, when sitting next to the then Queen and her daughter Princess Elizabeth, persuaded them to share ownership of a jumper to be trained by Cazalet at his grand Fairlawne stables in Kent. By finding and training Monaveen, he and Cazalet brought into the sport one of its true aficionados – the Queen Mother – and her

Trainer Peter Cazalet with the Queen and the Queen Mother at Sandown Park.

enthusiasm lasted until her death at the age of 101 in 2002.

Cazalet and Mildmay, who died tragically young at only 41, were a pair of true Corinthians. Cazalet was a fine tennis and racquets player, as well as having played first-class cricket for Oxford University and for Kent, and he also rode in three Grand Nationals. He set up training at Fairlawne, his 1,500-acre estate near Sevenoaks, soon after the war; he went on to become champion trainer in 1949/50, 1959/60 and 1964/65, when he trained a then record number of 82 winners, including 27 for the Queen Mother. In all, before his death in 1973, he trained more than 250 winners for the Queen Mother; her regular weekends at Fairlawne, where Albert Roux was Cazalet's private chef and where the trainer partnered her on the croquet lawn, were said to have been among the happiest times of her life. The company regularly included the likes of Noel Coward, and Elizabeth Taylor and Richard Burton. The Cazalet family's private joke was that the trainer, whose day started early on the gallops, was the only person allowed to fall asleep in Her Majesty's car on the way back from the races. The local vicar, whose sermons she apparently relished, was well aware that her visits tended to coincide with racing at the nearest course, and he was known to make reference to 'The feast of Saint Lingfield.'

Among the other owners for whom Cazalet trained successfully were Lord Abergavenny and Colonel Bill Whitbread, whose brilliant young chaser Dunkirk, twice a winner of the two-mile Champion Chase at Cheltenham, which was later to bear the Queen Mother's name, died at Kempton when trying to take on the mighty Arkle. In all, Cazalet trained more than 1,000 winners, ridden by jockeys including Bill Rees, Tony Grantham, David Mould and Dick Francis, who, of course, partnered the unfortunate Devon Loch in his Grand National disaster (see page 251).

They were different days, in more senses than one. There is a famous tale involving Lord Mildmay, who was a permanent steward at several West Country meetings as well as a regular competitor. One day at Exeter races he was 'waiting in front' (setting a steady pace to conserve energy) on his mount as they turned for home. In a small field of few runners one of two anguished professionals behind him who had been instructed not to overdo their efforts shouted, 'For God's sake go on m'lord. We're both not off.' (Not intended to win that day).

Major Cazalet, however, was very much of the old school, demanding the highest standards. He ran his stable with military precision and discipline. Once, when a cigarette end was found in the yard and all the grooms and stable lads denied ownership, the entire staff were given their notice, only to be reinstated when it was discovered that the errant butt had been abandoned by a visiting postman. The stable jockeys may have danced with the Queen at her celebration parties, but none of them was ever invited even to breakfast with the Major and his wife. The Queen Mother knew what a disciplinarian he was and acknowledged it when talking with stable staff. He had his rules about stable conduct, even with her, and jokingly she used to refer to him as 'The Führer.'

Cazalet died of cancer in 1973, a week after watching Inch Arran win the Topham Trophy for the Queen Mother at Aintree; the royal string of horses moved on to Lambourn and Fulke Walwyn.

Fred Winter

Champion Trainer 1970–75, 1976/78, 1984/85

Of all racing's heroes, few have been so universally respected as Fred Winter, not just for his ability to produce good horses to win great races, but also as a byword for sportsmanship and integrity – in his case, both as rider and trainer. As a rider, he was noted for his sheer physical strength. He would amuse his fellow jockeys by walking around the weighing room on his hands – with a cigarette in his mouth – and rivals said that he used to impel horses forward with his legs like a human clamp. One day at Newbury in his last season in the saddle, Winter rode four winners, at least two of

which, his competitors could see, had required every ounce of his strength. On his return to the weighing room, his battle-hardened rivals rose spontaneously to applaud him in. On one

The Queen Mother presenting the Whitbread Gold Cup to Fred Winter, trainer of Plundering.

occasion, the trainer of a horse Winter was riding was babbling on when the owner cut in, 'You needn't say any more. Winter is a master of his craft.' The owner was Winston Churchill. On his retirement from the saddle in 1964, Winter, already a titan of his sport, became the first jump jockey ever to be awarded an MBE. (It is an interesting sign of the changed times that, on his retirement, the award for AP McCoy was a knighthood.)

What Winter looked for first in those who worked closely with him was honesty. His own was never in question. Ryan Price, the trainer for whom Winter rode 450 winners, revealed how an owner in the paddock once instructed Winter to lose a race. Winter had glared fiercely at the man and told him, 'Listen, you had better go and back this horse – because it is going to win.' Which it then did.

The son of a trainer, also named Fred, who had won the Oaks on Cherimoya as a 16-year-old apprentice jockey in 1911, Fred Winter was champion jockey four times, with a strike rate of around 25 per cent of his 4,000 rides over 17 years. In all, he rode 923 winners from a much thinner fixture list than today's, including such horses as Clair Soleil and Saffron Tartan. Some jockeys are fearless; others are brave. The perceptive Brough Scott, who had ridden against him, once wrote of Fred Winter: 'He knew what fear was. He went to Mass every Sunday to find the courage to overcome it.' Winter himself told the American amateur jockey Tommy Smith, with whom he won a Grand National: 'Courage is like a bank account. If you draw too many cheques, sooner or later one bounces.'

In his 17 seasons in the saddle, as an idol of the small-time punter, Winter won three Champion Hurdles, two Cheltenham Gold Cups, three King George VI Chases, and two Grand Nationals. His victory on Fulke Walwyn's Mandarin in the Grand Steeplechase de Paris at Auteuil in 1962, coming after the horse's bit had snapped after

Fred Winter: a dominant figure in and out of the saddle.

just four fences, is rated by many as the best jump-racing ride of all time. But there was so much more to come. Winter went on to win twice as many championships as a trainer.

Fred Winter always admitted that he was not in love with steeplechase riding the way some others were, and persevered partly because he was determined to show he had the guts to go on after sustaining a broken back on only his 11th ride. He had not intended to become a trainer, but when he decided to stop riding, his application to become a starter, amazingly, was refused by the Jockey Club. The kindest explanation is that

officialdom feared that he would not be tough enough to impose discipline on fellow jockeys – lack of toughness being not something that ever became apparent to those who worked for him! The more probable explanation is that the elitists who were still running racing felt that jockeys should know their place – and that place did not include playing any part in the sport's administration.

The switch to training was not easy. Fred Winter had lived well and saved little during his riding days. Before his 1956 marriage to Diana Pearson, Winter and his fellow rider Dave Dick used to head for the south of France with their winnings at the end of the jumping season; there they stayed, enjoying the wine and the female company until the money ran out. As a prospective trainer, he wasn't just short of funds but of a key area of experience. Winter had never played a part in schooling horses at his retained yards. Ryan Price and Fulke Walwyn both rated him the best race rider they had ever seen but at the same time, they agreed he was useless as a schooling jockey, so they left that job to others. Nor was Winter's former loyalty as a rider much rewarded: only one of the owners he had ridden for, Michael (later Sir Michael) Sobell, sent him a horse to help him start up as a trainer, and he soon found the whole business a grind. Suddenly, he had to deal with people as well as horses. Instead of simply working out the best way to ride a particular horse, and winning on him, he now had to make the entries, buy the hay, find staff – and answer what he regarded as a ridiculous number of telephone calls. It did not make him ceaselessly charming.

Trainer Nicky Henderson, who spent five years as Winter's assistant, recalls, 'Fred in the morning was a different man to Fred in the afternoon. They were great times but he could be tough. Some mornings could be quite bruising when things weren't going right.' Winter certainly didn't waste words. Explaining his decision not to run a horse on unsuitable going, he declared: 'I want him in one piece three years from now and I'm not going to chuck that away by running for peanuts on concrete.' He had his likes and dislikes, too. Henrietta Knight, who used to prep some of Winter's horses, often went round evening stables with him. She says, 'He was very particular. He said, "I hate fat horses and I hate fat people." Once, he came and looked at the horses we had. They had been out to grass and just come in. He prodded one and said, "Too fat, too fat." And then he prodded my ribs and said, "a bit like you."'

Despite having said previously that he didn't believe he knew enough about horses to make it as a trainer, Fred Winter trained the winner of the Grand National (which he had won as a jockey on Sundew in 1957 and on Kilmore in 1962) in both his first and second years as a trainer, with Jay Trump (1965) and Anglo (1966). On the first occasion, he 'trained' the jockey as well, the American amateur Tommy Smith. By 1971, Winter had wrested the title of champion trainer from Fred Rimell, the only other person since the Second World War to have been both champion jockey and champion trainer. In all, Winter was champion trainer on eight occasions until a fall down stairs in 1987 and a subsequent stroke deprived him of his speech and mobility, thus forcing his retirement the following year.

Nicky Henderson gives an interesting glimpse of how different the methods were in Winter's time from today's vigorous workouts on all-weather 'precipices': 'We would walk through the village of Lambourn. We would trot out to Eastbury. Then you'd turn left or right up the hill as you came out of Eastbury and trot up the hill. You'd walk back down, trot back to the village and go home again. Lovely. Tuesday, you would set out for Mandown and that would be the start of the problem. We'd go round the bowl and up the hill and every single one of us would get carted, we were all run away with because the horses were so blinking fresh. On Wednesdays we went for a walk, we would walk through the village and trot up Sheepdrove. Turn round and walk home again. We wouldn't go 35 minutes, that was it: we'd turn and go home again. Every other Thursday, we'd trot up Hungerford Hill, trot up to The Hare and walk back down again. If you did that these days, you'd be killed. You wouldn't

have a cat-in-hell's chance. In those days, the roads around here were for horses, not for cars. That's all we did. Friday, we'd trot around again. Saturday, they'd go back to Mandown and everybody would get carted again because the horses hadn't set foot on grass for four days. It was extraordinary.'

What seems even more extraordinary now is that Winter's success was achieved from so few horses. Nicky Henderson again: 'When Fred was champion trainer, he ran something like 48 horses. Now we're all dealing in hundreds, but with around 48 horses he had 100 winners. Fulke Walwyn only had a similar number. They were the big yards. They were the all-powerful yards – but they still wouldn't have had 50 horses.'

Many of the stars Fred Winter trained – like Bula, Pendil, Lanzarote, Killiney and Midnight Court – became household names, living in the row of boxes at his Uplands Stables in Lambourn that became known as 'Millionaires' Row.' His number of horses may have been limited by today's standards, but with Bula (twice) and Lanzarote he won the Champion Hurdle (see page 86) three times in four years. In 1978, Midnight Court finally gave him the Cheltenham Gold Cup victory that had eluded him twice, once when the well-fancied Pendil fell, once when the same horse went down by a short head to The Dikler. Winter so nearly won another great Grand National in 1973 when Red Rum, in receipt of lumps of weight thanks to the handicapper's assessment of his chances that year, beat Winter's bold front-runner Crisp in one of the most memorable Nationals ever. Among his 28 successes at the Cheltenham Festival was Crisp's win in the Champion Chase in 1971. In all, he trained 1,557 winners over the jumps in 24 seasons.

He won the Gold Cup twice as a jockey and once as a trainer; the Champion Hurdle three times as a jockey and four times as a trainer; and the King George VI Chase three times as a jockey and twice as a trainer. He is the only person ever to have won the Gold Cup, the Champion Hurdle and the Grand National, both as a jockey and as a trainer.

Sometimes blunt in manner, Fred Winter bred a fierce loyalty in those who worked for him, notably jockeys Richard Pitman, Eddie Harty and John Francome, and also in his assistant trainers Nicky Henderson and Oliver Sherwood. Admired as much as Fred Winter's achievements, though, was his integrity. He would never, for example, criticise a jockey's performance in his discussions with an owner, before he was able to talk through the race with the rider.

Much has been made of Winter's rivalry with his Lambourn neighbour Fulke Walwyn, but it was always a friendly rivalry. Before Fred stopped riding, the Winters and the Walwyns used to holiday together in the south of France. The Walwyns provided a bed for their neighbours-to-be while Uplands was being prepared and Walwyn's head lad, Joe Lammin, would go next door in the evenings and help Fred Winter plan his training base. Winter's staff of four in the beginning included three who lived in caravans in a nettle bed: his long-time head man Brian Delaney, Derek King and Richard Pitman.

Pitman recalls, 'We were in little tow caravans – not mobile homes – with the woods for a loo. We only had 26 boxes at the time. When the yard became full, Fred Winter made it a priority to put up a lads' hostel before putting up more boxes. Most trainers would have said, "Fuck the lads, we'll have more boxes."'

Pitman believes that Fred Winter should have had two more Gold Cups with Pendil: 'Fred was a great man for discussing tactics. I would have breakfast with him nearly every day. On Pendil in his first Gold Cup, I said, "I want to come halfway up the run-in." He said, "No, that's too dangerous. If you miss the last [fence], then the race will be over – you will never get back on top in time. I want you in front at the second-last." So I went to the front at the second-last and was a couple of lengths clear. As a rider, the run-in looks like this little strip with a blaze of colour either side. But with Pendil being favourite there was this great cacophony of noise. Pendil was in front with no company and he froze – only for a stride – but he lost momentum. The Dikler

came back at me and Ron Barry passed us. Pendil fought back and we were in front again the stride after the line.

'It is typical of Fred Winter that there is a great picture of him hugging me in the winner's enclosure and there is a distinct handprint of Fred's on Pendil's quarters where he had patted the horse. He just said, "Richard, you did your best." The next year, there was exactly the same photo of the hug and the handprint after I won the Champion Hurdle on Lanzarote. He really was a man who could be the same both in victory and defeat.

'In 1974, he said to me, "You can ride Pendil exactly how you like." He was running away coming down the hill in second place. I was behind High Ken, an iffy jumper, and I was planning to pull out from behind him at the second-last and then go back in, but seeing that, The Dikler (Ron Barry) and Captain Christy (Bobby Beasley) rushed up on my outside and shut the door to prevent me pulling out. Perfectly legitimate, good race-riding tactics. They shut the door. No escape route. The horse came down.'

Part of that story is familiar to long-time racing followers. But Pitman supplies an additional element that is not: 'Before the race, Vince Brooks, the lad who looked after Pendil, looked really ill and I told him he did. He said, "Don't you know: I have slept with the horse in his box these last ten days because the IRA have threatened to shoot him if he hits the front." The poor kid said, "Please get him withdrawn at the start, don't let him race." I said, "I can't do that – he's odds on. Think of Fred and of the punters who have backed him." Then we fell, because High Ken fell in front of us and brought us down, at just the point the IRA might have carried out the threat. Fred must have thought initially that he had been shot. I told Terry Biddlecombe about it after the race and he said, "Hey, that's not very nice. They could have missed you and got me!"'

Even though his Uplands yard remained high on quality, Fred Winter had to cope with plenty more setbacks. When Bula and Lanzarote moved on from their Champion Hurdle successes to the bigger obstacles, Bula was put down following an injury in the 1977 Champion Chase and Lanzarote fell fatally in the same year's Gold Cup. Killiney, rated by Winter as potentially the best of all his charges after winning the top novice chase at Cheltenham, also died on the racecourse, at Ascot, depriving him of the chance to realise his potential.

The slightly fearsome Winter could be gruff to the point of rudeness with people. Even John Francome, who charmed him, could suffer from the Winter 'bark.' Once, when Francome had driven the trainer to the wrong destination and was trying to apologise, Fred Winter declared: 'That's all right, son; it's not your fault, it's mine. You're so bloody stupid that I should have put up a blackboard and written your instructions on it.' He did, though, care deeply about his horses. Says Richard Pitman, 'The one time Fred gave me a rocket I was on Beau Champ who ran away with me and finished legless. Fred tore me off a strip and it was all because he hated to see a horse that tired. His orders were nearly always the same: "Jump off in a handy position then settle him back to where you want to be, rather than jumping off slowly and having to fight your way through. Make sure you put him in the race – ask him to join the action two out. If you want to, give him one slap and then maybe another, but never more than two. If the horse doesn't go for two slaps, he won't go for 100. Once they're beaten, don't be hard on them because they've got to recover. I want them to come home thinking, 'That was nice…'"'

Uplands in Winter's day, recalls Peter Scudamore, had an atmosphere all its own. 'Fred was an older man before I joined him but it was just a privilege to go to that yard with all the great horses such as Lanzarote. Like Anfield or whatever, there was just a feeling about the place. You referred to Brian Delaney as "head lad", you never called him "Brian."' A man of unrivalled determination, Fred Winter was a model to many – both in the saddle and in the stable yard. It would be no exaggeration to say that for nearly 30 years he dominated the world of steeplechasing.

Peter Easterby
Champion Trainer 1978–81

Peter Easterby describes himself as a farmer and a horse dealer – yet nobody else in racing history has trained more than 1,000 winners both over jumps and on the flat. Miles Henry Easterby, known to all as 'Peter' since the woman helping his mother with the baby Easterby didn't like his given names, was champion trainer for three successive years in 1978/79, 1979/80 and 1980/81. The only person, apart from Michael Dickinson, to win that title from a northern base since 1957, his total of victories includes a quality haul of 13 at the Cheltenham Festival, including two Gold Cups, three Arkles, and no fewer than five Champion Hurdles. Still active in his late 80s, as assistant to his talented son, Tim – 'I need to be, to get in free' – Peter Easterby handled two of the most popular horses in jumping history in Night Nurse and Sea Pigeon. Like his trainer brother Mick, he has become a substantial landowner.

Peter Easterby is not a man to trumpet his victories. He is as careful with his words as he is reputed to be with his cash, never using ten if two will do, but sitting in the kitchen of the blue-shuttered Georgian farmhouse in Great Habton, which has always been his base, you can sense his quiet pride in a job incredibly well done. He clearly enjoys playing up to the Yorkshire image. 'Which winners did you enjoy the most?' 'The ones I made a bit of money on.' He admits, though, 'It used to be farming first and horses last, but now it's turned around.'

'My father was a horse dealer. How he managed on just 25 acres rented, I just don't know. The only time we had any money was in the war and just after, with black-market eggs and bacon – all cash. We used to get a licence to kill one pig and kill five!'

The Easterbys had hunters and point-to-point horses. 'I started with four horses. You had to have seven in your yard then, to get a licence. I had four plus one thoroughbred hunter, one I borrowed off my uncle who was a trainer, and a brood mare. None of them were any good and it took me four years before we had a winner.'

Nevertheless, after that first winner (Double Rose in a £102 hurdle race at Market Rasen in 1953) came more than 2,500 more. Alongside those famous Cheltenham victories were an Irish Sweeps Hurdle and a Schweppes Gold Trophy, a Gimcrack Stakes, two Chester Cups and three Ayr Gold Cups, as well as Ascot's King's Stand Stakes, which his top sprinter Goldhill, won two years after taking Ascot's Windsor Castle Stakes (Ascot in the intervening year having been washed out). It clearly still rankles – he mentions it more than once – that the prize money for what is now a Group One race was just £1,820 in the year he won it.

His best chaser and one of his best bargains was Alverton, the Gold Cup winner by 25 lengths after the front-running Tied Cottage had fallen at the last in 1979. 'I was the instigator of breeding him because I trained the dam. She cost a hundred and twenty quid and she did win a little race. I was on the lookout for a good stallion by a Cambridgeshire winner – which is speed and staying – and I spotted Midsummer

Night II. These days, they are all Group horses [winners of top class non-handicap races]. You wouldn't get away with a bloody handicapper as a stallion now.

'When he was a two-year-old, the owner ran short of money so I bought him off him for £720. He was a good horse on the flat. He was second in the Ebor but broke down badly as a four-year-old on both tendons. We fired him (an operation to strengthen a horse's tendons) and gave him 18 months off.'

Alverton had won an Arkle Chase the year before winning the Gold Cup – and at least one famous punter benefited from his Gold Cup victory. 'That morning, I went to give Alverton a canter and Peter O'Sullevan was with me. He was a big fan of Alverton. In that canter, Alverton just came alive. I can't describe it but I'd never seen him so well in his life. I turned to Peter and I said, "There you are. That'll win." Peter said, "It's too late for me" – he'd tipped something else – "but I'm going to back him."'

Since Alverton was set to carry only 10 st 13 lb in the Grand National the year of his Gold Cup victory, he was sent on to Aintree but tragically was killed at Becher's the second time around when simply cantering. Easterby believes to this day that he would have won the National, a race the Easterbys have never won (brother Mick was second with Mr Snugfit, and an uncle was beaten by a short head in the 1930s).

'Alverton was going well second time around at Becher's but he never took off. We think it was a heart attack. You can't prove anything. It happens and that's that.' For the following three years, Peter reveals, he got a telegram every year before the big race, telling him he was a 'horse killer' and that there was a curse on him.

In 1981, Easterby won another Gold Cup with Little Owl, ridden by amateur jockey Jim Wilson. Ironically, if Little Owl had not started, Peter Easterby's other runner that year, Night Nurse, who finished second, would have become the first horse ever to win the Champion Hurdle and the Gold Cup.

Night Nurse and Sea Pigeon, from an outstanding crop of hurdlers in their time (see section on Champion Hurdle, page 86), were two of jump racing's most popular horses of all time; they won 69 races between them.

'Night Nurse came up at the Doncaster Sales as a yearling. I bought him as a yearling with a view to him being a sprinter. He was by Tingle, who was sharp over five furlongs though the dam was stoutly bred. We buy horses to sell. That's what we do. The ninth man who came to see him was the late Mr Rudkin. He was 86 or 87 with glasses half an inch thick. Night Nurse ran on the flat and we pinched a little race at Ripon but he was no good on the flat really so we decided to give him a school (an educative practice run over obstacles) and he shaped very well. I told Mr Rudkin we were going to try him over hurdles. He said, "That's all right." A few minutes later, the phone went again and it was Mr Rudkin's lady. She said, "You run him over hurdles over my dead body" so I thought, "How do we get out of this one?" I rang him back and said, "Look, I'll take the horse and I'll give you your money back." He said, "That's good of you," and I sent him a cheque for £1,000. I then rang an old schoolfriend, Reg Spencer, who was a property auctioneer, and said, "He shapes well. He's £1,500." That's how he got him! I sold him Night Nurse for £1,500.'

Paddy Broderick rode Night Nurse to 19 of his 26 victories. Easterby recalls, 'Night Nurse was a miserable old bugger in his box. He would kick you if he could, but he was a good horse to deal with. I don't know whether he was a natural front-runner or whether Paddy Broderick was. Probably a bit of both. You couldn't give Paddy any orders. He never heard you. He never listened – and he was usually right. Paddy's style suited Night Nurse down to the ground. The one mistake I made with Night Nurse is that I didn't go chasing early enough.'

The biggest bet Peter Easterby ever had was when Night Nurse won his second Champion Hurdle. When the ground turned heavy, many thought that Night Nurse would not handle it. Having trialled him on the soft, Easterby knew better. As Night Nurse's price went out from 5-2 to 7-2, then to 7-1, he kept backing him. 'I had too much on for him to get beat but he drifted and drifted and I began to worry: "Has someone

Night Nurse and Monksfield – two great rivals over hurdles run a dead heat in the Templegate Hurdle at Aintree in 1977.

got at him?" There was a bit of doping going on then. But Keith Stone, who looked after him, then said, "I've never left him, guv'nor, night and morning." So I went and had some more on. We'd ten tons of potatoes left at the time. So I said to my brother, "Don't sell them taters. We might need them when I come back." When I left for Cheltenham, they were £100 a ton. When I got back after Cheltenham, they were £150 a ton – and the horse had won – so that was a good double.'

'I used to punt a bit. It got me into trouble. I was down at London [summoned to the Jockey Club] five times in two years. They tried to get me warned off, definitely. I was having a good run and they didn't like it. Other people got warned off.' Five times in two years. Did that put off any owners? With a chuckle, Peter Easterby replies: 'Maybe it even encouraged them. They thought they might make a bit of money.'

If the word 'shrewd' didn't exist, it would have to be invented to describe Miles Henry Easterby and his brother, Mick. Both of them are famous for having an eye for a deal and they have invested wisely. Tell him that he and Mick are reputed to own half Yorkshire and the reply is simply: 'Wish we did. It's a big county.'

Night Nurse and Sea Pigeon both won two Champion Hurdles; the two horses lie buried in a paddock within sight of the Great Habton office window. The plaque does not overstate the case in declaring them: 'Legends In Their Lifetime'; beside them, at her request, rest the ashes of Peter Easterby's late wife, Marjorie.

Sea Pigeon had originally been trained, for the wine-and-spirits importer Pat Muldoon, who paid £10,000 for the former Derby seventh, by Gordon W Richards in Penrith. Muldoon and Richards fell out over Richards' penchant for running two horses in the same race, and Sea Pigeon was moved to Easterby, who had sportingly urged Muldoon to sleep on it before transferring his horse. 'Pat Muldoon were a good client until he ran out of money. He was gaoled. He was in Edinburgh Gaol. I sent him a Christmas card: "Pat Muldoon, care of Her Majesty's Pleasure, Edinburgh Gaol" – and he got it. He was in the wine trade and it was

something to do with bonding. He was a good client but had too many bloody hangers-on.

'When I got Sea Pigeon – no detriment to the previous trainer – he hadn't got any brakes. I brainwashed him and got him relaxed. That's why he was so good. At first you couldn't hold him, but we cured him.'

Sea Pigeon had to be held up for a late burst of speed and his regular partner, Jonjo O'Neill, blames himself for the fact that Sea Pigeon did not win three Champion Hurdles. In 1979, Jonjo made the mistake of listening to the owner in the parade ring, who told him forcibly, 'Don't come too late.' Jonjo made his effort too soon, enabling Dessie Hughes on the tenacious Monksfield to come back at him up the run-in and win. Says Easterby, 'It was all Pat Muldoon's fault. With Sea Pigeon you could leave it to the last 10 yards and it wouldn't have mattered. You couldn't leave it too late with him. When they came in, Jonjo looked at me, and I looked at him. We never spoke. We both knew what had happened. I was never angry with him or anything.'

Peter Easterby achieved his results despite never having more than 47 horses in the yard or a clutch of large-scale owners behind him. Muldoon was the only one with several horses. Nor did Easterby spend a lot on his campaigners: Little Owl cost only £2,000; Ryeman, who, like Easterby's Clayside, was an Arkle winner, he bought for just £1,200.

Easterby says, 'I never set out to be champion trainer – it just happened. The name of this game is to sell them. If you keep too many of them, you go skint.' The same realism governed his decision to hand over in 1996 to his son, Tim. 'We were having a good time but it's no use hanging on until you're having a bad season and the horses are gone. You never see a young owner going to an old trainer. That's why Tim took the licence.'

Peter Easterby's response, when asked why the Cheltenham winners didn't keep coming after the glory years, is equally straightforward: 'We just ran out of ammunition. The replacements were nothing like as good as the previous batch. But it were nice while it lasted.'

Michael Dickinson

Champion Trainer 1981–84

The Easterbys might run them close – but perhaps the greatest of the northern dynasties in jump racing was that of the Dickinson family. There was little showmanship and no fuss as the hard-working Tony and Monica Dickinson sent out an impressive stream of winners through the 1970s and 1980s, first expanding the yard in Gisburn, Lancashire, which they rented from flat-racing trainer Jeremy Hindley's family, and then in 1979 moving across the Pennines to their purpose-built new base at Poplar House, Dunkeswick, near Harewood in West Yorkshire. True horse people who hunted, point-to-pointed, showed, and dealt in horses, they were turning out around 50 winners a year from a stable of 32 horses.

They had started, says Michael Dickinson, very much as amateurs. 'When my father first took out a licence, it took us from August to Easter to get the first winner. It was a culture shock. We didn't have a clue what we were doing. We were amateurs tripping our way through, but both my parents were very good horsemen [sic] and that helped us to get through. My mother [as Monica Birtwhistle] had showjumped for Great Britain.'

It was still very much the farming life. Michael remembers asking one rider at a point-to-point where they had won a race, 'Why didn't you run in the last race instead of this one early on the card – you would have won that.' The reply was: 'Couldn't do that. I had to get back in time to milk the cows.'

By 1976, Tony Dickinson was voted National Hunt trainer of the year by the Horserace Writers Association and, as the Dickinsons progressed, the duo became a triumvirate with their lanky son, Michael, becoming first, the champion amateur jockey and then for ten years a leading professional rider, before taking over the training licence. Of the early days, Michael remembers, 'We only ever saw Cheltenham on television. My first recollection of Cheltenham is that when I was 15 at school, I skipped a Latin lesson – and I liked Latin – to watch Dunkirk

Michael Dickinson back home with the five horses who helped him achieve the unprecedented feat of having the first five home in the Cheltenham Gold Cup.

run in the two-mile Champion Chase. Peter O'Sullevan was calling the race, building it up from a slow start, authoritatively, and I knew then I wanted to be in racing.'

When he was 17, Michael Dickinson's parents sent him to Cheltenham-based trainer Frenchie Nicholson, a famous trainer of jockeys as much as of horses. Says Michael, 'He had the reputation of being very strict, and that's why my parents sent me down there, to knock me into shape and teach me discipline. I was there for a year. I remember schooling over hurdles with Tony Murray and Pat Eddery. I used to go in 30 minutes before everyone else to muck out Frenchie's pony. I helped him build all the fences and hurdles with gorse, which we cut on the top of Cleeve Hill. [Nicholson used gloves, but didn't give any to his pupil.] To reward my efforts, he gave me some rides over hurdles. I doubt that my ability then warranted any rides. I wasn't really fit to ride a bicycle, but I worked hard and I was rewarded.'

There was another significant early influence. 'In those days there was a closed season of eight weeks. The other jockeys went on holiday to chase girls. I went to Vincent O'Brien at Ballydoyle. The two summers I spent at Ballydoyle were the two happiest times of my life. Vincent created the perfect world for horse and rider. Many people like to credit Vincent O'Brien's success to his attention to detail but they miss the main point. Vincent's main strength was that he got the fundamentals correct.'

At Ballydoyle the young Dickinson got to ride Classic horses – and a champion sprinter – and he soaked up all the knowledge he could absorb from O'Brien's head lad, Johnny Brabston. 'Johnny Brab took me under his wing and taught me. He had the gift of making complicated matters seem so perfectly simple. Watching the Ballydoyle machine work made training look so easy, when of course we know it isn't. We didn't really know what we were doing in our amateur days. You go to Vincent and suddenly all the answers were there. It was like going into a quiz and turning over the paper and finding the answers written on the back. It was just fantastic. The O'Briens were great to me.'

For a man as tall as Michael Dickinson, slim though he remains to this day, there were the usual problems as a hard-working young jockey.

Michael Dickinson at Cheltenham raising a Gold Cup goblet.

'I lived on Ryvita and Marmite because it didn't need much of that to give you a taste. It was that and a suck of my toothbrush. I used to go for runs at night in the countryside in the pitch black across the fields. I remember one day riding out two lots in the morning. I then drove 110 miles to Teesside Park and rode in five races before driving the 110 miles back. I did the list of horses for the next day then went for a sauna down the road at 7.30 p.m. First thing I knew was that at 2.00 a.m. Dad was banging on the door to wake me up. I was knackered.'

At that time there were still plenty of happy-go-lucky lads in the weighing room and a few bottles of Guinness to be found under the benches, but that side of the jockey's life was not for Dickinson. One reason was that Gisburn was 50 miles from the nearest trainer – and he was an assistant trainer as well as a jockey. Another reason was 'If I had half a glass of anything, I passed out.' As for the riding, he says, 'I wasn't very good over hurdles. If you wanted to be kind, I was better over fences. I had more JWs [the abbreviation meaning that a horse Jumped Well] than anybody in the race reports.'

The Dickinson horses did not always go unbacked. Michael confirms that in one particular year, father Tony, who in 1979 trained more winners than anyone else in the country, had nine bets – and eight of them won. 'When we moved to Harewood, we suddenly became better trainers, and all the horses were too short-priced to have a bet. We wouldn't get a price. So in the end, we had a big bet on Dad training the most winners because everything else was 4-5. In a field which included Fred Winter, Fred Rimell and Fulke Walwyn, we were about 10-1. We took all the prices down to 4-1 for Dad to be leading trainer. My last season [having succeeded his father with the training licence], we had 100 runners and 51 winners. We couldn't bet then.' Michael is not, however, averse to an occasional bet himself. His wife, Joan Wakefield, had £20,000 on a horse called Union One – and it paid for a mile of hard-top tarmacadam road on their Tapeta Farm estate. They call it 'Union Avenue.'

Tony Dickinson was affectionately known

as 'The Boss', while his wife Monica was 'Mrs D' to all. She was to train 149 winners in her own right but played a significant role too in the 941 trained by her son and her husband. Graham Bradley, one of their stable jockeys for ten years, puts it this way: 'It was a real family business. Boss bought them, Mrs D looked after them and fed them, and Michael, who also rode them early on, plotted up where they should run with the military precision of a field marshal.' Sir Peter O'Sullevan said on Mrs Dickinson's death in 2008 that the popular horsewoman had been 'a driving force in one of the most efficient National Hunt racing production teams in the country.'

Michael recalls: 'My mother was a brilliant feeder because she had passion for the job, a love of the horse, and she and Brian Powell, our head man, knew exactly how much each horse would eat at every meal on any given day. Some people like to say they work hard but not many people could outwork Mrs D. She would feed the horses – 55 of them – at 6 a.m., again at lunchtime and at 5 p.m. She would ride out first lot, cook us all breakfast, then ride out second lot. At the other end of the day, if any of the horses were late back from the races, she would always have some hot feed ready on her kitchen stove waiting for the runners that came back from the big southern meetings, even if it was 9 o'clock at night.'

Says Michael, 'My father and I liked the smaller, lighter, athletic horses. Because we were always outbid at the sales by the big southern trainers, many of our horses were by little-known sires. Every time we went to the sales, we were blown out of the water, and my father was fond of saying, "At least we haven't spent any daft money." There were times when I was frustrated with my father's conservative approach, and I went to Ireland myself several times and bought some unbroken three-year-olds with my own money. Aged 22, I obviously didn't know a whole lot, and I am sure the Irish dealers welcomed me with open arms: "Here comes this guy in short trousers." Putting up your own money is a learning experience and you learn quickly, but thankfully I did buy some good horses. My father would roll in his grave

at the prices now being paid for jumpers. It is madness. I wouldn't dream of training jumpers now in this environment. I wouldn't want to handle 200 horses and I wouldn't pay these prices for them.'

The Dickinsons also had a useful ally. Trainer and larger-scale punter Barney Curley used to look out for suitable purchases for them. 'Barney was very good at spotting horses and we would buy them. The condition was that we would let him know first time when we had them ready. I don't know if that would be allowed these days. Barney was great.'

Michael Dickinson was, and is, a true original, a restless thinker, forever experimenting with new methods and techniques. He would seek information from everywhere, talking to top athletes about conditioning, or football ground staff about turf quality: 'I had dinner with Michael Stoute during the Olympic Games, or it might have been the Commonwealth Games, when human athletes were breaking all the records. Stoutey said to me, "Wouldn't it be great if we could find out how they train all these people?" So I arranged to see the doctor to the British team and another guy who did all the testing. We had about eight meetings with these people, Stoutey and I did, and the next year he trained Shergar to win the Derby, and I won the Gold Cup with Silver Buck.'

Michael quit the saddle after a serious kidney injury. When he took over the training licence from his father, he rapidly became champion National Hunt trainer in Britain for three years in a row. In 1982, he trained the first two home in the Cheltenham Gold Cup (see page 38), and the following year, he trumped that by training the first five horses home in the Gold Cup: Bregawn, Captain John, Wayward Lad, Silver Buck and Ashley House. The remarkable thing is that neither Michael nor his wife, Joan Wakefield, were surprised by such an incredible result.

Michael explains: 'After the previous year's Gold Cup when Joan said, "Well done", I said, "You ain't seen nothing yet. Next year we will have the first eight." Every time we got in the car together, I would do a commentary in [radio commentator] Peter Bromley's style, anticipating the 1983 race and taking them from fence to fence. "Bregawn is forcing the pace. Now Wayward Lad is making steady and relentless progress. At the second-last, there is a mistake by Captain John … now they're coming to the last…" What I didn't do was to say which horse won. I used to end the commentary by saying, "The one thing that's certain is that the Gold Cup is going to Harewood." She had heard this commentary 50 times…'

Joan was then a schoolteacher in Durham and the school would not allow her to take the day off on Gold Cup day in 1983, so she smuggled in a radio and set her class a task to keep them quiet while she plugged in and listened to the race. She heard Peter Bromley virtually repeating, word for word, Michael's practice version, thinking, 'I've heard all this before.' The only thing that changed was that, at the last, Peter Bromley said, 'One thing is certain: the Gold Cup is going to the Dickinsons.' At which point, she burst into tears.

In fact, Michael was, and remains, a little disappointed by that famous Gold Cup result and still reproaches himself over it. On Boxing Day in 1982, he had achieved another phenomenal record by sending out 12 winners across the country's racetracks, including Wayward Lad's victory in the King George VI Chase at Kempton. Joan remembers: 'We'd only had seven of them when we got in the car and left Kempton to go home. Then they started interrupting the football commentaries to say, "Michael Dickinson has had another winner." We had to keep stopping as we passed betting shops so I could go in and check if we'd had another one…'

But the next day, as he began to prepare for Cheltenham, everything started to go wrong: 'Ashley House got beat, Captain John made a mistake in the Welsh National. He was favourite and he finished down the field. He was lame and, after that, they all went wrong. I said to [head lad] Brian Powell in mid-February, "Last year we had had first and second in the Gold Cup, this year I'm not going to have a runner." It was hero to zero. Leading up to Cheltenham, I lost 14 pounds with worry. I knew the horses

were good enough but I also knew the best two weren't right, and I felt really guilty about asking them to go into it when they were not fully prepared. To this day, I am not proud of myself. They weren't right. I was sorry to see Silver Buck jump the last in fourth place. It was distressing for me – and it still is.'

He won his first trainers' title by sending out 84 winners at a strike rate of 45 per cent, and his second in 1982/83 with 120 winners at a strike rate of 46 per cent, setting a whole new level of achievement despite being unable to match the prices paid at public auctions by southern-based trainers with big-money owners. Many of the victories were with horses by stallions nobody had heard of, bought out of a field in Cork or Tipperary. 'When we won the title, we attributed it to many things, lots of reasons, but essentially we marched to the beat of a different drum. We were non-conventional and made many changes from the norm. We were lucky enough to have good horses and a fantastic team of boys. 17 of our 22 lads had ridden winners.

'We only had 55 stables, that was all there was room for. Nobody had big strings like they do nowadays. That was the norm, and that was the way it should be really. You can only do the big strings with a good head lad who is in charge of another 25, and an assistant who is in charge of another 25. You have to have yard managers.'

Former champion jockey Peter Scudamore recalls that it was difficult to ride against the horses trained by Michael Dickinson because they were very fit and often made the running: 'We all had tactics to try to beat the Dickinson horses. If you rode up with them, your trainer would complain you were making too much use of your horse, but if you dropped in behind, you were accused of giving your horse too much to do at the end of the race. Consequently, there was a psychological challenge as well as a physical challenge in competing against his horses.'

As often happens with innovators, Michael suffered from jealous rivals, who spread unfounded rumours of drug abuse and blood doping, just as would happen later with a Somerset-based trainer making his way up, who sought out Michael Dickinson for advice and became a friend – a certain Martin Pipe. Michael has always gone his own way. In 2015, when he was planning a comeback to start training flat-racing horses in America, he decided he had better have a medical to ensure that he was fit enough to bear the strain of a relaunch. He tells the story himself: 'When I went for the check-up, I passed 29 of the 30 tests but the doctor said, "You need to keep exercising to keep a healthy brain. What do you do?" "Oh, that's fine. I run a mile a day, and 10 miles on Saturday when I go out with the hunt." "You mean you *ride* 10 miles with the hunt?" "No. I run it." "Well, in that case, you've come to see the wrong doctor – it's a psychiatrist you need!"'

The Pipe connection has continued over the years. Joan has not forgotten the sight when Martin and Carol Pipe came to stay with them in America: the two obsessives that were Martin and Michael went around the place talking constantly, one with a dictaphone in his hand, and the other with a notepad, comparing their views and experiences. Both have this continuing thirst for knowledge.

Michael Dickinson's domination of the British jumping scene might have continued much longer, except for the fact that – following his three championships – flat-racing tycoon Robert Sangster headhunted him to be his private trainer at the famous Manton estate in Wiltshire. That venture did not work out, but Michael later proved himself on the flat in America, winning the Breeders Cup Mile with Da Hoss both in 1996 and 1998, despite being able to race him only once in-between those victories. He also invented the Tapeta synthetic racing surface. Michael has recently returned to training in America.

By the time Michael Dickinson left Harewood for the south of England, his father was suffering health problems and it was his mother, Monica, who then took over the training licence in Yorkshire. She also did so well that – had it not been for the behaviour of Browne's Gazette, the odds-on favourite in the 1985 Champion Hurdle – it is likely that she would have been the first woman to become champion trainer in Britain.

Browne's Gazette had already won the Fighting Fifth Hurdle at Newcastle, the Bula Hurdle at Cheltenham and the Christmas Hurdle at Kempton Park, beating a certain Desert Orchid by 15 lengths. Browne's Gazette was ridden in the Champion Hurdle by Dermot Browne, then a talented Irish amateur; six years later, however, he became a racing outcast when in 1991 he was 'warned off' for ten years by the Jockey Club after admitting to doping a number of horses as the infamous 'Needleman.' As the starter despatched the 1985 Champion Hurdle field, Browne's Gazette lurched off violently to the left and missed the break. Even though he made up much of the lost ground, the effort cost him dearly and he had nothing left at the end of the race, finishing sixth. Nobody will ever know whether Browne's Gazette's behaviour at the start was by accident or design, but it was a cruel blow for the Dickinsons. Says Michael, 'I don't believe Mrs D blamed Dermot. My own reading of the matter was that the horse, the starter and Dermot were all a tiny bit to blame. The horse was highly strung, and I don't believe Dermot did it on purpose. Dermot was a good kid then; the troubles came later.'

The top jumpers trained at Harewood included Badsworth Boy, an exhilarating jumper, very quick through the air, who won the Queen Mother Champion Chase at Cheltenham three years in a row, including by a 30-length margin in the year of Dickinson's 'Famous Five.' Another star was Wayward Lad, a triple winner of the King George VI Chase. Other

Wayward Lad in the hands of Jonjo O'Neill.

stars included Bregawn, Gay Spartan, I'm A Driver, Rathgorman and Silver Buck, the nervy star known in the yard as 'Bucket', who tended to 'down tools' whenever he took the lead. John Francome said of him, 'He's a super horse until he hits the front. Then he wants ten men on him!' Michael agrees: 'Silver Buck used to stop when he got to the front. When he won his Gold Cup, he was cruising, but then he hit the front a bit too soon. He was an easy ride until he got to the front but he never lost a race he should have won. He never won by more than a length or so, but it was a great race, that.'

Graham Bradley's autobiography, *The Wayward Lad*, cast an interesting sidelight on Michael Dickinson's decision to accept Sangster's offer. One of Michael's senior staff, George Foster, who looked after any sick horses and later became a trainer himself, had asked for Saturday off to go to a wedding in Scotland, but when Saturday came, he was still in the

One of the Dickinsons' best horses, Silver Buck, with rider Tommy Carmody. The combination twice won the King George VI Chase at Kempton.

yard: why? The electricity bill had arrived and Foster told Michael Dickinson that he had faced a choice: he could either pay that or go to Scotland; he could not afford to do both. Says the trainer: 'It brought it home to me that despite all the success and training 100 winners a season, I couldn't pay these excellent people enough to make a decent living – so when the Manton offer came along, I took it.'

Nicky Henderson
Champion Trainer 1985–87, 2012/13

Nicky Henderson and his Steven Barrows yard are part of the weft and warp of jumping history. Nobody has trained more Cheltenham Festival winners than the 55 he had to his name by the end of the 2016 Festival, which – to the joy of thousands – saw Henderson's beloved Sprinter Sacre leap back on top of his pantheon. Nicky's father, Johnny, who has a Festival race named after him, helped to save Cheltenham from developers and he also set up the Jockey Club's racetrack-owning arm, which pours money back into the sport.

Nicky is sensitive to racing history: 'Do you know this is the first time that National Hunt horses have ever been trained at Seven Barrows? It's been flat since 1860. It's been here 160 years and it's the first time those gallops have ever had jumpers on them.' His love affair with racing, he told us there over lunch began early.

'At Eton, you didn't get expelled for smoking, drinking or women – not unless you were caught in bed with two women, smoking a cigarette and drinking whisky. But going racing really was a serious crime. We went to see Arkle in the Hennessy at Newbury, setting off in an old Morris Minor on the day when they play the Field Game against the old boys. We couldn't go into the Members, at least I couldn't, because Dad was stewarding, but we went down to stand by the last fence where Arkle jumped upsides Stalbridge Colonist, who went on to win. We got back in time for roll call and all was fine except that Arkle was the only horse in the world who could get his picture onto the front page of the Sunday papers. There he was, jumping the last fence, and there were three little men in the background, clearly identifiable. On the Monday morning, I met the headmaster, Anthony Chenevix-Trench, for the first and last time.' Nicky escaped comparatively lightly because his tutor, Michael Kitson, had accompanied the boys on what he persuaded the head was an 'educational' trip.

'All the other boys had pictures of naked

women on their walls, calendars or "page-three" girls. I had a picture of David Nicholson riding Mill House and winning the Whitbread. I finally got him to sign it two years before he died. I adored Mill House and always did.'

After a fruitless attempt by the family to get him to settle in the City, Nicky Henderson had a fateful meeting with Fred Winter, who was a friend of his parents. 'I was riding a bit, eventing and that kind of thing, and one summer I spent a couple of months with Lars Siederholm, who was a very smart eventing coach, a sort of Yogi Breisner of his day. It was all dressage, dressage, dressage, and he completely changed my style of riding. I'd just come back from Lars' and I was sort of poncing about like a Swedish dressage rider, and Fred came up and said, "Who in the world taught you to ride with your hands in your balls?" I said, "Lars Siederholm," and he said, "Come round to my yard tomorrow morning and I'll teach you to ride properly." I'd never sat on a racehorse in my life. I thought that was absolutely wonderful. That was it.

'The first ride I had was at Plumpton for Fred on a horse owned by my parents. Fred said to John Oaksey, "Look after the boy, would you." J. Oaksey did. He said, "Follow me wherever I go," and so I did. He was in the lead and I followed him, and we got to the water – it's gone now – which was three out. I was still following him, I had no idea where I was going. John Oaksey hated water jumps and he fell at the water and I did too. He had told me to follow him and I did. In the car going home, Fred confessed that in his riding days he refused to ride over fences at Plumpton.' By the time Henderson's riding career ended, he had ridden 75 winners, including an Imperial Cup on Acquaint for Fred Winter and the Aintree Fox Hunters' Chase on Happy Warrior.

Conversation at Seven Barrows tends to be interrupted by owners and others dropping in to the trophy-bedecked premises as if calling in to their favourite club. It might be 'Kimbo' – Malcolm Kimmins – part-owner of Gold Cup winner Bobs Worth, or 'Minty', David Minton of Highflyer Bloodstock, who sources many of

Sprinter Sacre gets up close and personal with trainer Nicky Henderson.

Henderson's stars. The trainer reckons himself lucky as he trains almost entirely for people whom he regards as friends. He admits: 'I'm quite a social animal. Yesterday we had 14 for lunch. Owners and mates, a huge dent in the cellar … you want to see people, it's fun. It's a lovely thing to do and it's fun to have people to do it with. There are no guarantees. All we can guarantee is a few laughs. There are plenty of things you can throw money at and it will work, but this isn't one.'

But when you join Henderson in the 4x4, slithering up to the gallops, or try to keep pace with him bounding across the yard to watch the string jig-jogging around the covered ride before heading out, there is no doubting the seriousness of purpose, the attention to detail, the restless energy that he devotes to his charges. It is easy to forget just how long he has been around the pinnacle of jump racing.

The Grand National apart, in which he has twice trained the runner-up, there is scarcely a race of consequence he has not taken. He won the Cheltenham Gold Cup with Long Run in 2011, and with Bobs Worth, a £20,000 purchase, in 2013. He took the Champion Hurdle three times with See You Then, from 1985 to 1987, and then with Punjabi (2009) and Binocular (2010). He won the Queen Mother Champion

Chase with Finian's Rainbow in 2012, and saw the spectacular Sprinter Sacre murder his field by 19 lengths in 2013 and then return after two years of injury to recapture his crown gloriously in 2016. He took the Arkle with the bold-jumping Remittance Man in 1991, and then with Travado (1993), Tiutchev (2000), Sprinter Sacre (2012) and Simonsig (2013). He has won the ultra-competitive Triumph Hurdle with First Bout (1985), Alone Success (1987), Zaynar (2009), Soldatino (2010), and Peace And Co in 2015, in which year he supplied the second and third as well.

Among his 2,000-plus winners, Nicky Henderson has won the King George VI Chase twice with Long Run (2011 and 2012), the bet365 Gold Cup (formerly the Whitbread) twice (with Brown Windsor in 1989 and Hadrian's Approach in 2014), and the Hennessy Gold Cup three times with Trabolgan in 2005, Bobs Worth in 2012 and Triolo d'Alene in 2013. Like his friend and rival, Paul Nicholls at Ditcheat, he has also given something back to racing by training a series of able assistants, who have since made their own mark on the

sport, in his case including Ed Dunlop, Charlie Mann, Charlie Longsdon, Jamie Snowden, Ben Pauling, Harry Dunlop and Tom Symonds.

One of the enjoyable things about spending time with Nicky Henderson is to hear him talk about those Festival winners, something he does with affection and with humour.

See You Then, who had legs like glass and could be raced so rarely that the racing press nicknamed him 'See You When?', was typical of Nicky's attention to detail. Steve Smith-Eccles, who rode him to all three Champion Hurdle victories, believes that See You Then's second success in 1986, a year when much racing was frosted off, was achieved only because his trainer drove a tractor at intervals through the night to keep the all-weather strip at his stables useable when many trainers were unable to work their horses. He said of Henderson's feat: 'Winning two Champion Hurdles with such a horse would have been an outstanding training achievement. To win three was a horseracing miracle.'

See You Then was not only a permanent potential invalid but a savage too. Henderson explains: 'He was a wonderful horse outside, but inside the box he was a brute. He would eat people. Glyn Foster looked after him all his life and got bitten and kicked to ribbons over the years. Corky Browne [Henderson's head lad] and I couldn't go in the box without him. Nor could vet Frank Mahon. We ran See You Then just once, in the last year, before Cheltenham. It was obviously going to be a tense night afterwards, waiting to see what was going to happen to his legs. I woke up in the early hours and thought, "I'm going to go into that box and take those bandages off," knowing full well that I couldn't really go into the box without Glyn. I went downstairs and to his box and, oh my God, the door was open ... there was Frank Mahon sat on the manger. I said, "What are you doing?" and he replied, "I couldn't sleep. I thought I'd come and take those bandages off and see how he was." "So why are you up there?" He replied, "He won't let me out!"'

Then there was the two-mile chaser, Remittance Man. 'He was a terrible worrier and box-walker. He used to pace round and round

See You Then: the horse with delicate legs whom Nicky Henderson trained to win three Champion Hurdles.

his box, so we put a sheep in with him. The first sheep was nicknamed "Alan Lamb" and then we had "Ridley Lamb" and "Nobby Lamb" – the sheep came from Dad's flock. When Nobby went home for the summer and joined his mates, another sheep was sent. Remittance Man flung it out, literally. He picked it up and chucked it out of the door. We put it back in. Much fur flew – and then out it came again. I thought, "We can't do this to the poor sheep," so I had to go back to Dad's flock and look for Nobby, not easy with four hundred of them. Amazingly, we sent in a horse, and 399 of the sheep went one way, and one came out, and that was Nobby. From then on, we used to put a blue blob on Nobby's backside when he went home for his summer holidays!'

Some comebacks take longer than others. George Foreman, the 'Punching Preacher', won the world heavyweight boxing title for the first time in 1973, lost it to Muhammad Ali (Cassius Clay) in 1974, and did not regain it until 1994, at the age of 45. When Nicky Henderson was champion jumps trainer in the 2012/13 season, it was not for the first time. Yet he had been

without the title for a while. The previous seasons in which he had been champion were 1985/86 and 1986/87. Before he regained it, briefly, the title had been divided for 22 years between Martin Pipe (15) and Paul Nicholls (7). 'Most of Paul's years, I've been second to him. One year, we were ahead of him before the National, and everyone said, "You'll get it now", and then he goes and wins the National!'

From 1974 to 1978 Nicky Henderson was assistant trainer to Fred Winter and he remembers vividly the Lambourn life of the Winter–Walwyn days.

'There was intense rivalry. Between [Fred Winter's] Uplands and [Fulke Walwyn's] Saxon House, there was only a wall. It was "over the wall" – that was how we talked about it. If we were talking about one of their horses, it was, "over the wall's going to be running that" or, "over the wall's doing this." But I am sure they were the best of mates.

'With Fred, I was second in the amateur thing [the jockeys' championship] a couple of times. When Fred was champion trainer, he ran

On Henderson's gallops at Seven Barrows, Lambourn.

48 horses. Now, we're all dealing in hundreds, but with around 48 horses, he had 100 winners. They were the big yards, the all-powerful yards, but he and Walwyn wouldn't have had 50 horses.

'There were two very defining eras, one when Michael Dickinson came along and changed National Hunt training quite a bit. He used to do relentlessly slow gallops, short work, miles and miles and miles of it. Then there was one period of post-Dickinson, pre-Pipe training life. Luckily I was learning in those years and we had two good years.

'I was champion trainer for those two years in-between, before someone called Martin Pipe turned up and did something completely different. He was just up and down, up and down a hill, nothing else. Totally opposite to Dickinson. But they were the two dominant trainers of that period.'

Zara Phillips embraces winning trainer Nicky Henderson after Sprinter Sacre's victory.

Didn't Peter Cazalet do something similar before them? 'He only had the park which was about five furlongs long. What they were all doing was training to the facilities they had got. We're very lucky here in that we've got these amazing grass gallops that have been here for 160 years. They've never been touched and they are just the most beautiful ground. I'd be pretty sure that if Michael Dickinson had had these gallops, he would have used them as you would. Martin trained as he did because that was what he had got. Nowadays anybody can train anywhere – and I don't mean this the wrong way. You don't need to have acres of land to train a horse. You used to have to, because you needed gallops. Now you only need an all-weather gallop, a six-furlong strip – up a hill, I'd have to suggest – and you can train.'

Feeding methods too have altered, he agrees. 'Again, that has changed dramatically. Science has come into this a lot. It's natural progression because people have become a lot more scientific. We've found out a lot more about why a horse does this, why it does that, what it needs. In the old days, they just lived on oats, that was it.' But didn't trainers pride themselves on their feeding with linseed mashes and all that? 'They used to have linseed mashes twice a week. Pendil used to have a bottle of Guinness. In fact, one of my jobs as assistant was to get the bottles of Guinness from the village for Pendil, Bula and Killiney. Brian Delaney used to dish it out every night. And eggs, Pendil used to have his Guinness and eggs. Arkle used to have his bottle of stout too.' That would probably be illegal today. Imagine a Gold Cup victor disqualified because the horse, not the jockey, had failed a breath test.

When he started up on his own in 1978, was he dealing purely with stoutly bred Irish horses? 'You were. Nowadays you can be breaking them in at three and four. In those days, at four, they'd be in a field unbroken. The game has completely changed. They were great big old-fashioned beasts and they were ignorant because they weren't touched until they were four.' But that was until the French-breds became fashionable? 'It has changed quite dramatically. It wasn't

long ago that you wouldn't buy a three-year-old because it was going to take you too long. Nowadays you wouldn't buy a four-year-old because you would assume that if it was any good, it would have been sold at three. So you wouldn't touch it.

'Johnny Harrington used to be my first port of call as a bloodstock agent in Ireland. Now we don't go over at all. We used to buy everything in Ireland, bumper horses, point-to-pointers. We used to go over there a lot. No point going now. If somebody rings up on Sunday and says, "I saw a seriously nice point-to-pointer winning the maiden at Ballygobackwards", you can guarantee ten others have seen it. It will have been sold on Sunday night – whoosh – and on the boat over. I used to go over and ride them and try them out. Now you don't even go over.

'Everything's changed. You used to put great big boots [gaiters] on the horses. You wouldn't do it now because science has told us why we were wrong to do it. It was creating too much heat in the leg so it was expanding. We don't even run horses in boots now. We would all say that we get far less leg trouble, tendon trouble, because we don't wear boots. We wear bandages at home but you can't race them in bandages because of the weight they'd finish up on a soggy day.

'We had some cracking old "backs men" but when a horse was lame nobody knew what was happening, and you just locked him up in his box until he was sound. You didn't have bone scans, you could hardly X-ray, you couldn't scan tendons. It was all down to the vets, who were spectacular men: Frank Mahon was a legendary vet here.

'You didn't have scopes. When a horse made a certain noise, you had him hobdayed [operated on, to clear his breathing passages]. We have learned so much more about how a horse operates. Research has discovered that if you do this, you'll get that. The big thing at the moment is ulcers. Five or six years ago, we knew nothing about ulcers, now every horse is being treated for them.'

Nicky Henderson used to duck out of work in the City in order to ride, but when the family was devastated by his mother's fatal accident

Nicky Henderson in 2012 with his long time stable jockey Mick Fitzgerald.

out hunting, he agreed with his father to enrol for an agricultural course at Cirencester. He had reckoned he would farm and have a few horses. But after his time with Fred Winter, it had to be training. Fred Rimell tried once to tempt him to Kinnersley but Nicky's friend, Roger Charlton, then a fellow Lambourn bachelor who owned the Windsor House stables, was offered a job as assistant to flat-racing trainer Jeremy Tree. Charlton then sold his stable yard and equine swimming pool to the Hendersons in 1978 – and a career was launched. As Nicky puts it now: 'I didn't do too badly at the end of the day – it didn't screw up the inheritance.' There was another big move in 1992 when flat-racing trainer Peter Walwyn wanted to move from Seven Barrows to Windsor House, and he and Nicky Henderson swapped premises. Amid many other changes, Henderson had to learn how to use those famous gallops to their best advantage.

'Millions of things have happened. We've got Sunday racing, which I don't agree with personally. I don't like it because it hasn't delivered what they promised we would get, which was proper racing. There's no good racing on a Sunday. It was virtually guaranteed to be a golden egg, and there's nothing golden about it.'

Schooling and riding techniques have altered too. 'Now, we've got Yogi Breisner [the jumping expert who has coached famous horses, jockeys and showjumping Olympians] for teaching. He comes and helps my young boys a lot. He sees the kids who will get onto a racehorse at some stage. He sees them in the indoor school and does showjumping with a lot of the horses in the indoor school now.

'And there's another change. Remember we had only 45–50 horses maximum at Fred's. In any given season, there were probably only four or five that had never jumped before. Now we are talking about 150. That's a lot of horses to educate to jump.

'[In Fred Winter's time] We'd have this old lead horse and you'd have a little hurdle, and the jockey would get on the three or four-year-old and the lead horse would canter up to the fence [hurdle], and the young horse would probably refuse. After three attempts, it would probably have clambered over this thing one-foot high. Then you followed up and did it again and again. Then you'd move up a size … and

that was the first day it ever learned to jump – with a jockey on its back. Just facing into a hurdle and saying, "get the other side." Since then, we've had Captain Charles Radclyffe, the pioneer of loose schooling. All the Queen Mother's horses started with him, and now we all start in loose schools.'

So how does the showjumping style help? 'It teaches you how to work it out and learn to make a shape. It's not just about how to get to the other side, it's about how to jump proficiently at speed. I'm pretty sure they've come on a fair bit. That was how we used to do it. The Captain used to do the loose schooling and that's undoubtedly very good. Now horses come from France and that's brilliant because they're used to jumping every day. They can jump with their eyes shut. They're racing them as two-year-olds, jumping them as two-year-olds. Jumping has changed and jockeys have changed a lot.

Nicky Henderson with Barry Geraghty in the Royal colours after winning for the Queen with Close Touch.

'All-weather racing has had a big effect on the whole racing scene. I don't think it's been totally detrimental to NH racing. It has affected it. I'm sure the flat boys are going to say it's great. But if everybody wants wall-to-wall moderate flat racing, there's no doubt it has chewed into the jump-racing programme. It's a substitute. It was meant to be there, in the first instance, to cover for NH racing when we lost days to a freeze-up. Now it's five days a week.

'There's no doubt it has impinged on NH racing. We get far less horses off the flat now, and don't buy them because they are not for sale half the time. The expensive boys, yes, but there used to be a lot of horses coming every year, switching codes. Now, trainers want to keep their horses, not have them sent off here during the winter.

'Sadly, the whole racing programme panders to mediocrity – and that is certainly the case in jumping. There are millions of opportunities for bad horses. They've got this amazing notion: they are absolutely paranoid about small fields.'

Asked what makes Henderson such a successful trainer, his long-time former stable jockey Mick Fitzgerald pays tribute, for example, to his acute race-reading. But he sums up the rest by saying simply: 'He's a good man to have dealings with. There's never any underhand business. He wouldn't take horses off other people. He's a gentleman.'

Which is perhaps why the largely traditionalist Henderson does have two grievances about how things are going. 'There are rules of etiquette in the game, which I think sadly have lapsed. Nowadays you have to keep your eyes open. There are hungry young guys on the lookout for horses. It wasn't the done thing when I began. If you did do that, you would always ring the other trainer. People don't bother any longer to do that. It is the same with staff. Rules of racing say that you should ask the previous employer for a reference. You would think that was common sense, and the rules state you have to, but it is amazing how few do. And another thing that makes me sad is that people say things on paper, in e-mails, they would never say to your face or on the telephone.'

The only blot on Henderson's record came in 2009 when a BHA panel found him in breach of the rules of racing over the presence of an anti-bleeding agent in the bloodstream of Moonlit Path, a mare he trained for the Queen. Even though he insisted that the drug had been administered for the animal's welfare, and not to enhance performance, an embarrassed Henderson was banned from having runners for three months and fined £40,000.

Nicky remains an optimist about the future of jump racing and the special atmosphere it can create – as it did for the late Lynn Wilson, owner of Blue Royal. 'Blue Royal actually jumped the last ahead of Istabraq in his third year. We were in the unsaddling enclosure, and when Istabraq came in, the Irish noise was quite ridiculous. Lynn is dead now, but he said to me, "This is one moment of my life that I will never, ever forget." The privilege was being in that unsaddling enclosure as part of the race that this amazing atmosphere was built around, being part of what had happened, Istabraq's third Champion Hurdle. Lynn had done lots of things in his life but he said that was his proudest moment. I understood what he meant and luckily we have been there when you see those Sprinter Sacre scenes. It's those sort of things that keep you going through the long, dark mornings in the middle of the winter when the horses are all wrong – and you wonder why you keep hammering away. People want to be part of it.'

If he does have one niggling regret, it is neither about a victory lost nor even about a horse. Many years ago, he relates, he and Barry Hills and Jimmy Lindley, and one or two others, enjoyed a fine lunch with owner Ernie Harrison, the boss of Racal, at the Dundas Arms in Kintbury. Afterwards, their host insisted, 'I'm going to show you something that will change your lives.' In the car park, he pulled out of a suitcase a prototype and said, 'Just watch. You won't believe this. Without any wires, I am going to make a telephone call.' He duly demonstrated the first mobile phone they had all seen – and offered one to each of them for £1,000. Says Nicky: 'We were all so full of his wonderful sales talk that most of us bought one. The phone was the size of a brick and the battery would have powered a car.' Within no time, their phones were obsolete. 'Somewhere in the attic, I've still got my original phone. I shall give it to my children, who will give it to theirs, and it will be worth a lot more than what we paid for it. But if we had each put that £1,000, instead, into shares at that time in Racal, we would have had something like £11 million pounds now. So weren't we stupid?'

David Elsworth
Champion Trainer 1987/88

Some top jumps trainers handle a few flat-racing horses on the side in summer. Some flat-racing trainers indulge themselves with a few hurdlers to keep the staff interested through the winter. Those who have achieved serious and consistent success both on the flat and over the

jumps can be counted on the fingers of one hand … you start with Vincent O'Brien, Ryan Price, Peter Easterby, and pretty well immediately you come to David Elsworth. Over the jumps, his successes included a Cheltenham Gold Cup a Grand National, four King George VI Chases, two Champion Chases, a Whitbread Gold Cup, and a Hennessy Gold Cup. On the flat, he has trained Classic and Group One winners, ranging from long-distance events to five-furlong sprints – and is still doing so. But 'Elzee' has a particular qualification: he shaped the shining careers of two horses who were adopted by the racing public as national treasures, the grey chaser Desert Orchid and the battling flat stayer Persian Punch. At times, he has seemed not far short of that status himself.

Racing folk have met all the versions of David Elsworth, a man who filled one career gap with a stint as a market trader, yet who is

Another of those frosty mornings. On the Seven Barrows gallops with jockey Jerry McGrath and Hunt Ball.

equally at home on any smart country-estate shoot. Some have encountered the cheery, hail-fellow-well-met, racecourse-bar raconteur, some the emotional and slightly chippy resenter of officialdom or the media. Whichever Elsworth is uppermost in their minds, all seem agreed that this complex man has an instinctive flair for understanding and bringing the best out of the horses who pass through his hands – from the crack two-mile chaser, Barnbrook Again, to In The Groove, the European champion filly of 1990, who won the Irish 1,000 Guineas, the Juddmonte International, the Champion Stakes and the Coronation Cup.

In 2006, David Elsworth relocated from Whitsbury in Hampshire to Newmarket, where in recent years he has handled smaller numbers but still proved capable of capturing big races, as when Jeff Smith's Arabian Queen caused the shock of the year in August 2015 by defeating previously unbeaten Derby winner Golden Horn in the Juddmonte International at York. Jumping fans remember him best, however, for the days when he handled nearly 150 horses at Whitsbury, when the Elsworth contingent was a squad to be reckoned with at Aintree, Kempton or Cheltenham. At one stage, he trained from another base, at Whitcombe Manor in Dorset.

Brought up by his grandparents in a Wiltshire council house, David Elsworth never got to suck on a silver spoon. He wasn't introduced to racing by a family pony, but by riding a bicycle with his ferret, his lurcher and an air rifle to the downland at Herridge to plunder the rabbits that he could skin and sell for half a crown a time to supplement his paper-round earnings.

Periodically occupying that same downland were the racehorses trained by the careful Scotsman Alec Kilpatrick; in January 1955, the young Elsworth knocked on the back door and got himself a month's trial with Kilpatrick, before returning with his suitcase on the handlebars of his bike. 'He [Kilpatrick] had around 25 horses, which was normal for trainers then, but the accommodation was basic and I nearly froze to death. I was paid £1 a week living in. He gave me five shillings and kept the rest as my "clothing allowance." If I asked for

David Elsworth, who now concentrates on the flat, in his Newmarket yard.

a new sweater, he would say, "I'll see if I can find one." It was supposed to be £2 a week in the second year and £3 a week in the third year of a three-year apprenticeship, but he overlooked the rise. I didn't have a holiday the first year. In the second year, after six months, he said, "You didn't have a holiday last year did you?" I said, "No, and you haven't given me my rise either", so I went on holiday with £100 or £150, which was a lot of money for a kid then.'

The yearning to be a trainer was there early on, but from 1957 to 1972 an itinerant Elsworth plied his trade as a jump jockey, looking for the opportunities and benefiting from the experience of such trainers as Toby Balding and Doug Marks. 'I rode mostly for small trainers, but while riding, I was helping them to train, I was advising them where to run their horses and so on.

'When I went to [Lieut. Col.] Ricky Vallance as an assistant, I had a couple of horses of my own. I couldn't get a licence because I didn't have the premises. He had some good horses – Red Candle won a Mackeson in 1972 and a Hennessy the next year. We had something like 12 winners from 12 horses. Officially, they were all trained by Ricky but he was the front and I did a lot of the training. Then one horse, Well Briefed, was backed down from a long price and won – and they took away his licence for a year. Johnny Haine rode it and they didn't do anything to him. They thought we had stopped it the time before, but we hadn't. It was unfair because we hadn't done anything wrong. I guess I've been a bit hostile to authority ever since.'

Owing to Lieut. Col. Vallance's perceived misdemeanor, Elsworth himself, despite repeated applications, had to wait for his licence until 1978; he probably only got it then thanks to a word in the right Jockey Club ears from Colonel Sir Piers Bengough, later the Queen's Representative at Ascot, who had known him from the time when one was a Captain and the other a stable lad. It was during that waiting period that David Elsworth worked as a market trader and as a guard at Stonehenge to make ends meet before opening a livery yard.

His first flat winner came with Raffia Set at Bath on the day when the legendary American jockey Steve Cauthen made his racecourse debut in Britain. Raffia Set had previously been with trainer Bill Wightman and was reputed to need firm ground. That day, backed down from

33-1 to 16-1, he won in a bog. From Elzee's first ten runners there were seven or eight winners. More than a thousand more came from his West Country bases and every year he seemed to find at least one good horse. 'I may not have always had the best horse, but I've had stacks of good ones.'

The first season at Whitsbury, he had two winners at Cheltenham, including Heighlin in the 1980 Triumph Hurdle, a race he won again with Oh So Risky in 1991. In the same year, Heighlin won on the flat at Royal Ascot. In 1981, Lesley-Ann won the Sun Alliance Chase and there were plenty more big names to follow. Desert Orchid's Gold Cup apart (covered elsewhere in this book), the eye-catching successes among Elzee's nine Festival victories were Barnbrook Again's two triumphs in the Queen Mother Champion Chase. The only one of Cheltenham's 'Big Three' that escaped Elzee was the Champion Hurdle, which Oh So Risky lost by only half a length.

Away from Cheltenham, Rhyme'N'Reason won the 1988 Grand National despite slithering on his belly at Becher's. Elsworth provides a realistic commentary: 'If you didn't produce him late, he was useless. He wasn't the best jumper but he could fiddle his fences. Brendan Powell gave him a fantastic ride. At Becher's he sat down and then got up again. Watching from the stands, when I saw his head go down, I thought that was it. But it was a blessing in disguise. Tom Morgan was well clear on Little Polveir but then he departed and Rhyme'N'Reason was left in front with five to jump. Coming to the last, he pitched up and down where Durham Edition pinged the fence and went on. But that was just what the other fellow didn't want. The other horse was a bigger shit than Rhyme'N'Reason was, and he also didn't want to be left in front, so Brendan Powell was able to come from behind and pass him.'

The star of stars, however, was Desert Orchid, who was brilliantly campaigned by Elsworth – in days when the racing programme took a rather different shape – to win 35 of his 72 races. Even though Dessie could suffer from corns, Elsworth kept him fit, fresh and enjoying

David Elsworth in thoughtful mood with interviewer Clare Balding.

the job for nine whole seasons. Few top chasers nowadays would be asked to do what he did, but the versatile Desert Orchid, whose best distance was perhaps over two-and-a-half miles, not only won his 1989 Gold Cup and four King George VI Chases, but also led all the way to win a Whitbread Gold Cup over three miles five furlongs, and then came back to Sandown the next year to win the Tingle Creek over just two miles. Owner Richard Burridge, marvelling that Desert Orchid stayed so injury-free with the cleanest of tendons, wrote: 'It was David's brilliant use of the Whitsbury gallops that deserved most of the credit, as well as his sheer professionalism. He never ducked a race but he never risked Des unnecessarily either; he had discovered that Des was a tough horse who thrived on racing, so that was what he did, he raced him.' It was a policy that meant Desert Orchid occasionally lost a race, but so what? – horses are judged by their best performances. In another yard, Desert Orchid might not have been a national hero: he became the most popular horse in jumping, not just because he was a grey with a spectacular jumping style, but also because the racing public had plenty of opportunities to see him.

Elsworth says now: 'These days, there are so many conditions races. Desert Orchid had to run in handicaps too, like the Whitbread and the Irish National. He won a Victor Chandler and a Tingle Creek. He was so flamboyant and widely talented, as good over two miles or three, and he was always out there mixing it. He might get beaten one day but he would win the next time. We ran him about eight or ten times a season and everybody loved to see him. It's all about the horse. If you've got the best around, you've got to make the best use of him. It's nice to be unbeaten but we were always ready to take on the best. People would ask, "Can he give X two stone over two miles?" It was either "Yes he can" or "No he can't" when we raced, but we wanted to find out. You can only win the battle not the war.'

It is also interesting to learn how Elsworth came to be Desert Orchid's trainer: 'The Burridges who owned him were a very talented family. Jim Burridge, a solicitor who had raced Dessie's dam, Flower Child, in point-to-points, needed to sell a bit of Desert Orchid and he persuaded his son, Richard, to come in. Richard, who was a film-script writer, said that he would do so, "provided that David Elsworth trains him." It seems that he had been doing a boardsman's job in betting shops – writing up the results – for some extra money. I must have had a good run with my horses which had impressed him!'

So why, after all that success, did Elsworth choose, in his mid-50s, to turn his back on jumping and concentrate on the flat? In part, it seems, it was the stress of the injuries to his horses and the pain of losing good horses. In part, there was a sense that he had 'done that.' Suddenly, there was less appeal in getting up on freezing, dark mornings to chase around Plumpton for a couple of thousand quid and get home again in the dark. He cannot envisage a life without horses but now he says: 'With age, I am pacing myself. I don't want to be working in the dark. You get the jumpers in, in September, then in March you are at full tilt, and you're getting in the flat horses. Jumping is tough: you've got short days, bad ground and injuries to cope with. There is more and more racing, and the ground takes a hammering. Even in my time, it was busy enough.'

Desert Orchid, one of the most popular horses ever, with the team.

Martin Pipe

Champion Trainer 1988–93, 1995–2005

Martin Pipe doesn't do serenity. Now in his 70s, he remains full of energy, full of questions, still relentlessly searching for any scrap of extra knowledge that might give that essential edge to the training operation these days conducted by his son, David, at their Nicolashayne base on the Devon–Somerset border. There is a laptop full of graphs open on a low table in front of the Cape Canaveral-style bank of televisions, each with their own recorder, beaming in racing from wherever it is taking place, including France. Apart from the equipment on the walls and the table-loads of trophies, the shelves are stacked with videos of every race in which they have had runners, and photographs of past triumphs. Sheets of statistics are summoned from the office to illustrate a point he is making. Now a welcome guest pretty well anywhere among his former rivals in racing, and no longer the upstart who upset the applecart of half a century of bland assumptions about training, he takes great delight these days in visiting other trainers. He grills them about feeds, about training methods,

about salt licks and inoculations, about ulcers and breathing operations, in a continuing quest for knowledge of how to make horses run faster and do so happily.

The chirpiness still resurfaces in recollection, the chuckle can still have an edge to it, but you can now discern a quieter sense of satisfaction, at a job supremely well done, in the man who rewrote racing's record books. The little bookmaker's son from Taunton knows that he came in from nowhere and – against a mountain of suspicion and prejudice – he changed the whole game.

First, the statistics: when Martin Pipe took out his first training licence in 1977, it was after a disastrous and painful period as a rider, which yielded just one point-to-point winner and a broken thigh that had to be re-broken and repaired. 'I was absolutely useless. I should not have been allowed to sit on a horse. That's why I've been fanatical about training the jockeys.' Nor was Martin Pipe an overnight sensation. For ten years he averaged no more than a dozen winners a year. But the results by the time he retired at the age of 60, in April 2006, were phenomenal. He had trained the winners

Martin Pipe, the punter's friend.

of 4,182 races, 3,926 of those over jumps. He had been champion National Hunt trainer 15 times; appointment as his stable jockey virtually guaranteed the chosen rider a jockeys' championship too. He took Peter Scudamore, Richard Dunwoody and, many times, AP (now Sir Anthony) McCoy to the title. Martin Pipe recorded the fastest 100 winners in a season, the fastest 200 winners, the most prize money won, the most winners trained in a lifetime – after just 25 years. On eight occasions, he trained more than 200 winners in a year. His record total of 243 winners in the 1999/2000 season will probably never be beaten.

Although he never trained a Gold Cup winner, Martin Pipe won the Grand National with Miinnehoma. He twice trained the winner of the Champion Hurdle; only Nicky Henderson, Willie Mullins and Paul Nicholls have trained more Cheltenham Festival winners than Martin's total of 34. But it was not just what he did that mattered; it was how he did it.

The first horse he bought at Ascot Sales for £300, Bobo's Boy, turned out to be the equivalent of a car with three wheels. He had a bowed tendon. 'I thought, "What do we do? How do I mend it?" I read all the veterinary books and gave him 18 months, and we won a race with him. It was a great introduction, it taught me an awful lot.

'I didn't know what you should do. I never thought about going to another yard to learn. Originally, I thought, "riding's easy, training's easy." I thought you just got in your car and drove. I was totally wrong about riding and I was totally wrong about training. I didn't know anybody in racing, though Tim Handel was a family friend, and Dad would ask Les Kennard for advice – he was a very good trainer.

Dad, the West Country bookmaker Dave Pipe, was a big presence in Martin's life and a questioning spur to his achievements. 'He had an illegal betting shop in the basement under the house, where all the local army camp used to come and place their bets. It was mostly cash, though he was taking credit bets as well there. I used to be upstairs in our billiards room listening to the commentaries. I used to go and work in the office even at 10, 11, 12. I used to help with the football coupons and all that. I was quite good at maths.

'I would go to the racing with Dad in the school holidays and we used to go dog-racing twice a week, four times a week in the end – Dad used to run Taunton dog track. We had a pitch there and he had a pitch at Exeter too. So there was the gambling side and the training side. When he had Taunton Dogs, he used to weigh the dogs twice a week. He had form cards for all the dogs – we still use the form cards now. That's how we evolved our system for keeping details of the horses. When we first came out here to Nicolashayne, we had a hundred greyhounds in the stables, six dogs to a box. He used to go round all the racetracks and the dog tracks, and I would go with him, and he would tell me, "This will win today" and "Don't back this one", and I loved it. I used to have my fiver on.'

Dave Pipe had horses in training in other people's names. One, called Royal Painter, was with Eddie Reavey, mostly a flat-racing trainer, and Terry Biddlecombe once won on it round Newbury. 'But if the horses got beat, Dad would lose two or three hundred quid, and the trainer would say afterwards, "I thought he might get beat, he didn't eat up last night." "So why didn't you tell us beforehand?" They'd say, "They didn't go fast enough for him." "So why didn't we make the running?" "Ah, you can't do that." Or, "He jumped badly." All the excuses. When I started training, I started to try and iron out these excuses.

'If the pace wasn't fast enough, why didn't we make the pace then? You can only do that if you jump well. So you've got to teach your horse to jump well. When I first started training, my horse would jump one hurdle. I'd think: "That's it. He's good. He's jumped it well, take him to the races." But, of course, racing's different and they didn't jump, so you had to go back and do it properly. You have to school them loads and loads of times. Jumping is all about jumping, it took me a time to realise. It's better that they hurt themselves at home, not at racing speed.'

Training had not been Martin's intended career path until, in the early 1970s, his job prospects altered: Dave Pipe sold his betting shops to William Hill. 'We were the biggest chain in the West Country. We virtually had a monopoly, it really was a licence to print money, and the big firms wanted to get in. We had Ladbrokes and Hills on the phone every ten minutes wanting to buy. Every time I picked up the phone, there was another hundred grand on offer. Dad had to sell up because the offer was so good.

'John Brown [later Hills' managing director] came down to oversee the takeover. He later wrote to me and said, "I'm glad you didn't come to William Hill, because if you had, you would have had my job." Dad wouldn't let me go. I'd never been outside Somerset except to the races.'

Working in his father's bookmaking business helped prepare him for a trainer's life, says Martin. It taught him method, and a respect for figures and for information. He learned to handle paperwork and organise systems. That is why son David now has a sheet for all the horses, listing the work they do. 'All our jockeys have to give written reports on their rides. We have a written report every day on every horse in the stables, so David can look and see this one has a cut on his knee, it's been treated with ointment, it's OK, or he can't run for four days ...

'Facts and figures, that's what life's all about. You must have your finger on the pulse and know everything. By 7.30 every morning, David knows the temperature of the horse, whether he's eaten up, everything.'

The trial-and-error road to the top for Martin Pipe, ready though he was to learn, was not a swift one, as he moved on from point-to-pointers to a full licence in 1973; nor was the target set too high to begin with. 'I wanted to win sellers [low-value races, where the winner is subsequently put up for auction]. I managed to win with cheap horses. I thought that if I could win sellers, since there's one every day, I could get 50 winners a year, wouldn't that be fun? I wanted to start at the bottom. The first 50 winners I had were all hurdlers. I couldn't

afford to buy a chaser. All my life I have just wanted to win. The prize money was only £300 or £500, but we knew they were going to win and they didn't go unbacked.'

On Cheltenham Festival days, in those early years, Martin Pipe was normally to be found somewhere he felt more appropriate, such as Newton Abbot. He didn't have the ammunition for Cheltenham. But in 1981 came the breakthrough – with Baron Blakeney's success at 66-1 in the Triumph Hurdle. The racing world greeted it as a flash in the pan. But they weren't surprised down in Nicolashayne and connections were well invested in the winner. 'We really fancied it. If it had been trained by a proper trainer like Fred Winter, it would have been about 14-1, but because it was trained by an idiot, an unknown, it was such a big price. We told everybody to back it. The owners' kids had £10 each way on it and all won nearly £1,000.'

But the ramifications went wider. 'We wanted to teach Baron Blakeney to jump so we took him to Captain Charles Radclyffe, who used to break in horses for the Queen Mother. He taught Baron Blakeney to jump.' Captain Radclyffe was one of the pioneers of the loose school in which horses run around teaching themselves to jump without a rider on their backs – and Martin Pipe had learned along with Baron Blakeney. 'We saw his loose school, saw what he did. We took all the measurements, came home and built a loose school like his.' It was incorporated into the Pipe method.

'We would loose school our horses twice a day. They would go round the loose school ten times in the morning, without a rider, ten times in the afternoon, so that meant they were doing 80 jumps a day for six days a week, that's 480, before they were ridden. We would do the same with the horses that we bought at Newmarket sales, "unjumped" three-year-olds.'

As the number of winners sent out from Nicolashayne soared, it became obvious not only that the Pipe horses could jump, but also that they were fitter than their rivals. For that, Martin Pipe gives credit to another workaholic with a questing mind, who became his friend and mentor – Michael Dickinson.

'One day, we went to Doncaster and looked at all the horses in the paddock. I always had an opinion of a horse. I would look at them all and say, "That's that, that can't win", and cross them off. I looked at one and thought, "That one's a skeleton, that can't possibly win." It was just skin and bone. But it was one of Michael Dickinson's and when I watched the race, it won [by] half the track. I thought, "Hang on, hang on. So that's what a fit horse is."

'To me,' says Martin, 'a fit horse is like a greyhound,' at which point, Martin's wife, Carol, very much part of the Nicolashayne team, pitches in: 'It's unfair to horses to race them when they are overweight, pushing them on. That's when they are going to break down.' That is why the Pipes developed intensive interval-training up and down a steep all-weather gallop – and where the profit Dave Pipe had made from the sale of his betting shops came in handy.

'In 1984, we got our first all-weather gallop (I spoke to Michael Dickinson about it – before then, we just had a rotavated earth strip). It is a woodchip gallop and it has stood the test of time. At first, it wasn't even two furlongs long, the strip at the end of the garden, and they used to go up and down it ten times.

'A company wanted £50,000 to lay the gallops, and Dad wasn't having that, so we built our own. We used washed stone, then a membrane, and then the woodchip, and we made it deeper and better than the usual specifications. After six months, we had it up to five furlongs.'

With his interval-training up steep slopes, and a meticulous eye for the opportunities offered by race conditions, Pipe entered his horses in the right races and sent them there leathery fit. As often as not, Peter Scudamore would make the running and leave fields strung out behind him.

The year when Baron Blakeney won at Cheltenham was the first time Martin Pipe had 20 winners in a season. Then things began to take off. 'In 1984, we had 50 winners for the

first time and in 1986/87, we had 100 winners for the first time [in what was then a ten-month season]. In 1987/88, we had 129 winners and in 1988/89, we had 200. That was from about 150 to 160 horses – the most we could take here was 160.

'I had a letter from [the Prix de l'Arc de Triomphe-winning trainer] Jonathan Pease, who told me, "If you want to be a proper trainer, you've got to move to a training centre" – Lambourn or Newmarket – and I thought, "Oh dear, I don't really want to do that." Dad said, "We'll make our own training centre," and that is basically what we have done with the loose school, the gallops, the swimming pool, the indoor canter etc.'

Another key factor has been the scientific approach. Martin Pipe, who always had his head in one veterinary volume or another, was an early convert to the efficacy of blood tests as a way of monitoring a horse's readiness to race. 'Here you are,' he says, pulling down a fat volume from the shelf, 'page 10 of *Modern Horse Management* by R.S. Timmis. I would have a horse ready and the vet would say, "This one can't win," and I couldn't understand why. I thought he didn't know what he was talking about. But we would run and it didn't win. I

Lady Cricket: yet another winner from Nicolashayne ridden by the man Pipe helped to win so many championships.

was converted the same way I was by Michael Dickinson over what was a fit horse. It was another section of my learning curve.' He told the *Racing Post* later, 'If we fancied them, we backed them, and if the blood tests said they were spot on, they usually won. It took all the guesswork out of it.'

Martin bought his own haemoglobin machine. 'The vet would say, "Basically, you've got to have a reading of 14.4 to win," and the bloody thing did win because its red blood cells were full of oxygen. That's the golden rule. That's why my lab got bigger and bigger, so you could take more and more tests. The blood tests weren't the sole reason for them winning, but they don't win at 12.5. Science counts – and nowadays we can get the results by 10.00 a.m...

Martin Pipe with Our Vic (left) and Celestial Gold.

'People laughed at us too, around the West Country, when we started weighing horses, but it's all for the welfare of the horse, so he can be as fit as he can and enjoy it. You don't want to run a horse 50 kg overweight.'

Following the success of Baron Blakeney, Martin Pipe had to wait another eight years for his next Festival winner – Sondrio in the Supreme Novices Hurdle of 1989. Sondrio had been sent for stud duties in the USA but was subsequently gelded and came to Martin to be trained. 'He had won nearly 450,000 dollars in America but he hadn't raced for some considerable time and he was a gross horse, he was very fat when we ran him at Hereford. I

remember apologising to the owner.' Not only that – on the way to Hereford, Sondrio went berserk in his horsebox and Martin, his car travelling upsides on the motorway, had to climb across into Sondrio's box to settle him.

Sondrio won all the same and was aimed at the Festival. Two weeks before that, he ran at Ascot. 'He was a certainty. He couldn't possibly get beat. Scu [Peter Scudamore] rode him, and he *was* beaten. He never jumped a hurdle. So Scu didn't want to ride him at Cheltenham; he'd been offered another ride in the race. Jonathon Lower, our second jockey at the time, came in and we schooled him every day, two or three times a day, trying to get him to jump.

'Come the day, Scu rode this other horse and fell early on. He was lying on the ground listening to the commentary as Jonathon made all. As they were going past the post and it was announced that Sondrio was the winner, Scu was beating his whip on the ground in frustration. The ambulance man ran across and said, "You're obviously in great pain." And he [Scu] was saying, "Go away, go away, leave me alone."'

Before Scudamore's retirement and the arrival of AP McCoy, Martin Pipe's association with Peter Scudamore was one of the most fruitful in racing. They shared the desire to win not just the big prestige races, but any race that was going, and the loyalty went both ways: when Scudamore broke his leg one year, Martin Pipe held back a number of his horses to give the jockey a winning burst on his return. Scudamore, in turn, respected Pipe's utter professionalism: 'If you didn't know the form of a horse you were riding and how it should be ridden, he'd be angry because he expected you to care as much as he did.'

Pipe's greatest victories at Cheltenham were the Champion Hurdle successes of Granville Again (1993) and Make A Stand (1997); Make A Stand's success epitomised the Pipe operation. He claimed the hard-pulling gelding from Henry Candy out of a Leicester seller in August 1995 for just £8,000. 'We sent out a letter to all our owners offering a half share for £4,000, and Carol told me off, saying no one else would buy the other half. Lo and behold, we couldn't sell it and we retained the half share. I am very glad we did because over the next year the horse won £250,000.' Well-known owner Peter Deal had taken the other half.

A natural front-runner had joined a yard where his jockey would be encouraged to take him to the front, make all, and dare the others to catch up. No longer held up, Make A Stand rapidly won three novice hurdles and a race on the flat. The following season, he ran at Sandown and Ascot and Kempton and never saw another horse, even in the normally hotly contested Tote Gold Trophy. 'He can't run like that at Cheltenham and win,' said the sages. 'He'll just be setting it up for others.' But Make A Stand did run like that. He set off in front, drew well clear – and proved joyously impossible to catch. This success came just a year after Pipe had won the Stayers Hurdle with Cyborgo, running his first race since coming second in the same race 364 days earlier.

'Make A Stand was a real athlete. It took him a while to get going, he wasn't a natural early on, but once he had the hang of it, he could really jump. AP got on very well with him, but loads of jockeys won on him. Jockeys just had to understand the pace, to allow him to dictate and conserve his energy. He was really exuberant, he really enjoyed his racing. In the Champion Hurdle we were really anxious, but it was great that he went on and kept going up the hill.'

Over a glass of champagne at Pond House, Martin Pipe has a legion of similar stories to tell about his winners. One of his favourites concerns Champleve in the Arkle Chase of 1968. Martin had been away racing one day and when he arrived home, Carol told him, 'I've been a naughty girl today, I've bought a horse.' She had seen Champleve, a handsome grey, win at Auteuil and had instructed their agent to buy it. Says Martin: 'The only one she's ever bought and, of course, he has to win at the Cheltenham Festival. It proves she's a better judge than me – and she never lets me forget it.'

Champleve was sold on to the late David Johnson, who at one stage had more than 100 horses in the yard, and who broke the record

A formidable combination – Martin Pipe and AP McCoy.

for winners in a season, previously held by Dorothy Paget, whose memorabilia Martin has collected.

Champleve won some small-value hurdle races nicely, and Martin told David Johnson they should put him chasing. 'One day, I said to him that I would give him a commentary over the telephone on Champleve's schooling and it went like this: "He's jumped the first well. A decent jump at the second, good again at the third, took the fourth brilliant ... and he's won the Arkle." That final comment, as he rung off, was intended only as a rhetorical flourish, but David Johnson had taken Pipe seriously, immediately calling Tote bookmakers and having £10,000 each way on Champleve at 33-1 for the Arkle Chase, the big novice-chase event at the Cheltenham Festival.

Come the next spring, Champleve ran in the Arkle. 'AP [McCoy] rode a terrific race on him. Champleve and Noel Meade's Hill Society drove up the hill together for a photo finish. I thought we were second. As we were waiting for the result of the photo, Noel and I had a friendly hug and I said, "It doesn't matter who wins." Suddenly, there is David Johnson beside us, saying, "Oh yes it jolly well does – I backed him at 33-1!" Luckily, the photo went the right way, and we all had a big hug with Noel Meade.'

Martin Pipe's successes on the racecourse were there for all to see, but the successful suffer from the jealousy of lesser men, and successful innovators incur added resentment from those who are too lazy to keep up to date in a changing world. As Pond House began churning out winners on an industrial scale, and bringing off some successful gambling coups, then, just as had happened with Michael Dickinson before him, Pipe became the subject of wild racecourse rumours that he was doping his horses, that he was 'changing their blood', that his training methods were wrecking animals and resulting in a high wastage rate. It aided the rumour-mongers and conspiracy-theorists that he wasn't based in a training centre but at a remote location on his own; that he was the first trainer to have his own blood-testing laboratory on site; and that he had a bookmaking background. Nor did it help that Pipe was a naturally shy man, brought up in a business where you don't give information away easily. For a long time he did not have many friends in the media.

For Martin and Carol, it was a painful business. Yes, they strove for winners; yes, they liked to have a bet; and they didn't mind having owners who shared that enjoyment, but all the energy and science that Martin Pipe put into training was designed to produce horses who were happy when winning their races, because their fitness meant they were not over-faced. As Martin says: 'I'm all about keeping the horses happy and well. You want the pupils to do well for you. Giving them a hiding isn't going to help.'

'It definitely put me off people,' Martin told one interviewer when he retired. 'There was so much jealousy, it became really hurtful. We were trying to keep our horses healthier and happier, and to have people say the opposite was quite shocking.' The lowest moment came with the Cook Report in 1991, a TV hatchet job that sought to make the case that Pipe's horses were cruelly treated. He condemns it as 'a very spiteful programme without foundation' but he still resents its effect, which was, he says, that 'the public never understood that we love our horses. We take their temperatures and wash their bottoms every day. We live with them as if they were our own children. And when they are gone, we miss them terribly.' Listen to him talk about how he and AP McCoy cried their eyes out over the loss of Gloria Victis and Valiramix, two potential stars who lost their lives at Cheltenham, and you don't doubt that for a minute.

Martin's long-time former jockey Peter Scudamore puts it this way: 'Martin was so far ahead. Other people pretended to be professional. Martin was professional in every aspect. No stone unturned. I loved that. He was always looking for that edge. The dislike other people had was because we were so far ahead. It almost gave you a siege mentality. They all think you're on something. They came down for

Gaspara, owned by Martin Pipe and trained by his son, David (right), collects a bonus after adding a Cheltenham victory to his Imperial Cup. Andrew Glassonbury in the saddle.

drugs – that's what they were looking for – and when they couldn't find any, they changed tack.

'Martin was so very different to anybody else I had been to, it was refreshing. At David Nicholson's, everything was done with such regimented style, cantering a mile and a quarter, then you go to Martin Pipe and you cantered up the gallop, and you cantered down on some small horse and I thought, "This man's an idiot. Cantering down a four-furlong all-weather gallop. What on earth is going on..." When I first went, I couldn't get on, I couldn't ride a winner for the first month, and I think they wanted to get rid of me, but then I think we had 50 winners before Christmas, 49 of them hurdlers.

'There were specialist jockeys down there [around the West Country tracks]. I needed M Pipe running horses on the firm ground before the season proper began, if I was going to have a chance of being champion jockey. Then he was giving me 50 winners before Christmas. He said, "Don't ever lie to me. Always tell me the truth and we'll never fall out." That was it.

'When I started off, I thought 100 winners in a season – that would be it. Then we were going for 200 winners with Martin, it must have been the next season. One hundred winners in a season was a lot of fun. Going for the first 200, I remember getting close to it and thinking, "We will never do this again. Stay sound. We don't want them coughing. We don't want anything to go wrong..."'

The rumour-mongering and the allegations reached ridiculous proportions, says Peter Scudamore. 'One trainer came to me and said, "I know what you be doing: you be taking the blood out of the good horses and putting it in the bad horses!" People had no idea how far ahead we were. The greatest tribute to Martin Pipe is that everybody has copied him.'

Even now, you can see the hurt behind Martin's eyes as he talks about the Cook Report and what it typified. 'I really was upset with the world. I wanted to get out. I had lots of support from trainers – and lots against me. I hated the whole world, I wanted to commit suicide, I hated the press. I was doing nothing wrong but after that, you don't trust anybody. I wanted to give up training. I went to a Devon-and-Exeter meeting and walked in, not wanting to speak to anybody. A steward, Percy Brown, came up to me. I'm not that sort of person but I wanted to punch him on the nose. I was saying to myself, "Try to keep calm, Pipe, try to keep calm", I was so upset. And then he said to me, "Mr Pipe, I'd like to send you a horse." Though I've done nothing wrong, I've just been on the Cook Report, but he sends me a horse. A steward sending me a horse. He brought me back to life – he really did. Fantastic guy.' Racing owes Mr Brown a debt, and, in the end, the racing establishment came to recognise just what the unshowy Martin Pipe had done for racing – even if the authorities did send a hit team into his yard one morning in 2001 to test his horses for illegal substances, tests that all came back clear. It must have smarted at the time but, in the end, helped to restore realism.

Fellow trainer Henrietta Knight says, 'Martin Pipe's horses were probably the fittest horses that ever raced,' and punters owe Pipe a vote of gratitude because, since his day, most horses from other yards have been sent to the races ready to run. French bloodstock agents too should bless him – Pipe was one of the first to spot the possibilities of importing early-maturing and early-schooled young horses from

Martin Pipe and Shirley Johnson, wife of Well Chief owner David Johnson in the winner's enclosure after Well Chief won the Betfred Celebration Steeplechase.

France, who could exploit the significant pull in the weights that four-year-old and five-year-old novice chasers enjoyed. Until Pipe began, no trainer had been quite so meticulously organised or so ruthlessly efficient in his planning, hence the on-site blood testing.

As his fellow West Country trainer Philip Hobbs said on his rival's retirement in April 2006: 'Martin changed the game. We all had to copy his methods to try to keep up.' And perhaps the ultimate tribute came from one of the most respected flat-racing trainers, Newmarket's Sir Mark Prescott. He declared: 'Only three people have changed their side of how the business of racing is conducted. The first was Admiral Rous, who worked out the weight-for-age and handicapping. The second was Tod Sloan, the American flat jockey who came over and changed the way jockeys rode. The third is Martin Pipe, who completely changed the way the National Hunt horse is trained. All those who whined and spread appalling rumours ended up training like him – and never had the good grace to either apologise or thank him.'

Like Nicky Henderson and Paul Nicholls, Martin Pipe has also nurtured a wide range of pupils and assistants who have become successful racing figures in their own right: those who gained valuable experience along the way at Pond House included trainers Len Lungo, Ralph Beckett, Gordon Elliott, Venetia Williams, Tom George, Tom Dascombe, Jeff Pearce, Ian Williams, Rod Millman, James Lambe, Alastair Lidderdale, Andy Hobbs, Jean-Rene Auvray, Dr Jeremy Naylor, Lars Kelp, Mary Sanderson and Florent Monnier, together with sports solicitor Rory Macneice and starter William Jordan.

David Nicholson

Champion Trainer 1993–95

There were few more readily identifiable figures on the jumping racecourses of the 1970s, 1980s and 1990s than David Nicholson, a passionate competitor, loyal employer and strong-minded individualist whose bulky sheepskin, trilby and red socks were often accompanied by a heart

worn on the sleeve. The stabbing forefinger that had helped to earn him the nickname of 'the Duke' from a stable employee in his youth was regularly employed to add emphasis to his forthright opinions, but even those who clashed with him acknowledged his vital contribution to the jump racing of his time.

The Duke came from a racing dynasty: his father, Frenchie Nicholson, had not only been champion jockey and ridden Golden Miller, but was also an outstanding tutor of young flat-racing jockeys, who once famously declared of those he coached, 'They came on bicycles and left in Rolls-Royces.' David's mother, Diana, was a trainer's daughter and great-granddaughter of William Holman, who trained three Grand National winners. Nevertheless, Nicholson had obstacles to overcome in pursuing a racing career: at 6 ft 1 in, he was painfully tall for a would-be jockey and he suffered terribly from both asthma and an allergic reaction to horses. Despite those handicaps, he rode 538 winners over jumps, including partnering Mill House to his hugely popular victory in the 1967 Whitbread Gold Cup. The Duke then went on to train almost 1,500 more, first from the yard he developed at his Condicote home in the Cotswolds, and then from the purpose-built splendour of Jackdaw's Castle nearby. He was never champion jockey but he was twice champion trainer, in 1993/94 and 1994/95, the only person to interrupt what would otherwise have been a 17-year run as champion trainer for Martin Pipe.

Nicholson first took out a training licence in 1968 and he combined the roles of jockey and trainer for six years before suddenly quitting the saddle in the middle of a racing day in 1974. As so often happens in top jumping yards, Nicholson was given invaluable help along the way by his wife, Dinah, who did everything from riding out to keeping the medical books and mending tack.

As a rider among the happy-go-lucky cavaliers of the 1950s and 1960s, scaling lamp posts, rubbing butter into fellow diners' hair, and sipping Guinness in the weighing room between rides, Nicholson roistered with the best; however, as a trainer and, like his father, a developer of jockey talent, he was an authoritarian traditionalist. A lad leading up a Nicholson runner would always be tidy, wearing a collar and tie, and expected to use the 'Sir' word. Nicholson's head lad Clifford Baker, who went on later to perform the same role for Paul Nicholls after Nicholson retired, noted that the Duke would never entertain the idea of employing girls as part of his stable staff.

Peter Scudamore recalls, 'You had to wear a collar and tie to go to the races, and when Peter Cazalet retired and the question was going around about who was going to get the Queen Mother's horses, the Duke was telling us, "When Sir Martin Gilliatt [her private secretary] talks to you, this is how you should respond." When I was with him, he was aspiring to be that kind of traditional thing. It took him some time to change but I think he settled down in himself as a person more later. Certainly, he instilled discipline in us – you looked smart, you cleaned your shoes, and he would check with you, "What time is your first race?"'

Nicholson was a traditionalist over his horses too. Bloodstock agent David Minton, whose Highflyer team bought many of them for him, recalls that until he acquired Broadsword, the Duke wasn't interested in horses off the flat: 'His attitude at first was, "What have you bloody well brought me this for?" Then we bought Mysilv from Chris Wall. The Duke rang after two days and said, "This can bloody jump!" She was a box walker [a nervous horse who expends precious energy walking agitatedly around its stable]. She ran in the Champion Hurdle and the World Hurdle at the same meeting – third in one, and fourth in the other. Sadly, she died on the gallops.' Dinah Nicholson says, however, that there were a few well-connected flat types from Sheikh Mohammed in the yard for a while: 'I don't think he realised we had them. It was all to do with [racing manager] Anthony Stroud, who was a dyed-in-the-wool jumping man and he kept sneaking them in. It lasted for a while and then dried up when Stroudie went

elsewhere. In those days, there wasn't any racing in Dubai. We did have the odd one from Prince Khalid Abdullah. That was through 'Badger' [Gavin Pritchard-Gordon]. We were invited to Prince Khalid's box at Ascot and introduced to him, and he said [to David], "Ah, you are the man with the funny coat." Well, you've got to be recognised by something.'

An all-round sportsman, David Nicholson had one other passion in life beside his racing – and that was for cricket. In those days, when the jumping season ran for ten months rather than all through the year, the National Hunt Jockeys Cricket Team had a full fixture list and raised plenty of money for charity with celebrity-studded matches. Fellow cricket-lover Peter Scudamore used to joke that the cricket was the reason he signed up with the Duke. As the team captain for many years, the Duke was a ferocious competitor in cricket – and also in the jockeys' football team, never worrying too much whether he connected with man or ball.

As a trainer, his major victories included a King George VI Chase with Barton Bank, Triumph Hurdles with Solar Cloud and Mysilv, an Arkle Challenge Trophy with Waterloo Boy, a Whitbread Gold Cup with Call It A Day, and two Mackeson Gold Cups with Very Promising and

David Nicholson, a great developer of jockey talent.

Another Coral. The victories that will be most remembered are those of Viking Flagship, who twice won the Queen Mother Champion Chase (1994 and 1995), and Nicholson's Cheltenham Gold Cup victory with Charter Party. Barton Bank might have won a second King George had he not fallen at the last. Following an irate confrontation with the photographer Ed Whitaker, who was taking pictures of Barton Bank's distraught rider Adrian Maguire, David Nicholson was fined £1,500 and censured by racing's authorities. 'It was a stiff fine – but nothing a large brandy wouldn't cure,' said the defiant trainer.

Like his friend Josh Gifford and Ireland's Noel Meade, Nicholson had endured a long wait for Cheltenham Festival glory: over the years he had seen many of his horses placed in Festival races since starting to train in 1968, before Solar Cloud's victory in 1986, unfancied at 40-1, gave him his first Festival winner. Ironically, the Duke had told jockey Peter

Scudamore to deliver his challenge on Solar Cloud, a horse of doubtful temperament, as late as possible, but Scu found that his mount was travelling so well that he went on a mile from home and just hung on after leading by six lengths over the last.

When the Fates relent, they sometimes do so with a bonus. Just two hours later, Charter Party won the National Hunt Handicap Chase to double Nicholson's Festival tally. The red socks the Duke had pulled on that day became a race-day tradition on the spot; it was also Charter Party who, in 1988, gave him his Gold Cup winner. To Nicholson's fury at the time (although they later became reconciled), Scudamore had left him to join Fred Winter at the end of the season in 1986, so it was Richard Dunwoody, the next top jockey to become the Duke's number one, who rode Charter Party, who was owned in partnership by Colin and Claire Smith with Raymond and Jenny Mould.

Training this initially clumsy jumper to win a Gold Cup was a considerable feat. Charter Party had fallen on his first visit to the Festival, then again in his next race at Cheltenham, and yet again in the 1985 Hennessy. Following wind problems, he was hobdayed and given a soft-palate operation, only to fall again in the 1987 Gold Cup after failing to win a race that season. In 1988, despite intermittent lameness, Charter Party did win the Gainsborough Chase at Sandown in February, beating Rhyme'N'Reason and Desert Orchid; he then filled his trainer with hope when running away from his speedier stablemates, Long Engagement and Very Promising, in a gallop before the Gold Cup. Nicholson had never lost faith that he would win a big one with Charter Party and, in Richard Dunwoody's hands, Charter Party took the Gold Cup in 1988 by six lengths from Cavvies Clown. If his trainer had shown faith, Charter Party had demonstrated courage – X-rays after the big race showed that he had been suffering from navicular disease (inflammation of a bone in horse's hooves), badly enough to put his future career in doubt,

The young 'Duke'.

although he did come back to finish third to Desert Orchid in the following year's Gold Cup.

David Nicholson had firm opinions on almost every aspect of racing. In training his jumpers, he was an advocate of sending them over gradually progressive obstacles, rather than loose schooling. In races, Richard Johnson recalls that his instructions seldom varied. The Duke liked his jockeys to settle in sixth or seventh place, get upsides the leader two out – and win if possible.

Nicholson took seriously his role in bringing on young jockeys and, commenting on the introduction of a system whereby a trainer took half of a conditional jockey's riding fee, he noted that with the previous set-up, trainers had not been able to afford to give opportunities to jump jockeys with little or no race-riding experience. The worry with that, he said, was how the leading jockeys of the future were to be found because with very few genuine amateur riders left, there would be no supply of future top jockeys except from Ireland: 'Over there, they have all these "bumper" [amateur flat] races, and so many of the children hunt. They're all half-made before they ever go racing. Add a flat apprenticeship and they are away.' His view was that National Hunt trainers had a duty to train young jockeys, as well as horses, and that meant sending them to Perth or Fontwell or wherever, even if it were only for a single ride. To promote a young jockey, the trainer must not be selfish – he must allow outside people to use him, he must excuse the young rider on occasions from 'doing his two' or from mucking out. It might be awkward for the riding-out rota and for the head man, but it was the only way youngsters could get going. It was right, then, in theory, for the trainer to be given half the fees, but he expected young riders who were going to make the grade to have the confidence to negotiate most of it back. Nicholson certainly had a good eye for jockey talent: those whose careers he helped to develop included Peter Scudamore, Richard Dunwoody, Adrian Maguire and Richard Johnson, as well as many lesser lights in the saddle.

Says the Duke's widow, Dinah Nicholson, 'Every lad who came in who was of a reasonable weight would get a chance if they behaved. David was always very open. Lots of waifs and strays would be in the kitchen. We were very fond of Richard Johnson. Richard Burton [a leading point-to-point rider] was a good cricketer and the Duke said to him, "You'd better stick to cricket." When he [Richard] won the Kim Muir at Cheltenham, the Duke said, "I was wrong, you were right."'

The Nicholson yard was not immune, however, to the musical-chair problems occasionally caused by upwardly mobile jockeys' ambitions and by other trainers' and owners' enticements. Says Dinah Nicholson, 'There was tension towards the end. Adrian [Maguire] kept getting hurt and owners were pressing to have Richard Johnson. It was quite tricky too when Adrian took over from Dunwoody. Richard Dunwoody said, "I'll keep coming and riding out", and Adrian said, "Don't you let him near the place. I know just what he'll do, he'll come creeping in..."' Then there was that falling-out between the Duke and Peter Scudamore. 'He

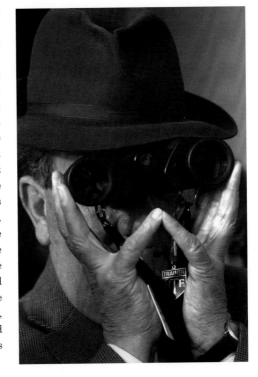

An early morning at Condicote. Jockey Peter Scudamore with David Nicholson.

and old man Scu were best buddies. Peter was a page at our wedding. It was just the way it was done. Freddie Winter had approached him without saying anything to David, and David had always been brought up to do these things correctly. The Winters asked us over, I think for lunch, and he was on about, "Who would you have as a stable jockey?" David said, "I think I'd go for Dunwoody," not imagining that Freddie Winter had already got Scu. It was extraordinary because Freddie was a very correct kind of person.

'When we got Dunwoody, he was with Tim Forster. He was an amateur at the time and David rang Tim and said, "Would you mind if I approached Richard Dunwoody to be my stable jockey?" Tim said, "Thank you very much for ringing. Carry on."'

Nicholson's training career had its ups and downs. For two years, he was plagued by a virus; on two occasions, he was nearly forced to give up because he had run his financial affairs into an embarrassing tangle. When the Duke's cheques started bouncing, stable jockey Peter Scudamore stepped in one week to pay the staff wages. A consortium of owners and friends took charge and created a company to run the yard. In the late 1980s, Charter Party's part-owner Colin Smith, with Nicholson's help, designed and built the state-of-the-art training establishment of Jackdaw's Castle (where Jonjo O'Neill now trains). Smith installed the Duke as a salaried trainer, taking over himself all the financial side of the operation. With those worries removed and with such wonderful facilities at his disposal, David Nicholson enjoyed the most successful period of his career at Jackdaw's. Dinah Nicholson says that the much-fancied Broadsword would never have gone down to Baron Blakeney (Martin Pipe's first Cheltenham winner) in the 1981 Triumph Hurdle if they had already been training at Jackdaw's Castle by then: 'The horses were so much fitter when we got there. We rather outgrew the facilities at Condicote. The gallops were a bit cobbled together. We did quite well out of it with the facilities we had, but things were so much better at Jackdaw's. Colin had bought the land; originally, his daughter was going to train point-to-pointers there, and David said, "You could make some bloody good gallops there." It was his concept.'

It was at Jackdaw's Castle that David Nicholson trained more than 100 winners in a season for the first time and won his two championships. Following his retirement from training in 1999, after a rumoured fall-out with Colin Smith, David Nicholson remained in racing, promoting British bloodstock. He continued to indulge his passion for all sport until his death in 2006.

Paul Nicholls
Champion Trainer 2005–12, 2013–16

When prosperous Somerset dairy farmer Paul Barber was looking for somebody in 1991 to take over the 24-box yard he owned in the picture-postcard village of Ditcheat, and train a couple for him, he knew what he wanted: 'Somebody who would eat, drink, and sleep horses.' In Paul Nicholls, he found a determined, driven and self-confident man who does precisely that. At the time, Barber's ambition was to milk 1,000 cows and win a Cheltenham Gold Cup. By 2008, Barber was milking 2,000 cows and Nicholls had given him his second Cheltenham Gold Cup victory with the mighty slugger Denman, the first having come with See More Business in 1999.

Nicholls radiates energy and commitment and isn't afraid to let the world see him enjoying his success. He has never lacked ambition either. But even *he* did not dream back in 1991, when he ended a seven-year riding career with just 133 winners and not much in the bank, that in April 2016 he would celebrate his tenth British trainers' championship after a gripping struggle that year with Irish-based Willie Mullins. By that point, he had trained more than 2,600 winners, including 110 Grade One victories, and 40 at the Cheltenham Festival. By then, still only in his mid-50s, Paul Nicholls had amassed for his owners more than £2 million in prize money every year for 14 years. His strike rate of winners to runners had by then been 20 per cent, or better, for 21 years.

The old cliché is that less successful jockeys make more successful trainers because they have more time to stand around and watch how it is done. Paul Nicholls wasn't that bad a jockey. He had ridden for Les Kennard and Josh Gifford and, during his time with David Barons, he partnered Playschool to win a Welsh National, an Irish Hennessy, and an English Hennessy Gold Cup. Barons and Nicholls collected another English Hennessy with Broadheath. What made him what Paul now calls 'exactly the kind of jockey I wouldn't employ' was not a lack of ability but the miserable grind he endured – as the son and grandson of well-built policemen –

Not as bad a jockey as he makes out. Paul Nicholls after winning the Hennessy Gold Cup on Playschool.

in struggling to get down to riding weights. He had always wanted to be a trainer and for his last two years with Barons he was his assistant, helping to prepare the yard's Grand National winner Seagram. In 1989, a kick that broke his leg finally forced Paul Nicholls to start pursuing his dream. Cue the advertisement in the *Sporting Life* from Paul Barber and the young horseman's interview promise, in the teeth of a looming recession, to fill those 24 Ditcheat boxes within a year. Neither Barber nor Nicholls looked at another option.

Ironically, it was riding a few for Martin Pipe, later to be his arch-rival, that had a key influence on Paul Nicholls' approach to training. 'His [Pipe's] horses were so supremely fit that it immediately struck me that fitness was the key to it all. When I came up here, it was a big appeal that Paul Barber had this uphill gallop. The hill was going to be a great fitness aid, and that was a big draw for me.' Soon he was declaring that his horses never had an easy day. 'I do more with a horse in a day than some trainers do in a week. I felt a lot of the horses I rode as a jockey failed because they were not fit.' One of Nicholls' key tutors had been point-to-point trainer Dick Baimbridge, who also trained his horses up a 'precipice' and who had emphasised to the young Nicholls that they were handling 'racehorses not show horses.' From Josh Gifford came the emphasis on intensive schooling, which was a feature too of Martin Pipe's approach. 'Josh used to say, "If they don't jump, they don't win." They're jumping fit and I like to think ours

jump particularly well. We do do a lot of practice. Not particularly a lot of fast schooling, but just a lot of jumping of different types of obstacles. I think some of the trainers in the past didn't do enough schooling.'

Again, there is a similarity with Martin Pipe in terms of the facilities: 'None of my gallops are more than five furlongs plus the 400-metre round. One uphill four furlong, one flat five furlongs. No grass gallops at all. You don't need massive long-grass gallops. You can get your horses fit, and with good-quality all-weather gallops, you can do so while massively reducing the risk of injury.'

Where Nicholls' and Pipe's methods diverge dramatically is in what a famous advertisement used to call 'the appliance of science.' For Martin Pipe, blood tests were almost a religious rite before he would take a horse to the course. Paul Nicholls says: 'We don't do blood tests and trach [trachea] washes, and we don't weigh them any more. We try to keep it simple. Weighing them just confused the hell out of us. Cliff [head lad Clifford Baker] and I know if they've worked hard and look hard. There have been times when we've taken a blood test and the vet has said, "Whoa, whoa. Don't run it: it's wrong." We've said, "Fuck that" and run it, and it has won – so what was the point in doing that? If one looks good and runs badly, then we will start to investigate why, and deal with it afterwards. But otherwise, no. You end up costing your owners a fortune and in the end your vet is training your horses – not you on your own instinct. You know when a horse is doing well and you're in business.'

In the Nicholls operation, blood tests and the like are tools for examining why a horse hasn't performed as expected, not predictors. 'We try not to make things too complicated. They've got to be extremely fit because everybody is catching up with everyone now. There isn't quite such an edge on fitness as there was with some yards.'

Nevertheless, he does believe that he and the others who have made the West Country such a focus of jump racing – Martin and David Pipe, Philip Hobbs, and now Colin Tizzard – have some advantages.

'There's a lot of benefit being on your own. It's been a big plus being away from a big training centre. I think that's massive.' Not just in avoiding equine bugs, he says, but getting away from a cut-throat atmosphere. 'Having a dairy industry in the area is a massive help as well. If I'd come up here and seen loads of corn and oilseed rape, I wouldn't have come. Dairy and horses work very well together. I see all these trainers in areas like Lambourn always moaning about oilseed rape. It's just a disaster. The West Country's got big roots in jump racing.' Many trainers believe that the dust from oilseed rape leads to equine respiratory problems.

Paul Nicholls does not share the fashionable view that horses today are more fragile: 'I don't think so. There used to be so many leg problems, and there are very few leg problems now. The biggest problem now is breathing, probably because we understand it more and it's not such a taboo subject – and we just get on and deal with it.' He does seem to have more wind operations performed than do other trainers. 'Probably because I'm the only one honest enough to say that I am doing it. Plenty of others are doing it, but just not telling anybody. If they want doing, they want doing.' So is there a case for compulsory declaration of wind ops? 'I wouldn't mind if we had a rule to say: "This horse has

had a wind operation since its last run." Not say it's had a "soft-palate operation" or whatever. Keep it simple. Just, "This horse has had a wind op." Then it is up to the punter to decide. I could probably give somebody a list of all my horses that have had a breathing operation in the autumn and say, "Back every one of these first time out", and somebody could make a quiet profit. It does make a huge difference to them. So why not? Just say, "This horse has had a breathing operation" and leave it at that. Just the first time.'

Having started with just eight horses and no big-money backers, Paul Nicholls trained his first Grade One winner when Paul Barber's See More Indians won the Feltham Novices Chase at Kempton in 1993. There was then what was to him an agonisingly long wait for his first Cheltenham Festival winner in 1999, although it was not nearly so long as those endured before him by the likes of David Nicholson, Josh Gifford and Noel Meade. When the breakthrough came, it was however, a spectacular one, with victories in three of the Festival's top races.

'I'd always felt that you judge people on Cheltenham. I'd only been training for eight years but it felt like 80. Then, on the Tuesday, we won the Arkle with Flagship Uberalles; on the Wednesday, we won the Champion Chase with Call Equiname; and on the Thursday, we won the Gold Cup with See More Business. It was what dreams are made of, the most phenomenal week. That got me going. New owners started coming in. Horses started coming in and things completely changed. Then I found Kauto Star and Denman, Master Minded, Neptune Collonges and Big Buck's, and we were flying. Those three winners changed my career.'

The victory with See More Business was especially sweet, not just because it was Paul Barber's horse, but because the year before See More Business, when well fancied, had been carried out of the race by Martin Pipe's Cyborgo as AP McCoy had to pull up the Pipe horse with an injury. Nicholls admits that he had to be physically restrained from 'clocking' Pipe over what he perceived as his fellow trainer's

Kauto Star and trainer Paul Nicholls in the winner's enclosure after winning the King George VI Chase at Kempton Park.

less than regretful attitude to the incident; it injected an animosity into the struggle over the next few years between the two men for the trainers' championship. For seven years, Nicholls occupied the runner-up spot behind Martin Pipe, before finally overhauling him in the 2005/06 season, since when Nicholls has lost the championship battle only once – to Nicky Henderson in 2013/14.

The exploits of Kauto Star and Denman are discussed elsewhere in this book, but there have been plenty of other stars at Manor House Stables. Few two-mile chasers could live with the speed of Master Minded, who won the Queen Mother Champion Chase of 2008 in breathtaking style by 19 lengths and went on to repeat his victory the following year, as well as twice winning the Clarence House Chase at Ascot. He became the highest-rated chaser in

the world that season – and Nicholls hailed him as the best he had trained.

Big Buck's, bought from French trainer Guillaume Macaire to go chasing, was diverted back to hurdling in 2009 after falling in a Hennessy Gold Cup; he proved to be possibly the greatest ever staying hurdler. Amid a sequence of 18 successive victories, Andy Stewart's champion captured four World Hurdles at the Cheltenham Festival and four Long Distance Hurdles at Newbury.

Rock On Ruby in 2012 became Paul Nicholls' only Champion Hurdle winner to date, while John Hales's Azertyuiop won an Arkle in 2003 and then the Queen Mother Champion Chase in the following year. At his local track, Wincanton, on 21 January 2006, Nicholls went into the record books as the first trainer to saddle six winners on the same card.

Ask him to name his own highlights and Paul Nicholls offers the Gold Cup of 2008, when he trained the first three home: Denman, Kauto Star, and Neptune Collonges. 'That was awesome. That was brilliant.' Then there were Kauto Star's two Gold Cup victories, and Kauto's incredible feat of winning the King George VI Chase five times. Nicholls now adds, 'Neptune Collonges winning the National was a different experience altogether. John Hales is a pal as well as an owner. I have to say, too, I got an enormous amount of pleasure out of Vicente winning the Scottish National [in 2016] because that put us right back in the bloody game.' The game referred to was the battle for the trainers' championship when it seemed – after Willie Mullins' seven successes at Cheltenham and his profitable Aintree, putting him some £200,000 ahead of Nicholls in prize money – that the Irish trainer was going to win the English trainers' championship. With typical tenacity, Paul Nicholls fought back with Vicente's victory and enough place money from a contingent of 17 sent to Sandown on the final day to hang on to the title in what had become the most thrilling contest ever (but without the bitterness of his battle 11 years previously with Martin Pipe). It showed the strength in depth of the Ditcheat horses, as Mullins had won 14 Grade One races

Elation from the Ditcheat team after Kauto Star wins the Gold Cup.

in Britain that season, compared with just two for Paul Nicholls.

The range of Paul Nicholls' success is extraordinary, thanks to his own training skills and thanks to the acquisition of some outstanding horses. As he says: 'You need a bloody good horse. If you haven't got horses of ability, you are not going to win races at the best level. You can get them fit, but if they're not good enough, you can't do it.' In an age when owners with deep pockets have become crucial to training success over jumps as well as on the flat, he has succeeded in attracting a clutch of those owners, but they would not be sending him expensive horses had he not achieved the results he has done. You have to write a best-seller, or two, to get the booksellers to stock their shelves in advance with your next book.

Paul reflects: 'They are once in a lifetime horses. You just keep trying with what you've got. I think a few people did well, then sat back and relaxed and took their eye off the ball, and it all went wrong. Kim Bailey had Champion Hurdles and Gold Cups and a Grand National and let it all go … You can't bask in glory, you've got to be even more determined. People do really well and think it's going to carry on for ever, and it doesn't. You have to keep looking for that next generation.' He does that relentlessly, week after week.

Several of that next generation have come to Ditcheat from France; Paul notes: 'When Ruby [his long-time former stable jockey Ruby Walsh] was doing well for me, Willie Mullins and people were green with envy, and wanted to have the same, and so they followed us to France and followed what we did. Now they've got a major team. Dan Skelton [Nicholls' former assistant, who trained 100 winners in 2015/16] will be following us. He's hungry. You can never rest on your laurels.'

Significantly, Paul Nicholls told me in April 2016, just after winning his tenth championship, 'I wouldn't want to start again. It's got to be harder. Dan Skelton is lucky, he has got his old man investing huge money in the business behind him – it's a massive help. My assistant Tom Jonason, who has just left: there's no way

he could start. You need to be in the right place with the right opportunity. It's very, very tough.' If younger trainers are to get to the top, says Nicholls, they need somewhere they can train 100 horses from.

One thing that is striking about talking to him and seeing the Manor Farm Stables operation is the focus on what he frequently refers to as 'Team Ditcheat.' An owner and friend is former Manchester United manager Sir Alex Ferguson and Paul insists: 'I talk a lot to Sir Alex. Much of what we do is very similar. You are only as good as the team around you. I've always thought that, so you've got to give everyone credit. You delegate and you've got to make people think they are all part of a team. It's my business and I've got to make all the decisions, but at the same time I need a really good team. Like Manchester United, it is both a sport and a business.' And there is another parallel with football. Paul Nicholls gets frustrated with owners who want to hang on to their horses for too long. 'Horses that have done nothing all year, you need to get shot of. Find another job. Start again. I've always been like that. Same as with a football team, some you need to get shot of. You've got to keep turning it over, otherwise you will end up standing still. At the end of the day, if they're no good or they've got problems, all they're going to do is to cost the owners money. I try to get people in that mindset.'

Paul Nicholls with Denman (left) and Kauto Star (right) at Manor Farm Stables, Ditcheat.

'Paul Barber always said to me, "It's a business first and foremost." All these people are reliant on you for their living. You've got to make the business work and the rest will follow. It's a business that has evolved around a sport.'

Of training at his level, he says that if you can't take pressure, you won't survive, and that delegation is the key. 'I get people to do stuff which gives me more time to concentrate on owners and entries and buying horses. The travelling head lad and Clifford Baker do everything without me having to say anything.'

As for the jockeys in his early years of training, he relied upon the experience of established stars like Mick Fitzgerald to ride his top horses, despite the presence in the yard of younger hopefuls like Joe Tizzard and, later, Sam Thomas. A key ally as the strength of Ditcheat developed was Irish jockey Ruby Walsh, whose services he shared with Willie Mullins in an unusual arrangement.

Says Paul: 'It's funny how that worked out. We offered Barry Geraghty the job before Ruby but he was going to be too expensive. Quite rightly, he wanted loads of expenses etc. Ruby was quite happy to come over on a gentleman's agreement, so that if I wasn't paying him anything, I couldn't insist: "I want you riding this", and he could stay in Ireland for the weekend and ride for Willie if he wanted. But it worked out really well for us. It was a great relationship and at the time I needed a really top jockey. I was just getting going. Now I've got a lot of youngsters with Sam ([Twiston-Davies] and co. A lot of people thought I was doing wrong, but we've had the championship with Sam here in the last two years. The year we lost it, Daryl Jacob was in charge. Daryl is a very good jockey but he is not a superstar jockey and he couldn't cope with the pressure. Sam's brilliant at it.'

Paul Nicholls' toughness showed when he dropped Sam Thomas, despite the young rider's Gold Cup success with Denman. 'Sam is a lovely guy. I'm fond of him. But things were going wrong and he was in tears half the time – and that's no good. He's too nice. You've got to have something about you. When he came in

the paddock after unseating on Big Buck's at the last in the Hennessy, he was literally crying. Ruby wouldn't have given a toss about it. He was arrogant and tough and hard.'

With Ruby long back in Ireland, the jockeys in Team Ditcheat who helped to win that tenth championship were Sam Twiston-Davies, Nick Scholfield, Sean Bowen, Harry Cobden and Jack Sherwood. Not one of them was older than 27 and three were still in their teens. All of them, incidentally, came up through the British pony-racing initiative.

Paul Nicholls likes to have a young team in a racing world that faces continual change. There is, he acknowledges, a change in the type of people owning jumpers and in what they expect. 'If you're doing it for commercial reasons, that's not going to work with jump racing. It's got to be your hobby. You've got to enjoy it. They all love the success but they've got to be patient. Training only two-year-olds might suit some because you've got an instant fix and you can turn them over quickly, but jump racing's different. Some horses, it takes you two or three years to get to know them properly. With Dodging Bullets, it took me ages to get there – and I won a Tingle Creek, a Champion Chase and a Clarence House with him. Even with Kauto, we never stopped learning about him.

'There's a lot of new young guys with money coming in: Johnny de la Hey, Chris Giles. They're the next generation, though they are a little bit more in a hurry. I have to say, "Hang on, wait five minutes, this is a baby ..."

'We are just beginning to get a few more who are prepared to take a longer view, to buy a "store" [an unbroken, potential jumper needing time to develop] or two on spec. Most people, though, like quicker action, and that's where the French horses do come into it a bit more.'

Paul used to say that the faster-maturing French horses suited his style of training because they came ready educated and you could crack on with them. Now he argues: 'The more time you give them, the better these French horses will be. You don't need to rush, rush, rush with them. Give them some time and let them mature.'

Point-to-point horses in Ireland are now almost impossible for outsiders to buy, says Paul Nicholls, because of Michael O'Leary's Gigginstown Stud, JP McManus and Willie Mullins. 'They've got it all sorted. But I've been buying some quite nice stores.'

As for the other ways a trainer's life has changed, he is no great fan of Sunday racing but will support a good-quality Sunday card. He acknowledges all-weather racing too has had a big impact on jump racing: 'Less and less three-year-olds are going to go jumping when they can stay on the flat and run on the all-weather. It's bound to have an impact.' Generally, he says, there is too much low-grade racing: 'If you've got nice horses, it's a hell of a job placing them, let alone running them. Bookmakers would rather have a 20-runner, 0–100 handicap than they would have a proper chase. There's too much. There must be a saturation point. There's more and more jump racing going on, less and less horses, and we wonder why there are small field sizes. These days, we can get horses fit, so there's no need to give a horse a run, or two runs, to get it fit. So they probably don't run as many times.'

If the master of Ditcheat is disturbed about how much the racing programme is arranged to suit the bookmakers' need to keep the betting shops churning, does he ever make use of their services himself? 'I backed Flagship Uberalles, See More Business and Call Equiname in a series of small doubles and trebles – and I won about £39,000. Then I had £1,000 on Big Buck's at 20-1 when he won his first World Hurdle and I put the lot on Kauto Star – and he won the Gold Cup. The only other big bet I've had was this year [2016] on Diego du Charmil in the Fred Winter and he won at 16-1. It was bloody close, and the second horse, which was a 25-1 shot, was another of mine. But I don't really bet.'

A 'lucky general' as well as a successful one: Napoleon would have approved.

Trainer Paul Nicholls with Denman, Kauto Star and Neptune Collonges – the three inmates of his Manor Farm stable who finished first, second and third in the Cheltenham Gold Cup of 2008.

5 Women in Racing
– the Long Battle for Recognition

'Get back to your knitting.'

One Jockey Club member to would-be licensed trainer Florence Nagle

A force to be reckoned with: Florence Nagle with her Irish Wolfhounds.

Women are important to the future of racing. The equestrian world is one of the few in which men and women meet on equal terms, and Jockey Club Chief Executive Simon Bazalgette told *The Times* early in 2016 that half the people who buy tickets to go racing and half of those who watch the sport on television are women – a different dynamic to almost any other sport. Apart from the success of women trainers, he pointed out, both Aintree and Epsom, hosts to the two most iconic races in the calendar, the Grand National and the Derby, would be chaired by women. But the Jockey Club has not always been so welcoming to the 'fairer sex.'

Women had farmed and ridden to hounds for centuries and competed in showjumping since the 1940s, but not until the late 1960s were women officially licensed by the Jockey Club to train racehorses.

In July 1966, when England was gripped by World Cup fever, the crucial case of *Nagle* v. *Feilden* was heard by the Court of Appeal, presided over by Lord Denning.

Florence Nagle, a daughter of the wealthy baronet Sir George Watson, was a feisty character who had been expelled from her girls' school for driving a car without permission, and who had risked disinheritance by marrying the gambling Irishman James Nagle, from whom she was divorced in 1928. Since 1938, she had trained racehorses successfully in Petworth, including a fast-finishing second in the Derby with Sandsprite, using the subterfuge to which the Jockey Club was prepared to turn a blind eye: in all official proceedings, the horses went down as being trained by her male head lad.

Mrs Nagle's fellow female trainer Norah Wilmot was forced to adopt the same demeaning procedure, despite previously having been assistant for 20 years to her trainer father, Sir Robert Wilmot. Miss Wilmot trained for the Queen, among others, and her record included victories in the Goodwood Cup and Doncaster Cup.

To add to their successes, in 1956 Helen Johnson Houghton, widow of the trainer Gordon Johnson Houghton, who had died in a hunting accident four years earlier, and the twin sister of the great National Hunt trainer Fulke Walwyn, had become the first woman to train a Classic winner when Gilles de Retz, a 50-1 shot, won the 2,000 Guineas. Because the Jockey Club refused to recognise women trainers, the success was credited in the record books to her male assistant, Charles Jerdein. He later became an art dealer in New York, in the words of his former employer 'selling Old Masters to old mistresses.'

The Jockey Club's responses to the efforts by women trainers to have reality recognised and to achieve equality varied from the insulting to the ridiculous. One Jockey Club member told

Florence Nagle, 'Get back to your knitting' and another declared, 'It would not be in the best interests of racing for women to be granted trainers' licences.' One wooden-headed member responded to the demand for equality with the asinine comment that 'Women are not persons within the Rules.'

Typical of the attitudes encountered by Florence Nagle, Norah Wilmot and Louie Dingwall, three leading figures in seeking a reversal of the ban, was that of the steward who informed them that officialdom could not run the risk of their falling into the hands of 'bad men.' As Norah Wilmot noted: 'We were all over 70 at the time!'

Things came to a head when in October 1961 the stewards of the Jockey Club told Norah Wilmot that she would not be allowed to supervise the saddling and unsaddling of her horses on the racecourse or superintend them in the stable block. Instead, those actions could be performed only by her head lad, R. Greenhill.

The racing public was well aware of the controversy and largely supportive of women trainers' efforts to achieve equality. When Norah Wilmot's three-year-old No Fiddling won at Kempton in 1961, the crowd began chanting, 'Norah, Norah' and Captain Charles Moore, one of the stewards of the meeting and the Queen's racing manager at the time, broke the rules himself by escorting Miss Wilmot into the winner's enclosure to greet her winner as any other trainer could have done. Given Captain Moore's connections, at least one racing scribe wondered at the time if a certain prominent owner was seeking to give her own gentle hint to racing officialdom.

Florence Nagle told the *Sporting Life* in 1965 that she was planning legal action against the Jockey Club: 'The stewards are not running a private men's club. It has to be borne in mind that racing is now existing on public money and should not, therefore, debar women from full participation in the sport.' All other attempts at getting the Jockey Club to see reason having failed, Florence Nagle finally took them to court, where the Jockey Club was soused as effectively as a high-summer winner having buckets of

Norah Wilmot, the first officially licensed woman trainer to win a race.

Henrietta Knight
with Best Mate,
Terry Biddlecombe
and Jim Culloty,
at home in West
Lockinge.

water poured over him in the winner's enclosure.

Lord Denning, who presided over the 1966 hearing, told Philip Feilden, the Jockey Club Secretary who had won an MC at El Alamein fighting against dictatorship, 'We are not considering a social club. We are considering an association which exercises a virtual monopoly in an important field of activity.'

He insisted: 'If Mrs Nagle is to carry on her work without stooping to subterfuge, she has to have a licence.' The Law Lords argued: 'The rights of a person to work should not be prevented by the dictatorial powers of a body which holds a monopoly,' and Lord Salmon commented that the Jockey Club's stand had been 'as capricious as refusing a man simply because of the colour of his hair.'

The High Court found for the plaintiff, but the Jockey Club was not a graceful loser. It said that Mrs Nagle could have her licence, provided that she recognised that it was granted 'in the exercise of the stewards' absolute and unfettered discretion.'

Miss Wilmot and Mrs Nagle became the first women to hold licences. Within days, Norah Wilmot became the first officially licensed woman flat trainer to win a race when her filly Pat took the South Coast Stakes at Brighton in the hands of Scobie Breasley. Meanwhile, the National Hunt Committee, in those days a separate body from the Jockey Club, had been just a shade more enlightened than the Jockey Club and, in early 1966, had decided to recognise women who trained their own hunter chasers: the first woman officially recognised as a winning trainer was therefore Mrs Jackie Brutton, who at the Cheltenham Festival on 16 March 1966 trained Snowdra Queen to win the United Hunts Chase.

Since then, women trainers have conclusively proved that gender has nothing to do with the ability to train horses. In 1983, Jenny Pitman became the first woman to train a Grand National winner with Corbiere. She repeated the feat with Royal Athlete in 1995. Mrs Pitman also trained Esha Ness, who was first past the post in the National of 1993, later declared void after a false start. Since then, Venetia Williams with Mon Mome in 2009 and Sue Smith with Aurora's Encore in 2013 have also triumphed in the National.

Jenny Pitman also won the Cheltenham Gold Cup twice, with Burrough Hill Lad in 1984 and with Garrison Savannah in 1991, a feat surpassed among women trainers only by the three Gold Cups collected between 2002 and 2004 by Henrietta Knight with Best Mate. Mary Reveley became the first woman trainer to train 1,000 winners on the flat and over jumps, and Pam Sly became the first woman trainer to win a British Classic with Speciosa in the 1,000 Guineas of 2006.

Venetia Williams, who was also only the second woman, after Jenny Pitman, to train a Hennessy Gold Cup winner (Teeton Mill in 1998), had originally hoped to progress as a jockey. She had ridden ten winners as an amateur when she was knocked unconscious by a fall in the Grand National at Becher's. Two weeks later, a broken neck in another fall brought her riding career to a premature end. She began training on the banks of the Wye in 1995, having spent time with Martin Pipe, with Colin Hayes in Australia, with Barry Hills, and after seven years as an assistant to John Edwards. Her talent was quickly obvious: in her second and third seasons, she had the best strike rate of any leading trainer with around a third of her runners entering the winner's enclosure.

If the prizes for the 'best turned out' horse were to be accompanied by awards for the 'best turned out' trainer, the coolly elegant Venetia Williams would win plenty of them, but visitors to her yard wouldn't always say the same of its inhabitants. As a great believer in turning out her jumpers to roll in what they will, she has been heard to boast that she has 'the filthiest horses in training.' In recent years, she has regularly seemed to enjoy a purple patch with her chasers when the ground is at its heaviest.

Women riders over jumps have so far found the going harder than have the trainers. Even Lord Denning highlighted some of the prejudice of previous times, during the Nagle case, when

Venetia Williams with jockey Aidan Coleman and the owners of Stan after winning the Mears Group Silver Chase at Cheltenham.

Carrie Ford, who gave as good as she got from Ginger McCain.

matter if they shared an ambulance if both were unconscious..."'

The first series of 12 races, on the flat only, for women amateur jockeys was finally introduced in 1972. In 1974, women were allowed to race against men in amateur races on the flat. Women were finally licensed to ride as professionals on the flat in 1975, and only when the Sex Discrimination Act hauled the Jockey Club into the twentieth century did officialdom permit them to ride over jumps. We did not see the first woman rider in the Grand National until Charlotte Brew competed in 1977, the year women members were first admitted to the Jockey Club. Geraldine Rees was the first woman rider to complete the course when she finished eighth and last on Cheers in 1982.

It hasn't only been officialdom that has displayed prejudice. Four-times Grand National-winning trainer Ginger McCain, forever associated with Red Rum, caused something of a storm in 2005 when he criticised the participation in the National of female rider Carrie Ford, riding Forest Gunner. She had ridden 75 point-to-point winners and had won the Fox Hunters' Chase over the National fences the previous year on Forest Gunner – just ten weeks after giving birth to her daughter Hannah. A professional character who enjoyed time in the media spotlight, Ginger declared, 'Horses do not win Grand Nationals ridden by women. Carrie is a grand lass but she's a broodmare now and having kids does not get you fit to ride Grand Nationals.' Carrie Ford dismissed most of the resulting hoo-ha on 'Ginger is Ginger' grounds, although she did call him a 'cantankerous old dinosaur.' In the event, she finished fifth, equalling the best-ever finish by a female rider up until then.

With women jockeys of the quality of Nina Carberrry and Katie Walsh (the best-placed woman yet in the National when she finished third in 2012 on Seabass) now participating, many believe that it is only a matter of time before a woman rides the winner of the Grand National. One of the most thrilling races seen at Cheltenham in recent years was the four-mile

he reflected: 'It is not as if the training of racehorses could be regarded as an unsuitable job for a woman – like that of a jockey,' and despite having been forced to license women trainers, the Jockey Club did not hurry to recognise women's rights to equality in the saddle.

Women had been riding professionally in the USA since 1969, while Italian racegoers saw their first female professional jockey, Tizziana Sozzi, in 1971. In that year, seeking to relieve the pressure, the Jockey Club agreed to look at introducing some women-only races for amateur riders. Opposition to giving women more opportunities came from several quarters: some men genuinely feared for the physical risks to women. Lightweight jockeys worried about the competition and claimed safety fears if women could not control their mounts. Others hid behind the smokescreen of added costs. The *Sporting Life* recorded a revealing snippet from Jockey Club discussions: 'One steward said that apart from changing rooms we would have to double up on many other things including first-aid rooms and ambulances. Another steward said, with a perfectly deadpan face, "It wouldn't

National Hunt Chase in 2010. Nina Carberry on Becauseicouldntsee and Katie Walsh on Poker de Sivola were the only two women riders in a field of 18. They managed their tactics so well that, as they turned for home, they were two lengths clear of the rest. They then threw themselves and their mounts at the final fence with utterly fearless abandon and battled every inch of the way to the line. Another step forward came when Lizzie Kelly, by riding Tea For Two to victory in the Kauto Star Novice Chase at Kempton in December 2015, became the first woman jockey to ride a Grade One jumps winner in Britain. Certainly, a look around any parade ring at those leading up the horses confirms that racing cannot now survive without the female input: girls outnumber boys in the intakes of both the Northern Racing School and the British Racing College. But Lizzie Kelly gives the necessary perspective: 'If I stood there and said, "I'd like to be a doctor," people would say, "Oh, you're so clever." When I said I wanted to be a jockey, people laughed. That gives you attitude.'

A new fillip was given to the debate about opportunities for women riders when AP McCoy suggested in November 2015, shortly after his retirement, and soon after Michelle Payne had ridden the 100-1 shot Prince of Penzance to win the Melbourne Cup, that they should be given a 3 lb allowance. The BHA, while considering some measures to increase opportunities for women, didn't give that idea any encouragement. Katie Walsh and Nina Carberry said they would be happy to take the allowance – but then they were speaking from the weighing room at Cheltenham! It remains to be seen just how much of a boost women riders will have been given by the creditable effort of the former Olympic cyclist Victoria Pendleton at the 2016 Cheltenham Festival, where, under massive media scrutiny, she rode Pacha du Polder into fifth place in the Foxhunter Chase, only 15 months after first climbing into a saddle with four legs, instead of two wheels, beneath it.

Katie Walsh (nearest camera) on Poker de Sivola and Nina Carberry on Becauseicouldntsee fight it out in the National Hunt Chase at Cheltenham.

Profile: **The woman who battled to the top**

'My owners had made an investment in their horses and I was paid to be their protector and their spokeswoman. Sometimes, Clerks of the Course were just pure liars.'

Jenny Pitman on racecourse officialdom.

No woman has made a greater impact on racing, and certainly on the Grand National, than Jenny Pitman, whose race-day interviews with Desmond Lynam became part of Aintree tradition. From an unprivileged farming background in Leicestershire, she did not have things easy in what was traditionally a man's world, especially after the breakdown of her first marriage left her with two children and little in the bank; yet she rose to become one of the best trainers of staying chasers in the country, not only winning the Grand National twice, but also twice succeeding in the Cheltenham Gold Cup. Emotional and forthright, Jenny Pitman did not suffer fools, or racecourse officialdom, gladly. She says now: 'We locked antlers a couple of times. They're paid to do a job, to get as many horses running as they can and as many people as possible through the gate. But I was paid to do a job, too. My owners had made an investment in their horses and I was paid to be their protector and their spokeswoman. Sometimes, Clerks of the Course were just pure liars.'

On one occasion, she called the Clerk of the Course at Newton Abbot, 20 minutes before she had to declare her horses, to check on the state of the ground. His wife answered the call and said, 'He's too busy, he's in the lambing shed! It's a very busy time of year for us...' Says Jenny, 'We were doing a professional job with a duty of care and trying to keep the horses sound, and he was in the lambing shed all morning. I reported him.'

In the Cheltenham car park one day with a course official, when the grass was in poor condition, Jenny relates how she asked him how much his smart car was worth. He told her. Having then asked him what he thought her horse was worth (about the same), she asked: 'Have you got any matches in your pocket?' What do you want matches for?' 'Because I'm going to light one

and drop it in your petrol tank, since that's what you're expecting me to do with my horses!'

Famously protective of the animals in her charge, she is furious to this day about being called in by stewards because one of her horses, Willsford, who had lost his form and needed encouragement, had been marked by a jockey's four strokes of the whip at Uttoxeter. Unusually, Willsford's coat had been clipped only the day before and she told the stewards that if he had still had a full coat, there would have been nothing to be seen. One of the stewards had a red beard, so she added, 'If I smacked the face of someone with a big bushy beard, it wouldn't show the hand-prints!' The stewards' secretary told her afterwards, 'Perhaps we don't want horses like him running again, Mrs Pitman.' Willsford went on to win another five races, including the Welsh and Scottish Nationals.

She could be just as direct with her owners. She told the flamboyant financial markets player Terry Ramsden, who had his own retained jockey: 'Your jockey is being too hard on these horses and I'm not putting up with it. Either you speak to him, because I've tried and it's not working, or you can get somebody else to train your horses.' She adds now, 'I know people thought I was neurotic about this, and I said it as though I cared more than they do. I don't know how much they care, I've got no idea. But how you measure success is not those trophies in the other room – it's by how big your graveyard is.'

She chuckles now, though, recalling her first meeting with the free-spending Ramsden, who had come to see his horse run at Haydock. They were to meet in the parade ring where his hurdler, I Bin Zadoon, was 'spooking' at the shafts of sunlight coming through the trees. 'I thought, "Shit, he's in good nick," and then, bugger me, if he didn't fall over. I nearly died. He stumbled and fell over. It's the first time I've met Ramsden, he's just come into the paddock and I have to say, "Well, that's the first time I've had a faller in the parade ring!"'

1984, Cheltenham Gold Cup winner Burrough Hill Lad with trainer Jenny Pitman.

She knows that some reckoned her to be better at getting on with horses than with other human beings; at one stage, she broke off relations with most of the media. But a sense of humour was usually there too. Once, after reading some press comment, she asked her vet, 'What the bloody hell is a virago?' 'A cantankerous old cow,' he suggested. 'Pretty accurate, then,' she replied – and they both burst out laughing.

Jenny Pitman's progress as a trainer came by stages. Initially, when her first husband, Richard Pitman, was riding for Fred Winter and they were living in a caravan at Hinton Parva, she would take in rest-and-recuperation cases for Winter, for Fulke Walwyn and Barry Hills, as she coped with a toddler round the yard and a baby in a tack-room playpen. 'They sent them to me because they knew I would be diligent.' Then she moved on to training point-to-pointers. 'I had to work. I didn't have choices. Life's difficult when you've got choices. If you haven't got any choices, you just keep marching down that road with the hope that the load on your back gets a bit lighter sometime.'

One of those to see her potential was Lord Cadogan. He had lent the young couple money to replace their caravan with a bungalow, and he asked her to train his Road Race. 'I won the Eton and Harrow race at the

Heythrop for Lord Cadogan, which meant the world to him. He wouldn't normally come racing because he felt that I was under enough pressure anyway. That day, the horses went past the line together, neck and neck, and he turned to me and said, "All we can do, Jenny, is to pray." It brought tears to my eyes – that's a chap who has won Gold Cups and so on, and it still meant so much.' The rider of Road Race that day, incidentally, was a certain Nicky Henderson.

With her second husband and long-time partner, David Stait, supplementing her stories, Jenny dismisses talk of other well-known names as pioneers of particular methods, saying, 'With the point-to-pointers, we had to do interval training because we didn't have any choice. We did a massive amount of roadwork. My horses were as hard as iron. I hunted them too. They were as fit as butcher's dogs.'

And what type of horses did she have? 'We had liquorice allsorts. We had the kind of horses other people didn't want!'

Another early patron was Tony Stratton-Smith of Charisma Records, who asked Jenny to be his private trainer and offered to buy her a Lambourn yard. She

Queen Elizabeth the Queen Mother presents the Gold Cup to Jenny Pitman, 1991.

felt that was too big a commitment but then gambled on buying the run-down Weathercock House herself. It became her base for a remarkable career with a full licence from 1975 to 1999.

Says David Stait, 'When they started the bumpers for four-year-olds, Jenny used to say to owners, "Look, there's two ways you can do this. If you want quick sport, you can buy something off the flat and hope it's going to go a little further. If you want a long-term prospect that maybe one day might be good enough to go to Cheltenham or Liverpool, we can buy three-year-olds, bring them in, turn them out, break them in, look after them, and give them a run in a bumper at the end of the season." We were up on the gallops one year at the start of the season and all the bumper horses were out, cantering up – we had about nine that year. Fred Winter comes bobbing along and Jenny asks, "Have you got any nice horses?" and he says, "No, I bloody well haven't because you bloody bought them all as three-year-olds!" It was the best compliment she was ever paid.'

There were, however, one or two horses of a different kind, such as Anais Anais, an Irish-owned horse sent over to Jenny with a string of duck eggs on his record. Jenny and David take turns with the tale: 'Mandy, Jenny's

sister, had what we called an electric arse – they [the horses] worked 7 lb better for her than for anybody else. They sent this horse over, saying it was a shagger. We exercised it with poor horses and it ran away from them. So we exercised it with slightly better horses. "It's not a messer, Jen," says Mandy, "This is all right." Whoosh – and it ran away. We exercised it with good horses and it ran away. "John Joe, are you taking the mickey?" "Oh, no, he's always done that. He's a morning glory. Only does it on the gallops."

'We keep entering the horse and it keeps getting balloted out. I'm pulling my hair out and I ring Weatherbys, saying, "I need to know when I am going to get a run." They say, "We can't really tell you because he's got a lot of noughts in his form, and the problem is when you run him, you're going to be in the same situation next time." I said, "Pet, don't you worry about next time – just let me run him this time," and we finally get in a race at Towcester.

'Mark [Jenny's jockey then trainer son] was riding and claiming 7 lb. His mother told him, "Jump the second-last, give it two smacks, and two smacks more when you've jumped the last. Don't look round, whatever you do." It won by half the track. Six Irish lads came over to back it. One big chap, Michael Cohen, goes up to one of the bookies and he says, "What's this – another fecker she's dug up from the grave!" They'd known all along. It took them four days to get home.'

Jenny Pitman's first big-race triumph came when Bueche Girod won the Massey Ferguson Gold Cup in 1980 but the horse who really took her into the big time was Corbiere, known as 'Corky' in the stable, who won the Grand National in 1983. Corbiere went on to finish third on two more occasions in the great race. Jenny won the National again in 1995 with Royal Athlete, then she had the first past the post with Esha Ness in the 'Grand National that never was.' She won three Welsh Nationals with Corbiere (1982), Burrough Hill Lad (1983) and Stearsby (1986); she won the Scottish National with Willsford (1995); and she completed the full set by taking the Irish National with Mudahim (1997). The greatest of all her champions, though, was surely Burrough Hill Lad, a big, athletic horse with 'difficult' legs; with this powerful horse, she won the Cheltenham Gold Cup in 1984, as well as that Welsh National in 1983, a Hennessy Gold Cup (1984) and a King George VI Chase (1984). Jenny won a second Cheltenham Gold Cup with Garrison Savannah in 1991 and came painfully close to training the first horse since the great Golden Miller in 1934 to win the Gold Cup and the Grand National in the same season.

Garrison Savannah won the Gold Cup in 1991 in the hands of her son Mark Pitman, beating The Fellow by the narrowest of margins in one of the most dramatic finishes ever seen. 'Gary', as the stable knew him, did so despite having spent six weeks at the height of winter confined to his box with a shoulder injury, and having undergone acupuncture almost until the day of the race. The victory was compensation for his jockey, who on Toby Tobias had been narrowly beaten by the 100-1 shot Norton's Coin in the previous year's Gold Cup. However, triumph rapidly turned to misery: in the last race of the day, the County Hurdle, Mark Pitman fell and broke his pelvis. His mother told him not to even dream of getting back to ride Garrison Savannah at Aintree – but the determined rider did just that. As Jenny Pitman vividly recalls, Garrison Savannah also suffered a setback in the run-up to the National. With equine coughs doing the rounds, she had decided to give Gary a course of antibiotics to ward off the bugs. Unfortunately, the assistant delegated to inject him stuck the needle not into his backside, but his chest. A huge lump came up, leaving the horse in great discomfort. It took four days to bring down the swelling with hot and cold compresses, and by keeping the horse constantly on the move, even directing car headlights onto the paddock at night so as to trot him on a lunge line.

Come the 1991 National, the brave Mark Pitman, who had taken another nasty fall on the previous Thursday when his mount had been killed, led over the final fence on Garrison Savannah but was heartbreakingly overtaken on that famous 494-yard run-in by Seagram. As Gary's petrol tank flickered to empty, his rival drove past to win in an agonising rerun of Richard Pitman's defeat on Crisp so many years before. Jenny Pitman says now: 'He was fit. I'd made the cake and got the plain icing on, but I just hadn't been able to finish dressing it properly. If we hadn't given him anything, if we'd left him, he'd probably have won – but then again, he might have got the flu.'

What really maddens Jenny was that in 1993, the year of the 'Grand National that never was,' when her Esha Ness was first past the post, she was convinced that she was going to win at Aintree with Garrison Savannah, a horse she had always seen as being a National horse. 'That year he was humming. When the owners had bought him and came to see him, they asked what kind of horse he was. I said, "He's Corbiere with a different colour." Because he was. He just happened to win a Gold Cup as well, and the Sun Alliance! Lots of other horses that had won Gold Cups ran in the Gold Cup the year he won. That's what a hero he was. But he'd had very little praise for his ability and what he'd done and I thought, that year, "Right, you lot: you are going to be on your knees worshipping him for what he has done." That's what I had planned that year.' Instead, it became a nonsense National, and Garrison Savannah was one of those pulled up before the second circuit. It was a cruel and absurd way to lose the chance of a third National winner.

After the void National, an angry Pitman sat down with a timer and a tape machine, and compiled her own painstakingly detailed report on the fiasco. She sent it to the racing authorities but never even received an acknowledgement. Never, ever, says the trainer, who retired in 1998, was she asked to contribute to any study by racing officialdom.

Jenny Pitman and Des Lynam at the BBC Sports Personality Awards in Liverpool.

6

The Jockey's Life

'Getting injured doesn't mess with your head in the same way that getting beaten does.'

Champion Jockey AP McCoy on jockeys' priorities

The jump jockeys of the 1960s lived in a different world from the riders of today. Back in the days of Arkle and Mill House, there were no agents finding them opportunities, no mobile phones chirping with the offer of extra rides, no video-players at home enabling them to wear out the rewind buttons, obsessively replaying the races they had been involved in, and to agonise over what might have been if they had chosen different tactics.

In 1961, at the jockeys' request, riding fees were changed from £7 for a loser and £10 for a winner to a flat fee of £10. Although there might, at the owner's discretion, be a 'present', there was no automatic percentage of winnings at that time.

The motorway network was in its infancy and travel times between courses were horrendous. The summer-racing circuit in the South West used to begin for the top jockeys with a stay at

Pensive before...
Jockey Sam
Twiston-Davies in
the weighing room at
Ludlow Racecourse.

the Palace Hotel in Torquay. Before the M5 was built, horses, jockeys and trainers had to lodge in the area if they were to get to the races at all through the holiday traffic. Against that, there was no Sunday racing (which was introduced in 1992) and the jumps season then lasted for ten months of the year rather than the all-year-round business it is today.

Few weighing rooms then boasted a sauna to help the early arrivals lose another crucial couple of pounds. There was no duty physio to stretch them out on a couch and ease the aches and pains of recent injuries before their daily duties commenced. In those cap-touching times, stewards, many of them ex-military men, expected to be addressed as 'Sir' and didn't use jockeys' first names when they were called in for an inquiry. When Fred Winter, as champion jockey, asked for a complimentary badge for his wife, Diana, when she accompanied him one day to Wincanton, the request was refused.

Many changing rooms had no showers or even hot water; jockeys would have to change standing on newspapers on cold concrete floors. Look at the pictures of Fred Winter and his contemporaries walking out to ride in races, and they would often understandably have overcoats on over their colours, the overcoat to be handed to the groom as they mounted.

As for safety, many courses still had concrete posts supporting the running rails;

some had strands of wire on the inside rails. Body protectors to help prevent spinal injury were unheard of and the cork skull caps that jockeys wore before proper crash helmets were introduced didn't even have a chinstrap. A jockey's cork helmet with colours attached came off one day at Cheltenham and free-wheeled through the air. In the distant stands, his wife screamed: 'Oh my God, his head's come off.'

Nor, in those days, were there always ambulances following the jockeys round the course, racing being the only sport, apart from motor racing, in which it happens now. In February 1970, Terry Biddlecombe fell on the flat in the last race at Kempton, well out of view of the stands. It was a shocking fall in which he split a kidney and crushed several ribs. It put him in hospital for weeks and resulted in Biddlecombe's missing a winning ride on Gay Trip in the Grand National. But it wasn't until his colleagues noticed that Terry hadn't returned to the weighing room that an ambulance was sent to look for him.

On the lighter side, the more happy-go-lucky brigade of jockeys in those days expected, with a few exceptions, to celebrate success with a few jars. They partied hard when there was the occasion for it – and sometimes when there wasn't. There was no threat of a breath test in the weighing room.

Then, as now, there was that special camaraderie among the jumping fraternity, born of the risks they face every time they ride. Perhaps the best example of that came a little later when, in 1982, John Francome and Peter Scudamore were battling for the jockeys' championship. Scu became sidelined before the end of the season with a broken arm; John Francome kept riding until he drew level with Scudamore's total and then took no more rides so that the championship was shared.

The insurance schemes to help jockeys when they did suffer such income-reducing injuries or worse were rudimentary in the 1960s and 1970s and then, as now, despite their greater risks, the jump jockeys were poorly rewarded compared with their flat-racing brethren. Before he gave up training to become a prolific racing author, Tim Fitzgeorge-Parker persuaded Jack Dowdeswell, the one-time jumps champion, to take out a licence to ride on the flat as well, when he was nearly 40 years of age. Dowdeswell won a mile race at Chepstow and the grateful winning owner handed him his 'present' in the shape of a fat brown envelope. The jockey opened it in the weighing room and gawped at the package of fivers, more than he would collect for winning three top three-mile chases: 'I held up the notes and asked the little flat fellows around me, "Do you always get lolly like this for doing so little?" They just smiled, so I suppose they must get it all the time.'

For jump jockeys, as for their flat-racing brethren, the past 50 years have seen a steady march to greater physical fitness and improved weight management. Says former top jockey Mick Fitzgerald: 'The biggest improvement is jockeys' awareness of their bodies. In the old days, they just grabbed a few "pee pills." Now they know how fit they need to be and regulate their liquids' intake.' Greater professionalism has been accompanied by significant – albeit sometimes hard-won – strides in jockey safety and effective insurance schemes. Nevertheless, partly through the concentration of power in a

Ecstatic after... Sam Thomas celebrates after winning in the 2008 Cheltenham Gold Cup on Denman.

Valet Adrian Heffernan in the weighing room during day one of the Galway Festival.

few big yards, partly through the dominating role nowadays of the jockey's agent, whereas rewards have increased significantly for those at the top of the riding tree, life has become tougher financially for the lower ranks. In the 1960s, the top jockeys would not have sought to ride at more than one meeting in a day, or in some lower-value races, unless it was for their retaining stable; nowadays, their agents, who take a percentage of what they earn, will book them for every race they can physically reach. The top riders now take a much bigger proportion of the rides.

In Ireland, particularly, so many rides are now going to the top ten per cent that it is very hard for young riders to build a career. Virtually their only hope is to become attached to one of the big stables, such as those of Willie Mullins or Gordon Elliott. If a smaller-scale owner or trainer stumbles across a good horse, they usually have to sell it to survive. If the buyer is the sporting JP McManus, the trainer could be lucky: he often gets to keep the horse in the yard. But JP and the other big owners have their own retained riders, whom they will want to put up on the new acquisition, so that the rider who has helped to make the horse will likely never climb aboard him again.

In England, Richard Killoran conducted an intriguing study, published in the *Racing Post* in March 2016, on the rewards and expenses of the 96 (out of 185) licensed jump jockeys who are outside the top 15 and who ride in more than 75 races a season. At £157 per ride, less deductions for insurance, agent, physio, valet, net of some £46, and motoring costs of £54, their take-home pay on average was less than £17,000 for the year, with a further £6,424 in prize-money percentages. Scant reward for risking life and limb on every ride with no job security.

Yet it is not only the rewards for race-riding that have seen considerable changes: lifestyles, relationships with owners and officialdom have altered hugely too, and so have riding tactics and styles as the great names of recent decades – Stan Mellor, Josh Gifford and Terry Biddlecombe, Jonjo O'Neill and Ron Barry, Peter Scudamore and John Francome, Richard Dunwoody, AP McCoy and Richard Johnson – have all put their stamp on the sport.

Lifestyles

Alcohol has long played a part in the racing life. Champagne bottles are regularly opened to celebrate victories and many jockeys used to start on the process well before the event: before he went out to win Gold Cups and Champion Hurdles for Vincent O'Brien, Aubrey Brabazon used to accompany his trainer to the bar for a port and brandy. Terry Biddlecombe, the dashing 'blond bomber' whose presence on the card probably doubled the female attendance at some race meetings, and who was three times champion jockey in the 1960s, was the epitome of the 'live hard, play hard' school in the last great age of the weighing-room cavaliers. He was tall and heavy-boned – and he struggled ferociously with his weight. Spending hours in Turkish baths to achieve a racing weight, he used to cheer the process by drinking champagne, Babycham or brandy, claiming that the alcohol made him sweat more.

He was a regular at Gloucester Turkish Baths, arriving at around 7.00 a.m. and reckoning to lose 6–7 lb in a couple of hours. When, at about 10.30 a.m., the manager asked if he wanted anything, Terry would ask for his 'usual' – a bottle of Worthington E, and a port and Babycham. 'I would pour out exactly half of the beer before going back into the baths. When I came out, I would finish the beer, have a quick shower and take off in the car to the races... Once in the car, I would sip my port and Babycham, which made me feel great.' Following a night out, a Turkish bath and a stiffener on the way to the races, jockeys such as Biddlecombe and those who celebrated and wasted with him could still be technically inebriated when riding the following day.

Following the introduction of weighing-room breath tests in 1994, it is no longer possible to do things that way. It does not mean, though, that the struggles to make the weight are any easier. In fact, they are probably becoming harder: medical science tells us that the average 18-year-old is increasing in weight by a pound every three years, and the weights set to be carried by horses in races are not rising on the same scale. With a weight range of 10 st to 11 st 12 lb in chases and hurdles, jump jockeys are not as constrained as flat-racing jockeys, who need to be able to ride at between 8 st 4 lb and 9 st to pick up enough mounts to make it worthwhile, but there is still pressure enough.

In his jockey days, champion trainer Paul Nicholls used to drive to the races in two tracksuits and an overcoat beneath an enclosing envelope of bin bags, leaving a pool of sweat on the floor of the car, as he struggled to lose

another pound or two. AP McCoy was, and is, a teetotaller, but he has outlined in biographies how, throughout his 20 years as champion jockey, he used to boil himself like a lobster in scalding hot baths to trim the crucial further ounces off his already spare frame.

Riders, nowadays, through the Professional Jockeys Association, have access to nutritional experts to help them frame sensible diets but the struggles still go on, with plenty of instances still of jockeys taking 'pee pills' to dehydrate themselves. Although it is less of a problem for jump jockeys, there is still serious concern about the number of young jockeys who, in order to keep down their weight, abuse their bodies too by 'flipping' – forcing themselves to 'sick up' the food they have just eaten. Apparently, it is so bad among US flat-racing jockeys that 'heaving bowls' are provided in the weighing room.

Overall, most jockeys now are physically fitter than were their forebears, running, working out in the gym and regularly walking the courses they ride. Better diet and better lifestyles have enabled a number of top jumps riders – Graham Lee, Jim Crowley, Timmy Murphy and Dougie Costello among them – to forsake the jumping world for the greater financial rewards, and lesser risks, of the flat-racing jockey's life.

If we all feel a pang for the loss of the weighing-room cavaliers who added so much

Terry Biddlecombe trying to lose weight at a Turkish baths.

colour to the racing scene, we should remember that the old 'glory days' of widespread drinking, often connected with weight loss, had a downside too. That was never better demonstrated than by the case of Bobby Beasley.

Before he was 25 years of age, Beasley had three times been Irish champion jockey. He had won the Cheltenham Gold Cup on Roddy Owen, the Grand National on Nicolaus Silver for Fred Rimell, and the Champion Hurdle on Another Flash. Beasley was a strictly brought-up Catholic: initially, he didn't drink. However, unsure of himself socially, he started drinking to 'be a man' among the weighing-room cavaliers – but he could not handle it. He wrecked his marriage, threw away his career and became a down-and-out alcoholic. In Beasley's case, there would be glorious redemption. He battled the booze, got his weight back down and climaxed a fairytale recovery by winning the Gold Cup again, at the age of 38, on Captain Christy, the tearaway that he helped to tame. Nevertheless, there are many other sad cases where there has been no comeback.

Since 1994, jockeys have been subject to random testing for drugs or excessive alcohol levels, albeit as Paul Struthers of the PJA points out, 'Testing in racing is purely for the safety of the individuals and others – there is really no such thing as a performance-enhancing drug for jockeys.' It is done to stop people riding while drunk or hung-over, when they could be a danger to themselves or others.

Safety

In jump racing, falls are inevitable. Jockeys' wives dread afternoon phone calls; jump jockeys are the only people who are likely to receive more 'get well' cards than birthday cards. Going back 20 years, one ride in 13 over the jumps resulted in a fall. The latest figures from the PJA put it at a fall every 14.7 rides. For the top riders who can afford to be choosy, or whose owners and trainers are keen to protect them, the average will be better than that. For the jobbing jockey on fewer than 15 winners a year, it will be worse: they simply cannot afford to turn down potential mounts who have a sketchy record of jumping and a row of Fs against their names. Of the 86 professional jump jockeys in Ireland, for example, only 15 had more than 20 winners by the end of January in the 2015/16 season. There were 24 riders without a single win: simply to survive they needed to take every ride they could get.

Interestingly, although some people, like the late John Oaksey, used to campaign against water jumps (which have been banned in Ireland), Richard Linley, the former top jockey who is now senior inspector of courses, insists: 'Water jumps are the safest jumps on the course.' If you put in a plain fence at Doncaster or Exeter, he says, where water jumps are the first obstacle after the winning post around the bend, 'I guarantee you would have more fallers and more injuries.' On courses like Perth and Wincanton, 'If you didn't have the water jumps,

the next thing people would be asking for is a camber on the bends, because horses would [then] be going faster and would slip up.'

It has all become much more scientific. In researching the best way of signalling troubles on the racecourse, Richard spent time with the Traffic Research Laboratory at Bracknell and on Thruxton motor-racing circuit. And things change all the time without most of us noticing: 'We got rid of gorse in hurdles and fences back in 1997/98. In 2002, we padded the guard rails on fences. Open-ditch guards have been painted a more-prominent orange since 2002.'

Safety standards have improved in most sports but you cannot build a hardened cockpit around race riders. Not all falls, fortunately, result in significant injuries. But jockeys can be their own worst enemies: many will seek to conceal injuries, including concussions, from on-course doctors – to avoid being stood down from a ride; if another jockey scores on what would have been your ride, the owner may be inclined to keep him on next time. Sometimes, such practices have been carried to extremes. Jonjo O'Neill only got to ride Sea Pigeon in the Ebor Handicap on the flat by conning the doctor who passed him fit into examining not the foot he had injured, but the other foot. There are pictures of Terry Biddlecombe winning a hurdle race at Cheltenham with an arm in plaster, and in the saddle at Hereford wearing a neck brace for a hairline crack in a vertebra.

Riders differ from most people in their attitude to risk. Amateur rider and racing journalist John Oaksey once recalled how, trying to present a horse's eye view of Aintree to television viewers, from a helicopter, for pre-National coverage, he kept urging that they must go lower and lower. Finally, the exasperated pilot had had enough. He protested: 'Look – if one of your bloody horses hits the fences, you get carried away in a nice comfortable ambulance. If we touch one, they scrape us up with a trowel.'

Jockeys, who are often not without their macho side, used to ride on with concussion if they felt OK, but nowadays the authorities in all sports, from boxing to rugby, are alert to the dangers, short-term and long-term, of sportsmen playing on with head injuries or resuming too soon after a concussion. Currently, jockeys who have suffered a concussion are automatically stood down for seven days and have to go through prescribed 'protocols' to get back in the saddle. Former champion Richard Dunwoody, who admits that after being concussed one day at Hereford, he couldn't remember that he had left his wife, and had to read the *Sporting Life* to remind him as to what he was riding in the next race, is now among a group of athletes from all sports helping the Concussion in Sport programme to research what long-term effects regular concussions might have in terms of future health – especially depression, Alzheimer's or Parkinson's disease.

Sometimes accidents can be truly bizarre. In July 2016, Northern Ireland jockey Chris Meehan was riding a hurldle race in Merano, Italy, where in a fall he broke his nose and

The most obvious peril of a jump jockey's life: even the best jockeys can expect a fall around every 14 races. Here (left to right) Richard Johnson takes a tumble from Alpha des Obeaux at Aintree; Andy Turnell parts company with Publican at Kempton Park, 1968; Richard Dunwoody and Spring Hay hit the ground; and Becher's Brook takes its toll in the 1989 Grand National.

gashed his chin. His worst injury, though, occurred when the ambulance sent to his aid reversed over his leg and broke it. 'You couldn't make it up,' said the remarkably good-humoured Meeham – especially since he comes from a family of ambulance workers!

Riders pay a heavy price for their addiction to the sport. Biddlecombe, for example, who retired from riding in 1974, broke a shoulder blade six times, his wrists five times, bones in his hand five times, his left collarbone, ankle, forearm and elbow once each. In addition to that, he had rib fractures, a split kidney, a dislocated ankle, and over 100 instances of concussion.

When Brendan Powell retired from the saddle in 2000 to start training, he declared: 'I've been pretty lucky with injuries.' He had only had two broken legs, a broken arm, two broken wrists, both collarbones shattered by repeated breaks – and a ruptured stomach, causing massive internal bleeding!

It happens even to the very best: when AP McCoy retired in 2015, his tally was one broken leg, a broken shoulder blade, broken middle and lower vertebrae, a broken sternum, broken ribs and a punctured lung, a broken wrist, too many broken collarbones and broken teeth to list, a broken cheekbone, a broken thumb and several concussions. Non-racing people might suspect that all jockeys are masochists but it is simply the different mindset that goes with the job. As McCoy noted in his autobiography, 'Getting injured doesn't mess with your head in the same way that getting beaten does.' Jump jockeys believe that the prizes are worth the pain; when they no longer feel that way, it is time to quit.

Some, of course, are forced to quit before they wish to, because of injuries. In the period covered by this book, compensation arrangements for those who pay a heavy price for the jumping life have been much improved. Since 1984, there has been a pension scheme operated by the PJA, which also operates several injury insurance schemes.

One key development, though, was brought about by a terrible accident to the popular Tim Brookshaw in 1963. Riding the inaptly named Lucky Dora at Aintree, he was thrown through the wing of a hurdle and, after a spinal

operation at nearby Walton Hospital, learned that he would never walk again. Then, in that year's Grand National, fellow rider Paddy Farrell took a sickening fall at The Chair and he too was paralysed. A public appeal for the two jockeys brought in £48,000, and when a further £6,000 came in after the closure of that specific fund, the money was used to set up the Injured National Hunt Jockeys Fund.

In 1971, that was renamed simply as the Injured Jockeys Fund (IJF), to include riders from the flat as well, and it has since been a major resource in helping injured riders and stable staff and their families. Largely through the efforts of the IJF, recuperation and treatment centres have been set up at Oaksey House in Lambourn and at Jack Berry House in Middleham (named after two of the most tireless campaigners). The IJF annually takes a number of injured jockeys and stable staff and their families for a holiday in the sun. In 1964, the Levy Board introduced its own insurance and pension scheme for all jockeys and stable staff, both on the flat and over jumps.

Given the inevitable perils in the sport of jumping, what is vital is that racecourses and the racing authorities do all they can to remove dangers and improve safety through the right conditions and equipment. Sometimes, though, it has taken campaigns by the Jockeys Association or by the media for sensible safety measures to be introduced. Many racecourses used to have concrete posts to support the running rails. If a mishap in a race caused you to be thrown against one of those, the consequences could be literally fatal, as they were for flat-racing jockey Manny Mercer at Ascot in 1959. Yet 30 years later, Monty Court, as editor of the *Sporting Life*, was still having to campaign for their removal: only 12 of the 59 racecourses then were concrete-free; others were still waiting for Levy Board funds to make the change.

One key issue has been that of the reactions on course to jockeys' injuries. In 1988, for example, Chris Grant fell and broke his leg during the first circuit of the chase course at Market Rasen. Even though warning markers had been put out on the approach to the fence where he lay injured, he had the same leg clipped by one of the three remaining runners on the second circuit. If horses had bypassed the fence where he was being treated, the race would have been declared void (that had happened at Stratford the previous season when a doctor waved the runners around a fence where an injured jockey was being treated: by missing out the fence, the riders and their horses were deemed to have 'failed to complete the proper course').

As Mark Dwyer, the northern jockeys' safety officer, asked: 'What if there had been 16 runners in Chris Grant's race?' The PJA pointed out that jumps could currently be bypassed if ground conditions were unsuitable or if low sun were blinding the riders, so why should they not be bypassed when injured jockeys were being treated? Agreement was reached eventually that doctors would be allowed to stop a race in

such circumstances, but the proposal that the jump concerned should simply be missed out was initially rejected because only seven of the 44 jumping courses had the necessary space to allow diversions around the fences. As Richard Linley points out, miles and miles of running rail had to be moved to make it possible for all fences to be bypassed: 'We don't sit around a table and try to dream up things to make life difficult for people. We try for something that is achievable within a three-and-a-half minute race.'

There is now much more training of groundsmen too. 'What we want,' says Richard Linley, 'is good sports turf in a condition

Mid-air Drama. Robert Lucey-Butler parts company with Elle Roseador at the last hurdle at Wincanton in 2005.

Profile: **John Thomas McNamara, 1975–2016**

No racing tragedy has more starkly underlined the perils faced by all jump jockeys than John Thomas McNamara's fall on Galaxy Rock in the Fulke Walwyn/ Kim Muir Chase at the Cheltenham Festival in March 2013. McNamara, an outstanding jockey who chose to ride – for love, not money – as an amateur, often for top owner JP McManus, had partnered more than 600 winners before the fall that fractured two vertebrae and left him paralysed from the neck down.

McNamara, the record-holder for the most wins in Irish point-to-points, was described by Jonjo O'Neill as 'the greatest horseman I've ever known.' He was hugely respected by professionals and amateurs alike. Among his famous victories was success on the quirky Rith Dubh in the four-mile National Hunt Chase at the 2002 Festival when he won by a neck after a duel with the wily Davy Russell on Timbera. He also won the National Hunt Chase on Teaforthree in 2012 and the Glenfarclas Cross Country Handicap Chase on Spot The Difference in 2005.

A tough man both mentally and physically, McNamara had been planning before the accident to retire from the saddle that summer at the age of 37. It took 15 months of treatment before he could be returned to his wife, Caroline, *and three children at their Irish home, a home that, in effect, became a 24-hour-a-day, high-tech hospital. Even though his sharp wit and brave spirit remained, he was never again to play with his children. The first jockey to have been paralysed on a British racecourse since 2008, McNamara developed complications in July 2016 and died at his home at the age of 41.*

for racing,' but the ground can take a hammering in winter and there is a good deal more racing than there used to be on some courses. Wincanton, for example, used to race 12 days a year with six races a day. Now it is 17 days a year with seven races a day. But who would have thought, 20 years before, that Cheltenham, for example, would be able to cover the whole course with frost covers, as it did in 2013.

One experiment that is unlikely to be repeated was that of hurdle races on the all-weather courses, which began in 1989 with the 'Ron Barry Hurdle' designed by Ron Barry and Jonjo O'Neill. Says Richard Linley, 'In France in 1991 they developed the brush hurdle and in autumn 1992 we had some brush-hurdle races at Cheltenham and Warwick. The thumbs-up was given for all-weather hurdling. We put in some more obstacles to slow up the horses a bit. We introduced brush hurdles in January 1993.

Then, because of a number of fatal incidents, the inspectorate team was asked to monitor hurdling on the all-weather. I was at Lingfield: we had a fatality in the first race – and that was the end of it. The key thing was that, on impact, there was no slippage. Where you landed was where you stopped. The jockeys seemed to get away with it – just. But the horses didn't. We had a few chases on the all-weather at Southwell, but it was ridiculous.'

Nicky Henderson, for one, doesn't believe we will ever see all-weather jumping again: 'A lot of people school on the all-weather, and the worst thing is that if you have a fall, you hit the ground and you go nowhere. Both for the jockey and the horse it's THUMP. You can't skid along the sand on the all-weather. With grass, you've got something you can fall onto. They never really got to a hurdle that worked really well, though I suppose those brush hurdles would do.'

When it comes to safety, jockeys don't always help themselves, though. Peter Scudamore has argued that the development of the body protector was a major step forward. These polystyrene waistcoats are the only protection in a fall for riders' kidneys and backs, but in their early days many jockeys did not wear them because they were poorly made and unsightly, making riders look amateurish. Jockeys prided themselves, says Scudamore, on having correctly fitting boots, breeches and equipment. 'There was a feeling that even if you could not ride like a professional jockey, you should look like one.' Typical of the macho culture was Terry Biddlecombe's remark: 'We wouldn't have been seen dead in a back protector. If you'd have turned up in the weighing room wearing one, the lads would have thought you were going to war or something.'

Scu was among the pioneers in developing body protectors. So was John Francome, whose mother sewed polyester-foam oblongs – 3½ in x 3 in – into a light shirt for him to wear under his colours. It took another Monty Court Sporting Life campaign to have back protectors made compulsory, as they were in 1988, and then further pressure from the Jockeys Association for the authorities to grant a one-pound weight allowance for them. Design improvements followed to allow jockeys still to be able to curl up in a ball having fallen. In 2016, however, body protectors were not yet compulsory wear for riders on trainers' premises when schooling inexperienced young horses – despite the fact that studies in France show they cut injuries by a third.

Injuries and incapacities, however, are not always of the obvious physical kind. Michael Caulfield, long-time chief executive of the Jockeys Association, argues that jockeys have to endure a working life of confidence-sapping mental harm and that the mental pressures can be immense. Dr Adrian McGoldrick, the Irish Turf Club's senior medical officer, said in 2015 that 49 per cent of jockeys suffer from some form of depression, many of their worries being financial ones. However, only in the past few years, and then thanks to the PJA, has any mental health care been made available to riders.

Finances

Most racegoers assume that jockeys are well paid for what they do, but that depends on your assessment of what should be built in for the risk factor; the average jump jockey in Britain is paid in a year what the average Premier League footballer receives for a week...

When the risk-oblivious Terry Biddlecombe started in 1958, a professional jump jockey received £7 10s. per ride, out of which he had to pay his travelling expenses and £1 to the valet who looked after his clothing and gear. There was no automatic percentage of prize money to add to that, although – dependent on the owner's generosity – there might be a nice 'present' for winning. By the time Terry published his book, *Winner's Disclosure*, in 1982, jockeys were receiving £36 per ride plus a percentage of the prize money. The valet's fee had risen to £4. In the 2015/16 season, the jump jockey's riding fee had risen to £161.51. Yet for a long time jockeys had to hang around the racecourse and accost owners to make sure that they were paid at all. The automatic payment of riding fees and percentages through accounts was not implemented until Weatherby's systems were computerised in the late 1980s.

There could be other hazards. Richard Pitman well remembers winning the Whitbread Gold Cup of 1970 for the West Country trainer Tim Handel. He had taken 'pee pills' to get down to the 10 st 0 lb riding weight. As was customary on big occasions, after his victory Richard bought a case of champagne for the weighing-room celebrations. There was by then no sign of Tim Handel, who had left the course to head back to Taunton. Later, Fred Winter, his boss, asked Richard, 'Did the old bugger give you a drink [a bonus]?' When Pitman said no, Winter advised, 'Go and see him and ask him.' Pitman did so, only to receive the blunt response from Handel, 'I've trained this horse for nine years and I trained the dam for 15 before that. I'm way out of pocket.' In desperation, the jockey changed tack. He tried, 'Won't you at least pay for the case of champagne?' only to receive an even more scornful retort: 'Look, those boys in there, half of them wouldn't even ride for me.' There were flat jockeys there too that day. 'That Lester Piggott wouldn't piss on me if I was on fire. No. You pay for the champagne!'

Most people assume that jockeys – both on the flat and over jumps – collect 10 per cent of the prize money that they win for owners. It is not quite as simple as that: in 2016, jump jockeys who rode a winner received 9 per cent of the advertised value of the winner's prize money. For placed horses in certain races, their percentage was from 4 to 4.5 per cent. However, Richard Killoran's study pointed out that in a number of races the winning jockey collects only 6 per cent, and for placing second, third and fourth, it can be as little as 0.86 per cent, 0.43 per cent and 0.22 per cent of the total prize money on offer.

Prize-money levels are therefore as crucial to jockeys, trainers and stable staff as they

Peter Scudamore on the trial scales in the weighing room in 1988.

are to owners; jump jockeys in Britain don't do nearly as well as those in France, for example. Take the career of James Reveley, who splits his time between riding in France and in the north of England, where his father, Keith, trains. In Britain in 2015, James Reveley rode 46 winners from 326 rides, earning prize money of just £371,025. In France that year, his 54 winners from just 162 rides brought in prize money totalling £1,734,462. In contrast, the 128 winners from 737 rides in Britain for Aidan Coleman, near the top of the list, brought in £1,237,824 – about £500,000 short of Reveley's total in France.

Of course, a few top jockeys winning big prize-money events do quite well; nevertheless, as the PJA's chief executive, Paul Struthers, points out, AP McCoy did not become the wealthy man he is purely from fees and prize money – it was sponsorship, combined with his retainer from millionaire JP McManus, that made the difference. According to the PJA, a jump jockey today with an average of 144 rides a year would be making £29,400 before taxes and expenses, and incurring about £10,000 of expenses in doing so. Not that much for risking your neck on a daily basis.

Jockeys pay 3 per cent of their riding fees to the PJA, which looks after their interests in many ways. It administers, for example, (together with a generous sponsor who meets half the costs) a career-ending insurance scheme to which jockeys contribute £1.60 a ride; sadly, there have had to be some £100,000 payouts from the funds. Another 75p per ride goes on group insurance to cover jockeys against being sued over accidents and other legal costs – as when a group of jockeys were fined over a false start at Aintree: taking the case to appeal cost them £9,000, even at the 'mates' rates' charged by a sporting solicitor.

It was the PJA that negotiated with the BHA an extra 1 lb weight allowance for warmer clothes in winter; the PJA also organises with the Levy Board the provision of on-course physios and nutritional advice; again, it was the PJA that finally, in 2014, won a compensatory payment for jockeys whose mounts are withdrawn after 9.00 a.m. on the day of racing.

Riding styles

Riding styles on the flat in Britain were revolutionised early in the twentieth century by Tod Sloan and other American riders, who rode with short stirrups and crouched over a horse's neck in contrast to British riders, who sat more upright and with much lower irons. Politely, it was known as the 'American seat'; critics called it 'the Monkey Crouch.' There have been arguments in jump racing over what is best practice, often centring on how 'short' a jockey is riding.

George Duller, a specialist hurdles rider in the 1920s, whose name was long given to a Cheltenham Festival race, was known as 'The Croucher' for keeping his weight well forward in the saddle and not shifting his position on take-off. His admirers argued that horses quickly recovered their cruising speed as the hurdle was jumped.

In the period covered by this book, the 'long or short' arguments continued, although in general it can be said that the bulk of today's jump jockeys ride with shorter stirrup leathers than those of the 1950s. Leading trainer and former champion jockey Fred Rimell, for example, while admiring the results obtained by his stable jockey Terry Biddlecombe, always maintained that Biddlecombe rode too short, a complaint made about many riders of Biddlecombe's period by the influential former trainer and racing biographer Tim Fitzgeorge-Parker. Biddlecombe was not directly critical of the older jockeys of his time, such as Tim Brookshaw, Michael Scudamore and Paddy Broderick, but when he said, 'They were good, tough jockeys who sat deep in the saddle and asked their horses to stand off well from their fences, but they got results,' it was clear that he favoured a different style. He admitted that many criticised him for riding too short but he maintained, 'If a horse is balanced and going forward for you, there is no need to kick him in the belly. If you can get your balance right and keep your hands down – hands are the most important thing of all, combined with balance and rhythm – if you can get all those together, then nothing else matters. I used to poke my toes down a bit, but riding

Jockeys (left to right) Daryl Jacob, Noel Fehily, AP McCoy and Tom Scudamore watch racing on TV in the weighing room during day three of The Open Meeting at Cheltenham.

that much shorter enabled me literally to kneel on my horses, which freed any weight from their loins and so distributed it over their forehand.' He used to slip his horses a lot of rein when they made a mistake, reckoning that unless they had blundered really badly they would often then manage to 'find a leg' and stand up. To Terry, jockeys such as Johnny Haine and David Mould were exceptionally stylish over hurdles or fences; polished hurdles specialists such as Johnny Gilbert and Jimmy Uttley, he noted, would walk the course and mark the best going with lollipop sticks – as well as loosening a few hurdles as they went!

Of course, trainers too play a part in jockeys' race-riding styles. Michael Dickinson and Martin Pipe, with their emphasis on super-fit horses, brought front-running back into fashion. Peter Scudamore was happy to use his judgement of pace on Pipe's front-runners, whereas during his time with David Nicholson, he had been given different priorities. Many trainers, Scu says, did not like to see their horses in front for too long. 'Very often, David [Nicholson] would say to me of the chief opposition, "you'll beat him for speed," and he liked to see his horses "dropped in" fourth or fifth,' conserving their energies behind the leader for a late burst.

Some jockeys have quieter styles than others; that can sometimes lead them into trouble. It even happened with John Francome. David Goulding, known as 'Gypsy Dave', in part because of the earring he sported, was a sensitive rider much admired by fellow jockeys for his patience in calming difficult horses such as the top hurdler Ekbalco. Goulding, who rode regularly in the 1970s for Gordon W Richards, believed that many horses labelled as rogues were simply one-paced; he would often use his judgement of pace to sit in behind on a slow horse and then come through the field to win – without recourse to any acceleration that his mount did not possess – as others ran out of steam in front of Pipe. Dave Goulding also believed in not giving horses too hard a race in second or third place when their chance of winning had gone, saving them to do better next time. He was not a great user of the whip and was furious with himself one day at Carlisle for persevering with a horse he had felt 'go' under him when in second place, rather than pulling him up, because he feared the stewards would accuse him of not trying.

That is where the betting background of horseracing comes into conflict with the welfare of the horse. With stewards keeping the betting public very much in mind, you could say that in his time there was an official prejudice against riders such as Goulding. In the 1979/80 season, he was called to Portman Square after 15 appearances that season before the stewards; he was warned to be more aggressive in the saddle and look busier in his riding style if he was to be granted a licence for the following season. Since he was a top rider, the officials explained, they feared that younger jockeys would copy his style and thus find themselves in trouble with racecourse stewards. It's not what you do, it's what you are seen to do...

Martin Pipe says that the use of video has made a significant difference. 'Everything is much more professional now in every walk of life. With television, we can now see all the replays and see what went wrong. AP didn't like it at first when we had the slow-motion replays although he later came to use video replays all the time. You can see the mistakes you make. I made loads of mistakes in entering horses in the wrong races. You have to learn by your mistakes. We have tutors now and mechanical

Jockeys' Agent Dave Roberts, seen in his office booking rides.

horses. We've always had one of those. We don't allow our jockeys or the lads to carry whips on the gallops so they can go and practise on the mechanical horses, and learn how to use their whips there and be instructed how to use them correctly, how to change their whip hands.' How appropriate it is that the race at the Cheltenham Festival named after him is the one for conditional jockeys.

Rise of the agent

Riding from 1978 to 1993 and winning eight championships, Peter Scudamore never had an agent to liaise with trainers and book his rides but by the time Richard Dunwoody was champion, several leading riders had agents. Today, even apprentices and conditionals have agents: top trainers and riders cannot manage without them. Mick Fitzgerald has no doubt that they have benefited most jockeys: 'All you want to think about is riding winners, not ringing around for rides.' So has it been good for trainers? 'Without a doubt,' says his former employer Nicky Henderson: 'They've helped enormously. Dave Roberts (agent to McCoy and Richard Johnson, and many other leading riders) is probably one of the most powerful men in National Hunt racing. He actually controls it. There are other good agents but he has the whole thing. He looks after all of ours. I speak to him three times every day. I speak to him at 9.00 [a.m.] every day and he helps me enormously. I don't have to book any jockeys. I say, "Can X ride that, can Geraghty ride that" ... if not, we just use our own. Otherwise, you've got to go ringing round. In the good old days, you'd get hold of Johnny Francome: "Will you ride mine in the novice chase?" "Oh, I'll have to check with the boss. Fred might be running so and so. I'll ring you back." Of course, this was in the old days when there were no mobile phones but then you didn't have to make the phone calls we make now because you only had 45 horses. You didn't have to make hundreds of calls a day. I probably make 60 calls on a Sunday morning.'

Three agents – Dave Roberts, Richard Hale in the north, and Chris Broad – would have up to 75 per cent of the jockeys on their books. Says one rider, 'Effectively, agents are doing the race entering and planning for some trainers and if you are not with that agent, you are not going to get a look-in.' The downside of that is that with one or two agents virtually able to fill a racecard on the quieter days, the lesser-known riders who might have been able to pick up a ride or two are crowded out. Another change in recent times has been the practice of owners, rather than trainers, having a retained jockey, as JP McManus did first with AP McCoy and then with Barry Geraghty, or David Johnson with Timmy Murphy. Paul Nicholls agrees: 'It is a bit of a nightmare. It makes it difficult with your stable jockey if somebody has ten or 20 horses with you and they've got their own jockey riding them if he is available. It's not easy.'

Jockeys' status

One change that has surely been for the better is the improved status of jockeys, particularly over jumps. In the governance of the BHA, there are four groups – the racecourses, the owners, the breeders, and the 'Licensed personnel' including trainers, jockeys and stable staff. Says Paul Struthers: 'Historically, jockeys have always been lumped with stable lads. There has been an element in racing's hierarchy which likes to keep riders in their place. There has been change but it has been slow. There is not quite so much "standing on the mat" in front of officials. Having a few superstar jockeys on a par with owners and trainers has made a difference. Some are valued for their input while others have the talent but

not the communication skills, and the old ways are still there in the pecking order.

'Riders have a more integral role in the development of jumping horses and there is more camaraderie in jumping because more of the officials have themselves been amateur riders and shared the risks.'

Richard Pitman, who rode from 1961 to1975, remembers how it used to be: 'They didn't consider us or our opinions. Terry Biddlecombe helped to change things a little. One day they put in some plastic fences with metal frames at Stratford. Biddlecombe saw them on walking the course and said, "Lads, we're not having this. I don't want any of you to ride." He led a deputation and the stewards reacted: the metal hurdles were taken away. Until then, jockeys were seen as uneducated, brainless – brave maybe, but not educated.'

Richard had to give evidence one day at Jockey Club headquarters in Cavendish Square over a trainer who had been called in because one of his horses had tested for drugs. 'I was a kid just six months out of school. The horse was 20-1 and unbacked. It hadn't run for some time and it sweated up badly. There was nothing untoward – it was entitled to pull up. With another witness, I was shown into a sort of broom cupboard with tobacco tins for an ashtray. The man who summoned us was wearing a

Jockey Richard Johnson (right) chats to trainer Philip Hobbs (left) after winning the Ryanair Novice Chase on Captain Chris.

morning suit. We went through double doors and across a room to three stewards sitting behind a table. It was definitely intimidating. The trainer concerned was found guilty and lost his licence. He went on the drink and it killed him. Nowadays, there are legal representatives, film from ten different angles...'

Richard too recalls the occasion when John Francome, whose quiet riding style irritated some officials, was summoned by the 'stipe' (the stipendiary steward). 'Francome. The stewards want you.' The jockey, not one to be cowed by authority, replied: 'If you want me to come and are feeling friendly, you can call me "John." If you are not, you can call me "Mr Francome."' Eventually, the stipe said, 'Come on, John.' Francome does not claim responsibility but, by coincidence, it was not long after that incident that in March 1983 the Jockey Club issued an order that, in future, jockeys and trainers were to be addressed as 'Mr.'

Another issue for jockeys, of course, is the public's view about how horses are treated, and there is no more sensitive issue on the interface between the racing community and the wider public than the use of the whip, both on the flat and in jump racing.

Racing and the whip

Trainer Sir Mark Prescott once noted that the greyhound races for the anticipated pleasure of sinking its teeth into a fluffy, white bunny tail ahead. The human athlete races for the hope of fame and riches. But what's in it, he asked, for the horse? One thing that has been in it for the racehorse has been the whip, the likelihood that if it doesn't do its utmost, a smack or two will follow, and the hope that if it does stick its head down and go all out, then that little demon on top will stop walloping away.

To some, what used to be euphemistically termed the 'persuader' or the 'attitude adjuster' is an essential piece of racing equipment, needed to help guide and steer a horse and to avoid dangerous situations. To others, including many first-time or potential racegoers, it is a cruel and debasing relic of past times. Michael Dickinson, an effective rider before he became champion trainer, says, 'After 11 years of riding, I was able to sell my whip at the nearly-new shop. I hardly ever used it. I once hit a horse three times – that was the most I ever hit a horse – and I was distraught. I wasn't very good in a finish because I didn't hit them. But you don't want to bottom them, and I knew I was going to be riding them next time. They were my father's horses.'

Other jockeys insisted that they could make horses go faster with sensible use of the whip; horsemen such as Peter Scudamore, sensitive enough to determine how horses were responding, did just that. Flat-racing trainer Mark Johnston likens use of the whip to a boxer's cornerman slapping his face to exhort him to extra effort in the final round. It reinforces the flight mechanism, he says, at a crucial moment. But there are bad jockeys – as well as good jockeys – carrying whips: too often we used to see tired horses flogged home unnecessarily by clumsy riders in a way that demeaned the sport.

The revered Peter O'Sullevan, broadcaster and *Daily Express* correspondent, campaigned constantly against excessive whipping. In 1979, he parcelled up a bundle of readers' and viewers' letters on the issue – after a visit to Scandinavia, where only minimal use of the whip was permitted – and sent them to the Jockey Club. In January 1980, the Jockey Club's Senior Steward, Captain John Madonald-Buchanan, issued a new directive to stewards about the increased instances of whipping and demanded greater vigilance, especially over the treatment of horses with no chance of making the first four. Nevertheless, at the Cheltenham Festival that year, even hardened racing writers were disgusted by several episodes of 'excessive use.' Ireland's champion jockey Joe Byrne and his compatriot Tommy Ryan were both called in by the Jockey Club and banned for three months after their brutal use of the whip: in Byrne's case, after a vet's examination of the damage he had done to Batista, his mount in the Triumph Hurdle, and, in Ryan's, after his thrashing home of Drumlargan in the Sun Alliance Hurdle. When Drumlargan landed awkwardly at the last, Peter O'Sullevan described his jockey's behaviour as that of a 'demented carpet-beater', while John Oaksey commented, 'What he [Drumlargan] badly needed was pulling together: what he got was a shower of blows down the neck and along the flank, including at least one after he had passed the post.' It became something of an England–Ireland issue, but by January 1981 the Irish Turf Club too had issued new regulations on the size of the whip and was deploring its habitual overuse.

Racing, both on the flat and over jumps, has long had rules on how and when whips may be used. The guidance from the BHA, as it was previously from the Jockey Club, is that the whip should be used for safety, correction and encouragement – not for making the horse go faster at the end of the race. But too often those rules have led to public-relations disasters. Contests for the biggest prizes bring the fiercest competition from jockeys trying to get their horse first past the post. If, in doing so, they break the rules and use their whips excessively, the penalties they receive and the implication of potential cruelty, rather than the excitement of the race, become the media focus.

One classic example, literally, was the 2,000 Guineas of 1996, a thrilling race in which three

The fiercely contested end to the King George VI Chase at Kempton in 2015, after which Paddy Brennan, the winner over Vautour on Cue Card (pink and blue colours) was banned for 11 days for what stewards called a 'win at all costs ride.'

horses drove to the line together, with Mark of Esteem prevailing by a head from Even Top with Bijou d'Inde only another head away. All three jockeys, Frankie Dettori, Philip Robinson and Jason Weaver, gave all they had. All three used their whips vigorously to encourage their horses into giving all they had – and the stewards suspended the three jockeys for eight, four, and two days respectively. The penalties were set to reflect the respective severity of the offences, the amount of times the jockeys had used their whips, whether or not they had applied excessive force, and whether or not they had hit the colts out of rhythm with their strides.

Horses do generally respond to the whip and such occasions raise many awkward questions. If you make excessive use of the whip and so break the rules to give your horse an advantage, then the difference between doing that and feeding it some prohibited substance to make it go faster is only a qualitative one. But doping would have you disqualified and banned.

So shouldn't you disqualify the winner whose jockey has broken the whip rules, especially if the losing jockey has not? Some say yes. But you would then be punishing not only the jockey, but also the owner, trainer and stable staff. And there is, if we are honest, another more commercial consideration: racing relies on betting to generate its income and, if any of the three horses in that 2,000 Guineas had been disqualified, there would have been an outcry from the punters.

Simon Clare of bookmakers Coral is clear: 'If horses start being disqualified as a result of whip misuse, it could be devastating in terms of the appeal of horseracing as a betting product.'

Racing is all about winning. In that 2,000 Guineas, to have handed the race to the fourth horse home, Alhaarth, would have been absurd. Yet if by whipping his horse another ten times, or harder, Jason Weaver could have improved his place from third to first, would that have been considered within the

A quiet word of encouragement at Philip Hobbs's Sandhill stables.

bounds as well? Where does trying to win end, and cruelty begin?

One day, the arguments may well be tested in a court of law. Top trainer Nicky Henderson says: 'If there is a big race where one guy has gone completely over the top and wins, having hit his horse more than the permitted number of times, and gets banned for three weeks, and the second guy hasn't broken the rules and says, "I could have won if I'd hit my horse too, but I didn't because I knew I'd got to my maximum [number of whip strokes permitted] and we got beaten a head: I object," there could be a trial case. There will be trial by jury in the press anyway.'

Jumps or flat, the more important the race, the bigger the prize, the more likely jockeys are to break the rules, whether by accident or design. There have been few more thrilling racecourse duels than the battle to the line in Sandown's Coral Eclipse in the year 2000 between Giant's Causeway and Kalanisi. On that occasion, George Duffield and Pat Eddery were each given ten days' suspension for 'excessive use.' And it is no different over jumps. One of the most exciting finishes ever to the King George VI Chase came in 2015 with a head-to-head battle to the line between Cue Card, ridden by Paddy Brennan, and Vautour, ridden by Ruby Walsh. For what the stewards described as a 'win at all costs ride' involving 16 strokes of the whip, Paddy Brennan was given an 11-day ban and fined £4,200, amounting to 40 per cent of his winning prize-money percentage. But Cue Card kept the race.

Periodically, there have been outcries, official reviews and revisions of the rules. There was one in 1988. Under pressure from the media and the RSPCA, the Jockey Club (then still in charge of discipline) issued rules saying that the whip was to be no more than 78 cm in length, a minimum width of 8 mm and with a flap no longer than 10 cm. No jockey was to be allowed to strike a horse more than ten times between landing over the second-last obstacle and passing the winning post. Peter Scudamore said that it proved unfair in operation, often penalising jockeys riding good finishes for the sake of stopping the 'cowboys' who hit horses unnecessarily. Local stewards did not all interpret the rules identically. Scudamore, like AP McCoy later, sometimes got into trouble early in his career for his use of the stick. 'Later, I was able to ride effectively with or without it. But it was experience and advice, not riding by the rule book which made me so. Some horses are best ridden with hands and heels, others respond to a couple of smacks.'

The rules were revised again in 1993 and there was another major review in 2011 after a 40 per cent increase in whip offences from 2008 to 2010. The BHA's objectives were clearly set out: to reduce the number of offences, to bring about a cultural change in riding style, to promote good horsemanship, and to safeguard the welfare of horses and public perceptions of the sport. The review took place soon after an outcry over Jason Maguire's riding when winning the 2011 Grand National on Ballabriggs. He was by no means a whip-happy jockey, but he was suspended for five days for hitting his mount 17 times.

Talking to great riders such as Dessie Hughes and Richard Dunwoody, as I did a few years ago for a history of the Cheltenham Festival, I found them regretting that the customs of the time had allowed, and even encouraged, them to use the whip to the extent they did on champions like Monksfield and Viking Spirit; when champion trainer Paul Nicholls gave his overall support to the new set of whip rules from the BHA in 2011, the key phrase he used was that 'the time has come' for change.

Traditions have their attractions but if we never accepted the need to reflect the mood of a new age we would still have ponies down pits, children up chimneys and landowners helping themselves by droit de seigneur to pretty peasant girls. The people we want to see thronging Britain's racetracks don't see the care and attention lavished on racehorses in stable yards by devoted staff: racing's image is determined for them by what they observe at the business end of races on the course.

Those new rules from the BHA in 2011 amounted to racing's acknowledgement that while the whip may be used for occasional correction, it is no longer appropriate beyond a very clearly defined point for coercion. Under the new rules, the number of times a jockey's whip could be used during a race was limited initially to seven times on the flat and eight times over jumps, with a maximum of five strokes in the last furlong or after the last obstacle. Jockeys breaking the rules faced automatic suspension and the loss of riding fees and prize-money percentages. It was to become an offence for owners or trainers to encourage wrongdoing by recompensing riders for what they had lost.

Unfortunately, the rules were introduced abruptly – without a trial period for riders to acclimatise themselves. The BHA also chose to start imposing the new rules in the week of maximum media exposure accompanying the new Champions Day at Ascot, planned as Britain's richest ever day of racing and featuring the wondrous Frankel. The big day became a fiasco, with visiting French jockey Cristophe Soumillon earning a ban and the loss of his £52,390 share of the prize money won by Cirrus des Aigles for delivering one stroke too many in the final furlong. The racing was almost forgotten as headlines for a fortnight were dominated by stories about whip offences. What the jockeys had done in most cases was to infringe a technicality: what the public absorbed from the headlines was that large numbers of jockeys were daily being found guilty of cruelty to their mounts. There were even threats of strike action by the jockeys: imagine how much good it would have done to racing to have the tabloids screaming: 'Jockeys strike for the right to thrash their horses harder.'

Mercifully, the BHA's new chief executive, Paul Bittar, gave the new rules several tweaks, both on numbers and on penalties, and handed back more discretion about their interpretation to local stewards. Armageddon was avoided. But the whole furore reminded me of a conversation at Kelso back in 1999 with veteran jockey Brian Storey. Discussing the change in training and riding styles, he told me, 'We used to go steady and chat for the first mile. Since Pipe and McCoy, the younger lads jump out and go from the start. But there are no records broken. They run faster at the start and slower at the finish. The horses finish tired and that's when all this business about the

sticks begins.' He himself had been penalised for only one whipping offence in 18 years.

Paul Struthers at the Professional Jockeys Association says, 'If you have travelled comfortably, you can easily keep track. When there is a pulsating finish in front of a baying crowd, I have sympathy with the jockeys [who transgress]. One or two strokes over does not look like blatantly cheating when you are going at 30 mph and are tired towards the end of a gruelling jumps race. You're not going to say, "I won't use the whip just in case I go one over."

'The new whip designed by Jim Mahon, (President of the Point to Point Owners Association and a horse lover who invented the air-cushioned whip), when used properly, should encourage the flight response by making a noise but should not hurt. Last year, out of 90,000 runners, just two horses were marked.' And to put things further into perspective, who better to rely on than TV pundit and racing guru Jim McGrath, a long time stalwart of Timeform. Amid all the figures circulating, he pointed out in a letter to the *Racing Post* that in races from January 2004 to April 2011 more than 99 per cent of runners had competed without any whip offence being perpetrated by their jockeys: 'Isn't that a statistic to be proud of?'

Use of the whip, fortunately, is just a tiny part of any jockey's range of skills. As we look next at the records of those who have won the coveted title of champion jockey since 1960, there will be plenty of other attributes to celebrate.

The trainers' championship is decided by the amount of prize money won in a season. Jockeys' championships, both on the flat and over jumps, have by contrast always been determined by the number of winners ridden, irrespective of the class of race in which they have scored their victories. Despite the interruptions caused by the injuries, which inevitably occur more frequently in a jump jockey's career, many title winners have managed to run up a significant sequence of victories. It is key, however, to be associated with a large stable producing plenty of winners.

7

The Champion Jockeys

'If we jump this well, Biddles, we'll be on next year's Christmas cards!'

David Nicholson to Terry Biddlecombe in the Cheltenham Gold Cup

Stan Mellor

Champion Jockey 1959–61

In the past few years, several of the lighter jump jockeys have switched from riding jumpers to plying their trade on the flat, where the financial rewards tend to be more generous and the risks of injury lower. In the 2016 season former jump jockey Jim Crowley became champion flat jockey. Were he riding today, Stan Mellor, the first jump jockey to ride 1,000 winners, a target he reached on Ouzo at Nottingham in December 1971, might well have joined the exodus. He never weighed more than 8 st 10 lb through his 20-year career and could well have made his career on the flat. But as he had been a showjumping champion at the age of 14, he never contemplated anything but a life over jumps.

Stan Mellor in 1963 at Stratford on Maxonna.

Small but determined, Stan Mellor used intelligence to make up for any strength he lacked. He had a method all his own, an ambush technique he called 'the real thing' and which he famously employed in 1966, on the lightly weighted grey Stalbridge Colonist, to catch Pat Taaffe napping and beat the great Arkle in the Hennessy Gold Cup. Approaching the last fence, Mellor would let his mount slip back behind the leader then wind him up and fling his partner over the obstacle. It did not always look pretty but it was effective, gaining precious momentum and wrong-footing his opponents. Getting the worst of a run-in battle, he would drop back just enough to switch and come at his surprised rival on the other side, the manoeuvre helping to convince an uncertain partner that he had it in him to win.

Very much a thinking jockey, Mellor believed a rider's duty was to be perfectly balanced and to get inside a horse's brain. He did, though, voice a frustration: 'If you win with strength, people see it, and if you win with style, people see it, but if you win with guile, people don't see it.'

The wonder was, after March 1963, that he ever got back in the saddle to deploy his techniques. In a 41-runner field that year (there was no safety limit) for the Schweppes Gold Trophy, then run at Aintree, Stan's mount, Eastern Harvest, was among the leaders when he fell at the first. Stan became a football for the following cavalry charge – and when the ambulance got him to Walton Hospital his lower jaw was almost detached. In this, the worst of his 750 career falls, he lost six teeth and had 14 fractures in his face. Colleagues, horrified by the spectacle, feared he would never ride again but by August he was back among the winners.

When later that year he married his wife, Elain, the directors of Schweppes sent him a silver cigarette box inscribed: 'To Stan Mellor – for falling heavily twice in one year.'

Before his accident, Mellor had been champion jockey for the previous three seasons and since, at the time of his accident, he was 20 winners clear of Josh Gifford, he would probably have collected a fourth championship only for that terrible fall.

Following his riding career, Stan Mellor took to training. Although he sent out more than 700 winners, including four at the Cheltenham Festival and two Whitbread Gold Cups, not to mention a Stewards Cup on the flat, he was surprisingly dismissive of his achievements; he reflected, on retirement, that he had not been ambitious or greedy enough, not having the mentality to urge owners to spend large sums. But what few forget is his significant contribution to his fellow riders' safety as a clear-minded chairman of the Jockeys Association in the years that saw the introduction of better crash helmets with chin straps, the early back protectors, and more effective insurance.

Josh Gifford

Champion Jockey 1962–64, 1966–68

There cannot be many jockeys who have won the championship while being only second choice for their retaining stable – but that was one of Josh Gifford's distinctions during a glorious 50-year career in racing, as both a jockey and a trainer. The explanation is that the trainer was Ryan Price and the number-one jockey in the Findon yard when Josh first became champion in 1962/63 was the great Fred Winter.

The son of a farmer and point-to-point enthusiast, Josh Gifford began as a child prodigy on the flat at the age of 11 and partnered his first winner, Dorsol, at Birmingham in July 1951 when only 14. By the end of that season, he had ridden for the Queen and also landed the Manchester November Handicap. Increasing weight, however, ended the speculation about his being 'a new Lester Piggott' and forced Gifford to switch to jumping, where he was soon snapped up by Ryan Price; Gifford became the youngest champion jockey for a hundred years.

Gifford won the championship for a second time in 1963/64, increasing his winner total from 70 to 90. Following a 15-month lay-off, having broken his leg twice, once in a fall and once in a car crash, Josh Gifford won the championship again in 1966/67, bettering by just one winner Fred Winter's record of 121 winners. He was champion for a fourth and final time in 1967/68, when his victories included the Mackeson Gold Cup on Charlie Worcester.

As described in the section on Ryan Price (see page 119), Gifford four times won the Schweppes Gold Trophy for the Findon maestro; the second time Rosyth won, Gifford was penalised, along with the trainer, being suspended for three weeks. His other big wins as a jockey, amid 642 over jumps and 700 in all, included the 1969 Whitbread Gold Cup on Larbawn. There might have been many more but when Josh was only 28, Ryan Price decided to switch to flat racing and offered him the chance to switch to training and take over his ready-made jumping yard. Gifford's seizing of that opportunity resulted in 1,587 winners as a trainer, including the famous Grand National victory with Aldaniti in 1981, a Hennessy, a Whitbread, two Mackeson Gold Cups and ten victories at the Cheltenham Festival. He might have added a trainers' championship to his four jockey titles had not his

Josh Gifford, then a young apprentice on the flat, in 1957.

Josh Gifford battling through a snowstorm at Warwick in 1962.

friend David Elsworth pipped him by winning both the National with Rhyme'N'Reason and the Whitbread with Desert Orchid in 1988.

There were few in racing who did not claim the popular Josh as being their friend. As a fearless opening batsman, he was a stalwart of the jockeys' cricket team run by David Nicholson. Along with the likes of Terry Biddlecombe and David Mould, he was one of the weighing-room cavaliers who would ride hard, party at night in London and spend the mornings in the Jermyn Street sauna baths, sweating down to the weight required to begin all over again the following day. Brough Scott, who rode alongside them, once wrote of Josh Gifford: 'Spending one evening on the lash with him and Terry Biddlecombe would fix most people. How they could do it week after week only their livers could tell.'

In 1993, when Josh became the first person to have both ridden and trained a winner of the Cheltenham race long known as the Mackeson Gold Cup, and later as the Paddy Power Gold Cup (with Charlie Worcester in 1967 and Bradbury Star in 1993 respectively), the BBC's Cornelius Lysaght asked Josh to compare the experiences. The popular trainer grinned and declared: 'I can hardly remember Charlie Worcester because I was still pissed from the Champion Jockey's Ball the night before.' Perhaps, though, it was his fellow cavalier Terry Biddlecombe who best summed up his abilities in the saddle. He insisted: 'Josh Gifford was a horseman in his own right. He had everything: style, ability, judgement and sheer guts.' The

trainer and journalist Tim Fitzgeorge-Parker, wrote that Gifford had a style over hurdles that was all his own. Most crack hurdle jockeys crouched low over the withers and went with the horse all the way over the obstacle, landing in the same galloping position; Josh, he said, seemed to swing back as he landed over hurdles and yet went all the way with horses over big fences. Sam Armstrong explained it this way: 'He picked his horses up before they touched down, so they landed balanced and straight into their action. They jumped quicker for him.'

Curiously, Josh Gifford never rode in the Cheltenham Gold Cup and never won a Grand National – the big race that got away from him was the Grand National in 1967, the year of the carnage at the 23rd fence when Foinavon was the only horse to pick a way through the chaos. Josh was riding the favourite, Honey End, who was among those brought to a standstill. He took his horse back 50 yards, jumped the fence and set off in pursuit of Foinavon. He got to within 15 lengths of the leader but by then, Honey End had nothing left. Josh remained convinced that with a clear round he would have won. A byword for loyalty to his jockeys – I once heard him tell a fuming owner he could take his horses out of the yard rather than blame a conditional rider unfairly for a horse's disappointing performance – Josh Gifford became an Aintree hero all the same, as a trainer, when he kept faith with the cancer-stricken Bob Champion and the patched-up Aldaniti to win the fairy-story National of 1981.

Terry Biddlecombe

Champion Jockey 1964–66, 1968/69 (shared)

When Terry Biddlecombe died at the age of 72 in 2015, it would have been unthinkable for the memorial service to be held at any venue other than Cheltenham Racecourse. More than 450 of racing's great and good, and a few of the other kind, turned up to mark the passing of one of the sport's great icons.

Riding in an age when jump racing was unquestionably still a sport, rather than a business, Biddlecombe as a jockey was the epitome of the swashbuckling camaraderie of a weighing room full of friends, who rode without fear, chased girls and drank with little restraint, and who abused their bodies with fearsome wasting (fasting) and disregard for a constant catalogue of injuries. Following a period of alcoholic decline out of the saddle, Biddlecombe then enjoyed a glorious resurrection in the fairy-story 'Odd Couple' romance with trainer Henrietta Knight and their joint campaigning of Best Mate to win three Gold Cups.

Tutored by his father, Walter, Biddlecombe's achievements in the saddle began early amid a country childhood of farming, fishing and shooting on the banks of the Severn. One family pony, Flyaway, won 3,000 gymkhana rosettes for Terry, brother Tony and sister Sue. Terry went on to ride 905 winners under rules and to be the first jockey to ride more than 100 winners in two successive seasons. He won the jockeys' championship three times, on the last occasion sharing it with his brother-in-law, Bob Davies.

There were early signs of what was to come: in his very first ride under rules, the 16-year-old Biddlecombe, partnering the 20-1 shot Burnella in a novice hurdle at Wincanton on 6 March 1958, beat a grumpy Fred Winter aboard the 4-7 favourite in a tight finish. Mr TW Biddlecombe then made sufficient impression when riding as an amateur over the following two years to be called in by the National Hunt stewards in February 1960 to be told that he was depriving professionals of income. He turned pro himself forthwith.

Biddlecombe was riding alongside hardened pros of the old school, such as Michael Scudamore, Tim Brookshaw and Paddy Broderick, who sat deep in the saddle and got their horses to stand well off from the fences. At 5ft 11in, Terry was tall and heavy-boned but from the outset he rode with his own short style, virtually kneeling on a horse and lying up on the horse's neck rather than bouncing about on the horse's back as some did then. He argued that if a horse was balanced and going forward, there was no need to kick him in the belly. His mounts often seemed quicker away from the obstacles. Much of it was instinctive rather than taught: Biddlecombe insisted that from the tension he felt in a horse, he could tell immediately whether or not the animal liked racing.

He suffered a huge catalogue of injuries while riding and wore guards on his arms after breaking both wrists badly, but he never lost his fearless attitude or his capacity for instant, bold decision. However, he was lucky not to have been killed after one particular fall – at the water on Hydra Dor in the Banbury Novices Chase at Stratford. Biddlecombe's foot had got caught in the stirrup iron and the leather had twisted, so that he finished up being dragged 200 yards – with hooves flashing by his helmet and his head banging up and down on the track. Luckily, as his partner prepared to jump the next fence, a manoeuvre that might have

Terry Biddlecombe dismounting after his success on Woodland Venture.

wrenched Biddlecombe's leg from its socket, the elastic-sided girths he had borrowed from Bobby Beasley before the race, and worn for the very first time, gave way, and the saddle slipped round to enable the horse to kick him free.

If that indicated a charmed life, it was more of a struggle when it came to paring down his frame to the riding weights he was required to achieve. When it came to wasting, Biddlecombe, who could not get on with diets, had a style all his own. At Terry's memorial service, his former fellow jockey David Mould noted: 'He always said that you can't waste on an empty stomach. I'd have a plate of oysters and a glass of wine. He would have two plates of oysters and a bottle of wine.' Mould also recalled one occasion after a freeze-up that had wiped out the racing programme, Terry was offered a ride in the richly endowed Schweppes Hurdle that required him to do 10 st 7 lb. He weighed 11 st 4 lb at the time but spent the night at the Turkish baths in a plastic sweatsuit and still had the strength to drive the winner home. Biddlecome would often stay in London between racecourse trips, eating at Jules restaurant or Wheelers Fish Bar, because they were conveniently close to the Jermyn Street Turkish baths where he spent many hours – fortified with copious quantities of champagne to aid dehydration.

Biddlecombe never had a problem finding female company – his amorous exploits with one hotel receptionist near Aintree nearly had his car engulfed by the rising tide on a beach; fellow jockeys used to tell of the day at Ludlow when Biddlecombe rode a treble during the afternoon, albeit only two of his mounts were equipped with four legs!

By the 1961/62 season, the canny Fred Rimell had signed up the eye-catching youngster as number-two jockey to Bobby Beasley. Soon he became number one; in all, Biddlecombe spent nine years at Kinnersley, riding for Fred and his wife, Mercy. Their greatest success together was with Woodland Venture in the Cheltenham Gold Cup of 1967, a race in which Biddlecombe should not have been riding at all. Following a fall the previous day, he could hardly walk, but on Gold Cup day Terry's friend, Dr Bill Wilson, sneaked into the weighing room and gave him a pain-killing injection in his knee before he rode in two other races. In the big race itself, Biddlecombe on Woodland Venture and David Nicholson on Mill House were together in the lead coming down the hill first time around; in an exchange symptomatic of those more relaxed times, the Duke told Biddlecombe, 'If we jump this well, Biddles, we'll be on next year's Christmas cards!' Both of them then clouted the next fence, and Biddlecombe shouted back, 'That's cocked up the Christmas cards!'

Mill House finally departed at the last ditch and Woodland Venture, left alone in the lead, began to look around. Coming to the last, Stan Mellor brought the grey, Stalbridge Colonist,

Game Spirit (right), Terry Biddlecombe up, clears the last fence to win from Solonus (left), Richard Pitman up.

once Arkle's conqueror, to challenge him. For a few strides, the grey, with Mellor shouting his mount on, headed Biddlecombe's mount, but then Woodland Venture responded to his jockey's urgings, regained the lead and held on to the line. The emotional Biddlecombe's face was running with tears at their triumph.

Then came the moment of fear, which in later years Biddlecombe loved to relate. Amid the crowd celebrating Woodland Venture's triumph was Doc Wilson, waving his hypodermic syringe and yelling, 'This is what did it. This is what got you round, Terry!' Fearing disqualification, Terry urged him to shut up – but it was too late. Officialdom heard about it and the rider was called in by the stewards, who told him that under the rules he should have been treated only by the course doctor. Had he sought treatment through those official channels, Terry knew, he would not have been allowed to ride. Fortunately, he was dismissed with only a caution and the result stood.

He won many other great races at Cheltenham and a memorable Welsh Grand National on French Excuse in 1970 after he had lost 9 lb in two hours and was dizzy with dehydration after riding a frantic finish. On that occasion, it was the course doctor whose proposed remedy was a pint of Guinness – with added salt. That remedy, however, induced such colic spasms that Terry had to be given an injection. He never did win an Aintree Grand National, though – the year Gay Trip won it for Fred Rimell, he would have been Terry's mount, but he had been injured and missed the race.

As a jockey, Biddlecombe had formidable strength. But Richard Pitman recalls that Terry did lack one weapon in a jockey's armoury: 'He could only ride with his stick in one hand. He could never swap his stick to the left. He used to have a hand up near the horse's ears. He'd be pushing its head down as he was swinging his stick. That was his unique style. If you can get them to lengthen, that is the key. Nowadays, the post-race analysis is so strong that it wouldn't be tolerated to be a one-handed jockey now.'

Any imperfections in style, Terry more than made up for with his courage and strength.

But even good sports are not above a little gamesmanship. Richard Pitman discovered in his novice days that Biddlecombe could talk a good race too. 'Once, I beat Biddlecombe and he objected. They all loved him and he was God. I hadn't ridden a winner. I said, "Why are you objecting, I haven't done anything to you", and he said, "You've got to try, haven't you?" I knew straightaway I was going to lose it. It was Man in the weighing room, Boy in the weighing room. The stewards were like, "Terry, what have you got to say?" "Ah, yes." "And you, Pitman, what about you?' It was all over. Terry said afterwards: "I told you it was worth objecting."'

Another day at Haydock, Richard recalls, 'Biddles and Josh Gifford brought in a bottle of red liquid and they were sipping away. It was evident by the final race they'd had a fair bit [to drink] and the rest of us went out to watch. It was a long run-in and, three strides from the line, Biddles' hands fall off the horses' ears. He comes in and tells Fred Rimell, "That's as good a race as I have ridden. Such a pity the horse put his foot in a pothole just as we were finishing … Weren't we unlucky."'

Terry Biddlecombe retired from the saddle at Cheltenham in March 1974, cheered to the echo by the Festival crowd as his fellow riders, led by Richard Pitman, held back and let him canter to the start alone.

Bob Davies

Champion Jockey 1968/69 (shared), 1969/70, 1971/72

The West Country has always been a bedrock of jump racing and Bob Davies, who shared the jockeys' championship with Terry Biddlecombe in 1968/69 with 77 winners each, and then won it twice outright, launched his career from a typical background.

His father, Eric, who had served with the Shropshire Yeomanry, had been a sergeant-instructor at the Weedon Cavalry School, otherwise known as the Army School of Equitation, thus Bertram Robert Davies was introduced early to the horsey life. He hunted with the South Shropshire at the age of eight,

Bob Davies, a Grand National winner on Lucius in 1978.

and rode a point-to-point winner for his permit-holding father before he was 15.

When he told his headmaster that he was leaving school to go racing, he met opposition: 'No, you will not,' said his headmaster. 'You will go to university. Here are the forms.'; so while he rode as an amateur, Bob Davies collected a BSc in agriculture from Wye Agricultural College to qualify him for a later life in farming if need be. Even so, he spent more time on the racecourse than in the lecture room, taking more than 200 rides for Les Kennard in one season while still a student. When the Jockey Club stewards asked how he could afford to remain an amateur, Davies told them, 'I get a student grant, my father pays my petrol, and as the principal spends more time hunting than he does in college, he doesn't mind.'

His ascent was swift: by the end of the 1966/67 season, a vintage one for gifted amateurs, he was in fourth place in the table to Chris Collins, Nick Gaselee and Brough Scott, with John Oaksey behind him. In 1968, when Brough Scott suffered an injury, the Chepstow-based Colin Davies asked Bob Davies to ride most of his horses. His career founded on the West Country circuit of Newton Abbot, Exeter, Taunton and Wincanton, Bob Davies, who was also taken on by Devon trainer David Barons, was well up the jockeys' table before racegoers

at Sandown, Kempton and Haydock had begun to take note of him.

Some may have thought it a fluke when he tied for his first professional jockeys' title in 1968/69 with Terry Biddlecombe, whose sister, Sue, he would marry, but Davies soon proved it was no such thing, winning the title outright in 1969/70 and in 1971/72. He rode good horses for Bury St Edmunds trainer David Morley, for whom he became first jockey.

One memorable victory that helped to establish him in racegoers' minds was that on Solomon II for David Barons in the Imperial Cup at Sandown in 1970. Bob Davies had walked the course in advance and found the driest ground, which his mount needed, to be on the outside. He drove Solomon II up on the wide outside nearest the stands to sweep past Paul Kelleway riding Pendil and then held off Josh Gifford, who was renowned for his strong finishes, on the Ryan Price-trained favourite, Potentate.

Bob Davies's most famous victory, however, was that on Lucius for Gordon W Richards in the 1978 Grand National (see page 100), a last-minute spare ride after an injury to Dave Goulding. In a close finish involving five horses, Bob Davies had held up his challenge until well after the final fence. He was in contention at the final fence the following year too, on another last-minute spare ride, but aboard

Bob Davies on Havanus leads Graham Thorner on Rajmataj.

Nicky Henderson's Zongalero, he went down by a length-and-a-half to Rubstic.

Film of the aftermath in Lucius's year shows the winning rider chewing: as a jockey who battled with his weight, Bob Davies used to stick a Polo mint behind his front teeth at the start of a race to help counter dehydration and a dry mouth. Keeping a Polo going for over 9 minutes 30 seconds is an achievement on its own. Apparently, he also used to fight the cramps – liable to develop with wasting to lose weight – by sipping from a bottle of Guinness in the changing room during the afternoon. 'I'm not sure it was allowed,' he told the *Daily Telegraph*'s Marcus Armytage, himself a Grand National-winning jockey, 'but we all did it.'

In all, Bob Davies rode 912 winners before retiring, in his case, not to take up training or farming, but to become a Clerk of the Course, first at Bangor on Dee, and then at Ludlow, where he has held various positions for more than 30 years.

Graham Thorner
Champion Jockey 1970/71

AP McCoy was champion jockey for 20 years. At the time when Graham Thorner, the champion jockey in the 1970/71 season, was riding, there were nine jockeys who had won the title riding against each other. He was reputed to be among the toughest of them and little wonder: his early days are a reminder of how unromantically brutal the stable life could be for those at the bottom.

Graham left school at 15 in 1964 and joined Captain Tim Forster in Letcombe Bassett. Graham still lives nearby but, speaking in a sitting room with his Grand National-winner Well To Do's colours framed on the wall, he recalls the kind of brutal initiation ceremonies and bullying rife in those days, with tar and grease a-plenty available to stable sadists: 'I had my balls blackened twice. I don't know what it is like to be raped but after that, I've got a bloody good idea. You are in total shock.

'It was the norm in hostels. Some of them were Liverpool lads who'd been smacked round the ear by the police. I was a country bumpkin

Royal Marshall II, ridden by Graham Thorner, heads to victory in the 1974 Hennessy Gold Cup.

greenhorn. I was scared shitless. I used to go on the Ridgeway and cry my eyes out. The lads would sleep in the afternoon, drink all night. Then they'd come and pick on the kids. "Let's give him a cold bath, this bastard lad who is getting a few rides." One guy spoke up at the breakfast table and said, "Joe, I've been watching you. You're bullying that kid. Leave him alone." I was chuffed. It was barbaric but it didn't half do me good because racing's a tough game. But they loved their horses.'

'The loyalty the lads had was to the two, and then three, horses they looked after. There would be fights if one lad mocked the ability of another one's horse. "You put my horse away?" Smack! Where's all that gone? It was a learning curve. It sharpened me up. I wasn't stupid but I certainly wasn't streetwise.'

There certainly wasn't much relief to be had from the trainer. 'He was very much old school. He bollocked the hell out of the lads. We all had to have a cap and had to touch our caps to the owners. Some of the owners wouldn't even say "hello" to a groom or a lad.'

Between 1964 and his retirement in 1979, Graham Thorner rode 650 winners, including his success on Well To Do in the 1972 Grand National, the first of Forster's three wins in the race. Yet despite the shared success there was never any intimacy.

'I had dinner with Captain Forster twice in

17 years. I never went with him in the car to the races. At one stage, I went to him and said, "If I am riding all these horses, I don't want to 'do my three.' I am champion jockey but I am still on a lad's wage." The reply was: "Fucking hell. I shall have to write to all my owners..."

'He said, "well done" to me no more than three times in 17 years. Apparently, he said good things about me to other people. He would tell them, "He wins me 25 races a year that no one else could." Why didn't he say it to me just once?'

Racing relationships reflect their times. Despite such treatment from a man who didn't like others to get too close to him, Graham reflects: 'Captain Forster didn't give a shit but he was the gov'nor and at the same time I respected him enormously. I had gone to him straight from school at 15. He couldn't see me as a champion jockey: he could only see me as a state schoolboy who'd left at 15. When John Francome came down to school one day, he went in the Land Rover with the Captain. I was riding work. I should have jumped off and said, "Fuck you, gov'nor." He was a snob. It was my privilege to knock him. But if you knock him, I will say, "Shut up, he was my gov'nor."

'Once, when I was offered some outside rides, I said to Captain Forster, "Mr Winter would like to know where I'm going to be on Saturday and you don't want to mess Mr Winter about." Forster replied, "I pay you a retainer. I'll let you know Friday at five to eleven. It's my privilege to fuck you about."

'We never really had a chat, a conversation. He's there, I'm here. That's it. He didn't want you to get close. Nowadays, nobody would work for a trainer who behaved like that. I wouldn't stand for it now.'

Stable jockeys today, especially in jump racing, are very much part of the decision-making. For Graham Thorner, there is wry amusement when he hears the TV commentators say, 'Jockey X has chosen to ride this one'; 'I rode everything. I never got off a horse. I never had a choice in what I was riding. He told me what I was riding. There were no safety numbers. I never missed a novice chase.'

Graham Thorner praises Captain Forster for treating every horse the same and for being scrupulously honest; he was not a gambler. The loyalty, however, was pretty one-sided. When Graham Thorner retired, Captain Forster gave him a dinner in the Cavalry Club in London where he told their fellow diners, 'I know Graham was irritated that I didn't give him chances to begin with, but I was very clever: I waited and let him make his mistakes on other people's horses.' Yet Forster also declared publicly, 'It was perfectly obvious from the beginning that Graham was going to be a fine rider. He immediately displayed natural ability, horsemanship and a racing brain.'

To go with that racing brain, Graham Thorner had a physical and mental toughness. At one stage, when a surgeon told him that his leg was too badly broken for him to continue riding, the rider jumped off a table onto the supposedly irreparably broken leg; the surgeon agreed he should take the second opinion that kept Graham in the saddle. One day he rode on with three broken ribs. He won the race but was in such pain on the journey home with three other riders that he screamed at them to take him to hospital.

His uncompromising style in a finish earned him the nickname of 'Whanger' but he points out to those who criticised him for whip use that might have brought him into trouble with today's stewards, that Captain Forster's horses nearly all had long careers. One riding memory he cherishes is not, though, of a Forster horse. He once rode Tingle Creek in the Colonial Cup (a top US race), a legendary bold-leaping animal who would take off further from his obstacle than almost any other horse: 'He had a gene no other horse possessed. You can stand off or have an exceptional stand-off. He stood off the fences further than any horse I rode. You just said, "go on" and he would come up for you.'

For some years after his riding career ended, Graham Thorner tried his hand at training but eventually pulled out in 1999. An energetic workaholic, he admits: 'I tried to do it all myself. I never asked a lad to do anything I couldn't do better but I wasn't enough of a delegator. I was old school doing it properly. I was down the yard with the horses when I should have been having a drink with the owners.'

Tommy Stack

Champion Jockey 1974/75, 1976/77

Tommy Stack's mother had wanted him to become either a vet or a priest. Unlike most Irishmen who have come to prominence in the sport, Tommy Stack had had little contact with racing before his late teens when Barry Brogan invited his school friend, then an insurance clerk, home for the weekend to his father Jimmy Brogan's stable. Tommy Stack was captivated by the racing life and when Barry Brogan took over the yard on his father's sudden death, Stack helped out and turned his back on the insurance world.

In 1965, Stack wrote off to a dozen English trainers seeking a job. Only Captain Neville Crump bothered to reply, in the negative, but Tommy Stack flew over anyway and soon joined the Ripon-based veteran Bobby Renton, starting life as an amateur; two years later, he was effectively ordered by the the authorities to become a professional. When Renton decided to retire in 1971 at the age of 83, he persuaded Stack to take over the training licence and handle Mrs 'Muffie' Brotherton's horses; within a matter of months, however, the Irishman found that the training duties were jeopardising his riding career and handed over the training side to Tony Gillam.

By the 1973/74 season, he was enjoying more rides than any other jockey – in that season, his 76 winners came from 458 rides (compared, for example, to the southern-based Richard Pitman's 316 rides for 79 winners). In the following season, 1974/75, Stack took the championship with 82 winners from his 577 rides, having become stable jockey to WA (Arthur) Stephenson's powerful Bishop Auckland yard.

Among the big races that Tommy Stack won were the Schweppes Hurdle in 1977 on True Lad and the Whitbread Gold Cup in 1978 on Strombolus; his rides that most people will

remember were those on Red Rum at Aintree in 1976 and 1977.

Ironically, Tommy Stack had been associated with Red Rum at an early stage in both their careers: in 1969/70, Stack had ridden Red Rum over hurdles for Bobby Renton 14 times –

Tommy Stack on Saggart's Choice (13) leads early at Newbury.

without winning. He had also ridden Red Rum in all 12 of his chases in the following season, leading the yard to conclude that the Aintree legend-to-be was no more than a decent division-two north-country horse.

After Ginger McCain had bought him and toned up his dicky legs in the Southport shallows, Red Rum had already won two Grand Nationals under Brian Fletcher before a falling-out between trainer and jockey saw Tommy Stack, now a star of the northern circuit, reinstated in the saddle. In 1976 the pair finished a gallant second to the lightly weighted Rag Trade, a 14-1 shot, but in 1977 Tommy Stack received a hero's welcome after riding Red Rum to his third National victory.

Colleagues rated the popular Irish jockey as shrewd, careful and businesslike, noting that in his early days he had bought a little black Austin for £40, run it for a couple of years and then sold it for £70. Michael Dickinson, a weighing-room

Red Rum ridden by jockey Tommy Stack.

Ron Barry

Champion Jockey 1972/73, 1973/74

Ron Barry was twice champion National Hunt jockey. Had there been a championship for leg-pullers, he would undoubtedly have won that too. He used to introduce his young friend Jonjo O'Neill to owners in the north of England saying that he had endured awful trouble persuading his fellow Irishman to wear shoes on his arrival in England: 'When he came off the boat, I had to march him up the quayside – left, right, left, right…' He loved winding up their sometimes irascible boss Gordon W Richards but built stable camaraderie in the process.

Ron Barry would also have been high up on any championship table for celebrations. He was the northern leader of a generation of jockeys who rode hard and played hard; as the teetotal Jonjo says, Ron Barry was always the man to take the champagne bottle by the neck and make sure his many friends enjoyed his success. The most famous example occurred after his courageous victory on The Dikler in the Cheltenham Gold Cup of 1973.

The race itself was remarkable: Ron Barry had broken his collarbone only ten days earlier and was worried that Fulke Walwyn's hefty hard-puller of a horse might run away with him on the way to the start. In fact, they arrived at the start without any problem. In the race, Barry knew he could not fight his wilful mount and he modestly said afterwards that this had allowed The Dikler to 'go to sleep' and relax on the first circuit. Others rightly ascribed that to his horsemanship. Pendil, ridden to Fred Winter's orders by Richard Pitman, hit the front two out and at the last fence was a good three lengths clear of his pursuers. But as the crowd cheered him up the finishing hill, Pendil began to falter. Ignoring the pain from his collarbone, the man they called 'Big Ron' drove on The Dikler with every fibre of his considerable strength and began reeling Pendil in. It was only 50 yards from the post when he got The Dikler's white nose in front – and there they stayed to win an enthralling contest by a short head.

contemporary, recalls, 'Stackie was our leader in the north. He sussed everybody out. He looked after us. He was riding for Arthur Stephenson and he was very good, very smart. He would always say: "We'll go in your car and I'll drive." That way, he didn't have to pay for any petrol. The rest of us were glad to let him drive because we were always so tired. Financially he always came off best.'

Tommy Stack was a friend of Coolmore's John Magnier; while he was still riding, he owned five or six mares and invested in stallion shares. Says Richard Pitman, 'He was well ahead of his game. He was earning ten grand and borrowing fifty grand to invest in stallion shares. Coolmore spotted him.' Indeed, on retiring from the saddle in 1978, Tommy Stack became manager of Longfield Stud, the Cashel, Tipperary outpost of Coolmore. In 1986, however, he took out a flat trainer's licence and had significant success, winning the 1,000 Guineas with Las Meninas in 1994 and the Irish equivalent with Tarascon in 1996, as well as the Prix Morny with Myboycharlie. In 1998 there were fears for Stack's life as he was rushed to hospital with meningitis. He survived but was rendered deaf by his illness. Undaunted, he taught himself to lip-read so as to be able to understand the feedback from jockeys and owners, even if he could no longer hear the cheers of the crowd.

After that day's racing, Barry maintained tradition by buying a case of champagne for his weighing-room colleagues. A boozy sing-song followed in The Cellar, the storeroom where caterers used to keep their supplies (that much-loved home of jockey celebrations disappeared in the 1980s amid rebuilding schemes). More celebrations followed at the Queen's Hotel and Ron Barry, who had been wasting to do a light weight at Uttoxeter on the following day, was led to bed feeling decidedly queasy. A morning glass of 'hair of the dog' failed to improve things; when Ron Barry arrived in the parade ring at the Midlands course, his deathly pallor alarmed trainer Gordon Richards, who had gone for a 'big touch' with the hurdler Pneuma.

Jonjo O'Neill confirms that after a lurch at the first hurdle his great friend patted Pneuma on the neck, muttered 'Look after me' and relied on his fellow jockeys. 'Our instructions from Ron were that one of us was to make the running, and one of us was to tell him when the hurdles were coming up, and when we'd jumped the last. It worked out somehow and he won the race.' Afterwards, with the weighing room still spinning, Ron Barry appealed to the course doctor: 'I won the Gold Cup, had a great celebration and now I'm dying of alcoholic poisoning. I can't possibly take the rest of my mounts.' The entry sportingly penned, in red ink, in his medical book read: 'Off colour. Headache. Should be all right tomorrow.' As Jonjo says: 'They were proper people then. They knew the craic. You thought you were pulling the wool over their eyes but they knew. They played along with it using common sense at the end of the day.'

Richard Pitman remembers Ron Barry for his bravery and his humour, even though, he says, few could understand Barry's Limerick accent.

Spectators forget that jump jockeys talk to each other in races; Richard recalls an occasion when he and Barry were riding in the Grand National alongside the pretty Geraldine Rees. As they were approaching Becher's, Ron Barry called out to her with an earthy enquiry about how she had spent the night before. When Richard later questioned his conduct, the Irishman replied, 'I knew what I was doing. It made her look across. The next thing was she didn't even know she had jumped Becher's. Her horse handled it fine.' Gallantry, it seems, can take many forms...

Nerves would be jangling before the National but Ron Barry had his way of dealing with that too. Says Richard, 'There would be 40 of us in that little room, flat jockeys too amid the smell of saddle soap and sweat. At about 2.30 Ron Barry would pin a notice on the loo door saying, "Reserved for R Barry for the next 45 minutes."'

If such anecdotes seem to stamp Ron Barry as a carefree reveller, nothing could be further from the truth. To win two championships while based in the north was proof of that; no one was more respected for his toughness and professionalism in the saddle. His horsemanship was exemplary: when Gordon W Richards acquired from Neville Crump a hurdler called Sheil, the horse would not consent to leave the stable yard for anybody else; Ron Barry not only took him up to the gallops, for Ron, Sheil would 'shake hands,' eat sweets from his mouth – and even lie flat out with Ron on his back. When Barry set a record of 125 wins in his first championship-winning season, it was regarded as an amazing total that would last for years. Ron Barry also had a great record in big races. He won the Whitbread Gold Cup three times on Titus Oates (1971), Charlie

Ron Barry on The Dikler (red and white colours) in touch with Tommy Carberry (4) on L'Escargot and Barry Brogan (6) on High Ken.

Potheen (1973) and The Dikler (1974). In 1969 he won the Scottish Grand National on Playlord, the Massey Ferguson Gold Cup on Titus Oates, and he won the Mackeson Gold Cup on Man Alive ten years later. He also went over to South Carolina to win the Colonial Cup twice on Grand Canyon in 1976 and 1978.

Ron Barry weighed only 6 st 5 lb when he first rode on the flat at the Curragh. As his weight increased, he came to Britain and joined Wilf Crawford in Scotland in 1964. He then spent most of his life working for Gordon W Richards, despite an attempt by Fulke Walwyn to tempt him to Lambourn as his stable jockey. When his riding career ended, he set up a business in the Lake District building boxes and became the Jockey Club's inspector of courses in the north. One safety improvement down to him was the replacement of the wrought-iron 'chair' on the right-hand upright beside the Aintree fence of that name with a lightweight replica.

Ron Barry's Irish accent never notably diminished over the years; when his fellow ex-jockey Richard Linley was being interviewed by the Jockey Club for his long-held position as inspector of courses, he was asked, 'Would you be able to understand Ron Barry on the telephone?' Having frequently had in-race conversations with Ron on a variety of tracks, Linley replied, 'If I could understand him on horseback down the back straight at Hexham in a howling gale, then that wasn't going to be a problem.'

John Francome

Champion Jockey 1975/76, 1978/79, 1980/81, 1981/82 (shared), 1982–85

You don't get to be champion jockey without ability and determination but some champions have something more: they are the landmark jockeys who become models for the next generation. Says trainer Nicky Henderson, 'To me, jockey styles turned around John Francome's era. He was the first one.'

As assistant trainer to Fred Winter, Nicky was one of the first to see the new star in action: 'I can remember Fred saying to his dear old mate Dave Dick, "I want you to come over one morning. I've got something to show you.' He brought him along and said, "Hey, watch this, it's quite extraordinary", and it was Francome schooling. It was quite extraordinary. He could see things: his art of producing a horse at an obstacle was completely different to how it had been done before.

'Fred's own style was fearless. It was strength and bravery. Those good old jockeys just threw horses at fences, there wasn't a lot of finesse to it. Francome to me was completely different and I think Fred would agree. It's been carried through and now jockeyship has changed a lot. They've certainly had to change their attitude and behaviour since they had breathalysers in the weighing room. Now they walk the course and run and they're all on specialist diets. They've got Oaksey House and they've got fitness men, they've got dieticians, they've got everything under the sun – and so they should have. That's natural progression. It's all changed very rapidly; the styles have changed and I think that change started with Francome.

'Francome didn't have the dedication and the focus of the Scudamores and Dunwoodys and APs and these guys who came after. It wasn't that professional then but, Christ, he was good. He was the game-changer.'

John Oaksey, too, used to say that there was no one better than Francome at making the instant calculations required to present a horse perfectly at a fence, and it was John Francome's horsemanship that Fred Winter admired as much as his tactical racing skills, so perfectly demonstrated when – in Jonjo O'Neill's absence through injury – he won the 1981 Champion Hurdle on Sea Pigeon.

Francome came to racing almost by accident from a showjumping background; with typical modesty, the fact that he had been part of the British team that won the European junior showjumping championship when Francome was 17 years old receives only a passing mention in his autobiography, *Born Lucky*.

Richard Pitman and John Francome were best men at each other's weddings and Richard, whom Francome eventually succeeded as stable jockey, still remembers his first arrival.

'He walked into the yard, a chubby little thing, an international showjumper. Fred looked at his hands and feet and said, "You'll get too big. I think you should go home."'

Richard recalls that when Winter asked the would-be rider 'What's the lightest you've ever been?' Francome replied as quick as a flash, '7 lb 3 oz.' 'We've got enough clever little fuckers in here already.' growled the trainer. But he took him on and he loved him.

Says Richard Pitman of Francome, 'He was so brilliant at fences because of his showjumping. You never saw him correcting a horse coming into a fence. There was no, "Come here, come here, come here" shortening up or calls of, "Go on, my son" to get a big one. You can evaluate your horse's stride and John Francome met every fence on the right stride, saving a lot of energy. He was just always right. At first, he couldn't ride a finish but being a clever man he worked on that. Like Fred Winter he too became my hero. He could do anything – put a new window in Millionaires' Row, whatever.'

John Francome won the Cheltenham Gold Cup for Winter on Midnight Court in 1979 and what is now the World Hurdle on Derring Rose; the best chaser he ever rode, however, was Jenny Pitman's Burrough Hill Lad. On him, Francome won the Welsh National, the Hennessy and the King George VI Chase. (He could not maintain the partnership when Burrough Hill Lad won the Gold Cup in 1984 because of his commitment to Fred Winter.) Francome also rode such good horses as Wayward Lad and Bregawn for Michael Dickinson.

John Francome was champion jockey seven times in his 15 seasons and retired on 9 April 1985 with a record 1,138 victories to his name. The one episode that brought him adverse publicity, in 1978, was his friendship with the flamboyant bookmaker John Banks. Questioned by Racecourse Security Services, Francome freely admitted that he had discussed some of his mounts with Banks, saying that he had not realised it was against the rules to do so. Banks was 'warned off' for three years for paying for information; Francome was fined £750 and suspended for six weeks.

That the episode had little or no effect on Francome's career owed much to Fred Winter's solid support for his stable jockey. He declared: 'It just never occurred to me that John might have done anything wrong.' When a shaken Francome emerged from his first interview with the authorities, he told Fred Winter, 'I want you to know I have never stopped a horse in my life.' Winter's reply was a classic: 'Son, if I ever thought for a moment you had, then you wouldn't be standing there. You'd be lying down.' Winter clearly had a significant influence on his young jockey. Peter Scudamore notes: 'Fred and John Francome rode out in collar and tie – and John does to this day. John is so rebellious in so many things that he does, but when you've instilled a discipline in somebody…'

In jump racing's history John Francome was more than a riding-style model and a record-breaker: as deference faded, his attitude and lifestyle reflected the changing times. He did not take himself or anybody else too seriously. He wore his hair long; officialdom was often the target of his sharp wit. He did not endear himself to the stewards by referring to them in a speech as the 'cabbage patch kids' or by asking sarcastically as they rolled film of an incident several times in one racecourse inquiry if an usherette would soon be coming in with ice creams and popcorn. Says Nicky Henderson:

Rag Trade, ridden by John Francome, during the 1975 Grand National.

'I wouldn't say Francome's dedication to being a jockey was absolute. There was a fair bit of rascal in him. When we came to the era of the Scudamores and Dunwoodys and guys like that, they were amazingly focused. They took it to another level.'

Definitely the wittiest champion we have ever had, Francome has been racing's equivalent of a Renaissance man. He enjoyed other things in life besides jumping fences (which he still does for fun) – his football, his tennis, his friends, writing racing novels, making money from fish-and-chip shops, buying land and building things – and he wasn't going to stand any nonsense from puffed-up officialdom.

Francome did seem to be something of a target for officialdom but he admits that he didn't always help his own case because he was disinclined to give placed horses a hard time. Nor did he bother to hide his contempt for the racing knowledge of some stewards: not altogether surprising, when on one occasion a steward came to confront him in the weighing room over 'pulling up' his mount; the mud-plastered Francome had not pulled it up at all – the horse had fallen and then rolled on him!

Following his retirement, Francome tried his hand at training for a couple of years but then decided it was not for him. He was then, for 25 years, an illuminating and amusing

Perfect poise: John Francome on Uncle Bing at Cheltenham in 1980.

member of Channel Four's racing team while also writing a series of Dick Francis-style racing novels; however, when Highflyer Productions, led by Andrew Franklin, surprisingly lost the television contract to IMG Sports Media in 2012, he retired from our screens too.

Jonjo O'Neill
Champion Jockey 1977/78, 1979/80

Many good jockeys become popular with punters because of their results. Just a few, though, are taken to the hearts of the racing public and achieve some kind of mystical bond with racegoers. Jonjo O'Neill was one of them, admired for his driving ruthlessness in the saddle and for his self-deprecating charm when out of it. There was also a special sympathy that has lasted into his successful training career because of his courage in adversity – a leg broken so badly that there was a likelihood of amputation, followed by a battle against lymphatic cancer.

The two key influences on Jonjo O'Neill's early career in England were trainer Gordon W Richards and Ron Barry, the senior stable jockey at Greystoke, where Jonjo was based from 1972 to 1977. Jockeys who had to battle against the finished article he later became would have been surprised to learn that, in his early stages as a jockey, Jonjo's confidence was fragile. More than once, especially after a last-fence tumble in the 1972 Mackeson when he had the race at his mercy on Proud Stone, he nearly retreated to Ireland in despair. But the better times were not long in coming.

In his second season, Jonjo's first 50 rides produced 21 winners. He wound up the 1972/73 season with 38 winners, taking the conditional riders' title, while Ron Barry was champion jockey with 125 winners. No intelligent young jockey could have failed to benefit from long hours travelling to and from the races with Gordon W Richards and Ron Barry, although the hard taskmaster would castigate either of them fiercely – even after a win – if they had not scrupulously followed his orders. Despite the progress he made at Greystoke either side

of a broken leg in 1975 and the steady stream of winners, Jonjo felt stifled; so it was that, at the end of the 1976/77 season, he told a surprised Richards that he was leaving.

His decision to go freelance could hardly have paid off more spectacularly: his advisers had reckoned that by leaving Richards, Jonjo's winners' total might drop in the next season to around 30. Instead, with a third of his successes provided by another major northern force in the shape of Peter Easterby, Jonjo ended the 1977/78 season as champion jockey with a record 149 winners. He rode five in just one afternoon at Uttoxeter. There was fevered media speculation at the end of the season as to whether he would reach what then seemed a magical total of 150; in the final week, however, Jonjo twice 'lost' races he reckoned to have won. First, at Hexham, fellow jockey Dennis Atkins carved him up on a section of the track where there were no patrol cameras, bumping him so hard that Jonjo's mount was turned

sideways, but somehow managing to persuade the stewards that it was Jonjo, in the quest for the 150 winners, who was being economical with the truth at the subsequent inquiry. Then, on the last day of the season, Jonjo was delayed when flying to Market Rasen and was still circling the course and watching from above as the rider who had been substituted for him won on Pleasure Seeker.

Peter Easterby called Jonjo the strongest jockey he had seen, and Timeform described him that year as the most reliable of all jockeys over jumps. The racing annual added: 'He is also by some way the most masterful finisher in the game: his driving power on the Flat is phenomenal. His overwhelming determination to get to the line first at all costs seemed at times to inspire his mounts to do the impossible for him in a tight finish: time and again he won races that lesser riders would have lost.' At the time, let us remember, Jonjo was riding against the likes of champions Ron Barry, Tommy Stack and John Francome.

In the weighing room the teetotal Jonjo, with his impish smile and gentle manner, was one of the best-liked riders; in a race his opponents knew there was no one more ruthlessly determined. In that championship season, his winning percentage through 545 races was 27.33. Yet it was another kind of determination that saw him through 13 months of agony after he broke his leg at Bangor in October 1980. The limb was shattered like crazy paving in four places. After his surgeon, Hugh Barber, had patched him up, Jonjo was so desperate to get back in time to ride Sea Pigeon and Night Nurse at the 1981 Cheltenham Festival that he disregarded his surgeon's orders and climbed back prematurely into the saddle. The leg was so badly damaged and so hideously painful as a result that Jonjo, a deeply religious man, even contemplated suicide and gave the Swiss surgeon who picked up the pieces permission to amputate during a corrective operation if that proved to be the best course. Amazingly, he was back race-riding at Wetherby in December 1981, his return bringing a record crowd to the Yorkshire course.

Jonjo's most famous successes in the saddle, on Sea Pigeon in the Champion Hurdle and on Dawn Run both in the Champion Hurdle and the Cheltenham Gold Cup, are described elsewhere in this book. Fellow champion Richard Dunwoody calls Jonjo's ride on Dawn Run the best-ever at Cheltenham: 'She was by no means a natural jumper and to keep her in contention after making mistakes in a strong field before driving her back to the front on the run-in was amazing. It was a brilliant ride.' But there were so many more. Sea Pigeon's trainer, Peter Easterby, says, 'I never gave him orders much. A good jockey doesn't need orders. Waste of breath. The thing about him was his will to win. He was just very good at his job. He quite often won on horses that shouldn't have won.'

As well as his famous victory on Dawn Run, Jonjo also won the Cheltenham Gold Cup in 1979 on Alverton. His hoodoo race, though, was the Grand National: in eight attempts, he never managed to complete the course, albeit he made up for that as a trainer by supplying AP McCoy

with his only National winner, Don't Push It, in 2010. At JP McManus's Jackdaw's Castle, Jonjo O'Neill has also been one of the most successful trainers at the Cheltenham Festival: among current trainers, only Nicky Henderson, Willie Mullins and Paul Nicholls have trained more than his 26 winners.

Peter Scudamore

Champion Jockey 1981/82 (shared), 1985–92

'All I wanted,' says Martin Pipe, looking back on the riders who helped him win 15 trainers' championships, 'was a jockey who wanted to win.' For many years, of course, he had the perfect example of that in AP McCoy; nevertheless, if there was one jockey–trainer partnership that epitomised the years of Pipe's domination, it was his association with Peter Scudamore. Martin remembers clearly how that all began.

'At Warwick, Jonathon Lower [the stable's number-two jockey] made it all on My Dominion after barging his way in to the rail. He was a £300 purchase. We'd told him, "You make all, on the inside." Then he won another on Bob And Peter, a useless article. Peter Scudamore saw it and said to himself, "I know what I'm doing wrong – I'm not riding for that chap." Paul Leach [at that time Pipe's number-one jockey] was injured and Scu said, "Can I come and ride for you?"

'The first one was Hieronymous [at Haydock on 2 March 1985]. I told him, "Go out and make all." He did – and he was coming into the home straight as the others came out of the back straight. He went on and on and won. It was what I expected, it was no surprise. That was the idea: we train them to win. Scu kept saying, "Do you know, that's the fittest horse I have ridden all season." He must have said it half a dozen times and I kept saying, "Go away!" We became acquainted after that basically.'

'Scu', as the racing world knew him, had been based previously with David Nicholson and had then ridden for Fred Winter. He retired at Ascot on 7 April 1993 after riding Sweet Duke to success in his last race with a then record total of

Eight-times champion jockey Peter Scudamore celebrates winning his last race at Ascot.

1,678 winners and eight jockeys' championships behind him, another record. Of those 1,678 winners, 792 had been trained by Martin Pipe; on Pipe's horses over the years, Scudamore's strike rate was a remarkable 37 per cent. In the extraordinary season of 1988/89, that strike rate rose to 44 per cent, with 158 winners for Pipe among Scudamore's record total of 221.

Scudamore, often leading all the way, from start to finish, on the 'superfit' horses from Martin Pipe's base at Pond House, Nicolashayne, became the punter's friend: 353 of his Pipe-trained winners were odds-on favourites. As Pipe says, 'He was a terrific judge of pace. He went out, he knew the pace, knew the horses would jump and got them jumping and going. He used to ride the racecourses the proper way, same as AP McCoy. They know where the wet ground is. The courses haven't altered. Now I see the kids do it wrong...'

Peter Scudamore's reputation was already established before he linked up with Martin Pipe. As the son of Michael Scudamore, who won the Grand National on Oxo, he had spent time with Willie Stephenson before joining the David Nicholson academy at Condicote. He respected the Duke and was loyal to him – once, when Nicholson had got his finances in a tangle, Scudamore signed a cheque to pay the stable's wages. After the trainer's long wait, Scu gave Nicholson his first Festival winner in 1986, taking the Triumph Hurdle on the 40-1 shot Solar Cloud and then winning the Ritz Club National Hunt Chase with Charter Party for good measure. But the next year an offer from Fred Winter to start partnering his stable stars was too good to refuse and, to the chagrin of David Nicholson, Scudamore moved on.

Peter Scudamore, who had been chasing all around the country in pursuit of rides, shared his first jockeys' championship in the 1981/82 season, but only thanks to the sportsmanship of previous champion John Francome. Scu had been well in the lead but broke his arm in a fall at Southwell. Francome, as he had promised, kept riding until he had drawn level with Scudamore's 120 winners just four days before the end of the season and then stopped

so that they shared the championship. With the Nicholson yard suffering from the virus and going through a lean period, it was not until the 1985/86 season, with Francome no longer riding, that Scu won his first jockeys' championship outright, beating off a challenge from Simon Sherwood; the championship then became his personal property for the next six seasons, during which the highlights included a Queen Mother Champion Chase on Pearlyman (1987), a Champion Hurdle on Celtic Shot (1988), Welsh Nationals on Bonanza Boy (1988 and 1989) and on Carvill's Hill (1991), and a Scottish National on Captain Dibble (1992).

Celtic Shot's Champion Hurdle victory was a poignant one: with Fred Winter incapacitated after a fall down stairs and a subsequent stroke, his Uplands yard was being run, although still in Winter's name, by his young assistant, Charlie Brooks, who leaned heavily on Peter Scudamore's experience. Scu himself had three times been second in the race so this was a victory to be relished.

Certainly the 1988/89 season was special. Scu won the Mackeson Gold Cup on Pegwell Bay, the Hennessy Gold Cup on Strands of Gold, the Welsh National and the Racing Post Chase on Bonanza Boy, the Imperial Cup on Travel Mystery, the Welsh Champion Hurdle on Celtic Shot, and the Grand Annual Chase

Broadsword, ridden by Peter Scudamore, going down to the start at Cheltenham.

at the Cheltenham Festival on Pukka Major. Bonanza Boy's victory in the Racing Post Chase was a tribute to Scudamore's determination. He had been virtually tailed off last but his rider never gave up and, in the end, he came through the field and won going away. Like a number of other top riders, however, including John Francome and Jonjo O'Neill, Scudamore never won a Grand National.

Throughout his period in the saddle, Scudamore was renowned for his will to win. For the equally talented and win-hungry Richard Dunwoody, who also became David Nicholson's number-one rider, Scu was the role model: 'I was weaned on Scu's hardness. In the weighing room of my youth he was the epitome of the great jockey. For as long as he was there, Scu set the standard. To beat him you had to need winners as badly as he did. Losing had to hurt you as much as it did him.' Dunwoody rated Scudamore

as even stronger in the saddle than AP McCoy. Scu himself says he was probably at his best when he was young: 'You're full of confidence, you don't believe you are going to get hurt. Your enthusiasm eliminates danger.'

And who was Scu's own role model? 'Piggott really. His professionalism was what I could grasp to take you on to another level. His diet. His attitude. If you were paying someone to come into the weighing room or the paddock, you didn't want someone who said, "I was pissed-up last night and it was a lot of fun." That's why Martin Pipe and I got on so well.'

For a time after his retirement from the saddle, Peter Scudamore joined his long-time friend Nigel Twiston-Davies in his training operation. Later he became a partner and assistant to leading Scottish trainer Lucinda Russell. In February 2016 Peter's son, Tom, who has continued the family tradition as

stable jockey to Martin Pipe's son, David, at Nicolashayne, rode his own 1,000th winner.

Talking to Scu gives a real sense of the continuity of jump racing. He is proud of Tom, he has genuine respect for the professionalism of AP McCoy and his contemporaries, but he is full of admiration still for his own father and that generation of jockeys. 'I remember Father talking of a Hereford race with 40 runners, so many that they could not line up. In those days, starters would say, "Triers at the front, non-triers at the back" and let them go. There were no safety factors and at that time they wore no helmets. Then they brought in those cork helmets with no chin straps. If you had a fall, they would hit the floor before you did. Father said that when helmets first came in, if you wore one for schooling, people said your nerve had gone.

'There was no overnight declaration of horses. It was like a point-to-point. You would turn up.

You went to the races without a [booked] ride and you might end up with a hatful. He [Scu's father] won a Gold Cup in 1957 on Linwell because Terry Biddlecombe had said to him, "Come on, Michael, drive me to Kempton," and when he got there, he picked up a spare ride on a horse which was later to win him a Gold Cup.

'There was no all-weather racing taking horses out of the jumping system and there were a few jockeys who only rode over hurdles.

'There were no motorways in those days. If you went to Newton Abbot in the summer, he said, it would take you eight or nine hours to drive down. In London they lived in the Turkish baths, went out to Wheelers for a steak and went back to the Turkish baths. They got to know the cricketers who'd be staying there ... Nowadays, you couldn't stay all night in the Turkish baths – it would be a very different kind of gentleman staying.

'My father was booked to ride Legal Joy in the National for Dorothy Paget. She sent a message to him via a secretary who had been ordered, "Tell Scudamore he's not to stay in the Adelphi because of all the partying that goes on there." He was riding in 1951 with people most of whose rides had been taken away from them by the war. These people had had their youth taken away from them and they were fearless. Their minds were different. They were not afraid. They had seen death and stuff and some of them couldn't come to terms with themselves being alive. That's why they went and did things like climbing the Himalayas.'

That had its effect on the next generation too. Says Peter: 'Concussion didn't count. A collarbone was three days. We hid injuries because we didn't understand the consequences. People like my father who had come out of the war only a generation away set such an example of toughness that you felt you had to show toughness too.

'We go on now about how much softer the fences are than when we rode and in my father's day. Dave Dick had three falls at Leicester where in those days the fences were notoriously stiff. After the third fall, the doctor came up to him and said, "Are you OK, Mr Dick?" He replied, "It's not me you want to test, it's the fucking

Peter Scudamore leads over the water at Fontwell in 1992.

idiot who built those brick shithouses out there."

'My father rode in the National before they built the sloping aprons in front of the fences. The Dorothy Paget papers which Martin Pipe has say she was going to offer Dave Dick £700, or it might have been £500, to ride in the National. In those days, you could get a car for £250 and I think my father paid £9,000 for his farm. Father got £250 to ride in the National because he wasn't as good as Dave Dick.

'They didn't get paid through Weatherby's in those days. A lot of jockeys didn't get paid for their winners. You had to go to the bar or somewhere to get your cash for riding. You had to chase up the money yourself.

'In the days when father won the Grand National, it used to be on the Pathé News. If you look at the old newsreel, you can see Tim Brookshaw breaks his iron. Father and Tim land over Becher's and you can see Tim look over to Michael and he says, "Look, Michael, no legs. We'll be on the pictures now." They showed the Grand National from Becher's the second time onwards, and the jockeys used to go to the cinema to see themselves.'

Although he smashed up his face before he retired, Michael Scudamore never broke a limb in his 13-year riding career. Ironically, the only time that happened was when he fell down a manhole outside a bookshop in Ross-on-Wye!

Move on a generation to Scu's own time and he remembers how it used to be before every race was on camera. 'If the trainer sent you off to, say, Fakenham, there was no television. All they had was the audio commentary in the betting shop, so if you fell off one, you'd grab the thing, wipe a bit of grass on the horse's nose, give the travelling head lad a tenner – and say it turned arse over tip. You had to get to the travelling head lad real quick if you got beaten a short head and give him a tenner, saying: "Tell the trainer I rode a brilliant race."'

The workload and the opportunities have changed too. 'Coming up to Aintree one year, I had had 600 rides. Somebody came and said, "You've just broken Stan Mellor's record for the number of rides in a season." These days, they are having 1,200 rides.

'Now they've all got agents. We had to book all our own rides. The coming of mobile phones made a difference. I bought one of the early ones for £250, a lot of money then, and spent a lot of time driving around trying to get a signal. You wanted to ring to book a ride to justify spending £250 on a mobile phone. But three days after I had bought it, John Edwards rang me and gave me the winning ride on Pearlyman in the Queen Mother Champion Chase – so it paid for itself.'

For those with championship ambitions, there were other considerations too. 'The big trainers would rarely go to Exeter or Newton Abbot at the beginning of the season. I was riding for Fred Winter or David Nicholson. So I needed some little West Country trainers. We were all nice to them in the summer. Once the rain started, we didn't speak to them again until the spring...'

Richard Dunwoody
Champion Jockey 1992–95

When you read jockeys' autobiographies, one thing becomes clear: it is unwise to become emotionally involved with a top jockey. Former champion Richard Dunwoody entitled his book *Obsessed* and that title would be equally appropriate if applied to the volumes produced by Peter Scudamore, AP McCoy, Mick Fitzgerald and a number of others. The all-consuming quest for winners and for the demonstration that you are top of the heap results often in a total loss of perspective: all those named have revealed how badly they behaved on occasion to wives, partners and girlfriends.

Alone among top sportsmen, jockeys not only have to cope with the media spotlight but often have to struggle with their weight, starving themselves and spending hours in the sauna. They have to drive thousands of miles in the course of the year to get to the racecourses where they ply their trade and they have to work all hours, not just travelling to far-flung meetings but also being on the gallops soon after dawn to ride work for the trainers whose horses they would like to partner in races. It requires massive single-mindedness and the strains of a jockey's life ensure that single-minded is what they become, at least until children arrive or they hang up their boots.

Richard Dunwoody has revealed with remarkable honesty what the pursuit of perfection in the saddle can do to a man. On New Year's Day at Newbury in 1994, in a televised race, he was unseated at the last hurdle. Worse for him, the race was won by Adrian Maguire, his rival for that year's jockeys' championship. Richard came home and had a row with his then wife, Carol, in which all the aggression came from him. He then watched the incident a hundred times on the video recorder, beating himself up mentally. He wrote: 'That evening I loathed myself. Full of rage and frustration, I literally knocked and banged myself against doors and walls in our house. I wanted to damage myself, punish myself for a stupid and costly mistake.' The black eyes and bruising he exhibited on the racecourse were not all the result of falls.

When he was warned that he could lose the use of his right arm if he carried on, Richard Dunwoody had to end his career at the age of 35, five or six years before he would have expected or wished to. His retirement deprived us of one of the most accomplished and stylish riders we have ever seen. Richard was the epitome of professional cool in the saddle and many young pros modelled themselves on him. He was three times champion jockey and he ended his career having ridden more winners than any jockey before him, including his personal idol, Peter Scudamore. But if there is one thing about his career that racegoers will never forget, it is the relentless, punishing season-long battle for the jockeys' championship between Richard and Adrian Maguire in 1993/94. To outsiders, it was one of the greatest duels in sporting history. Dunwoody has since described it as a 'journey through hell' that left both of them utterly drained.

The championship began at Bangor on 30 July 1993 and ended on 4 June 1994 at Market Rasen. Dunwoody's season was complicated by an uneasy relationship with Martin Pipe, his main supplier of rides, and by splitting acrimoniously with his agent, Robert Kington. So depressed was he at times by trailing Maguire, who at one stage had a lead of 43 winners and whose main retainer was with David Nicholson, that Dunwoody even consulted a sports psychologist, who noted that Richard talked more about his rival than himself. It reached the stage, Dunwoody concedes, that he and Maguire were riding more and more against each other, rather than the other jockeys in a race, both feeling impelled at all costs not to lose to the other. They paid an obvious price: it was the intensity of their rivalry rather than anything else that earned Maguire a six-day suspension for excessive use of the whip on one occasion (riding a finish against Dunwoody) and Dunwoody a two-week enforced holiday for 'causing interference' (to Maguire), which resulted in his missing the Cheltenham Festival. Ironically, that event finally led to a more or less friendly drink between the two, which took some of the bitterness out of the struggle.

In one racing week, Dunwoody rode 18 winners. On another occasion, from Monday to Saturday, he had 34 rides at ten different meetings for eight winners. More concentrated and committed than they had ever been in their lives, sometimes conjuring victory from horses that had no business winning their races, on

Richard Dunwoody takes the 1994 Grand National on Miinehoma.

Richard Dunwoody aboard Florida Pearl after winning the 1999 Hennessy Gold Cup at Leopardstown.

one crazy day Dunwoody and Maguire each rode at three meetings: Hereford, Southwell and Huntingdon. In the end, after 890 rides (and 47 falls – although he never missed a single race through injury), Dunwoody emerged the victor with 197 winners, his biggest ever total, to Maguire's 194 winners. In *Obsessed*, he says that by the end he was sick of the battle. 'It had been too long, too punishing and in the end too cruel. Adrian rode 194 winners and lost. I was glad it wasn't me but I also knew it was ludicrous to speak of a winner and a loser at the end of a race in which both riders had reached into God-knows-what reserves to surpass themselves. My 197 winners to Adrian's 194 didn't make me a better jockey.' Maguire, much of his career interrupted by injuries, figures high on the list of top riders who never became champion jockey.

With a career total of 1,699 winners from 9,399 rides, Richard Dunwoody rode more than 100 winners for ten consecutive seasons and was champion jockey in the seasons of 1992/93, 1993/94 and 1994/95. He won the Champion Hurdle on Kribensis, the Cheltenham Gold Cup on Charter Party, and the King George VI Chase four times (twice each on Desert Orchid

and One Man). In all, he rode 18 winners at the Cheltenham Festival. His record in the Grand National was remarkable: altogether, he rode in 15 Grand Nationals from 1985 to 1999, finishing in the frame eight times from 14 valid rides. Only once did he fail to reach the frame when completing the course. His first five rides in the National were all on West Tip, who, as well as winning the race in 1986 (when Dunwoody was the youngest jockey in the race), finished second once and fourth twice. His other winning ride was on Miinnehoma for Martin Pipe.

In his early days, having made himself anorexic in his desire for a racing career, Richard Dunwoody rode out for flat trainers in Newmarket and, in December 1981, signed up as a pupil assistant with Captain Tim Forster in Letcombe Bassett, where Hywel Davies was the stable jockey. Progress was slow as an amateur rider until one memorable day at Hereford brought Mr R Dunwoody rapidly to public notice: the return from his seven mounts was four winners, a second and two thirds.

By the 1985/86 season, Dunwoody was second jockey to both Captain Forster and David Nicholson (where stable jockey Peter Scudamore was a formative influence), while also having the pick of Michael Oliver's horses. Within the year, Scudamore had moved on to Fred Winter and Dunwoody, with a National victory behind him on West Tip, became Nicholson's number one, riding horses such as Very Promising, on whom he won the Black and White Whisky Champion Chase at Leopardstown, the Duke's first winner in Ireland.

In 1988, he won the Gold Cup for Nicholson on Charter Party, a horse that was difficult to keep sound, and the next year in a memorable race he took the Arkle Challenge Trophy on the 20-1 shot Waterloo Boy in a close finish with Southern Minstrel and Sabin du Loir, ridden by Peter Scudamore. In confirmation of Dunwoody's rising status, he was then asked to partner Nicky Henderson's top horses. With Simon Sherwood retiring, he took over on Desert Orchid for David Elsworth; at the same time, he was asked to ride Highland Bud, the best jumper in the USA, for Jonathan

Sheppard. (Dunwoody twice won the Breeders Cup on him.) With Nicholson's Viking Flagship coming to his best, and Dunwoody linked too with Michael Stoute's top hurdler Kribensis, it was a period of high opportunity. The search for winners was also becoming addictive, so much so that one day Dunwoody booked himself a helicopter at a cost of £350 for a single ride at Hereford – on which his percentage for winning offered no more than £130.

With Peter Scudamore riding for Martin Pipe, who was training 100 more winners per season than most other leading trainers, it was virtually impossible for Richard Dunwoody to win the jockeys' championship. When Scudamore retired at the age of only 34, Pipe asked Richard to replace him as his jockey; Dunwoody knew that he faced a choice between being guaranteed enough winners to be champion and continuing to win a good proportion of top races on the equine blue bloods that Nicky Henderson and David Nicholson trained. Nicholson and Henderson gave him retainers, Martin Pipe would not. Having finished second in the table to Scu for the previous three years, Richard Dunwoody went to Pipe, even though he sensed that their relationship might not be like the one he had enjoyed with David Nicholson, who, in turn, took on Adrian Maguire as Dunwoody's replacement. The next season, 1993/94, then saw that epic struggle for the championship between Maguire and Dunwoody. In the end, the Pipe firepower helped to clinch a second jockeys' title for Dunwoody: in return, one of the best Aintree jockeys we have seen won Pipe a Grand National on Miinnehoma.

Their relationship was never, though, the kind of harmonious partnership Martin Pipe enjoyed with Peter Scudamore before Dunwoody, or with AP McCoy after Dunwoody: Pipe felt that Dunwoody was fine for the big occasions but not quite as interested as the other two in winning every race possible, however small. Relations were not helped in January 1995 when Dunwoody earned himself a 28-day suspension, and when he told Martin Pipe he was no longer prepared to waste to do the 10-stone minimum but would manage only 10 st 4 lb at best. Having

clinched a third championship, Dunwoody then surprised much of the racing community by deciding to leave the Pond House winner factory and to ride as a freelance in future. The jump jockeys' championship, he had decided, took more than it gave.

AP McCoy
Champion Jockey 1995–2015

There never has been another sportsman quite like Sir Anthony McCoy – still 'AP' to most in racing – and there never will be. Other great sportsmen have achieved remarkable, sustained success – Steve Redgrave's five consecutive Olympic rowing golds from 1984 to 2000, hurdler Ed Moses' unbeaten run of 122 races – but they were not competing in one of the two sports in which participants are followed, day-in, day-out, by an ambulance, and in which regular and painful injury is inevitable. Nor were they driving their bodies every competitive day well below their natural weight on a starvation diet. To achieve his riding weight, McCoy regularly boiled himself in hot baths like a lobster. His results were achieved despite the formidable list of injuries related in the section on jockeys' safety. He once said, "I dream of things and then I convince myself they are possible." He also had the capacity to lock away in the recesses of his mind any fear of pain.

AP McCoy – a 20-year champion.

My abiding memory of him will be that of Ascot on a November afternoon in 2012. The previous day, AP had been kicked in the face at Wetherby. His injuries required the extraction of two teeth and hours of work by a plastic surgeon stitching up his mouth and nose. But because he wanted that day to ride the promising My Tent Or Yours, McCoy had insisted on having no general anaesthetic. His face, swathed in medical tape, had a ghostly pallor. Trainer Nicky Henderson was only half-joking when he told us: 'I wanted a jockey, not the Phantom of the Opera.' No one else would have ridden that day but McCoy's high pain threshold, sheer guts and all-consuming thirst for winners ensured that in the next few minutes My Tent Or Yours became his 101st winner of the season.

Typically, when he broke back vertebrae and endured kriotherapy, the blasting of freezing nitrogen in an icy chamber, to get back in the saddle in time for the Cheltenham Festival, he enquired as to who previously had endured the lowest temperature. Told it was a footballer, McCoy of course then went several degrees lower and set a new endurance record. Revealingly, when his aide, Gee Armytage, was running the

London Marathon, AP asked, 'Are you going to win?' and when she replied in the negative, the puzzled jockey followed up: 'So why are you doing it?'

Having been apprenticed first in Ireland to Billy Rock (1987–89) and to Jim Bolger (1989–94), AP McCoy, as the British racing public first knew him, came to Britain to join Toby Balding's academy of young would-be champions. He had not even ridden in a chase at that point; yet with Balding he was champion conditional jockey in his first season in 1994/95. He was then British champion jump jockey every year for the next 20 years, for many of those years riding as first jockey to Martin Pipe, and then taking on a retainer from Irish owner JP McManus to race in his famous green-and-gold colours.

First, the blaze of statistics: following his nine successes on the flat in Ireland, McCoy then rode 4,348 winners in Britain and Ireland. As well as his record of 289 winners in a British season, he scored the most wins in a calendar year (307 in 2002), the most wins in a European season (290 in 2001/02), and the most prize money in a British season (£2,753,453 in 2001/02). His other records include the fastest 100 winners in a British season (by 21 August in 2014) and the fastest 200 (by 20 December in 2002). The record McCoy prized most highly himself was beating

AP McCoy on the way to Cheltenham victory aboard Albertas Run.

Sir Gordon Richards' total (on the flat) of 269 winners in a season, a record that had lasted for 56 years. But McCoy always set himself a new target: the moment he had ridden 4,000 winners, he focused on the 4,182-winner total accumulated by his friend and patron, Martin Pipe, as a trainer: 'I never forget that one: 4,182. Take 41 and double it. Martin had better feel worried...' There has never been a rider so thirsty for winners at all levels. But it was all about so much more than numbers.

At Sandown in April 2015, a crowd of twenty thousand turned up, most of us there in order to cheer on McCoy as he took his last two mounts and collected his 20th trophy as champion jumps rider. Many a grown man admitted to damp eyes that day and even the ultimate iron man himself shed a tear or two as he rode back on the third-placed Box Office. Only affection and admiration were to be seen that day but it had long been thus. What was remarkable about AP's achievements was that nowhere in jump racing could be found any resentment or jealousy: there was only wonder at his application and will to win on stages big and small. A keen Arsenal fan, he once declared: 'I admire dedication more than flair. Thierry Henri is brilliant but people don't realise how hard he works...'

A non-drinker (although never a party-pooper and often the last to leave) and nowadays the proud father of Eve and Archie, who, along with his wife, Chanelle, have tempered his obsession, McCoy became the model sportsman: modest, professional and just plain likeable. Typically, his first week of retirement included visits in Ireland to two badly injured jockeys, cousins Robbie and JT McNamara. By announcing his impending retirement at Newbury two months beforehand, AP gave racegoers their chance up and down the country to say goodbye and, on the day, he signed autographs and posed for selfies with an endless good grace as they queued to do so.

It had not always been quite like that. There was a moody selfishness in his early obsession with winners; with his starvation pallor and sucked-in cheeks, he could look the picture of misery on the racecourse when thwarted. After one Cheltenham Festival where the winners had failed to flow, McCoy wrote to the *Racing Post* apologising publicly for his grumpiness, wryly adding, 'Think yourself lucky. I have to live with me all the time.'

The young thruster of the early days became depressed when regularly penalised by stewards for contravening guidelines on the use of the whip and effectively being ordered back to riding school. He felt he was being picked on and publicly vented his fury by throwing his whip into the crowd as he returned to the winner's enclosure on Cyfor Malta after winning the Murphy's Gold Cup in 1998. But he accepted the inevitable and, to the immense relief of those same authorities, remodelled his style, becoming an example to every young professional. He went into racing, he admitted, to ride winners, not to be popular or win accolades – but he came to realise that he could do both. The tumult of delight when in 2010 he finally kicked his Aintree hoodoo and won the Grand National on Don't Push It convinced McCoy how much the racing public admired and respected him; when he in that same year became the first jockey to be voted BBC Sports Personality of the Year, it

The Grand National 2010 – AP McCoy celebrates his win on Don't Push It.

'I wanted a jockey, not the Phantom of the Opera' said trainer, Nicky Henderson on seeing this apparition in the parade ring.

was clear that his appeal had transcended his own sport.

The Grand National was just one of many big race successes. Back at the Cheltenham Festival of 1997, among his 31 Festival winners, AP brought off the Champion Hurdle–Gold Cup double by winning the hurdling crown on Make A Stand for Martin Pipe and the top steeplechase on Mr Mulligan for Noel Chance. McCoy won another Gold Cup and the Welsh National on Synchronised, and the Scottish National on Belmont King. He won a King George VI Chase on Best Mate, and further Champion Hurdles on Brave Inca and Binocular.

We all have our favourites among his great rides. McCoy himself took particular pleasure in the 1998 Aintree Hurdle when on the quirky Pridwell, a horse very much with a mind of his own, he managed to beat the Champion Hurdler Istabraq, ridden by Charlie Swan. In his autobiography, AP explained: 'There were certain stages of the race at which he tried to drop himself out but I just kept at him, gently asking him to go forward, coaxing him into it, making him feel like he wanted to do it, not because I wanted him to ... they took it up and went on over the final flight, looking all over the winner but I managed to get Pridwell to dig deep, as deep as he had ever dug before, and we got back up and nutted Istabraq in a head-

bob on the line.' It was a triumph of persuasion more than domination, but the stewards reacted by suspending him for four days for his whip use. When he appealed, the Jockey Club added another two days to the punishment.

Other victories McCoy recalled with special pleasure included the Grand National victory for which his patron, JP McManus, had waited so long and Synchronised's Gold Cup victory after a bad jump at the first had forced AP to niggle and squeeze and cajole for three miles to get the horse back on terms.

Most of us would add his 2009 Festival victory in the William Hill Chase on Wichita Lineman. Again, he nursed the horse around through a series of blunders then rallied him at the end to win in the last stride. And then there was the Queen Mother Champion Chase of 2000. AP used to call it 'the professionals' race' and see it as the ultimate test: 'You need speed to win it and you need to jump fast. It's the 100-metre Olympic final of National Hunt racing. I love riding in it: I love the thrill of going as fast as you can over fences.'

Riding Edredon Bleu that year for Henrietta Knight, AP was in a classic duel with Norman Williamson on Direct Route. They jumped the last level, then Direct Route inched ahead. Edredon Bleu relished a battle so McCoy put his head down and asked for everything. The two horses matched stride for stride in frantic concentration and it was 'on the nod' at the line. As they pulled up, neither jockey knew who had won – but Edredon Bleu had prevailed. 'It was a hell of a race in which to be involved. It was one of those signature Cheltenham Festival races that people remember and it was even better to win it.' Better still for McCoy was that it gave him at last the full set of Champion Hurdle, Gold Cup and Champion Chase.

McCoy, thank heaven, went out at the top, more or less intact and without anyone ever having suggested that he had lost a scintilla of his fire or his bottle. He set the standard: sports writers are often too hasty with the word 'legend' but with McCoy that description truly fits.

Richard Johnson

Champion Jockey 2015/16

If there was one thing the world of jump racing wanted in 2016, it was for Richard Johnson, at the age of 38, to be crowned as champion jockey for the first time in his career. For two decades, until the retirement of his good friend and rival, Johnson had to play second fiddle to the man who had made the championship his personal property – AP McCoy. It was a tribute to Johnson's character that he never let it get to him, but it must have been galling to know that in any other age his achievements would have made him champion jockey many times over. He finished second to AP in 16 championships.

Richard Johnson, like his rival, has been a model of consistency. Up to the 2015/16 season, he had ridden 100 winners in every one of the previous 19 seasons with a peak of 186 in 2003/04, but the closest he ever came to beating McCoy was in 2005/06 when he achieved 167 victories to McCoy's 178. In January 2016, however, Richard Johnson ticked off an achievement that puts him without doubt alongside McCoy on the pantheon of the greatest jockeys: when he rode Duke Des Champs to victory at Ascot on 23 January 2016, he became only the second jump jockey ever to ride 3,000 winners in Britain and Ireland. (We are going with the figures of John Randall, the

Racing Post guru who is the 'statistician general' of British racing. Some reckoned Richard Johnson's 3,000th winner came a few days earlier at Ludlow on Garde La Victoire but that was only if you included two cross-country victories in France on Balthazar King.) In his career, Johnson had then ridden more winners than the combined total of two previous great champions, Peter Scudamore and John Francome.

Jump-riding careers, however, are about more than quantity: on the quality front, Johnson is one of the few jockeys, alongside Ruby Walsh and Barry Geraghty, to have ridden winners of all the Cheltenham Festival's 'Big Four' races. He won the Gold Cup in 2000 on Looks Like Trouble for Noel Chance, the father of Johnson's wife, Fiona, and he won the Champion Hurdle in 2003 on the popular grey, Rooster Booster, for his long-time friend and employer Philip Hobbs. A Queen Mother Champion Chase victory came on Flagship Uberalles for Paul Nicholls in 2002, and he had already tucked away a World Hurdle victory in 1999, when it was still known as the Stayers Hurdle, getting up by a neck on Anzum in a thrilling finish. Johnson has always been a byword for loyalty; it meant a lot to him that not only was that win on Anzum his first Festival victory (with 19 more to come and still counting), it was also the final Festival win for David Nicholson, the man who had given him his first big break.

Richard Johnson on his Champion Hurdle winner Rooster Booster.

Richard Johnson with his first Champion Jockey's trophy at Sandown Park in April 2016.

In April 2004, when Martin Pipe was left looking for a new stable jockey, Richard Johnson could have moved to the man whose stable strength had already helped three others to win the jockeys' championship but he chose instead to remain with his long-time supporter, Philip Hobbs. On the day that Johnson reached a significant landmark, the first time he rode 200 winners in a season, on 24 February 2016, trainer Henry Daly noted: 'He has been coming to me every Tuesday and Friday since I started training and he never changes. All the staff love him. He is both amazingly phlegmatic and unbelievably competitive. It's an odd combination but it sums him up.'

Many saw Johnson's Champion Chase ride on Flagship Uberalles, an athletic but quirky character with a mind of his own and a less than perfect jumping record, as the perfect example of Johnson's diehard, never-give-in qualities. On going that did not suit, Flagship Uberalles had never appeared to be giving his all and then he hit the third from home, but Richard Johnson has never been one for throwing in the towel. On the stamina-sapping ground and in a performance that left the rider utterly drained at the winning post, as you could see from the pictures on the day, Johnson never stopped reminding his talented mount that he had the quality to do the job; in the end, he got enough response to

come home three lengths to the good. The last thing his fellow jockeys want to see, after the last, is Dicky Johnson ranging alongside them ready to challenge: it is not just his strength in a finish but the indomitable will to win and to keep fighting that he seems able to impart to his mounts. At the Cheltenham Festival in 2014, he won by a short head in the cross-country race on the Hobbs' stable favourite, Balthazar King, and later by a nose on Fingal Bay in the Pertemps despite a blunder at the last fence that had seen Southfield Theatre go ahead of him up the run-in. The motivation showed too after one shocking final-obstacle fall at the Festival in 2012 when Wishfull Thinking crashed through the rails after a fall at the last fence and collided with photographer Jean-Charles Briens. Bystanders recalled that as trainer Philip Hobbs reached his bloodied but still determined rider, as Johnson was being borne away on a stretcher (despite the horrific fall, he escaped with only soft-tissue injuries), the jockey's first words were: 'And don't you start giving away my rides!'

Richard Johnson may have had to settle for second place all those years behind McCoy, but he never lost his readiness to compete against him. McCoy was not just being polite when he insisted, 'Without him pushing me, I wouldn't have achieved anything like so much as I did.' When Johnson was leading the field to win the first post-McCoy championship by 70 winners, his old rival noted: 'He is out in front because he makes less mistakes than anyone else. It's as simple as that.' Ruby Walsh noted: 'When AP retired, he saw that chink of light and threw himself at it. He hasn't let anyone else have so much as a sniff of the title.' There have been two other advantages: like McCoy, Richard Johnson has enjoyed the services of the leading jockeys' agent Dave Roberts; and, as an articulate and friendly man, he has won a reputation too for talking a good race after he has ridden it. His post-race debrief tells owners and trainers exactly what they need to know. Roberts says he is just as motivated as AP: 'There is never any question for him of having a day off or not going somewhere for one ride.'

When I asked Richard at Warwick on that

200-up day what set him and McCoy apart from the rest, he grinned and replied, 'Greed.' What he meant was that many of the other jockeys want to win big races; he and McCoy want to win every race.

McCoy always appreciated his rival's competitive urge, insisting, 'If you've somebody that talented on your tail, it doesn't half drive you on.' In an age when so many sports are disfigured by sledging and by professional fouls, by bitter rivalries and financial jealousy between teammates, the genuine friendship between the two greatest riders we have seen has been heartening. So too has Dicky Johnson's own attitude. Hate, he says, is no part of his inspiration: 'I don't need anger against someone to compete with him.' And he is shining proof that nice guys don't always finish second.

For some time, Richard Johnson was harried by the tabloids as the boyfriend of the Queen's granddaughter Zara Phillips, who later married the rugby international, Mike Tindall, but the farmer's boy had the tact and style to negotiate even that ordeal without ever managing to provoke the wrong kind of headlines.

England's best jockey comes of traditional Herefordshire stock. His father and both grandfathers were amateur riders, and both his parents, Keith and Sue, have farmed and trained, although it was grandfather Ivor Johnson who gave Richard his first winner under rules on Rusty Bridge at Hereford on 30 April 1994. He came through the point-to-point world, rode as an amateur, and then served his apprenticeship with David 'the Duke' Nicholson in the Cotswolds, winning the conditional jockeys' championship the year after McCoy did so. He has since been a byword for his loyalty to a small cluster of trainers including Philip Hobbs, Henry Daly and Tim Vaughan; what other trainers like about him is that you can expect the same unremitting effort whether it be a big Festival race or a selling hurdle at Fontwell or Ffos Las.

As well as the 'Big Four', Richard Johnson has victories to his name in most of the other key Cheltenham Festival races; he has also ridden winners of the Welsh National (Edmond in 1999) and the Scottish National (Beshabar in 2011). However, up to 2016, success in the Grand National has so far eluded him. He did, though, finish second in the Aintree spectacular, on What's Up Boys in 2002 and on Balthazar King in 2014.

Richard Johnson on Village Vic in Aintree's Topham Chase.

8 Ireland
– Jump racing's great provider

'It is very influential to have a Festival winner, to show you can go over there and do it against the top of the British Isles. If you can repeat the dose, then people say you can train top horses for the top races.'

Irish Champion Trainer Willie Mullins on Cheltenham

Without the Irish contribution, British jump racing would be hugely diminished, and the Cheltenham Festival would probably never have become the racing Mecca and the glorious celebration of the equine arts that it is. That Irish racing has developed so far owes a lot to one man, Vincent O'Brien, and to a horse, Arkle, who became an institution.

The trainer, Tom Dreaper, and owner, Anne Duchess of Westminster, in high spirits after seeing Arkle win the Gold Cup.

Not only are many of the horses running over jumps in Britain of Irish origin, so are many of the stable staff and jockeys who tend and ride them. In the 2015/16 season, Willie Mullins, despite being based in Ireland, trained the winner of so many big races in Britain that he came a close second to Paul Nicholls in the contest for Britain's champion trainer, a contest that lasted until the final day of the season. Around a sixth of the horses that contest races at the Cheltenham Festival travel from Ireland to do so. At the 2016 Festival, 14 of the 28 races were won by Irish runners. Seven of those 14 winners were ridden by Irish champion jockey Ruby Walsh, who was leading rider at the Festival for the tenth time, and seven were trained by Willie Mullins. Six of the ten biggest stakes' winners over the season in Britain were Irish-based horses, five of the top ten jockeys in the British championship were Irish, and four of the top ten owners in Britain were Irish.

The Cheltenham Festival is the best going-stick for measuring the Irish involvement; the training legend Vincent O'Brien, the first trainer to fly horses to Britain, was the man who inspired the friendly but fierce racing invasion. He started persuading some Irish owners to hang on to their horses and have a go for English prizes themselves, rather than cashing in on early promise. Before he switched his attention to flat racing and training Derby winners, he amassed four Cheltenham Gold Cups, three Champion Hurdles, ten

Gloucestershire Hurdles (a race that used to be divided into separate divisions and which is now the Supreme Novices), and six other victories in Festival races, all in the period from 1948 to 1959. The triple victories of Cottage Rake (Gold Cup 1948, 1949, 1950) and of Hatton's Grace (Champion Hurdle 1949, 1950, 1951), at the time when the Gold Cup was becoming valued for itself rather than as a warm-up race for the Grand National, and when the Champion Hurdle was becoming exactly what its name says, encouraged a burgeoning Irish attendance and inspired other Irish trainers and owners to travel to Gloucestershire to seek the top prizes.

Between 1946 and 1971, Tom Dreaper scored 26 Festival victories in days when the Festival was confined to three days (it only expanded to four days from 2005). Edward O'Grady, beginning in 1974, and still training, has 18 Festival wins to his credit; Dan Moore had 14 wins between 1953 and 1979; and Willie Mullins, who began in 1995, has 48 wins already. Trainers such as Noel Meade, Jessica Harrington, Mouse Morris and the fast-emerging Gordon Elliott have all won important races at Cheltenham too. Says Edward O'Grady: 'The Irish come as a team. It is the only place I know where every Irish trainer is hoping that if he does not win, another Irish trainer does.' Jessica Harrington agrees that they come wanting to beat the English horses; going under to another Irish runner isn't nearly so bad. Mouse Morris trains almost exclusively with Cheltenham in mind; anything else he wins on the way is a bonus.

The battles these days are comparatively good humoured but the Irish contingent, even if England is giving them a home or a job, like to see their champions not just as horses, but as warriors taking the battle to the old colonial enemy. Yet even Vincent O'Brien did not mind putting up an English aristocrat, Lord Mildmay, to ride one of his horses to Festival victory. In truth, there is a touch of artificiality about the whole thing in that Jonjo O'Neill, formerly champion jockey and now a highly successful trainer, who is as Irish as they come, has his victories counted on the English side of the

Captain Christy ridden by Bobby Beasley before winning the 1975 Gold Cup.

tally because he trains at Jackdaw's Castle in Gloucestershire – in premises owned by the equally Irish JP McManus!

It was the triple Gold Cup-winner Arkle, trained by Tom Dreaper and ridden by Pat Taaffe, who really fostered Irish national pride and set the tone of the sporting rivalry between two racing nations. Public interest saw the Gold Cup switched to a Saturday in March 1964, ensuring a massive TV audience for the much-hyped contest between two great horses. The imposing Mill House, a precocious winner of the previous year's Gold Cup at the age of only six, had beaten Arkle on their only previous encounter and, in his famous commentary, Peter O'Sullevan caught the public mood, pitching it in terms of 'Mill House for England and Arkle for Ireland.'

Mill House had been looking good, but suddenly, two fences out, he failed to shrug off Arkle as he quickened. Suddenly, it was not the news the English audience wanted to hear … 'as they come towards the last fence, it's Arkle for Ireland. Both riders are hard at it. Here they come into the last. Arkle over first. Mill House over second on the run-in with 150 yards to go. It's Arkle for Ireland...'

Arkle won by five lengths and from then on he was Ireland's hero and an object of admiration among racegoers of every nationality. From then until a career-ending accident at Kempton, Arkle was only ever beaten twice, when giving massive lumps of weight away: first, to Flying Wild and Buona Notte in the Massey Ferguson Gold Cup, and then to Stalbridge Colonist in the 1966 Hennessy Gold Cup. He won two more Gold Cups, a King George, a Whitbread, and two Hennessys carrying 12 st 7 lb.

Politics have probably had as much to do with Ireland's racing resurgence over recent times as the innate talents of its horses and horsemen. Back in the 1960s, the Irish economy was weak. Decades after independence, jobs were scarce; there was too much dependence on agriculture and the young were emigrating. Irish breeders and trainers mostly had to be sellers of their horses. English owners and trainers would scour Irish studs and point-to-point meetings, looking for useful prospects to purchase and take home to be trained in England. Paddy Mullins, for example, reckoned that Fred Rimell obtained the subsequent Grand National winner Nicolaus Silver far too cheaply at 2,600 guineas but lamented, 'I had no owner to buy him.' The resentment showed when he declared, 'From the way Fred spoke after the race, you would think that he had foaled the horse himself and trained him ever since. I could never bear Fred after that.' Through the 1970s and 1980s, Ireland's raids on the Cheltenham Festival weakened. In both 1987 and 1988, Galmoy, trained by John

Davy Lad with Dessie Hughes in the saddle takes the last fence in the lead on the way to winning the Cheltenham Gold Cup.

Mulhern, was the only Irish winner; in 1989, there was not a single Irish winner.

It was not just a Cheltenham phenomenon. After Vincent O'Brien's Grand National victories with Early Mist (1953), Royal Tan (1954) and Quare Times (1955), there was not another Irish-trained winner at Aintree until L'Escargot, owned by the wealthy American Raymond Guest, won the race 17 years later in the hands of Tommy Carberry. There was then another gap of 24 years before Bobbyjo, trained by Tommy Carberry and ridden on his Aintree debut by Paul Carberry, won in 1999. Since then, Ireland has had a stream of National winners including Papillon, Monty's Pass, Hedgehunter, Numbersixvalverde, Silver Birch and Rule The World. There was a similar picture with the Cheltenham Gold Cup. Between 1968 and 1977, Ireland won seven Gold Cups with Fort Leney (1968), L'Escargot (1970, 1971), Glencaraig Lady (1972), Captain Christy (1974), Ten Up (1975) and Davy Lad (1977). There was then no Irish-trained winner until Fergie Sutherland, an Old Etonian who had trained in Newmarket before moving to his mother's estate in Ireland, won with Imperial Call in 1996. Ireland then had to wait until 2005 for another winner in the shape of the Mouse Morris-trained War of Attrition.

There were several factors behind the Irish recovery. The late 1960s saw the introduction of free secondary education. After Ireland joined the European Union in 1973, Irish farmers benefited from the Common Agricultural Policy, trade increased 90-fold and foreign inward investment soared. By the early years of the twenty-first century, we were talking about the 'Celtic tiger' economy as Ireland became a more urban society and the property market boomed. However, there were to be recessionary bumps on the financial road ahead: when the 2008 recession hit, more than 1,000 Irish owners pulled out of racing; the industry was largely saved by JP McManus's steady expansion to a training bill of more than £4 million a year. Nowadays, the continued strength of the Irish bloodstock market suggests that there are enough Irish-based owners with money to spend on Irish horses.

Another key change was that the Irish Turf Club, the equivalent to Britain's Jockey Club, handed over its powers to the Irish Horseracing Authority, and then Horseracing Ireland, in return for the Irish Government's allowing the racing industry to receive the entire proceeds of the off-course betting tax. Suddenly the Irish horses didn't all have to be sold abroad but could be campaigned at home for improved prize money. In the 1960s and 1970s, Irish racegoers would be pleased with anything more than three or four victories at the Cheltenham Festival. By 2006, there were now ten Irish winners, in 2013 there were 13, and in 2016 there were 14. The success was also spread more widely. In their day, Vincent O'Brien and Tom Dreaper had been dominant. By 2009, there were a dozen Irish stables producing Cheltenham Festival winners. In recent years there has been another factor: the arrival on the jumping scene of millionaire owners prepared to spend big to win big, despite the fact that there is little hope of recovering the sums expended: however many big races a particular horse might have won, you can't send a gelding to the breeding sheds. As currency dealers, property men, hedge funders and sold-up entrepreneurs have brought their fun money to the jumping scene, Irish trainers have done particularly well.

JP McManus spends more to support jump racing than any man alive and although Jonjo O'Neill's Gloucestershire yard is his biggest British outpost, much of JP's funding goes to an ever-widening group of trainers in Ireland. When their link with northern-based British trainer Howard Johnson was ended by Johnson's disqualification, big-money owners Graham and Andrea Wylie sent some horses to Paul Nicholls in England, but even more to Willie Mullins in Ireland. Ryanair tycoon Michael O'Leary and his brother Eddie, who runs the Gigginstown House Stud for him, are buying 20–30 quality potential chasers every year and they have all their horses trained in Ireland. Likewise, wealthy owners Alan and Ann Potts, for whom Henry de Bromhead scored significant successes with horses like Sizing Europe, have until recently had most of their string in Ireland. And

Florida Pearl ridden by Adrian Maguire jumps the final fence to go on and win the King George VI Chase at Kempton Park.

then there is Rich Ricci – the free-spending and boldly suited American banker whose horses run in the pink and green-spotted colours of his wife, Susannah – he has not seen the need yet to look beyond the Willie Mullins yard. Ireland is now far from being the poor relation.

Willie Mullins's three principal owners (until his sudden split with Michael O'Leary last autumn) covered all the bases in terms of sourcing good horses. Rich Ricci buys mostly ready-made jumpers from France, the Wylies purchase winning Irish point-to-pointers and Michael O'Leary and brother Eddie swept up the best of the unbroken store horses.

As Irish racing has developed over the past half century, some considerable talents have emerged. The young Aidan O'Brien was Irish champion jumps trainer in his very first season of 1993/94 – and champion amateur rider to go with that. This quiet workaholic had his first Cheltenham success in 1996, a year before his first Ascot winner on the flat, and he won the Whitbread that year with Life Of A Lord. With the mighty Istabraq, ridden by Charlie Swan, Aidan won the Champion Hurdle in 1998, 1999 and 2000; no doubt Istabraq would have been favourite to take a fourth title in 2001, had not that year's Festival been wiped out by foot-and-mouth disease.

Son of Dawn Run's trainer Paddy Mullins, Willie Mullins rode his first Cheltenham Festival winner, Hazy Dawn, in the National Hunt Chase in 1982, and he repeated the feat on Mack's Friendly in 1984. His first Cheltenham winner as a trainer was Tourist Attraction in 1995, and he caused some excitement the following year by insisting, at the age of 39, on riding Wither Or Which – to victory, as it turned out – in the Weatherby's Champion Bumper, a race he later came to dominate as a trainer.

Willie recalls the early Cheltenham success clearly. 'Wither Or Which was special because he was an Irish banker. Tourist Attraction, who won the Supreme Novice Hurdle the year before, was my first Festival winner as a trainer. I enjoyed that. However, bringing Wither Or Which the following year, which was a horse we made ourselves, and coming over as favourite

Trainer Willie Mullins and owner Rich Ricci at the 2016 Cheltenham festival.

and winning was hugely beneficial to us. It immediately showed we could buy, make and train a horse to win at the top level. Whereas Tourist Attraction the previous year was 33-1 and a lot of people thought it was a fluke, we actually couldn't believe the price. In the eyes of the public, Wither Or Which was a bigger benefit to us because it is very influential to have a Festival winner, to show you can go over there and do it against the top of the British Isles. If you can repeat the dose, then people say you can train top horses for the top races.'

The following year, in 1997, although Richard Dunwoody was angling for the ride on Florida

Pearl, who won that year's bumper before taking the RSA Chase in 1998, Mullins put up, instead the amateur Mr R Walsh, who has since become an even more regular visitor to the Cheltenham winner's enclosure than the trainer has been, and who is now exclusively Mullins' stable jockey, having previously combined that role with being number one also for the Somerset-based Paul Nicholls.

Florida Pearl never managed better than second place in the Cheltenham Gold Cup but he scored eight Grade One victories; with Adrian Maguire in the saddle, he beat Best Mate in the King George VI Chase in 2001 in a tremendous contest. Along with the likes of Dawn Run, Danoli, Doran's Pride and Beef Or Salmon, Florida Pearl was one of the Irish racing public's all-time favourite horses, winning four Irish Hennessy Gold Cups.

There have since been any number of success stories for Willie Mullins, one of them being Quevega's remarkable record of winning the OLBG Mares Hurdle for six years in succession from 2009 to 2014. Although the Gold Cup has, to date, narrowly eluded Mullins, he has won Champion Hurdles with Hurricane Fly (2011, 2013), Faugheen (2015) and Annie Power (2016). He has won the RSA Chase four times with Florida Pearl (1998), Rule Supreme (2004), Cooldine (2009) and Don Poli (2015) and the JLT Novices Chase three times with Sir des Champs (2012), Vautour (2015) and Black Hercules (2016). He also trained Hedgehunter to win the Grand National in 2005.

Other Irish trainers who have made a significant mark in leading English races are Mouse Morris, trainer of the Gold Cup winner War of Attrition (2006) and of the Grand National-winner Rule The World (2016); and Gordon Elliott, responsible for the 2007 Grand National-winner Silver Birch and the 2016 Gold Cup-winner Don Cossack. Jessica Harrington has eight Festival victories to her credit, including the 2014 Champion Hurdle with Jezki, and an Arkle Chase and two Queen Mother Champion Chases with the spectacularly talented Moscow Flyer. The 'Flyer' did take the occasional chance with his fences but – in four years from April

2001 – he was never beaten in a race that he completed, collecting ten Grade One victories in association with jockey Barry Geraghty.

One Irish-based trainer with a unique record is the former champion amateur jockey Enda Bolger. In 2015, the 'King of the Banks', as the cross-country expert is known, trained On The Fringe to win the Foxhunter Chase at the Cheltenham Festival, the Fox Hunters' Chase at Aintree and the Champion Hunter Chase at the Punchestown Festival. As if that treble were not enough, he then captured all three races again with On The Fringe in 2016, a quite extraordinary record. In all but one of those races, when she was suspended, Nina Carberry was the rider.

If Ireland has contributed some first-class training talent to the jump-racing scene, it has produced an even higher proportion of the jockey talent. Irish-based riders such as Tommy Carberry, Dessie Hughes and Charlie Swan proved successful raiders at Cheltenham and elsewhere, and a series of young jockeys who first swung their leg across a saddle in Ireland have come across the water to become champion jockey in Britain, among them Ron Barry, Jonjo O'Neill, Tommy Stack and the incomparable AP McCoy. There are many more who have figured at the top level and who could have been gunning for a championship if the cookie had crumbled a little differently: the likes of Adrian Maguire, Mick Fitzgerald, Norman Williamson, Timmy Murphy, and even the talented but flawed Barry Brogan. It is a measure of the Irish talent that both Paul Nicholls and Nicky Henderson have been content in recent years to have number-one jockeys who were based in Ireland – Ruby Walsh and Barry Geraghty.

Ruby Walsh (Ruby is short for Rupert, not an early parental confusion) is the son of trainer and commentator Ted Walsh, who was 11 times Ireland's champion amateur jockey. An all-round sportsman who played Gaelic football and had a trial at scrum-half for Leinster's under-16s, Ruby followed his father as champion amateur – in a country where that amounts to a full-time job – while still in his teens. One role model was Richard Dunwoody, whom he admired for his poise in the saddle, coupled with an implacable desire to win, but Ruby was also a huge admirer of Charlie Swan's tactical sense, and it was Swan's nine-year term as champion jockey that came to an end when the 20-year-old Ruby Walsh took the title in 1998/99, his first year as a pro. Ruby won the Grand National at his first attempt, riding Papillon for his father in 2000, and he later won another National on Hedgehunter for Willie Mullins. If he had spent more time riding in Britain, rather than splitting his efforts between Paul Nicholls and Willie Mullins, Paul Nicholls believes that Ruby could have given AP McCoy a real run for the British championship. Ruby has become the most successful Cheltenham Festival jockey of all time, with seven wins in 2009, and another seven wins in 2016, contributing to his total, to date, of 52 victories, and he was associated with most of the successes of Kauto Star, Master Minded, Big Buck's and other Nicholls' stars (see page 171).

You don't see as much of what Ruby is doing to a horse as you did with McCoy, partly because he believes in the need for stillness. You need, says Ruby, to allow the horse to flow and jump beneath you. 'If you have it right, only the arms are really moving.' In an excessively modest rating of his own contribution, he insists that 99 per cent is down to the horse. 'You want to give a bit of a squeeze, a bit of encouragement, but I'm not really a big "one, two, three bang"

On The Fringe (17) ridden by Nina Carberry clears the Chair on their way to winning The Fox Hunters' Chase.

jockey. Horses don't like falling, so the less you interfere, the better.' A sharply intelligent rider, Ruby Walsh doesn't suffer fools gladly. He is so much the epitome of concentrated cool that he could play patience on horseback in a hurricane. He argues that it is a crime to come too early – 'You are giving a race away' – and he is hard to beat in a finish. In short, he is the complete package, and the only restrictions on his career have been the periods out through injury. He has broken or dislocated an ankle, a leg, both hips, both shoulders, his left arm, both wrists and a collarbone. But, like McCoy, he is brave too. He once returned to riding just 27 days after being kicked in the stomach and having his spleen removed. One of his King George VI victories on Kauto Star was achieved the day after his return from a dislocated shoulder. Charlie Swan's verdict

War of Attrition pictured with (left to right) trainer Mouse Morris, owner Michael O'Leary and jockey Conor O'Dwyer after winning the Cheltenham Gold Cup.

is: 'He's the best we will ever see. He's got everything. He's a good judge of pace, he's got great hands, he's brave: it's all there.' Ruby's diplomatic skills also came in handy during his 'One Man, Two Masters' role with Nicholls and Mullins, but he was helped by the fact that, over time, more and more of Ireland's major fixtures seem to be taking place on a Sunday, unlike the situation in Britain. It is an intriguing sign of the camaraderie of the sport that when he was commuting to Britain, sport that when he was commuting to Britain,

Ruby would stay with his great friend and rival, AP McCoy, in Lambourn.

A bouncier, noisier character than Ruby Walsh, Barry Geraghty once summed up his attitude by telling Jessica Harrington that 'Pressure is for tyres.' As he declares: 'If you don't believe in your own ability, then who will?' He too was Irish champion, at the age of 20, seizing an opportunity when Paul Carberry was injured. He will forever be associated with the career of Harrington's brilliant two-miler Moscow Flyer, on whom he twice won Cheltenham's Queen Mother Champion Chase, albeit his attempt to emulate Frankie Dettori's flying dismount after one of those victories landed him on his backside. Perhaps that was appropriate, seeing as Moscow himself developed the curious stat of failing to complete every fourth race. Asked once at a Cheltenham preview whether Moscow Flyer would win, Geraghty needed only two words in reply, 'Doing handstands', and you could understand his confidence: he rode Moscow Flyer in 38 races and won 25 of them, sporting those famous black chevrons.

Barry Geraghty was in the top echelon of Irish riders from the start and, after Charlie Swan's departure, he became the go-to man for Irish trainers at Cheltenham when the money was down. Associated with the yards of Jessica Harrington, Edward O'Grady and Tom Taaffe, he won a Cheltenham Gold Cup in 2005 on Taaffe's Kicking King, the horse travelling so well that Geraghty was even able to take a pull (giving his horse a pause for breath) at the top of the hill. He also partnered Kicking King to two victories in the King George VI Chase, at Kempton in 2004 and at Sandown in 2005 when Kempton was undergoing alterations.

When a neck injury forced Mick Fitzgerald to retire after 16 years as Nicky Henderson's stable jockey, it was Barry Geraghty's big-match temperament that prompted the trainer to turn to Geraghty as his replacement, and it worked well for both of them. Geraghty was hugely impressed by the Seven Barrows set-up and Nicky Henderson's ability to 'peak' his horses, while Henderson appreciated the calm professionalism of his new stable jockey. A string of successes followed: Arkle Chases with both Sprinter Sacre and Simonsig, another Gold Cup with Bobs Worth, and Champion Chases with both Finian's Rainbow and Sprinter Sacre. When, in 2015, AP McCoy announced his retirement, there was little surprise when Geraghty was the man selected to replace him in the coveted position of number-one rider for the multi-horsepower JP McManus. Because Ireland's leading jumps patron has so many horses, riding for him involves making choices, choices such as the ones that even AP got wrong – between More Of That and At Fishers Cross for the World Hurdle, or between Jezki and My Tent Or Yours for the Champion Hurdle. Geraghty was the beneficiary of a wrong choice when thus getting to ride both More Of That and Jezki. Now he has to make the choices but as he has never been one to bother with the 'what ifs' of life, he will probably find that role easier than AP did.

Another leading Irish rider who impacted periodically on the British jumping scene was Paul Carberry, son of the three-times Gold Cup-winner Tommy Carberry, for whom he rode Bobbyjo to win the Grand National of 1999, and brother of successful jockeys Nina and Philip. A passionate devotee of hunting and a man who appeared to be fearless in the most basic sense of the word, Paul Carberry was a naturally gifted horseman with 14 Cheltenham Festival victories to his credit. When McCoy, Walsh and Geraghty were once asked on a racing panel as to who was the best jockey of all, they all three replied: 'Paul Carberry.' But Carberry is also a party animal who likes a drink, and says, 'I love racing but not at the expense of everything. I like to have a life as well.' He has attracted nearly as many headlines for non-racing events as for his achievements in the saddle. Unhitching somebody's horse from a trailer and riding it into a local bar amid 150 drinkers was one thing; setting fire to fellow jockey Davy Condon's newspaper on a flight to Dublin in October 2005 was quite another. That thoughtless prank initially brought him a gaol sentence, later ameliorated to community service.

JP McManus, AP McCoy and Jonjo O'Neill celebrating Synchronised's 2012 Gold Cup victory.

Early in his career, in 1995, Carberry was spotted by Yorkshire millionaire Sir Robert Ogden, who brought him to Britain as his retained rider, but after three years Carberry went home. His extraordinary ease in the saddle communicates itself to his mounts and Carberry says, 'I cannot sit on a horse without wanting to jump something on it,' a temptation he apparently indulged even on Jim Bolger's two-year-olds when the trainer wasn't watching. Carberry was associated with Michael Hourigan's successful chaser Beef Or Salmon, but the mainstay of his career was his long association with trainer Noel Meade. It was Carberry who gave Meade his first Cheltenham Festival success by winning the Supreme Novices Hurdle on Sausalito Bay – despite a haematoma on the jockey's back bursting agonisingly on the drive up the run-in.

Out of the 39 Grade One races Paul Carberry won, five came aboard the tricksy hurdler Harchibald, who had to be held up until the last possible moment. In later years, Carberry was dogged by injury, ruefully admitting, 'I break easy.' After one break too many, a 'gutted' Carberry reluctantly announced his retirement in 2016 at the age of 42. British racegoers will long remember his outstanding ride to win the Welsh National in 2013 when he slowly crept through the field on Monbeg Dude despite a series of jumping errors, and collared AP McCoy on the line.

9

Finding the Horses
– Ireland versus France

'Patience was no longer a key word for the jumping owner. If you were prepared to pay good money, you could get yourself a ready-made Saturday horse.'

Bloodstock agent Anthony Bromley

ometimes the economics of jump racing just don't seem to make sense. On behalf of owner Clive Smith, Paul Nicholls wanted to keep the impressive Million In Mind syndicate horse Garde Champetre, when, as is the syndicate's policy, they sent it to the sales at the end of a jumping season. He thought it might fetch 400,000 guineas and his last throw, as the bidding rose, was 490,000. Irish millionaire JP McManus bought it for 530,000. Having lost that horse, Clive Smith and Nicholls went to France and, through agent Anthony Bromley, bought a certain Kauto Star instead for 400,000 euros.

Kauto Star in his career won £3,776,000. Garde Champetre never became the kind of Gold Cup horse that connections had originally hoped. Nor did he win back his purchase price. But

McManus never regretted his purchase. Garde Champetre became one of the multi-horsepower millionaire's all-time favourites as he won five times in a rather different discipline, racing over

Cheltenham's cross-country obstacle course. It isn't just about the money – and in jumping it never has been. Nevertheless, how people have made their money is changing things.

No less an authority than Anthony Bromley believes that jump racing, in recent years, has been going more the way of the flat. Bromley is well placed to make such observations since, along with David Minton and Tessa Greatrex, he runs the leading bloodstock agency Highflyer, responsible for finding five Grand National winners and stars such as Kauto Star and Master Minded. It is becoming a numbers game dominated by owners with big strings of horses. Look back, for example, to a typical year in the 1980s. In 1982/83, the leading owner was Sheikh Ali Abu Khamsin. He had 13 horses who won 32 races and collected £132,000 in prize money, twice as much as the next owner in the list, who happened to have owned the Grand National winner. Of the other top 12 in the list, none had more than three horses in training.

In the 2015/16 season, the leading British jumps owner, following victories in both the Gold Cup and the Grand National, was Michael O'Leary's Gigginstown House Stud with seven victories from 46 horses campaigned in Britain. They collected more than £1.5 million in win and place money. In second place was JP McManus with 59 wins from 152 horses; third came Rich and Susannah Ricci with seven high-class wins from 22 horses; and fourth were Paul and Clare Rooney with 31 victories from 78 horses. In Ireland, virtually all the top races fell to a small group consisting of Gigginstown, McManus, the Riccis, and the families of Graham and Andrea Wylie and Ann and Alan Potts. JP McManus's many trainers in Ireland ran 253 horses for his 95 victories, Gigginstown's team 170 for their 91 wins – and those are only the ones that actually made it to the racecourse.

Willie Mullins, the champion trainer again at the 2016 Cheltenham Festival, had 185 horses in training that season and 231 to start the present season. The equivalent figures for Gordon Elliott, trainer of the Gold Cup winner, Don Cossack, were 92 and 128, while Horses In Training listed the inmates of Paul Nicholls' yard at 131 and 157

– and those numbers don't include horses on the sick list or in pre-training.

So where are these horses coming from? Traditionally, there have been four main sources. Firstly, there were the Irish 'stores', horses that were sold unbroken to spend a couple of years in a field growing up before being introduced to racing. Secondly, there were horses bought after winning 'bumpers' (flat races for jumping-bred horses) or point-to-points in Ireland. Thirdly, there has been a growing demand for more precocious jumpers bred in France, who have often been taught to tackle obstacles from two or three years' old. Finally, there was a steady demand for stoutly bred horses who were being sold off after campaigning on the flat by Newmarket yards that were finding space for a new influx of two-year-olds.

There have always been some English trainers who bought French jumpers: in the 1950s and 1960s, Peter Cazalet and Ryan Price did well with such imports; but Anthony Bromley now says that the demand for French horses increased massively in the 1990s. One factor behind that was the new style of owner.

In the past, many jumping owners were from the landed classes, people accustomed to the rhythms of the countryside. In the last two decades, more owners have been people who have made money in the City or in industry. 'Suddenly,' says Anthony Bromley, 'patience was no longer a key word for the jumping owner. If you were prepared to pay good money, you could get yourself a ready-made Saturday horse.' (That is to say, a horse likely to win the bigger prizes available at weekends for sponsored – and televised – races.) The ready-made French horses, he said, appealed to City men with well-

Anthony Bromley.

Opposite: Jockeys parade at the start before the Presidential Stand at Auteuil.

developed analytical skills, who were used to
making quick business decisions. Trainers, led
by Martin Pipe and Paul Nicholls, adjusted to the
new mindset, as did bloodstock agents such as
Highflyer. It was, says Bromley, a revolutionary
change. It didn't mean that it became impossible
for smaller yards run by farmer/trainers to find
bargain buys or homebreds to rival the Mullins
hotpots and achieve good results occasionally
'but the guy coming in and paying proper money
could buy Grade One form.' Unlike the situation
in England or Ireland, where most people are
putting mares to Coolmore stallions who raced
predominantly on good going at places such as
Royal Ascot, half the French stallions themselves
raced over jumps in the mud of Auteuil, starting
at the age of three, and they are covering mares
who did the same. The result is that the French
have more proven horses for sale.

Says Bromley's Highflyer partner, David
Minton, 'The French horses in the 1980s
were coming just as the Irish horses got more
expensive and they started keeping more of
them. In France they have no problem with
running them every fortnight at Auteuil as a
three- and four-year-old. Not what you'd find
Nicky Henderson doing. But I think you will
find the new generation in England will run
their horses more often.'

Another factor, says Bromley, is the growing
dominance of the Cheltenham Festival and its
extension from three days to four, giving seven
more chances of somebody having a Cheltenham
winner – a bit like the scurry among Middle

Eastern owners on the flat to buy themselves
a prospect before Royal Ascot. 'Everybody
thinking of buying a jumper wants to know, "Is
this one with a chance of being a Cheltenham
contender?"' David Minton, says that Saturday
horses are what it is all about. Their Highflyer
agency will have bought 70–80 of the horses
that run over the four-day Festival – and
success there is crucial: 'The spin-off in terms of
one's credibility is huge,' although he says that
Aintree is catching up. 'You don't have to go to
Cheltenham now to prove you've got a decent
horse; there's no disgrace now in saving it for
Aintree or Punchestown.'

There is no end-value for a gelded jumper at
the end of his career but Anthony Bromley says
that does not deter the big owners: 'This is a rich
man's sport, pastime, pleasure. Once they have
been bitten by the racing bug, that does not
matter. The desire to have a nice horse outweighs
commercial sense. Middle-aged guys need kicks
of different sorts and, with so much information
available to people about racing, it becomes an
intellectual puzzle which they enjoy.'

When Sheikh Mohammed and his colleagues
first moved into British racing in a big way, there
was something of an exodus from the flat by
smaller owners who felt they could not compete
with oil money. Now, says Bromley, that trend
may have begun to reverse. Small owners are
again willing to buy flat-racing horses in the
hope of winning a race or two and funding their
racing hobby by selling them on to the Qataris
and others. In the same way, there has been a

boost to prices and production in Ireland, where they have traditionally been sellers of jumping horses. Everyone wants the next Best Mate and, thanks to McManus and Gigginstown and the scouts for big English yards, Irish horsemen are now putting enormous effort into producing point-to-point winners who will have a hefty and guaranteed sell-on value.

At the same time, the supply of potential jumping horses from English flat-racing yards has decreased. For agents such as Anthony Bromley, there is less to look at in the autumn sales because everybody across the world now loves to get their hands on European stayers; whereas Godolphin and other massive players in the 1980s and 1990s used to sell nice jumping types, they are now keeping more of the horses they might once have discarded to race in Dubai or Australia.

Says David Minton, 'We used to love the Horses In Training Sale, we used to flock there. Now we hardly bother to go because the Australians, the Kuwaitis and the Qataris are buying all the staying-type horses.'

As for the debate between strong-boned horses bred on Irish grass and the more precocious French horses with early racing experience, that will surely go on for ever. Perhaps Best Mate was the perfect compromise: French bred but bought after Henrietta Knight and Terry Biddlecombe had seen him jump in an Irish point-to-point.

Paul Nicholls' backer, Paul Barber, who owned See More Business and Denman, warns: 'You are breeding for a bit more speed. Everyone wants to go a bit quicker because everyone wants to win. If you are going to breed for more speed, you are going to produce less bone. If you produce less bone, you will get more problems.'

Nicky Henderson says, 'I'd rather go and buy a store, but the value is in France. You can get a maiden hurdle winner from Auteuil for £100,000, the same as a three-year-old which has won a point-to-point round Ballybunion or Ballygobackwards.' He notes that you can expect to get about four years out of a jumper. If it is French, you run it at four, five, six and seven. If it is Irish, you run it at six, seven, eight and nine.

A sobering thought, however, is one offered by Michael O'Leary of Gigginstown House Stud. He says that the attrition rate among jumps horses means that you get one good one for every ten you buy. Then the question is whether he is good enough for Cheltenham. 'I'm comfortable with that. I know what I'm getting into. I like the good days and that's why I'm involved in it.'

Henrietta Knight and many others believe that Ireland's milder climate produces outstanding horses for racing, showjumping and eventing: its rich grass and mix of essential minerals give them stronger bones. She and Terry Biddlecombe preferred to buy horses they had seen run in point-to-points or had been able to view being ridden or loose schooled at their owners' establishments: they picked out Best Mate among 16 youngsters contesting a race for maiden four-year-olds at the West Waterford point-to-point at Lismore on the banks of the Blackwater river.

As she noted in her memoir of life with Terry Biddlecombe, *Not Enough Time*: 'He always insisted that horses should have strong hindquarters and be athletic individuals. He liked to watch them move from their shoulders as well as from behind. He maintained that if horses were tight behind their elbows, they would not bring their forelegs forward with a good jumping technique.'

Most trainers have their likes and dislikes: Hen liked individuals with a big, bold eye and no white showing around the edge. It did not stop her, however, encouraging Sir Martin Broughton to buy Eastthorpe, a horse with two white eyes, from Mick Easterby – and going on to win 15 steeplechases with him. There is an exception to every rule.

David Minton.

10 The Royals and Racing

'When she pulled up at the end, I asked, "Does it hurt?"
She replied, "Yes", so I instructed her to go round again.'

Trainer David Nicholson on tutoring the Princess Royal

The British love their royals and royal patronage has been of enormous advantage to horseracing. Even Queen Victoria, contrary to her prudish image, revivified the Royal Stud and enjoyed a flutter, and few monarchs have been more involved in the sport than Queen Elizabeth II. The Queen is a knowledgeable owner-breeder who, as we write, has horses in training with Nicky Henderson, Richard Hannon, Andrew Balding, Roger Charlton, Michael Bell and Sir Michael Stoute; she is said to be rarely happier than when visiting stables and studs. She takes a camera with her on most of those visits and rarely forgets a horse or the names of stable staff whom she has encountered.

When the Queen is with racing people, there is an acceptance on both sides that she is a natural part of the scene and can be treated as such: on a visit to Richard Hannon Senior, she once remarked that his house was one of the few places she ever visited that did not smell of new paint! She is a prolific writer of letters to her trainers and is careful when visiting stable yards not to wear scent that might excite the colts. In Royal Ascot weeks, when a number of the races are named after her ancestors, those people out early on the track, watching foreign contestants being put through their paces, would often encounter Her Majesty and a few friends who had ridden over from Windsor Castle with her.

Labour's former Foreign Secretary Robin Cook, a fellow enthusiast, won the Queen's gratitude once on a foreign visit by passing on to her the *Racing Post* he had read on the plane and which she would normally have digested over her morning cornflakes. Among those who have hosted the Queen on private visits is the French trainer Alec Head; she has, too, much enjoyed visiting the horse farms of fellow breeders in the lush Kentucky countryside. One of her Press Secretaries told me once of the occasion on one of those visits when he had drafted a press release to help the local media. He originally entitled it: 'Queen to visit US studs.' When he was

reminded how our two nations are as divided as they are by a common language, it was hastily redrafted as: 'Her Majesty to tour US breeding establishments.'

The Queen's first love has always been flat racing, but the first horse that she raced was the steeplechaser Monaveen. She shared Monaveen with Queen Elizabeth The Queen Mother, and it was her mother who was for so long revered as the most considerate and sporting of owners on the jumping scene with horses in training, first with Major Peter Cazalet at his famous Fairlawne stables in Kent, and then with Fulke Walwyn in Lambourn.

At a dinner during Royal Ascot 1949, the day the King's filly Avila won the Coronation Stakes, the charming and persuasive Anthony Mildmay, a good friend of Peter Cazalet, who shared with him an ambition to lift the social and sporting status of jump racing, was seated between the Queen and her daughter Princess Elizabeth. He left the table with the Queen's instructions to find for her and her daughter a chaser to be trained by Cazalet at Fairlawne. The interest grew to a point at which the Queen Mother at one time had 25 horses at Fairlawne. In her lifetime she enjoyed nearly 500 winners, each half-century landmark celebrated with a lavish party into the early hours with friends and stable staff. On those occasions she would insist on dancing with her jockeys, even doing so on one occasion with the elegant David Mould who had a broken leg in plaster at the time and who had slit his evening trousers to accommodate it.

The popular Mildmay (in those more deferential days, racing crowds apparently used to shout, 'C'mon My Lord') was her first racing manager but tragically drowned off the Devon coast, after only two years in that role, when taking a pre-breakfast swim, possibly assailed by the same debilitating seizing-up of his neck that on occasion had left him riding the last mile of a race able to see nothing but the turf beneath his mount's feet.

Like all owners, the Queen Mother had her ups and downs on the racecourse. No 'down' could have been more calamitous than the spectacle of Devon Loch in the 1956 Grand National. The gelding was over the last fence and well clear of his pursuers when he did the splits, almost in the shadow of the winning post. His collapse allowed ESB to gallop past him to win. In Lord Sefton's private box, the Queen Mother, the Queen, Princess Margaret, and

Zara and Peter Cazalet had been cheering home what would have been the most popular winner ever of the big race when they were stunned into silence by the spectacle. Devon Loch's jockey, Dick Francis, later the phenomenally successful author of racing novels, a genre he virtually invented, said in his memoirs of the moment before Devon Loch's collapse: 'Never had I felt such power in reserve, such confidence in my mount, such calm in my mind.' The shock could not have been crueller but the Queen Mother's behaviour was exemplary. First, she consoled the distraught Francis and then smilingly and gracefully she presented the trophies to winning trainer Fred Rimell, jockey Dave Dick and owner Mrs Leonard Carver. On the day, the Queen Mother said publicly of Devon Loch's still-unexplained collapse, 'Oh, that's racing,' but in a letter to Cazalet afterwards, she did reveal, 'I will have an ache in my heart for ever.' Although she never attended a Grand National again, she made a point of going down to Fairlawne after that 1956 race to give presents to all who had been involved. They were, she told them, 'Mementoes of a terrible yet glorious day.'

The Queen, who was then Princess Elizabeth, admires Monaveen, the horse she owned in partnership with her mother, in the winner's enclosure at Fontwell Park.

A mystery he didn't write: royal jockey Dick Francis, later a phenomenally successful thriller writer, walks dejectedly from the course after the collapse of Devon Loch just short of the Grand National winning post in 1956.

Far from being deterred by the tragedy of Devon Loch, she instructed Cazalet soon afterwards to find her more horses.

Conflicting theories have been advanced as to what caused Devon Loch's collapse: many felt that he had seen the shadow of the water jump and tried to jump an obstacle that wasn't there, while his jockey believed that Devon Loch might have been spooked by the roar from the crowd anticipating a royal winner, or suffered a sudden attack of cramp. The experienced Rimell, however, believed that Devon Loch, who was about to set a record time for the race, was like a long-distance runner who had suddenly 'hit the wall' and become disoriented. He had, Rimell believed, suffered a spasm or heart attack, even though Devon Loch went on to win other races. With more courage than tact, he told the Queen Mother that ESB would have been terribly unlucky not to win, having been badly interfered with at the third-last.

Peter Cazalet never had much luck at Aintree. Monaveen, the horse owned together by the Queen and the Queen Mother, finished fifth in the 1950 Grand National won by Freebooter and looked a good prospect for the following year; however, after winning four races, he then broke a leg at Hurst Park the following year, ironically in the Queen Elizabeth Chase.

Cazalet had also trained Davy Jones who, in the hands of Anthony Mildmay, was in the lead two fences out in the 1936 Grand National, only for the reins to snap and the horse to run out. The beneficiary of Davy Jones's mishap was Reynoldstown, ridden by Fulke Walwyn, the man who was eventually to succeed Cazalet as the royal trainer. Twelve years later, in 1948, Mildmay's mount Cromwell finished third to Sheila's Cottage in the National and might have won had not Mildmay's neck seized up several fences from the finish.

David Mould was convinced that the Queen Mother was robbed of victory too in the 1967 Champion Hurdle at the Cheltenham Festival, where her record was comparatively poor. He was riding her Makaldar, who was on the heels of the leader up the final hill but was then carried off a straight line by the St Leger winner Aurelius, veering left as if to run another circuit. Saucy Kit won and Makaldar was placed second when Aurelius was disqualified. With a chuckle, Saucy Kit's trainer Peter Easterby remembers, 'When you won the Champion Hurdle, she used to send for you for a drink afterwards. That year she didn't send for me.'

The Queen Mother did not win as many Cheltenham Festival races as she might have done partly because Peter Cazalet, whose gallops were no more than three furlongs up a steep rise, ran her horses regularly in the early part of the season when the royal diary gave her more opportunities to get to the races. You can go to the well only so often, even with a royal horse.

The Queen Mother's colours of blue with buff stripes, blue sleeves, and black cap with a gold tassel had originally been those of her great-uncle Lord Strathmore, who rode in four Grand Nationals as an amateur. The first time she saw them, on Manicou, she remarked, 'The blue is not quite royal enough and that is because they have been copied from a set 50 years' old in which the blue has faded. In time, I intend to have a new set and this time the blue will be truly blue.'

Those blue-and-buff colours, though, were carried to some great successes as when Manicou, under Bryan Marshall, won the King George VI Chase at Kempton on Boxing Day 1951. Marshall, having suffered the same casualties as many jump jockeys, used to like to have his false teeth handy when meeting the royal owner. That meant having the stable lad, leading up a horse, keeping them in safe custody and handing them over at a suitable moment. The Queen Mother enjoyed teasing him when she saw him smuggling the dentures into his mouth behind a handkerchief.

Gay Record was another classy horse, albeit a nervous one who was difficult to train. He was moved from Fairlawne to less grand premises in the little yard just off Reigate High Street maintained by Jack O'Donoghue, a Grand National winner but a man also famed as an animal lover who won countless prizes with his donkeys. Calmed by sharing his new premises with cows, sheep and donkeys, Gay Record went on to win nine races for his royal patron. O'Donoghue also won for her with Colonello.

Another of the Queen Mother's favourites was The Rip, not only because he won 14 times as well as coming third in the Hennessy Gold Cup,

David Mould (right), another of the Queen Mother's favourite jockeys, takes the last fence in the Topham Trophy at Aintree on Inch Arran.

Profile: Special Cargo's Whitbread win
– the race that had everything

It was once written of the great cricketer WG Grace that he had 'exhausted all superlatives.' Steeplechasing has plenty of candidates for 'the best race ever seen' but most spectators at Sandown for the Whitbread Gold Cup on 28 April 1984 were convinced that the contest that unfolded in front of them that day deserved that accolade. It was the race that had everything – a popular rider riding his last race on a previous winner, a blanket photo finish involving three contestants, two of them with dodgy legs. To add to that, there was a touch of comedy followed by a secret drama and, of course, there was victory in the end for the sport's most popular owner.

The Queen Mother at Sandown with her horse Special Cargo.

Those who worked with him, such as his one-time assistant Mark Bradstock, marvelled at Fulke Walwyn's ability to patch up old veterans and keep them enjoying their racing: that year, Walwyn ran two of them. One was Diamond Edge, with whom he had twice previously won the Whitbread, traditionally the climax of the jumping season, but who was now 13. The other was the 12-year-old Special Cargo, whose pottery pins had kept him off the racecourse for two years before he had returned to win the Grand Military Gold Cup at Sandown the previous month. Diamond Edge was beating Special Cargo out of sight on the gallops in Lambourn and the firm going would not suit Special Cargo, so not surprisingly stable jockey Bill Smith, who had decided it would be his last race, had opted for Diamond Edge; thus his quiet but capable understudy, Kevin Mooney, was given the ride on Special Cargo, who would probably not have been risked if the Queen Mother had not been present with her racing friends Colonel Bill Whitbread and his wife, Betty. Favourites for the race were Plundering, trained by Walwyn's Lambourn neighbour Fred Winter, and Ashley House, trained in the north by the gifted Michael Dickinson, who also ran Lettoch.

There was a moderate pace around the first circuit and when Bill Smith let Diamond Edge stride on at the first of the railway fences down the back stretch, Special Cargo was caught out. Kevin Mooney, kicking and pushing, thought his chance had gone and considered pulling him up. But he took his mount to the inside and

the pair flew the Pond Fence. Special Cargo, then in seventh place, changed his legs and began to forge up to the leaders, Diamond Edge, Plundering and Lettoch, who had been badly hampered by a faller early on. Special Cargo hit the second-last without losing momentum and bore down on Lettoch and Diamond Edge, who led 50 yards out, as they tore up the hill. At the line, with four jockeys and their mounts straining every sinew, it was a blur with Special Cargo, Lettoch, Diamond Edge and Plundering flashing past the post apparently inseparable. There was an anxious wait for the judges to consult the photograph and then came the announcement: Special Cargo had won, with Lettoch second and Diamond Edge third. The distances separating the trio were a short head and the same. To the Queen Mother's concern, both the Walwyn pair were lame in the winner's enclosure. When the Queen Mother invited Bill Smith and Kevin Mooney up to the Royal Box for a glass of champagne, they watched a rerun, with the successful royal owner emphasising what a marvellous race Bill Smith had ridden. As for Fulke Walwyn, his staff recalled, he kept bursting into tears for days afterwards.

And the touch of comedy? Special Cargo suffered regularly from an ailment that, about six months into the season, caused large lumps of his hair to fall out. Having consulted his vet, Bob McCreery, Walwyn had his team cover the bare patches with Cherry Blossom boot *polish – and Special Cargo strode around the parade ring with the crowd commenting on his glossy black coat. When the Queen Mother patted her victor after the race, she made no comment over the blackening of her glove, but for Walwyn and his wife, Cath, there was a worrying aftermath. He was contacted by the Jockey Club to say they were unhappy with the routine drug test. Walwyn, in his wife's words, 'Did his nut,' castigating the vet who had advised him there was no risk, and fearing that a tin of boot polish could see his old horse denied a famous triumph. Fortunately, the second test confirmed that there were no performance-affecting substances.*

but also because she had spotted him herself in a field beside the Red Cat pub in Norfolk, near the Sandringham Estate. Once, as photographs were being taken at Fairlawne, the Queen Mother was holding The Rip. When he was spooked by Cazalet's head lad Jim Fairgrieve, waving his cap to make him look up, she was pulled off her feet. Worried lads dashed forward to help but she calmed them by remarking, 'Now I know how a National Hunt jockey feels.'

Other prolific winners for her and Cazalet were Chaou II, who scored 17 times between March 1967 and December 1972, Makaldar with 15 victories, and Laffy with 13 wins plus a third place in the Whitbread Gold Cup. Racegoers with long memories will remember too a series of victories for Irish Rover, Ballykine, Escalus (also third in the Champion Hurdle), Super Fox, Sun Rising, Lunedale and Inch Arran, who won 13 chases for her with Cazalet and another when moving on to Fulke Walwyn after Cazalet's death from cancer in 1973.

One of her best jumpers was Game Spirit, still commemorated in the title of a Newbury race. He died on the Berkshire course after a race, forestalling his owner's plan that he should, on his retirement from the racing scene, become the Queen's hack. At Cheltenham he was third in the Gold Cup and second in the two-mile Champion Chase while on other tracks he won 11 races for Cazalet and another ten for Fulke Walwyn. Colonius opened his winning account under Cazalet and won 13 more races with Walwyn. Isle of Man, another prolific winner from the Walwyn days with 14 victories, was also placed in the Champion Chase, the race that in 1980, the year she became 80 herself, was renamed by the Cheltenham authorities as the Queen Mother Champion Chase. Ever since

it has been known to racing folk in short as 'the Queen Mother.' She would have liked that.

In all, Fulke Walwyn trained 115 winners for the Queen Mother and his widow, Cath, trained six more after he died in 1991. When Cath retired, the royal baton was passed to Nicky Henderson, also in Lambourn. He won five chases for her with Nearco Bay who, by triumphing in a three-and-a-quarter-mile chase at Uttoxeter on 30 May 1994, became her 400th winner. A one-time winner of the New Zealand Grand National, Nearco Bay was the slowest horse in the Henderson yard when he arrived – but clearly improved. When Channel Four racing chief Andrew Franklin realised that the feat was looming, he arranged for their coverage that day to include the one race from Uttoxeter in which the Queen Mother had a runner.

At an Ascot party to celebrate the 400 winners, David Nicholson noted that he was one of 32 proud jockeys who had ridden to victory in the royal colours.

Insular, winner of the 1986 Imperial Cup at Sandown.

There were hurdle victories too for Ian Balding with the dual-purpose Insular, who ran on the flat for the Queen and over hurdles for her mother, winning the William Hill Imperial Cup among his other successes. When Insular's racing career in two royal colours came to an end, his connections with royalty did not. Told by Lord Carnarvon, the Queen's racing manager, that Insular would otherwise be put down after running two bad races, Ian Balding had taken him on as a lead horse for his youngsters, and when Timeform sponsored an amateurs' race named after the Queen Mother during their charity meeting at York, Balding was persuaded by Timeform chairman Reg Griffin to let Insular participate. This he did to good effect, lifting the £10,000 prize for his half-embarrassed, half-delighted trainer in the hands of Princess Anne. She held him up behind a fast pace, came through one-and-a-half furlongs out and won by 12 lengths. Modestly, his rider said afterwards, 'Insular knows more about racing than I do. I just sat and let him get on with it.'

The day that Insular won the Imperial Cup, the Queen Mother had one of her finest day's racing. She scored a treble, with Special Cargo capturing the Horse and Hound Military Gold Cup for the third year running and The Argonaut claiming victory in the Dick McCreery Chase. The Argonaut was ridden by Fulke Walwyn's assistant trainer, Mark Bradstock (now better

known for training the novice chaser Coneygree to win the Cheltenham Gold Cup in 2015 from his own small yard at Letcombe Bassett), and he won twice more on The Argonaut for her. The Queen Mother's jockeys were always under orders to use the whip only if absolutely necessary. She liked the way that Mark rode without using his whip and he kept the ride on The Argonaut outside amateur races.

The Queen Mother adored her visits to Peter Cazalet's Fairlawne, particularly an annual expedition for a three-day Lingfield meeting when the Cazalets would assemble a house party not just of racing people but also of show-business personalities, such as Noel Coward and Chan Canasta, to help entertain her and play croquet. They were cooked for in the grand house by Albert Roux. Cazalet always made sure he had plenty of runners primed for the meeting. One year, when there was a threat that the ground would be too wet to race, Cazalet was heard telephoning Lingfield's Clerk of the Course, Peter Beckwith-Smith, and declaring: 'We simply have to race, Peter, even if the horses have to swim.'

The Queen Mother was always very good at putting at their ease those who were introduced to her on the racecourse. Trainer Jenny Pitman has never forgotten the first time she was invited to the Royal Box after Burrough Hill Lad had won the Cheltenham Gold Cup. Nearby officials looked shocked when she asked, 'Would you mind if I do the horse's legs first?' and then went off to wash and bandage them, but the Queen Mother was not fazed in the least. It was Jenny who was fazed a little later. As the attendant in the Royal Box asked, 'May I take your coat, madam?' she remembered that she was wearing a sweater with a large hole burned into it by an ironing accident. 'I wrapped the coat around me and said, "No, thanks, I won't be staying long..."'

When Burrough Hill Lad won the King George VI Chase at Kempton, the two met again. 'She was looking round like a meerkat saying, "Where's Jenny?"' the trainer remembers. 'She said, "I know you'll want to see to your horse first. Have you got any one else with you?"' and so her mother and father enjoyed a long talk with the Queen Mother before Jenny joined them. 'Forget about trophies and stuff,' says Jenny. 'Those are the real memories,' and she recalls that the Queen Mother even expressed an interest in buying Corbiere. The message relayed back through intermediaries was that Her Majesty could have a half-share, so long as the horse remained in Jenny's yard – and no more was heard.

When Cazalet died and the Fairlawne operation was dismantled (the house was to become the property of the Saudi Prince, Khalid Abdulla, later the owner of the mighty Frankel), the Queen Mother came down to Fairlawne and spoke to all the members of Cazalet's staff individually. All were presented with mementoes: cigarette cases, cufflinks, etc. bearing her coat of arms. When the Fairlawne horses were sent to Fulke Walwyn, David Mould tried to have Game Spirit routed instead to Tom Jones in Newmarket, for whom he was riding at the time. It is a comment on those times that such a move for a horse in royal ownership did not happen largely because Tom Jones had recently been divorced. Similarly, when the Queen Mother became the owner of Matuba Matuba, named after an African chief reputed to have had 600 children, he was rapidly re-registered as Harbour Master.

It was not just as an owner that the Queen Mother benefited jump racing. Her obvious enthusiasm as a spectator was equally valuable. In all weathers she would be there, if necessary under a transparent umbrella or, when age began to take its toll, in her version of the 'Popemobile.' The year Channel Four took over Festival coverage from the BBC, her household contacted Cheltenham chairman Lord Vestey in a panic: they had set the video for the BBC and only had children's programmes on the tape. A copy was run off from Channel Four's master and despatched to Clarence House – with an off-air comment about her, during an advertisement break, by John Francome dubbed out.

If the Queen Mother's patronage was an important factor in raising the profile of National Hunt racing, it seems that indirectly

The Queen Mother presents the 1990 Gold Cup to Sirrell Griffiths, owner and trainer of 100-1 winner, Norton's Coin.

she did the sport another big favour. In the early 1960s, racing was plagued by a notorious doping gang led by the bookmaker and gambler Bill Roper. With mobsters pressing him for their cut, the emboldened gang began sending Roper's Swiss mistress to a number of stables in a chauffeur-driven car, posing as a potential owner to spy out the boxes occupied by their targets. As Jamie Reid revealed in his impeccably researched *Doped*, Fairlawne was one of the targets visited by Micheline Lugeon – and the Queen Mother's Laffy was one of the horses that the gang's enforcers succeeded in reaching. Fortunately, Laffy received only a mild dose of what they were administering. The positive factor was that Cazalet, appalled by the prospect of one of the Queen Mother's horses being drawn into a squalid affair, had the clout that some other targeted trainers did not. The amateur administrators of the Jockey Club had been handling the doping no more effectively than the Macmillan government had been handling sex and espionage scandals, but the enraged Cazalet was an establishment man himself who knew most of the key figures personally. He spoke to the Senior Steward, Lord Crathorne, a former Cabinet Minister, about his concerns. The result was a meeting with the Metropolitan Police Commissioner,

The Princess Royal in action at Uttoxeter.

Sir Ranulf Bacon, followed the next day by a gathering of Jockey Club and National Hunt committee chiefs with Richard Jackson, the head of the CID. At last, the likes of Major-General Sir Randle Feilden and Lord Willoughby de Broke had recognised that they were incapable of coping with the doping menace alone and that Scotland Yard was needed. In the end, Bill Roper and his mistress were convicted, Micheline Lugeon's first appearance in a Brighton court coinciding with the Old Bailey trial of Stephen Ward for living off immoral earnings, at which Mandy Rice-Davies gave her famous 'He would, wouldn't he?' response when told that Lord Astor denied having had sex with her. At the Roper trial, Peter Cazalet and his head lad, Jim Fairgrieve, gave evidence, but, as agreed with the Jockey Club and Home Office in advance, said nothing about the attempted doping of the Queen Mother's horse.

Following the Queen Mother's death at the age of 101 in 2002, and with the Queen remaining focused on flat racing, albeit she has had jumpers with Nicky Henderson, jump-racing enthusiasts have had to look elsewhere for royal patrons. Perhaps as an encouragement, the Queen gave Prince Charles and the Duchess of Cornwall a horse called Supereva, a young brood mare by Sadler's Wells, as a wedding present; however, even though Prince Charles did have six rides as an amateur in the early 1980s, including one on Upton Grey for his grandmother, he has never displayed the same enthusiasm for jump racing that he did for polo. Things might have taken a different course if his favourite horse, Allibar, with whom he had become familiar in the hunting field while being tutored by Lambourn trainer Nick Gaselee, had not, sadly, dropped dead.

The royals are rarely permitted to take a step without media scrutiny and there was a ridiculous media fuss in March 1981 after television recorded two racecourse falls for the heir to the throne within a week, both while riding the perhaps inappropriately named 12-year-old Good Prospect. Nobody made the same objections when he was taking the same

risks as others while scuba-diving, parachuting, windsurfing or skiing.

Princess Anne, the Princess Royal, has been the most prominent royal on the jumping scene. A fine rider who was part of Britain's eventing team for five years, she competed in the Montreal Olympics; in 1971 she was voted the BBC Sports Personality of the Year after winning the individual three-day event at the European championships at Burghley on Doublet. She too has ridden in races. TV presenter Clare Balding, daughter of Ian Balding, has recorded how she crossed another rider on the way to winning a contest for amateurs at Beverley in 1989 and heard some most unladylike language behind her. It was only afterwards that Clare realised that it was the Princess whom she had 'cut up.' On that occasion Balding's mount, Waterlow Park, prevailed in a photo finish. Two years later, Princess Anne had her revenge in the same race when riding Croft Valley to beat Balding's Knock Knock by a neck.

The Princess Royal had a fine tutor as a race rider, the former jockey and champion trainer David 'the Duke' Nicholson, for whom she began riding out at his Condicote stables in March 1985. After he had advised her to pull up her leathers and do a long, steady canter, he recorded in his autobiography: 'When she pulled up at the end, I asked, "Does it hurt?" She replied, "Yes,"

so I instructed her to go round again.' The Duke once prepared a female rider, Joan Barrow, to compete against male jockeys for a BBC series called The Big Time. As part of the training, he advised her to ride a bicycle everywhere without a saddle. When he made the same suggestion to Princess Anne, it was less well received.

With the Duke's friends rallying round to provide suitable mounts, Princess Anne rode in flat races at Epsom, Goodwood, Redcar and Chepstow in her first season. The second season brought her first winner on Gulfland at Redcar for Gavin Pritchard-Gordon. There were more winners at Ascot, in front of the Queen, on Ten No Trumps for Michael Stoute, at Newmarket on Vayrua for Barry Hills, and at Nashville, Tennessee on Wood Chisel. In all, she won six races on the flat; when she turned her attention to steeplechases, she won at Worcester on Cnoc na Cuille for her mentor, David Nicholson, having driven the horsebox to the races herself. She has remained close to all equestrian pursuits, working with a number of racing charities such as Riding for the Disabled. The Princess became the first royal to appear on the quiz programme, A Question of Sport, and was a member of the organising committee for the London Olympics. Her daughter, Zara Phillips, has taken after her, winning individual and team gold medals at the European Eventing Championships in 2005.

The Queen Mother presenting the Royal Artillery Gold Cup Steeplechase trophy in 2001.

The Queen at Cheltenham with Chairman, Sam Vestey who led the modernisation of the course, which contributed greatly to the popularity of the sport.

11 Running Racing

– from a Jockey Club fiefdom to the British Horseracing Authority

'What can you expect now that we're in with the National Hunt Committee?'

Lord Sefton, after his binoculars 'disappeared' one day after the merger of the Jockey Club and the jump racing authorities

For more than 400 years, the Jockey Club was the supreme authority in British horseracing. Its members, largely drawn from the aristocracy and the establishment, alternated between running horseracing and running the country: at least six prime ministers were Jockey Club members, and the Club's members provided most of the finance that developed horseracing in Britain. Those who were not members of the aristocracy tended to have spent time in the armed forces: as late as the 1970s, the application forms for posts as stewards' secretaries asked candidates to state their rank and regiment.

It is easy to caricature the old-style Jockey Club and its members, who were woefully slow at moving with the times over such issues as equality for women, but the Club did contain a number of figures who, usually unrewarded, made a genuine contribution to racing's development, and many more who believed they were doing so. The Club, though, was Newmarket-oriented and jump racing was rarely at the top of any Jockey Club list of priorities. Some of its grandees had a low opinion of the jumping fraternity. When Lord Sefton's binoculars 'disappeared' one day after the 1969 merger, he was heard to protest, 'What can you expect now that we're in with the National Hunt Committee?' Others, however, welcomed the fact that many of the National Hunt stewards had greater race-riding and training experience compared with their flat-racing counterparts.

At the start of the 1960s, recognising that the laws on gambling had become an unenforceable farce (see Betting chapter), the Government began framing new laws on betting. Some racing historians, looking longingly at the lavishly funded racing in places like Hong Kong, have blamed the Jockey Club for failing then to mobilise its political friends in support of the kind of Tote monopoly that applies in France or in Hong Kong. The Jockey Club failed to support a Tote monopoly apparently on the grounds that there was little enthusiasm for the idea among racegoers or the general public. Cynics, meanwhile, suggested that some Jockey Club members had over-cosy relationships with their bookmakers. Certainly, the bookmakers proved effective in their lobbying efforts among Parliamentarians to stave off any threat to their existence: the Mirabelle restaurant and the Hyde Park Hotel dining room became virtual extensions of the House of Commons' canteens as they made their case. Nor was there much pressure on Home Secretary Rab Butler to provide adequate funding for the racing industry.

The 1960 Betting and Gaming Bill, which was to legalise betting shops initially, included no plans for a levy on off-course betting to help provide for the costs of running and policing racing, as the Jockey Club stewards had sought, and to compensate racecourses for the expected loss of attendances as high street betting shops came into existence. The racing authorities were fobbed off instead with the setting-up of a committee to 'consider the desirability and practicality of bookmakers contributing to racing and breeding' and, if that committee favoured the principle, how the money should be raised.

The departmental committee, set up by Butler under Sir Leslie Peppiatt in December 1959, did however report by April 1960 in favour of a levy, and Butler pushed through the legislation with support on all sides in the Commons. Butler said on the Second Reading of the Levy Bill in December 1960 that he had always thought the new betting legislation wouldn't be complete without a levy and that the Peppiatt Committee had found an 'almost unanimous' opinion on all sides of the racing industry, including the bookmakers, that a levy was necessary. He quoted Peppiatt as saying, 'The United Kingdom has for a long time been in the lead in horseracing and we think the infusion of fresh money should be regarded not as serving to bolster a declining industry, but as an aid to improving it.' Butler refused, incidentally, to give greyhound racing a levy too.

The legislation to introduce a levy , the precise sum to be agreed each year between bookmakers' representatives and the racing industry, was duly completed in 1961 but while the Jockey Club had hoped for £3 million in the first year, only £892,617 was raised for technical services, prize money and the improvement of racecourses.

Although it has become increasingly 'unfit for purpose,' the Levy Board, whose activities are covered in more detail in a separate section, has been one of the success stories of the 60 years covered by this volume. Established by the Betting Levy Act 1961 and operating in accordance with the revised 1963 Betting, Gaming and Lotteries Act and subsequent gambling legislation, the Levy Board is unlike most other non-departmental public bodies: it doesn't receive any money from the government or any funding from the National Lottery. Covering both flat and jump racing, its statutory duty is to collect money, by agreement, from the

bookmakers and to spend it to improve horse breeding and veterinary science; to support the provision of horseracing; and to generate increased betting turnover (thus enhancing the levy and the funds it has to distribute). Collected in recent years at an agreed rate of 10.75 per cent on bookmakers' profits it is, along with the BBC TV licence fee, a rare example of ring-fenced taxation but its very existence means that racing is not simply organised to provide a spectator sport: it is also organised to promote betting and so increase its levy income. The existence of the Levy Board has also been an incentive to the various pressure groups in racing, such as the Racehorse Owners

MAJ-GEN SIR RANDLE FEILDEN, C.B, C.B.E, K.C.V.O.

Association (ROA), speaking for the owners who provide racing's basic commodity, and the Racecourse Association (RCA), speaking for the racecourses on which the sport takes place, to become both efficient and vociferous. Each pressure group has to be both well-organised and noisy if its members are going to win their share of the cake.

In the 1960s, the Racehorse Owners Association began to emerge as an effective pressure group, calling for lower entry fees, an increase in the prize money for placed horses, and a better spread of prize money, rather than its concentration on top feature races. It also drew attention to the high costs of transporting horses to meetings. The ROA became increasingly frustrated with the Jockey Club but it lacked weight: by the end of 1969, it still had only 800 members. During the 1960s however, the ROA increased links with the Racecourse Association (RCA) and won concessions, including free parking and improved lunch facilities, which it saw as an acknowledgment that owners were a vital part of the industry. The ROA also began collecting and organising statistics on which to base its arguments.

By 1976, the ROA, which had started advertising itself in the *Sporting Life* and publishing its own magazine, had swelled to more than 3,000 members, representing more than 6,000 horses in training. But there were constant clashes with a sometimes openly contemptuous Jockey Club. When Lord Leverhulme became the Jockey Club's Senior Steward he promised that the ROA would be listened to but, finding things no different, the ROA began campaigning for direct representation on the Levy Board. It widened its range of concerns to include better racecourse maintenance and the improvement of pay and conditions for stable staff. In

1973, when the introduction of VAT brought new concerns, the ROA joined other racing bodies in negotiations with HM Customs and Excise over the effect on racing and breeding.

Steadily the ROA's voice became more prominent and, in the mid-1970s, it commissioned a report from the International Racing Bureau that demonstrated that although Britain had probably the highest betting turnover in the world, the return to racing was among the lowest. Joining with others, such as the RCA and the Thoroughbred Breeders Association, the ROA proposed in a submission to the Royal Commission on Gambling that the Jockey Club's control of the industry should be ended in favour of a British racing board more properly representative of all those involved in the industry. It took a while but that aim was eventually to be achieved.

The 1980s, however, were little happier than the 1970s in terms of relations with the Jockey Club, which, for example, denied the ROA a voice on the Sunday Racing Working Party in 1984. There was only limited improvement before the creation of the British Horseracing Board (BHB) in 1993 finally gave the ROA a legal and practical voice in the governance of racing. The ROA worked with others like the RCA to pressurise the government into giving racing a better return from betting revenue, and in 1998, Peter Savill became chairman of the BHB after his ROA presidency ended that year.

The ROA backed Savill's plan to base the funding of racing not on the Levy Board formula but on the sale of database rights – the detailed information on fixtures, race conditions, riders, weights etc – to interested parties like the bookmakers and the media. The legality of that plan was, however, successfully challenged in the European Court by bookmakers between 2002 and 2004 and uncertainty about its future financial base has plagued racing ever since.

The original Levy Board consisted of two Jockey Club representatives and one from the National Hunt Committee, the chairmen of both the Tote and the Bookmakers Committee, and three impartial civil servants. The Jockey Club considered that while it was the Levy Board's

Lord George Wigg, Chairman of the Betting Levy Board, signing copies of his autobiography at a press conference, London, 11 May 1972.

duty to raise the money, they should decide how it was spent. When Lord (George) Wigg, one of the prime movers in uncovering the Profumo scandal, succeeded Lord Harding as chairman of the Levy Board on Wigg's retirement from politics in 1967, Major-General Sir Randle Feilden informed Wigg that that was how they saw it. The Duke of Norfolk instructed Wigg that he must never talk to the press on turf matters without clearance from the Jockey Club. To the testy Wigg, who clashed equally fiercely with the bookies, that was not so much a red rag as a crimson blanket; he informed the Club representatives bluntly that if they wanted to speak to him in future, they could find him at his offices.

To ease the confrontations, the Joint Racing Board (JRB) was set up in 1968, including representatives of both the Jockey Club and the Levy Board. It was one of a series of worthy bodies that sought to reconcile interests within an industry often divided by the conflicting demands of owners and breeders, trainers, jockeys, racecourses, stable staff and bookmakers. One of them was BRIC, the Bloodstock and Racehorse Industries Confederation, which was set up in 1975 on the initiative of flat-racing trainer John Winter to tackle the slump in the bloodstock industry and the chronic shortage of prize money. To counter the perceived threat of BRIC, the Jockey Club set up RILC, the Racing Industry Liaison Committee. Then there was JALC, the Joint Association Liaison Committee, which had been tackling racing's concerns since 1964…

An important development was the establishment of the umbrella organisation, the HAC (Horserace Advisory Council), in 1979, but the HAC, like the other worthy bodies, had influence but no executive authority over racing and it did not include any bookmakers' representatives.

Another key development was the brainchild of Lord Porchester (later the 7th Earl of Carnavon) the Queen's racing manager. At his instigation in 1970, the Jockey Club was granted a Royal Charter, putting it on a par with

Lord Porchester, the Queen's racing manager at Newbury.

the BBC, the Theatre Royal, and many learned societies. The Charter, which senior steward Major-General Sir Randle Feilden announced on 11 February that year, was crucial because, despite its dominant role in racing, there had been no legal or constitutional basis for the Jockey Club's authority. The Royal Charter (which is, for example, the mechanism by which towns become cities) was welcomed by some Jockey Club members as a defensive measure that protected them from enforced change (any modification to a Royal Charter requires the consent of Queen and parliament). But the Charter conveyed another advantage: it gave the Jockey Club the legal status to begin reforming, and to implement some of the recommendations of the Benson Committee report in 1968, which had examined the role of horseracing as an industry. (That, in itself, has always been an underlying tension: some of those involved in it see racing as a sport; to others, it is an industry that employs some 20,000 people directly and is responsible for another 80,000 jobs in ancillary trades.) Then there is the question of public perception: because of its association with gambling, some sections of society associate racing with knavery and crime. At the same time, it is the one sport that undoubtedly carries the social cachet of royal approval: it has long been the Sport of Kings – and especially Queens.

The committee under Sir Henry (later Lord) Benson, the leading accountant of his generation and one of the government's go-to figures for Royal Commissions, identified nine different bodies with varying degrees of responsibility for racing and urged the creation of a single racing authority. The Royal Commission on Gambling took a similar view but wanted the Levy Board to remain responsible for revenue-raising. One Benson recommendation was swiftly implemented: in 1969, the Jockey Club and National Hunt Committee amalgamated. That nearly doubled the size of the Club since there had been 46 Jockey Club members and 53 National Hunt Committee members, with 18 individuals belonging to both bodies. The amalgamated Jockey Club thus became responsible for the rules of flat racing, jumping and point-to-point racing.

A key figure in the next stage of racing's development was Lord 'Stoker' Hartington, later the Duke of Devonshire. As the Jockey Club's senior steward from 1989 to 1994, he put some steam behind the reform efforts: in 1989, Christopher Haines was appointed as a salaried chief executive and the post of finance steward was created. Crucially, Stoker Hartington realised that racing needed a more representative body to help it make its case to government, and the next key development was the setting-up of the BHB, the British Horseracing Board, in 1993, to take over many of the functions that the Jockey Club had performed over the previous 241 years.

With representatives from many sectors, the BHB, with Lord Hartington as its chairman for the first three years, gained responsibility for the day-to-day conduct of racing, for licensing, security and integrity, fixtures and finance. But the Jockey Club retained responsibility for discipline. The foundation of the BHB was greeted by a triumphant *Racing Post* banner

headline on 11 June 1993: 'WE'RE IN CHARGE.'

It was not until 2006, however, that the Jockey Club finally let go of the reins. As of 12.01 a.m. on 3 April that year, it finally lost the power to tell anybody what to do. That moment saw the birth of the Horseracing Regulatory Authority (HRA), with veterinarian Peter Webbon as its first chief executive, to take over the Jockey Club's regulatory and disciplinary powers. Many of those on his payroll had previously worked for the Club but their contracts were now transferred to the HRA, which had three members independent of the Jockey Club on its five-strong board. Licensing, law-making, rules and penalties, safety measures and security concerns were now all a matter for the HRA.

The BHB, which had strictly defined representation for all racing's special-interest groups, was to last until 2007. Various chairmen included the former Conservative Minister Lord Wakeham, once one of Lady Thatcher's chief fixers; Sir Thomas Pilkington (as a caretaker when Lord Wakeham resigned); self-made millionaire Peter Savill; and former British Airways and CBI Chairman Sir Martin Broughton. The most energetic and forceful of them was the cruise-ship-magazine mogul, Peter Savill, formerly a leading light in the ROA, who sought to move the BHB (which had no marketing or commercial director) from a civil-service mentality into a more commercial organisation.

Savill's first financial plan highlighted the relatively low proportion of betting turnover returned to racing in Britain and argued that racing needed an extra £105 million a year, some £80 million of which, he suggested, should come from an increased share of that betting turnover. His agenda included the abolition of the Levy Board (an agenda shared openly by the government from 2000 onwards); the transfer of the Tote to racing; and the spinning-off of the BHB's commercial interests to a separate company, which he hoped could realise £140 million a year from the sale of data rights. He also wanted a reduction in sectional interests on the BHB board and a 'modernisation' of racing that included more Sunday racing, the limiting of field sizes to 14 for all but a few races, and a 20 per cent increase in fixtures within three years.

There was a spat with the media when the BHB, in 2002, sought a huge increase in data charges from newspapers. After some publications began to drop racecards from their pages, the scheme was rapidly withdrawn.

When his confrontational style was questioned, Peter Savill said he was amazed that anybody could have thought his aims ever could have been achieved 'over a friendly cup of tea.' When his term ended, Savill concluded: 'Racing couldn't have gone from where it was when I arrived to where it is now without someone taking things by the scruff of the neck.' He left a more streamlined board, with commercial and governance functions separated, and a more businesslike approach. When he first arrived in 1998, bookmakers were paying less than £56 million in the levy. In 2003, they paid almost £100 million. Prize money had increased from £60 million to almost £94 million, media rights' income was up, so were racecourse attendances and, marginally, the number of horses in training.

Savill's biggest service to jump racing came after a bombshell announcement in 2003 when the Office of Fair Trading (OFT) issued a notice to the BHB and the Jockey Club saying that their rules and orders breached the Competition Act. The OFT wanted a complete free-for-all, allowing racecourses to open their gates whenever they wanted to. David James, then the chairman of Racecourse Holdings Trust, said that if all the OFT's plans were introduced at the same time, it could produce 'a state of complete anarchy.'

Savill recognised that they would virtually give the bookmakers the whip hand because they would decide which races to fund. He realised that, in particular, there was a dire threat to smaller jump tracks because, even though they do provide the vital feeder races leading through to the pinnacle of the Cheltenham Festival, novice hurdle races on their own do not do too much for the bookmakers.

Savill restructured the BHB and introduced a scheme to allow racecourses to compete for some fixtures. A deal was done: the OFT was satisfied that a non-exclusive, non-discriminatory policy was being operated at a fair marketing value, and the BHB kept the right to make orders and rules for the sport. The *Racing Post* headline on 11 June 2004 simply read: 'VICTORY.' To the delight of those running tracks such as Fakenham, Ludlow and Market Rasen, Savill was able to announce: 'We have convinced the OFT that jumping should be treated in the main as a separate sport to flat racing. By doing so, jumping will be able to flourish, as will the many small community-driven racecourses that showcase this important part of country life.'

Savill's wider plans to finance racing by the sale of data rights and scrapping the levy were scuppered, however, by a decision of the European courts. Firstly, a provisional deal worth £600 million over five years was signed in April 2002; this followed a move in the previous October when the government had switched from a levy based on turnover to one based on bookmakers' gross profits. Then, in November 2004, the European Court overruled a British-court decision and found that bookmakers William Hill had not infringed the BHB's data rights by publishing details of runners and riders on its website. That issue became linked with a football-pools case and, effectively, British racing found itself on the opposing side to a number of

The Jockey Cub, horse racing headquarters.

European governments who wanted to protect their pool-betting operations and didn't want to pay football for its fixture details.

The government had, many years before, asked the BHB to find an alternative to the levy, and the BHB had proposed a commercial system based on licensing data rights: now the BHB was left with nothing to sell. Says one BHB insider: 'The rug was pulled from under us and government had already passed legislation to wind up the levy. We had to go back to the Labour government and say, "Sorry, we don't have a clean bill of health on replacing the levy."' Governments of different colours still have not abolished the levy, although both the desire to do it – and the legal powers to do so – remain in place. What to replace it with has remained the problem.

By the time the British Court of Appeal refused to overturn the verdict from the European Court of Justice, Sir Martin

Peter Savill, Chairman of the BHB.

Broughton was the BHB chairman. He noted that the bookmakers were making £1 billion a year from using the data while racing was getting just £100 million in levy. Lord Donoughue chaired a BHB-inspired Review Group, with the backing of the government,

to find an agreed and sustainable system to replace the levy. The Group recommended a combined selling of pictures and data (known as 'bundling') but the advice of legal counsel was that this was not 'legally robust' on competition grounds – and everyone was back to square one. The government (which had passed legislation ready to abolish it) agreed to Donoughue's urging that the levy should continue while the search went on.

As Savill had declared, 'No major racing industry in the world can, or does, function without the majority of its funding being provided by a percentage of betting turnover,' and without the sale of data rights there was little alternative. In September 2005, Broughton declared: 'The government doesn't want a statutory agreement and we don't either but, interestingly, every other country in the world has got one, so nobody else has cracked it.'

The quid pro quo for the government retaining the levy was the final removal of the Jockey Club's role of regulating racing and the arrival of a new set of 'initials' to take over responsibility. The BHA emerged as a unified body assuming the responsibilities of the BHB and of the HRA, which in 2006 had taken over the regulatory and disciplinary functions of the Jockey Club. The BHA's first chairman was Paul Roy, who had previously coped with revenues of $10 billion while running the Global Markets and Investment Banking Division of Merrill Lynch, and the chief executive was Nic Coward, former director of corporate affairs with the Football Association.

It was an awkward time, with racing overshadowed by the Old Bailey trial of champion flat-racing jockey Kieren Fallon on alleged race-fixing charges. Paul Roy promised a fresh start but hardly burnished the sport's image by warning, 'Racing won't get the investment it needs until it makes it clear to the outside world that it is no longer a closed shop where people whisper behind their hands and rich outsiders are considered as mugs for fleecing.' He emphasised that racing had an 'economic impact' of £3 billion a year and employed 88,000 people directly or indirectly.

The board he took on was 'de-factionalised' by design; the old BHB had succeeded in achieving a significant boost in prize-money levels and also boosting attendances to a 40-year high. At the other end of the scale, it had also taken a step, which was long overdue, in setting up Lord Donoughue's Stable and Stud Staff Commission to examine working conditions.

Despite his own working background, Paul Roy made clear in an interview with the *Racing Post*'s Howard Wright that the BHA was specifically set up to have nothing to do with the commercial aspects of British racing. Income generation was to be driven by Racing Enterprises Ltd (REL). A year or so later, Roy reminded Howard Wright's readers that he had warned, on taking over, that racing had been standing still while the broader economy raced ahead – where were the owners and other participants from China, Russia, Brazil and India, where were the hedge funds and private-equity companies? – 'I also said my fear was that if racing had only managed to stand still in a period of unprecedented prosperity, what would happen in a period of economic decline. Now it is happening.'

Some were surprised at the BHA's stepping back from the commercial side when taking on a chairman with Paul Roy's qualifications but the priorities were clear: the government and the BHA recognised that, as in motor racing, you cannot allow a body that owns the commercial rights to be also responsible for making and enforcing the rules on the safety and welfare of its participants.

One of the BHA's first actions, following the embarrassing collapse of the Old Bailey trial (when Fallon and two other flat-racing jockeys were found to have no case to answer), was to set up a review under Dame Elizabeth Neville, former Director of the Serious Fraud Office, to review racing's security operations, taking into account any issues raised by the trial. The BHA was not party to the decision to prosecute or involved in any part of the case but it had passed information to the City of London Police. Dame Elizabeth's report described the BHA's integrity and licensing services as 'a model for the effective investigation of corruption in sport.'

Chief Executive Nic Coward declared that the BHA assessed a 'fair and reasonable return' from the betting industry to be £135 million to £153 million even though the full value of racing's product to the betting operators was more. He urged the government to increase the levy from 10 to 15 per cent of bookmakers' profits and he also insisted: 'We should be getting £20 million from the betting exchanges. The current mechanism wasn't designed to cope with the exchanges.' He and Paul Roy also instituted a root-and-branch fixture review, looking at the effect of the increased number of races on the horse population and on stable staff and hoping to cut out some of the dross. But not for the first time, racing's central authority was forced to accept that with racecourses 'owning' many of the fixtures, it did not have the power to make major change there.

Since then, if anything, more powers have been devolved from the centre to the racecourses and to the Horsemen's Group, a group set up in 2006 and now chaired by Philip Freedman, comprising representatives of owners, trainers, jockeys and stable staff, which exists 'to ensure an equitable share of racing's income is returned to the horsemen through prize money, to secure a racing programme that supports the requirements of the horse population and to provide a single voice for the horsemen in areas of common interest.'

In both 2010 and 2011, the Group, whose consultant chief executive was then Alan Morcombe, clashed fiercely with a number of racecourses after setting its own minimum tariff levels for prize money in every category of race to replace levels that had previously been recommended by the BHA. Amid an atmosphere of bitterness and furious debate, there were threats of strikes and stay-aways by owners, trainers and jockeys if courses did not offer prize money at the level that the then decidedly confrontational Group deemed appropriate.

As one insider put it: 'The Horsemen's Group took the attitude: "Let's take on these racecourses, they're awash with money from television picture rights and we're not getting

Johnny Henderson, founder of Racecourse Holdings Trust with Zara Phillips at Cheltenham.

a fair return. Here is the price we're going to put against each race. That's our tariff and we'll be looking at boycotting certain courses. That's how we'll drive up prize money." It was a pretty messy time.'

Out of the disputes, however, eventually came an effective compromise. With both sides recognising that it was better to create a bigger cake rather than bicker about how to slice the existing one, formal Prize Money Agreements were struck between the Horsemen and the racecourses. The BHA, under then Chief Executive Paul Bittar, was happy to concede some power to the racecourses and to the Horsemen, provided that they agreed between themselves: they had to recognise that if the sport became a constant conflict between courses and horsemen, then it had no future.

In a sport or industry that, historically, has been notorious for the internal squabbling of its interest groups, it is perhaps symbolic that in a single office block at 75 High Holborn you can now find the BHA, the ROA and the Jockey Club and the Horsemen's Group, together with a significant presence also from the RCA, which is based in Ascot.

The creation of the BHA strengthened racing's hand in negotiating with the government or other bodies vital to its funding: it had thrown off the sled the baggage, good and bad, which the Jockey Club had brought along with it. But the Jockey Club too had been on a different direction of travel: it had been freed to develop its own commercial role and it has become the

country's biggest racecourse operator.

In 1964, Johnny Henderson, a leading figure in the City and the father of later champion trainer Nicky Henderson, formed a group to purchase Cheltenham Racecourse and thus preserve it from the threat of property developers and urban sprawl. That group was entitled Racecourse Holdings Trust (RHT). Likewise, the Jockey Club was instrumental in rescuing Aintree from developers (see section on Grand National, page 100). In due course, RHT morphed into Jockey Club Racecourses, which now operates as a trust running a portfolio of 15 racecourses, flat, jumping and all-weather. There is no distribution of profits to shareholders; instead, all the money is reinvested in racing. Between 2010 and 2015, the Jockey Club injected £103 million into prize money and was due to inject £20.9 million in 2016.

Jockey Club Racecourses are currently involved in a £145-million investment programme to improve the quality of racing and widen its appeal to new audiences. The group has pioneered the use of frost covers to preserve racing programmes that might in the past have been lost to bad weather, and they seek to set the standard in turf management. As well as running the National Stud and the Racing Welfare charity, the group stages 25 per cent of the UK racing programme, including the Cheltenham and Aintree Festivals and the Epsom Derby meeting. Of the group's 15 racecourses, 11 stage jump racing: Aintree, Carlisle, Cheltenham, Exeter, Haydock Park, Huntingdon, Kempton Park, Market Rasen, Sandown Park, Warwick and Wincanton. (The others are Epsom, Newmarket's two racecourses – the July course and the Rowley Mile course – and Nottingham.)

Britain, in the famous words of US Secretary of State Dean Acheson in 1962, had once 'lost an Empire and then failed to find a role.' The Jockey Club, whose motto is 'For the Good of British Racing,' lost the right to make and enforce the rules in British racing, yet it has found a role that enables it to do more good for racing than at any time in its life. As Chief Executive Simon Bazalgette told the *Racing*

Post in February 2016, 'One can argue about the relative importance of governance and commercial aspects but I would say in the long run it is commercial that gives you the most robust future.'

The Jockey Club, which was once an empire built on land, has developed a new empire based on intellectual property, media, new media and catering. In the latest annual review, it reported its sixth year of turnover growth on a record turnover of £171 million with an operating profit of £21.7 million. And since it is incorporated by Royal Charter, all its profits are reinvested into racing's prize money and amenities. Its property arm, Jockey Club Estates, still holds 5,000 acres of land, including training grounds at Newmarket and Lambourn. As well as running the National Stud and the charity Racing Welfare, it is a major shareholder in the Qipco British Champions Series and, of course, it runs those 15 racecourses, profiting not just from race meetings but also from all the ancillary opportunities such as conferences, antique markets and exhibitions.

Beside the catering business, another subsidiary, Jockey Club Live, is claimed to be the sixth-largest music promoter in Britain. The very thought would have some of its founders spinning in their sarcophagi. Another subsidiary, Jockey Club Services, brings in more income from consultancy on issues such as turf management and ticketing from clients including the Football League and county cricket clubs. It was also the Jockey Club that launched the first retail bond in British sport, raising £25 million towards the £45-million grandstand development at Cheltenham.

Another major force is the Reuben brothers' Arena Racing Company (ARC). They too have ten jumping courses among the sixteen they run including Chepstow, Doncaster, Newcastle and Uttoxeter and are responsible for nearly 40 per cent of racing fixtures. A significant influence on the whole racing scene is the Racecourse Media Group (RMG), set up to manage the media rights of 34 of Britain's courses, including the 15 owned by the Jockey Club. As the owner of the tracks that run the Cheltenham Festival, the

Grand National and the Derby, the Jockey Club inevitably has a significant voice on the RMG. Chief Executive Simon Bazalgette came to the Jockey Club from RMG, having also helped to found TurfTV (half-owned by the RMG courses), which, by introducing competition, revolutionised the market in betting-shop picture rights to racing's benefit. It now provides the major flow of income into racing from the bookmakers.

All in all, the Jockey Club remains a major player in racing, able to influence – if not always to determine. It did, for instance, give its enthusiastic backing to the Authorised Betting Partners strategy embarked upon by the BHA of refusing to allow bookmaking companies that did not pay full levy contributions on their overseas profits to sponsor events on race courses, even though some major tracks such as Ascot, Newbury, Goodwood and York did

Simon Bazalgette, Chief Executive of the Jockey Club.

not fall into line, despite their having boards or race committees heavily sprinkled with Jockey Club members. Nor do the Jockey Club's policies always coincide with the commercial considerations of ARC. The year 2018, when Betfred's exclusive licence on pool betting runs out, will provide the next test of its new role. The Club has been looking at ways of running its own Tote, but a number of the larger independent courses within RMG are thinking of running their own individual operations.

Profile: **The lost racecourses**

An explosives factory, sheepwire electric shocks and the jockey who won after drinking three bottles of champagne – life at Britain's departed racecourses.

Jump racing takes place at 41 of Britain's 60 racecourses. There used to be many more jumping tracks but the pressures of housing demand, increased competition for the leisure pound and, in some cases, poor management have seen the number decline. In 1939, there were 79 courses licensed by the National Hunt Committee. By 1947, that was down to 46, with some, such as Newbury, which had been handed over to the USA as an Army depot and marshalling yard, still to be reclaimed from war service.

In 1963, the Levy Board carried out a cull, having decided that a number of flat-racing and jumping courses were uneconomic. In some cases, local efforts saved the condemned tracks – at least for a while. Stockton, for example, survived at first, partly by adding jumping to its flat-racing programme, but the course, also known as Teesside, finally succumbed in 1981.

Other jumping courses that have been lost include Buckfastleigh (1960), Hurst Park (1962), Manchester (1963), Woore Hunt (1963), Birmingham Bromford Bridge (1965), Rothbury (1965), Bogside (1965), Wye (1974) and Folkestone (2012). Some other courses have continued as flat-racing tracks while ceasing to race over jumps. Nottingham, for example, stopped staging jump racing in 1996, Windsor in 1998 and Wolverhampton in 2002. Windsor did stage racing over fences for two years from 2004, taking over Ascot's fixtures while its near neighbour was rebuilding.

Fortunately, it has not all been a story of decline. Two very welcome developments were the decision by Ascot to stage jump racing from 1965, and the creation in 2009 of a new dual-purpose course, on the site of a former opencast mine, at Ffos Las by Welsh entrepreneur and racehorse owner Dai Walters, although with

In Hurst Park's heyday, patrons of East Molesey's Upper Deck swimming pool got a good view. Jockeys with an eye on bikini belles sometimes missed the break at the start.

climate change seemingly dropping even more rain on Wales, they may have to stage more summer jumping than winter jumping there.

Arena Leisure announced the closure of both Folkestone and Hereford in 2012, having been unable to get planning permission for housing developments at Folkestone to fund the investment needed to keep the course open – thus leaving Kent without a racecourse. In October 2016 however, to the joy of the jumping community, Hereford, which had been staging point to points and Arab racing, was reopened. Market Rasen and Warwick have bucked the trend by becoming a jumping only course.

Many people have happy memories of the departed racetracks, so attractively chronicled in Chris Pitt's book A Long Time Gone. As a boy living in East Molesey, I was hooked into racing for life when standing on my bicycle saddle and peering over the Hurst Park perimeter fence. After its closure, at least some of the turf eventually went to Ascot and the stand was bought by Mansfield Town FC.

Birmingham Bromford Bridge, where the fences – and usually the fields – were big, was a popular track, but perhaps not Josh Gifford's favourite. In November 1961, he was riding a horse called Timber and had been having a few words with rival jockey, Tim Brookshaw, on Joss Merlyn. Gifford had started to laugh as he went past his rival, still cantering, but overdid it so much, that he swallowed his dentures and nearly choked,

allowing Brookshaw to get back up to win. Josh always rode without his teeth after that. The refreshment bar in the centre of the course once boasted the longest bar in the world but the course closed when Birmingham City Council made an offer that could not be refused, in order to build houses on the land.

Some jockeys would not have been sorry to see the course at Wye being closed. Those who fell at the course could find themselves tangling with the electric fence used to keep sheep in, getting six-volt shocks to add to their injuries. It was also a dangerously tight track, which closed in 1974 after the inspector of courses insisted on the end out of the back straight being banked to counter an adverse camber. The owners were not prepared to fund the £40,000 cost.

At Bogside, 14 miles from Ayr, which used to be the home of the Scottish Grand National, loose horses sometimes finished up in the estuary. With an explosives factory nearby, there were fears for crowd safety, which helped to make it an early casualty when the Levy Board was looking for cutbacks. In the 1950 Scottish National at Bogside, Ken Oliver won on board Sanvina but broke his wrist in the process. Due to ride again in the last race, he retired to the ambulance room where, it was rumoured, he consumed three bottles of champagne. The price of his mount, Johnnie Walker, drifted from the original 1-3 but, having had a decent bet, Oliver emerged and won easily.

The now silenced stands at Folkestone.

Paying for Racing
– Levy Board largesse
and the quest for a 'racing right'

'No major racing industry in the world can, or does, function without the majority of its funding being provided by a percentage of betting turnover.'

Peter Savill, former BHB chairman.

Running racing is an expensive business. Racecourse turf has to be nurtured and maintained, new grandstands and toilets built, tractors employed to pull motorists out of muddy car parks, and turnstile attendants paid. Human and horse ambulances, vets and doctors have to be on hand. To maintain the 'integrity' of the sport, the jargon word for ensuring that the punter is not cheated, racecourse stables have to be guarded, photo-finish cameras and patrol cameras have to be supplied, dope tests carried out.

Crucially, too, prize money has to be found to incentivise owners to keep their horses in training at a cost of something like £22,000 or more a year – and that applies even more to jumping than to flat racing. In flat racing, owners and trainers have the solid foundation of a breeding industry behind them and a – more or less – guaranteed international demand for their products. The jumping end of the sport does not have this advantage. Because most equine participants in jumping are geldings, the sell-on value of even a champion jumper at the end of their career is peanuts.

Racing over obstacles has two elements. The bedrock is provided by the relatively small yards in rural communities across the country, where farmers and other countrymen combine their daily business with training a few jumpers for themselves and their friends for fun. At the top end is a layer of full-time professional trainers handling most of the potential stars of the sport. They depend on the readiness of a group of comparatively rich enthusiasts (or syndicate groups) to pay large sums of money, with little

hope of profit, for the privilege of owning a jumper – and on the readiness of others to pay money to watch their expensive purchases.

Rich or poor, every one of those owners has an endurable level of expenditure with a 'blow this for a game of soldiers' cut-off point at which they decide their passion or hobby has become just too expensive to justify. So, with racehorse owners in Britain on average getting back only 21 pence in the pound of their running costs, let alone what they have spent in buying a horse (compared with the equivalent of 54 pence in France and 73 pence in Japan), prize-money levels are crucial. Once again, as with the racecourse costs listed above, it is the Levy Board that is expected to help.

Governments sometimes take their character as much from the person who is Chancellor of the Exchequer as they do from the person who is sitting in number 10; in this way, even while the Jockey Club saw themselves as racing's 'ruling authority,' the Levy Board, as racing's treasury, was beginning to exert its influence. Through its history, Levy Board priorities have changed, sometimes due to changing pressures within the industry, sometimes according to the differing priorities of different Levy Board chairmen.

At its inception, the Board took on, from the Tote, some responsibility for veterinary research. For a while, it owned the National Stud; it took over from the Jockey Club such racecourse technical services as photo finishes; and it became responsible for racecourse security, including dope testing. Made up of three Jockey Club/NHC members, three members (including the chairman) appointed by the Home Office, and one each representing the Tote and the bookmakers, the Levy Board was arguably, through the 1960s and 1970s, the most influential administrative body in racing – and some chairmen had hobby horses alongside real ones. When the abrasive Lord Wigg, formerly a minister in Harold Wilson's Labour government, became chairman in 1967, he was determined to improve the lot of the ordinary racegoer, and there followed furious clashes with the Jockey Club. Relations were smoother during the reign of Sir Desmond (later Lord) Plummer, the former Leader of the Greater London Council, under whose leadership a higher proportion of levy funds went to increasing prize money. His successor, Sir Ian Trethowan, formerly of the BBC, shifted the emphasis from boosting the prestige flat races to aiding smaller courses and jumping fixtures.

In its early days, the Levy Board used a significant chunk of its funds to subsidise the costs of travelling horses to the racecourse; soon, however, the emphasis switched to boosting prize money and giving racecourses loans and grants towards improving scruffy and outdated grandstands, toilets and refreshment facilities. In 1979, transport subsidies were dropped for all runners except steeplechasers being sent more

than 100 miles, and that concession too was dropped in 1983.

Flat racing seemed to be granted rather more than did jumping from the Levy Board: in 1983/84, for example, the split was £6.7 million for flat racing and only £3.9 million for the greater number of jumping courses. However, flat racing regularly produced more of the betting turnover on which the levy funds depended. That was not the only circular argument: crucially, the smaller meetings and midweek fixtures depended on their levy payments and would often have run at a loss without them, but without that intervention, effectively using the big weekend meetings to subsidise the others, there would have been nothing for the midweek punters in betting shops to bet on, which would have soon had the bookmakers up in arms...

It did not, however, always make sense to outsiders: the Royal Commission on Gambling in 1978 argued that the racing industry had become 'hopelessly addicted to subsidy.'

The levy process, based on negotiation, has never been an easy one to operate. Year after year, racing has said, 'we need more,' often 'we need much more.' Year after year, the bookmakers have said, 'Sort yourselves out. We can't afford what you are asking,' lately adding, 'especially since we have to pay for media rights

A close finish in the 1978 Grand National, with the winner Lucius (left) ridden by Bob Davies, ahead of Sebastian V (centre) and Drumroan (right).

too' through mechanisms such as TurfTV.

Neither the government nor the racing authorities are comfortable with the levy system. It is a funding formula that nobody likes but to which no effective alternative has been found. As BHB chairman, Peter Savill sought its removal, saying that there were two major flaws for racing: the bookmakers effectively decided how much would be raised, and the Levy Board then decided how to spend the money.

With both sides questioning each other's figures, threats are bandied about and accusations of bad faith hurled across the table. Bookies have complained that racing keeps seeking subsidies from them to prop up an ineffective business model. At the same time, the bookmakers call for more fixtures for which racing has to bear the integrity costs, including cameras, drug-testing, vets and others. Bookmakers have for some years argued that with much more betting nowadays on other sports, much less of their business is now

Mares and foals at the National Stud, Newmarket.

derived from horseracing, but that doesn't seem to stop their calls for more racing and bigger fields. Meanwhile, racecourses and others have bemoaned the bookies' meanness while pulling in much greater fees for media rights for the televising of the races they put on.

There have been years when the haggling between racing's representatives and the bookmakers has gone on until nearly midnight on the last day of October, by when the annual agreement is supposed to have been reached. Sometimes, an irritated Home Office minister (more lately, a Department of Culture, Media and Sport minister) has had to step in and impose a settlement, 'determination', as that process is called. But somehow racing has kept the system going.

If the Levy had not existed since 1961, we would not have much of the racing we have today, and the levy channel is efficient: no VAT or service charge is attached – the money goes straight through to racing. With racing's media

rights income – bookmakers pay the racecourses for the right to show races in their betting shops – a much smaller proportion of the money raised actually reaches racing. However, it is now generally agreed (in 2016) that the Levy Board model is no longer working and that a new mechanism for the support and funding of racing is required. As early as November 2008, after yet another round of knife-edge levy negotiations had been settled by the BHA (reinstating some Sunday racing that was to have been cancelled), its then chairman, Paul Roy, declared: 'The whole process is pretty archaic and there is room for fundamental change.'

With smaller receipts from bookmakers some years, levy funding has had to be cut. In April 2010, for example, the Levy Board announced cuts of £4.6 million. Sharing the pain, it cut the prize-money contribution that year by £2.8 million, while appearance money for Sunday runners was reduced from £155 to £120. In addition, there were cuts in breeders' prizes and the money available for drug-testing.

The levy funding never has been truly predictable or stable, and technological advances and careful tax-planning by the bookmaking industry have undermined the system. Funds made available by the Levy Board have been dropping from more than £105 million in 2004/05 to a forecast £53 million by 2017/18.

Paul Lee, the Levy Board chairman in 2010, warned that the Board couldn't keep on spending more than it was raising and eating away at its reserves. 'By Christmas this year, we will have spent £60 million more than we have collected over the last five years and reserves will be less than £20 million.' That year, racing was looking for £130–150 million, the bookmakers were offering £83 million and, in the end, the levy raised £91 million.

One other major change has intensified the arguments. By 2015, online betting was responsible for 40 per cent of betting turnover, and all the 'Big Four' bookmakers – Hills, Ladbrokes, Coral and Betfred – and most others have been taking those online bets offshore, where their turnover is not subject to the levy.

Reminding people that the money from the levy underpins fixture funding, prize money, regulation, integrity and welfare, the BHA chairman, Nick Rust, warned early in 2016, 'Quite simply, racing will not be able to finance a fixture list of anything approaching the current scale if we continue to lose levy funding.'

Nick Rust, who had been managing director of Ladbrokes retail before becoming Chief Executive of the BHA in 2015, had earlier set out his determination to close the loophole that was enabling bookmakers to avoid paying £30 million of their dues to the racing industry. In a classic example of the poacher turned gamekeeper, he outraged the layers by introducing an initiative called Authorised Betting Partners (ABP), whereby those bookmakers who did not have a 'mutually sustainable funding relationship with the sport' (i.e. those who didn't pay levy on their offshore operations) were to be banned from commercial deals such as race sponsorship and racecourse Wi-Fi partnerships. The scheme had the backing of the Jockey Club and of Arena Racing Company, who between them own half the country's racecourses.

Bookmakers opposing the scheme, led by Coral and Betfred, argued that they were already paying £75 million in levy and £173 million in media rights – on top of the £12 million they contributed to sponsorship – and that racing was asking for too much.

With bookmakers responsible for around 40 per cent of the money invested in sponsored races, the ABP scheme was a bold move. Some leading figures applauded Rust's nerve, while admitting privately to fears that it could all end in tears. However, when Betfred's chairman, Fred Done, announced that his company would not become an ABP and would therefore no longer be sponsoring racing's top prize, the Cheltenham Gold Cup, Tim Radford, a racehorse owner with horses in the care of trainers Henrietta Knight and Mick Channon, swiftly announced that his company, Timico, would take over the sponsorship. The first fence had been jumped, although Fred Done countered that the BHA would not find it quite so easy finding alternative sponsors for Wincanton on a wet Tuesday afternoon.

The government and racing's authorities have had much discussion about the introduction of a 'Racing Right' as an alternative to the levy, ever since the European Court decision in 2004 that bookmakers were entitled to use BHA data on runners and riders without paying for it – in effect, that there were no 'data rights' (see section on Running Racing, page 260). Effectively, the Racing Right is a Government-backed legal stipulation that bookmakers must pay for the right to take bets on British racing, whether those bets are processed in Britain or abroad. Doubts remain, however, about its precise definition and enforceability. Nick Rust told *The Times* in February 2016: 'We have been working tirelessly with government to try to find a different way of funding our sport and in 2015 government expressed its support for the implementation of a racing right. We continue to work with them on the delivery of this but whether or not we end up with the Racing Right, or an alternative system, it must meet a series of tests: primarily, that it is fair, that it gives racing more control, and provides more certainty than the current voluntary environment.'

At the time of writing, the levy payment is based on 10.75 per cent of bookmakers' profits.

That has applied since 2001. In Ireland, the levy has continued to be based on turnover, at 1.0 per cent, and some argue that a turnover base provides a more consistent and predictable income stream. The advantage for bookmakers of a turnover-based system is that it would encourage racing's authorities to frame race programmes likely to increase that turnover. Betting exchanges, which rely on low margins and a high turnover, would be less keen on a turnover base.

Running alongside the usual battles is the bookmakers' argument that the betting exchanges – and some of the bigger gamblers who use them – operate effectively as unlicensed bookmakers, unencumbered by the tax and levy payments that the government and racing demand from traditional bookmakers. Betfair, bet365, 32Red and others counter that they pay tax and levy on their gross profits in the same way as bookmakers do and that people who 'lay' horses on the exchanges, that is, who accept or 'match' the bets of other gamblers, are not acting as bookmakers in doing so. But BHB and then BHA leaders have argued that the exchanges need to pay more. As Peter Savill put it: 'Racing cannot live on ten per cent of the exchanges' three per cent commission.'

Bookmakers at Ayr Racecourse.

The Levy Board has looked into the issue and, in framing the 2003/4 levy, it accepted a proposal by the Bookmakers Committee that the levy on exchanges should be on gross profits of successful layers. The Sporting Options exchange sought a judicial review and the Levy Board's move was ruled unlawful. The Treasury said in 2004 that while some betting-exchange users did have high volumes, 'there is not sufficient evidence to characterise them as running a business as opposed to merely being high-volume gamblers who have traditionally been outside the tax net.'

At the time of writing, the battle over Authorised Betting Partners is still running. Large-scale owner Michael Tabor, owner of Betvictor, signed up, but when the traditional bookmakers Paddy Power and the Betfair exchange merged, Paddy Power stayed out of the scheme while Betfair retained its ABP deal. As a number of smaller online companies signed up to become authorised betting partners, Coral complained that its rivals were being let in on paying 7.5 per cent or less, providing them with a commercial advantage over the 'Big Four.'

In March 2016, the government formally announced plans to introduce a new funding system for horseracing that would derive income from all betting on horseracing, whether it was conducted with British bookmakers or remote operators based offshore. Racing called it the establishment of the long-sought 'racing right' and many praised the latest BHA chairman, Steve Harman, for having improved racing's clout with government. Bookmakers called it an extension of the levy. Martin Cruddace, ARC's chief executive, called it a vindication of his company's policy and the ABP scheme. In October 2016 Sports Minister Tracey Crouch indicated that she was looking at a rate of ten per cent of bookmakers' profits to hand over to racing. It appeared that any deal, however, would continue to be subject to European Union state-aid rules so long as Brexit has still to be implemented.

Racing was alarmed however when the Government also announced a major new review of gambling, hinting at restrictions on the FOBTs (Fixed Odds Betting Terminals) which significantly boost bookmakers betting shop profits and on daytime gambling advertisements (a move which could precipitate a sharp fall in the amount of TV coverage of racing). For racing it could be: you win some, you lose some...

Profile: The 'Nanny' – Churchill's gift to racing

'They've nothing to sell and I've nothing to buy from them, and if they think they are going to have some sort of control, that is not on.'

Bookmaker Fred Done, purchaser of the Tote, on the BHA and the Horsemen's Group.

Inside the tote facilities.

As well as legalising betting shops, The Betting Levy Act 1961 also facilitated the pool-betting operation of the Tote, by then known as the Horserace Totalisator Board. There had been legal pool betting on racecourses since Winston Churchill, later a racehorse owner himself, pushed through the Racecourse Betting Act in 1928, creating the Tote as a statutory corporation to provide a safe pool-betting alternative to illegal betting. It was then known as the Racecourse Betting Control Board and it was given a monopoly of on-course pool betting on condition that its profits would be ploughed back into racing.

The 'Nanny', as it became known in Cockney rhyming slang (nanny goat = Tote), produced some popular bets, notably the six-leg accumulator bets: the Placepot on six consecutive races, and the Scoop6 on six nominated, televised races, which created a few betting millionaires over the years. In 1972, the Tote began opening betting shops and, from 1992, Tote Direct enabled other high-street bookmakers to channel bets into its pools.

In 1999, the government formally reviewed the future of the Tote, and in 2001 Labour's election manifesto pledged to sell it to a racing trust. An Act in 2004 converted it into a limited company, effectively nationalising the Tote so that it could be privatised.

In 2006, a racing trust offered £400 million for the Tote but was rebuffed by ministers and in that same year the EU declared that a cut-price sale to such a trust would be an abuse of state-aid rules.

In 2008, the government rejected another bid from a racing consortium and then scrapped an open-sale process run by Goldman Sachs. In 2010, the coalition government revived the promise to privatise the Tote and, in February 2011, the government, forcefully nudged by the then BHA chairman, Paul Roy, formally pledged that

half the proceeds of any sale would go to racing. It stated that potential bidders must deliver value for the taxpayer, maintain a financial contribution to the sport, and safeguard jobs at the Tote's Wigan headquarters.

Eighteen potential bidders for the Tote showed interest, with the racing community largely backing a charitable foundation devised by the Tote board. That was soon eliminated and, before long, the competition had narrowed to two: bookmaker Fred Done, owner of Betfred, and the Sports Investment Partners bid led by Sir Martin Broughton, the former chairman of the British Horseracing Board.

Fred Done was a self-made millionaire, who had started with a single betting shop in Salford; with his brother, Peter, he went on to build a £4-billion-turnover business with 843 outlets. Sir Martin Broughton, a former chairman of British Airways, President of the CBI, and a successful racehorse owner, was a man who walked easily in the corridors of power. Fred Done's bid was cash-based; Broughton's bid involved raising funds through the stock market and through high-net-worth individuals involved in racing, but if his SIP group had won, racing would have had to give up its right to 50 per cent of the sale proceeds. Despite worries that major shareholders in SIP would have been more interested in maximising the return on their investment than in funding racing, the BHA, the Racecourse

Association and the Horsemen's Group (representing owners, breeders, trainers, jockeys and stable staff) all wrote to the government backing Broughton's bid. The racing establishment, however, had backed the wrong horse in a two-horse race: Betfred won out with a gross-value bid for the Tote of £265 million, reduced to £180 million net after provision for debt and pension commitments. For that, Fred Done acquired the 514 Tote betting shops, the call centres, and an exclusive licence to continue offering pool bets, which will end on 12 July 2018. Effectively, that meant £90 million each for racing and for the taxpayer. Fred Done's company pledged to limit redundancies at the Tote to a maximum of 150; they also promised to give racing £11 million in the first year and a minimum of £9 million a year for the next six years during which the Tote pool licence monopoly remained. Speaking about his victory, Fred Done emphasised that his deals were going to be with the racecourses, and not with BHA chief Paul Roy or Horsemen's Group chief Paul Dixon: 'What commercial terms can I speak to them about? They've nothing to sell and I've nothing to buy from them, and if they think they are going to have some sort of control, that is not on. No one's going to have power of veto over how we run our business.'

Fred Done's bitterness towards his bidding opponents showed when he told the Racing Post, 'If I gave certain people in racing the world with a cherry on top, I'd never get them on side. My priority is to make a massive success out of the combined business and if that's the case, racing will also be massively successful. If they don't help me, it's on their own heads.'

The Horserace Totalisator Board was formally wound up on 17 July 2011, the day Betfred made a down payment to the Treasury of £150 million. In 2010/11, the year before its demise, when it was struggling to compete on telephone and internet business

Racegoers place their bets during Ladies Day at the Crabbie's Grand National.

with competitors who had mostly gone offshore, and with more than 500 high-street betting shops to run, the Tote had put over £18 million back into racing. It paid £6.76 million as its Levy Board contribution, and made a direct contribution to racing of £11.30 million. It also sponsored 724 races at 172 race meetings at a cost of £5.23 million.

The Tote had helped to keep going some of the lesser lights among Britain's 60 racetracks, since it paid a percentage of gross profits made to every racecourse, even if it made very little money at places like Kelso or Cartmel. John Heaton, a former Tote chief executive, was one of those who expressed fears that privatisation would lead to those tracks that generated most Tote revenue demanding a bigger share. He saw a danger of racing going the way of football, with the Premier League dominating. It is still early days, but the growing concentration of TV attention and of the big sponsored prizes on the larger tracks' Saturday meetings, the closure of Folkestone and the temporary closure of Hereford tend to underline Heaton's worries.

13 Betting on Racing
– from barber shop backrooms to betting exchanges

'Someone leaving a betting shop should feel like they are leaving a brothel.'

Home Secretary RA Butler, driving through legislation to legalise betting

Glamorous television advertisements entice us noisily to bet on any sport we fancy. Open your laptop and a betting-bargain opportunity will wink at you amid the cookies. Clusters of garish betting shops, outnumbering even the charity outlets in the high street, beckon us inside to have a wager. Even in the corner shop you will be tempted to purchase a Lottery ticket alongside your daily paper or packet of mint humbugs. Gambling is in our faces, every day. Yet until 1960 it was illegal to gamble anywhere in Britain except on a racecourse or a dog-racing track. Even those playing bridge and other card games for pin money would tend to settle up in the bus shelter rather than on public premises. But everything changed on Monday, 1 May 1961: that was the day it became legal to open a betting shop – and our lives have never been quite the same since. The flamboyant Scottish bookmaker, John Banks, famously declared it 'a licence to print money.'

Conservative Home Secretary RA Butler, the man who legalised betting shops – and wanted them kept dingy.

There had been betting shops before. When racing began to attract large audiences in the first half of the nineteenth century, there were bookmakers on course and a credit service was available off course for the well-heeled. To cope with the demand from small-stakes off-course punters with their 'tanner' singles or penny doubles, betting operations were set up in various premises where people gathered – such as barber shops and tobacconists. As these operations began to attract more customers, some venues began to provide comfortable furnishings, and lists of runners, together with their odds, on the walls. Those early betting shops were known as 'listers' or 'list shops' but as they developed their business, unscrupulous underworld characters moved in to take a cut and instances of failing to pay out winnings increased.

One well-known London establishment, Dwyer's in St Martin's Lane, disappeared literally overnight after the 12-1 shot Nancy, carrying 4 st 12 lb, won the 1851 Chester Cup (then known as the Tradesmen's Plate). The Chester Cup was in those days the biggest betting handicap of the season. Dwyer's was set to pay out a total of £25,000 to winning punters, but when they turned up with their betting slips, even the furniture had gone: all that was to be found was the shell of the cigar shop that the premises had once been. Nancy, incidentally, went on to win 12 of her 13 races in that year, including the Ebor and the Goodwood Cup.

It wasn't just racing that gave people a chance to enjoy themselves in a world in which only drink and gambling seemed to offer the poor some relief from grime and daily tedium: many sports, such as wrestling, boxing and running, grew on the backs of the gambling opportunities they offered, and their rules in many cases developed in an effort to ensure that the punter had a fair chance.

Victorian authorities began to worry, however, that the working man might become less reliable if tempted into too much gambling; so, in 1853, Parliament passed a law suppressing betting shops and outlawing the promotion of betting lists in pubs. The predictable result was to drive gambling underground and to boost organised crime. For the next century, clandestine betting flourished, with 'runners' ferrying bets from workplaces to bookmakers' offices. Illegal backroom betting shops were rife and attempts by the authorities to curb their activities were half-hearted; in fact, the police often 'tipped off' proprietors about proposed raids on the behind-the-counter betting facilities supplied by such as fishmongers, pie shops, butchers and barbers. The fines imposed on law-breaking individuals were mostly at a token level. Such penalties were looked upon as 'honourable scars' and many policemen were encouraged, by regular 'bungs' from the proprietors, to turn a blind eye. In some quarters, people would ask a local bobby the way to the nearest back-street bookie with no more reluctance than asking the way to the gents' lavatories. The Street Bookmakers

Federation estimated that you could find somebody to take your bet in 64,000 of the country's 76,000 pubs. Finally, after three Royal Commissions and regular complaints from senior policemen that such ridiculous laws were resulting in the corruption of police officers, the authorities bowed to reality.

Not all Parliamentarians at the time were in favour of the Betting and Gaming Bill of 1960, which was passed by 211 votes to 42 on its Third Reading. RA 'Rab' Butler, the Home Secretary in the Macmillan government that had thus fulfilled its 1959 election promise to legalise betting shops, was certainly not in favour of making them attractive. He declared that 'someone leaving a betting shop should feel like they are leaving a brothel.' In his autobiography, he noted that MPs were so intent on making betting shops as dreary as possible that they ended up looking like undertakers' premises.

The legislation stipulated that there should be 'no television, radio, music, dancing or refreshments on the premises,' with the result that punters used to slip into nearby TV shops to watch the races. The 'wire service' commentaries available in the better-class shops were rudimentary. Televisions, seats and refreshments were not permitted in betting shops until a relaxation in the law in 1986. A tax was levied on bets: initially, it was 10 per cent,

1956: Perched high in the grandstand at Alexandra Park racecourse, the 'tictac men' signal betting information to bookmakers below.

but it was later reduced to 9 per cent. While the tax situation lasted, most shops gave punters an extra gambling option: you could choose to pay the tax either on your stake or on your winnings. For all the time that the tax continued to be levied, it helped to sustain illegal bookmaking operations.

The benefit to bookmakers of the new law was obvious despite William Hill, the head of one major bookmaking firm, setting his face against betting shops. Although the company bearing his name was later to acquire more than 2,400 street premises, he described betting shops as 'a cancer on society' and did not apply for any licences initially. It was said that Hill had left-wing views: while he was happy to take money from the rich via credit betting, he did not want to fleece the poor. But he, like others, bowed to the inevitable: betting-tax receipts demonstrated that, within ten years, more than 90 per cent of the betting on horseracing was taking place in betting shops.

The boost given to the gambling industry by legalising betting shops increased pressure on the bookmakers to help to fund the racing industry that presented them with such opportunities. Acknowledging that pressure, Rab Butler finally followed his Betting Bill with a Levy Bill to force bookmakers to make a contribution to racing. The principle was established and confirmed in law, but the arguments between racing's authorities and the bookmakers about precisely how much bookmakers should pay into the sport have raged ever since.

As betting shop – and particularly online – business boomed over the years, some bookmakers chose to cut their tax liability by taking part of their operations offshore. The government's reaction in 2001 was to scrap betting tax and to impose instead a 15 per cent levy later reduced in level on bookmakers' profits. They also introduced more gambling legislation in 2004, designed to level the playing field and tighten rules for betting on the Internet. The taxation switch massively widened the appeal of betting and provoked an explosion in fixed-odds betting terminals. It boosted gambling-industry turnover and profits, and helped to promote the setting up of betting exchanges, such as Betfair, which connect gamblers with other gamblers of opposing views, enabling them to match their bets. Betters can thus 'lay' a horse to lose, previously a function only the bookmaker could perform, as well as backing it to win, transactions taking place in a free market, rather than with odds set by a bookmaker. The exchanges take a guaranteed commission from what the winner collects.

Whether the taxation switch was good for racing in the long term is more doubtful. The then chief of the BHB, Peter Savill, regarded

Boardmen chalking up the changing odds available for punters in a 1963 betting shop.

it as a disaster. He declared: 'With government switching to gross profits tax, the levy switched too. As exchanges grew and grew, margins shrank, bookmakers had to compete with exchanges, and racing's income got squeezed more and more. Failures in gambling regulation, tax and levy avoidance by offshore bookmakers, an unlevel playing field for betting exchanges, and an explosion in FOBTs (fixed-odds betting terminals) diminished racing's finances.'

The provision of more FOBTs in betting shops, giving punters the chance to play roulette and other casino games on slot machines, has helped to maintain bookmakers' profits. However, it has also seen a reduction in the sums wagered on horseracing and, as the racing authorities have battled continually to extract from the bookmakers enough money to keep the show on the road, the bookies have been able to counter that the proportion of their turnover that comes from racing is in decline. In recent years, they have also had to pay more to racecourses to show pictures of the day's racing in betting offices.

When the government abolished the betting duty and instead began taxing gross profits, most bookmakers 'came home' to Britain under a 'gentleman's handshake' agreement. In the ensuing economic downturn, however, they headed abroad again to avoid the 15 per cent profits' tax on their online and telephone betting operations, albeit their betting shops obviously remained at home. Ralph Topping of

William Hill, announcing his company's offshore move, denounced the government, claiming that they had sided with the betting exchanges, which were allowing unregulated, unlicensed operators to act as bookmakers through them – without paying a penny to the levy or to racing.

Interestingly, most of the trainers who have voiced an opinion, whether being people who like a bet themselves or not, seem to have reservations about the betting exchanges, about the potential for people to bet on horses to lose, as well as trying to pick winners.

Hunting for a winner: a Cheltenham punter at a Tote window.

Bookmakers' boards shine bright for the last race of the day.

Epilogue

Jump racing since 1961 has been shaped by the levy, the volume of races, currently at over 3,700 each year, determined by the bookmakers. Prize money averages more than £10,000 per race but that figure is distorted by the £1 million Grand National, Cheltenham and Aintree festivals, other Grade One races and big Saturday handicaps. Between them, Ascot, Aintree and Cheltenham deliver prize money averaging £50,000 per race. Many lower grade courses average £6,000 and winning owners frequently come away with less than £2,500, little more than 10 per cent of their annual expenditure on training fees.

The objective that the levy might generate in excess of £150 million has become a distant dream as racing struggles to get by on a third of that amount. Fortunately, new media platforms and commercial rates for picture rights have brought racecourses new revenue streams. Without valuable sponsorship attracted to flat racing from Middle East investors, jumping is relying on 'Son of Levy' to provide strong and broad foundations for the immediate future.

Of the top 25 races in the British racing calendar in terms of betting turnover, no fewer than 19 are jump races. The media, encouraged by the betting industry, capture the public imagination on the narrative of high profile races from November through to April.

The good news story of our period has been the resuscitation, recovery and return to rude health of the Grand National. From fears that the next National might be the last, our shop-window event has fought back quite brilliantly to weave its magic on successive generations. Standing alone, high above the parapet of public awareness, the National has led on equine welfare, turf management and, perhaps most importantly, attitudes of outsiders towards our sport. We have their licence to operate.

Racehorse owners, who prime the pump, continue as individuals, partnerships and, increasingly as syndicates to buy into a lifestyle that is progressively more about the experience than financial return. The remote possibility of winning the Grand National, or more realistically having a runner there or at Cheltenham will always be tucked away in that dark corner of the imagination entitled 'hope' as the runners go to post for the second division of the maiden hurdle race on a dank afternoon. Four and a half minutes is all it takes to start dreaming or resorting to Plan B.

That is the nature of all sport, vast involvement at grassroots level focusing on fun and a tiny community at the pinnacle who strive to make a living from their investment and commitment. Margins are tighter than in any previous decade. Whether it be for a breeder, bloodstock agent, trainer, jockey or racecourse, very few show a profit. They survive because they love the seasons, the people and, above all, the horses.

Thanks mainly to the efforts of Nicky Henderson and Paul Nicholls, young men and women continue to set out on training careers more in hope than expectation. A few more doing so in the north will redress the gravitational pull towards the M4 – M5 corridor.

It will be intriguing to see how the assault on British racing from the big Irish teams plays out. Can Paul Nicholls, who is streets ahead of his domestic colleagues, continue to resist the efforts of Willie Mullins or might another assailant, Gordon Elliott or Joseph O'Brien perhaps, breach those walls and emulate his namesake Vincent?

In Thistlecrack, God willing, we already have a steeplechasing hero to keep us warm through the winter. As for the next AP, he or she could already be moving up the ranks or – hold on a minute – that might be her, peeping through a crack in the racecourse fence to catch the glimpse of the action, enthralled by the colour, sounds, spectacle and thrill of this extraordinary sport.

Edward Gillespie

Bibliography

Armytage, Marcus and Cottrell, John (2008), *A-Z of the Grand National*, Berkshire: Highdown.

Biddlecombe, Terry (1982), *Winner's Disclosure*, London: Stanley Paul and Co.

Bose, Mihir and Sharpe, Graham (2014), *William Hill,* Berkshire: Racing Post.

Bradley, Graham with Taylor, Steve (2000), *The Wayward Lad*, Great Britain: Greenwater Publishing.

Bromley, Peter (1982), *The Price of Success: The Authorized Biography of Ryan Price*, London: Hutchinson.

Buglass, Dan (1994), *Ken Oliver – the Benign Bishop*, Berkshire: Marlborough Books.

Burridge, Richard (1992), *The Grey Horse*, London: Pelham Books.

Clower, Michael (2007), *Kings of the Turf: Ireland's Top Racehorse Trainers*, London: Aurum.

Dunwoody, Richard (2000), *Obsessed*, London: Headline.

Fitzgeorge-Parker, Tim (1971), *Steeplechase Jockeys: The Great Ones*, London: Pelham Books.

Fitzgeorge-Parker, Tim (1980), *Jockeys of the Seventies*, London: Pelham Books.

Francis, Dick (1986), *Lester*, London: Michael Joseph.

Green, Reg (1997), *National Heroes: the Aintree Legend*, Edinburgh: Mainstream.

Green, Reg (2002), *Kings For A Day*, Edinburgh: Mainstream.

Herbert, Ivor and Smyly, Patricia (1989), *Winter Kings*, London: Pelham Books.

Lambie, James (2010), *The Story of your Life: A History of 'The Sporting Life' Newspaper,* Leicester: Matador.

Muscat, Julian (2012), *Her Majesty's Pleasure*, Berkshire: Racing Post.

Nicholls, Paul (2009), *Lucky Break: The Autobiography*, London: Orion.

Nicholson, David with Powell, Jonathan (1995), *The Duke: The Autobiography of the Champion Trainer*, London: Hodder & Stoughton.

O'Neill, Jonjo and Richards, Tim (1985), *Jonjo*, London: Stanley Paul.

O'Sullevan, Peter (1989), *Calling the Horses*, London: Hodder & Stoughton.

Peters, Stewart (2003), *Festival Gold*, Gloucestershire: Tempus.

Peters, Stewart (2006), *The Hennessy Cognac Gold Cup*, Gloucestershire: Tempus.

Pinfold, John (1999), *Gallant Sport,* Halifax: Portway Press Ltd.

Pinfold, John (2016), *Aintree*, Surrey: Medina Publishing Ltd.

Pitman, Richard (1976), *Good Horses Make Good Jockeys*, London: Pelham Books

Pitman, Richard (1995), *Fit for a Queen*, Chorley, Lancashire: Pride of Place.

Pitt, Chris (1996), *A Long Time Gone*, Halifax: Portway Press.

Powell, Jonathan (2010), *Kauto Star and Denman*, London: Weidenfeld & Nicolson.

Richards, Tim and Paul, Stanley (1985), *Jonjo: an autobiography*, London: Stanley Paul and Co.

Rimell, Fred and Mercy (1977), *The Aintree Iron: an autobiography*, London: W.H.Allen.

Scudamore, Peter (1993), *Scu: The Champion Jockey's Story*, London: Headline.

Smith, Adrian and Porter, Dilwyn (eds) (2000), *Amateurs and Professionals in Post-War British Sport*, London: Routledge.

Smith, Martin (ed.) (2011), *Kings, Queens and Four-legged Athletes*, London: Aurum.

Smith, Sean (2001), *Royal Racing: The Queen and Queen Mother's Sporting Life*, London: BBC Books.

Tanner, Michael (2002), *The Champion Hurdle*, Edinburgh: Mainstream.

Tyrrel, John (2001), *Running Racing: Jockey Club years since 1950,* Shrewsbury: Quiller

The first fence in the 2007 John Smith's Grand National won by Silver Birch for Irish trainer Gordon Elliott.

Index